井 上 雄 彦

Takehiko Inoue

I JUST GOT TO MEET MAGIC JOHNSON!! THE
LAKERS' SUPERSTAR–WHO WEARS THE NUMBER
32–IS LIKE A *GOD* TO ME. I WAS SO EXCITED
THAT I COULDN'T SLEEP THE NIGHT BEFORE!

I WANT TO THANK EVERYONE WHO MADE THE
MEETING POSSIBLE AND OF COURSE MAGIC,
WHO GREETED ME WITH HIS INIMITABLE SMILE.

Takehiko Inoue's *Slam Dunk* is one of the most
popular manga of all time, having sold over 100
million copies worldwide. He followed that series
up with two titles lauded by critics and fans
alike—*Vagabond*, a fictional account of the life
of Miyamoto Musashi, and *Real*, a manga about
wheelchair basketball.

SLAM DUNK
Vol. 4: Enter the Hero!!

SHONEN JUMP Manga Edition

STORY AND ART BY TAKEHIKO INOUE

English Adaptation/Kelly Sue DeConnick
Translation/Joe Yamazaki
Touch-up Art & Lettering/James Gaubatz
Cover & Graphic Design/Sean Lee
Editor/Kit Fox

Published by VIZ Media, LLC
P.O. Box 77010
San Francisco, CA 94107

10 9 8 7 6 5 4
First printing, June 2009
Fourth printing, August 2018

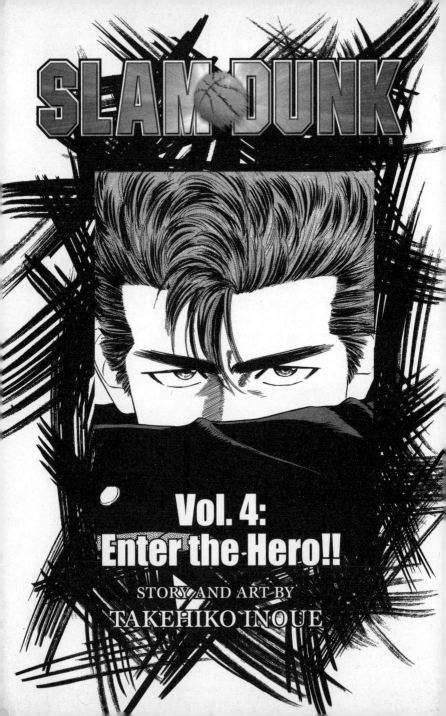

Character Introduction

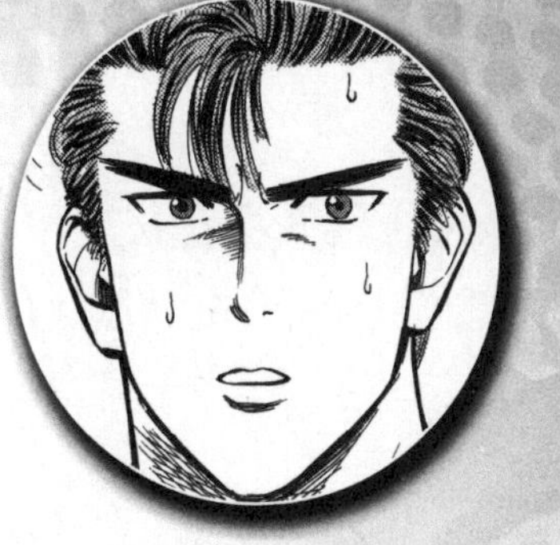

Hanamichi Sakuragi
A first-year at Shohoku High School, Sakuragi is in love with Haruko Akagi.

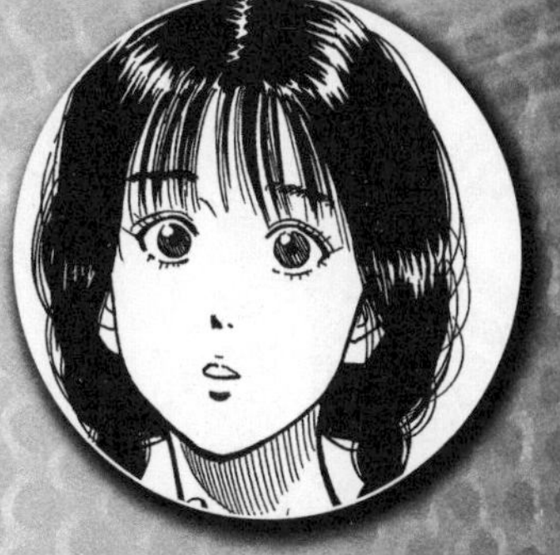

Haruko Akagi
Also a first-year at Shohoku, Takenori Akagi's little sister has a crush on Kaede Rukawa.

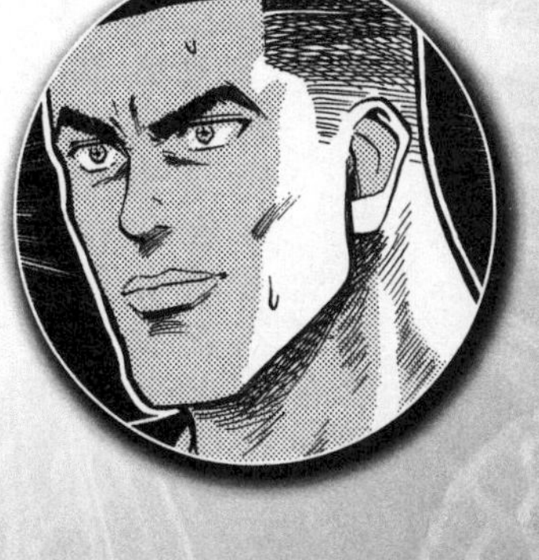

Takenori Akagi
A third-year and the basketball team's captain, Akagi has an intense passion for his sport.

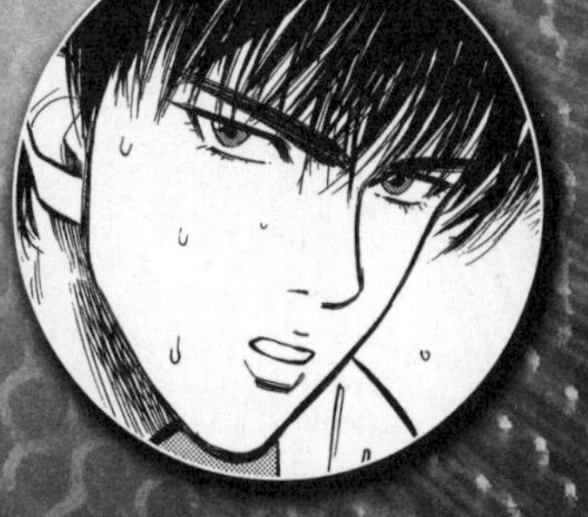

Kaede Rukawa
The object of Haruko's affection (and that of many of Shohoku's female students!), this first-year has been a star player since junior high.

Sakuragi's Friends

Ohkusu Mito Takamiya Noma

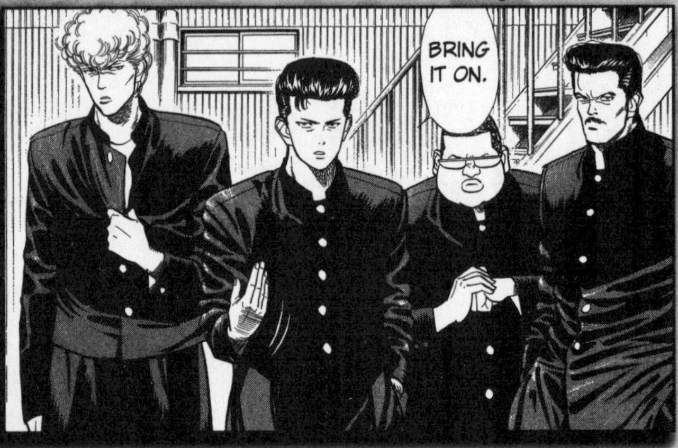
BRING IT ON.

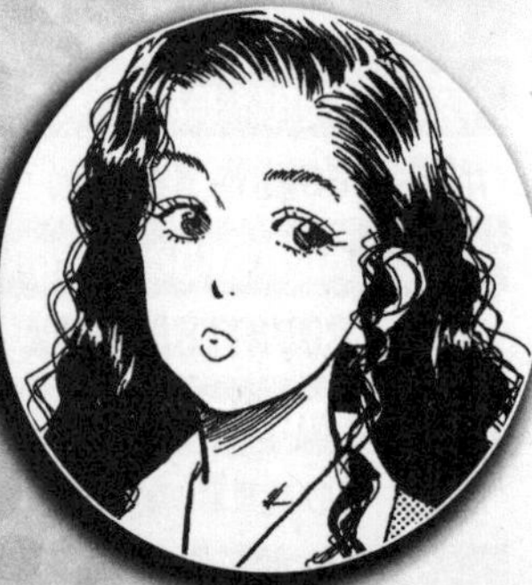

Ayako

Basketball Team Manager

Our Story Thus Far

Hanamichi Sakuragi is rejected by close to 50 girls during his three years in junior high. He finally becomes a high school student, but the 50th girl he asks out tells him that her heart belongs to Oda from the basketball team. Hanamichi is still trying to overcome the shock when he meets Haruko Akagi. Haruko approaches him in the hallway and asks, "By any chance, do you like basketball?"

Sakuragi joins the basketball team for Haruko, but the endless fundamental drills don't suit his personality. He continually butts heads with the team's captain, who also happens to be Haruko's brother. It's not clear whether Akagi will let Sakuragi play in the big practice game against their Ryonan rivals...

Vol. 4:
Enter the Hero!!

Table of Contents

#27 CAPTAIN ALL FIRED UP

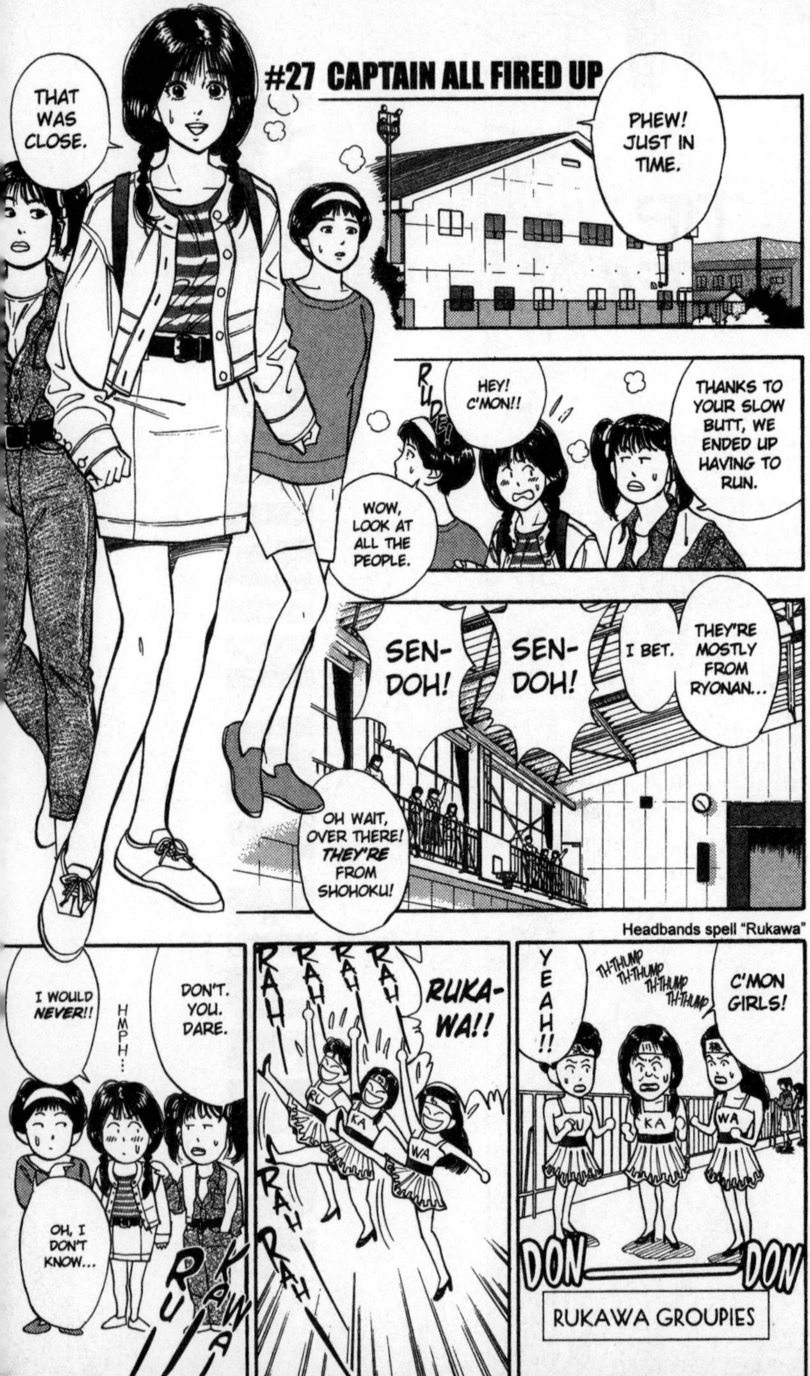
PHEW! JUST IN TIME.
THANKS TO YOUR SLOW BUTT, WE ENDED UP HAVING TO RUN.
HEY! C'MON!!
RUDE!
WOW, LOOK AT ALL THE PEOPLE.
THEY'RE MOSTLY FROM RYONAN...
I BET.
SEN-DOH!
SEN-DOH!
OH WAIT, OVER THERE! *THEY'RE* FROM SHOHOKU!
THAT WAS CLOSE.
C'MON GIRLS!
TH-THUMP TH-THUMP TH-THUMP TH-THUMP
YEAH!!
DON
DON
RUKAWA GROUPIES
RUKA-WA!!
RAH RAH RAH RAH
RAH RAH RAH
RU KA WA
DON'T. YOU. DARE.
HMPH...
I WOULD *NEVER!!*
OH, I DON'T KNOW...

Headbands spell "Rukawa"

#27 CAPTAIN ALL FIRED UP

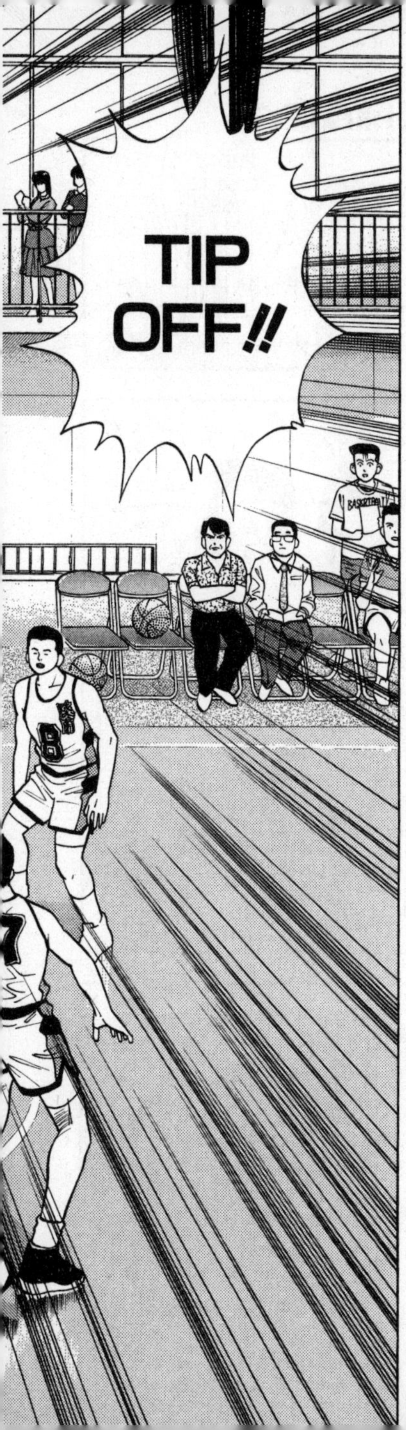
TIP OFF!!

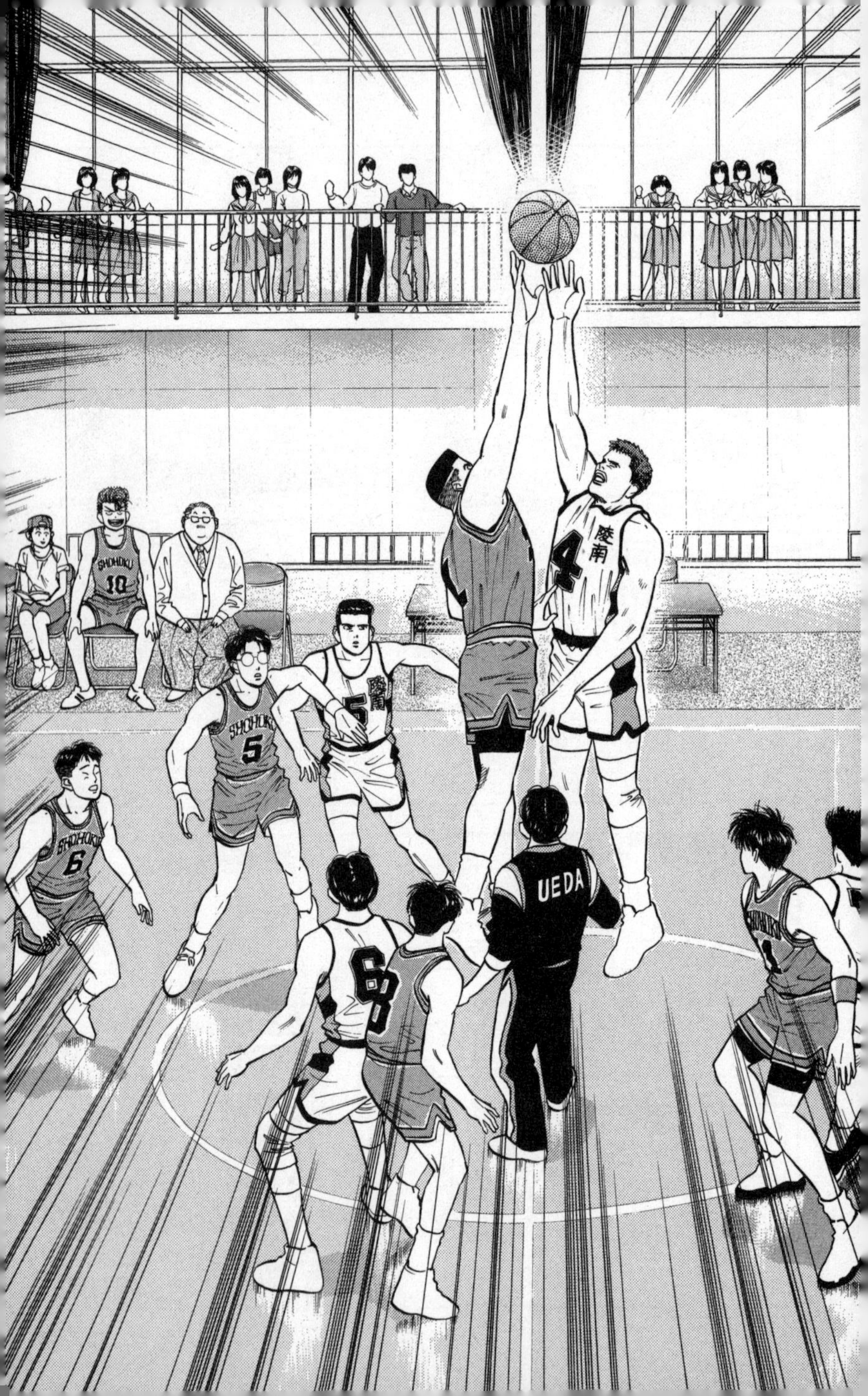
陵南
SHOHOKU
UEDA

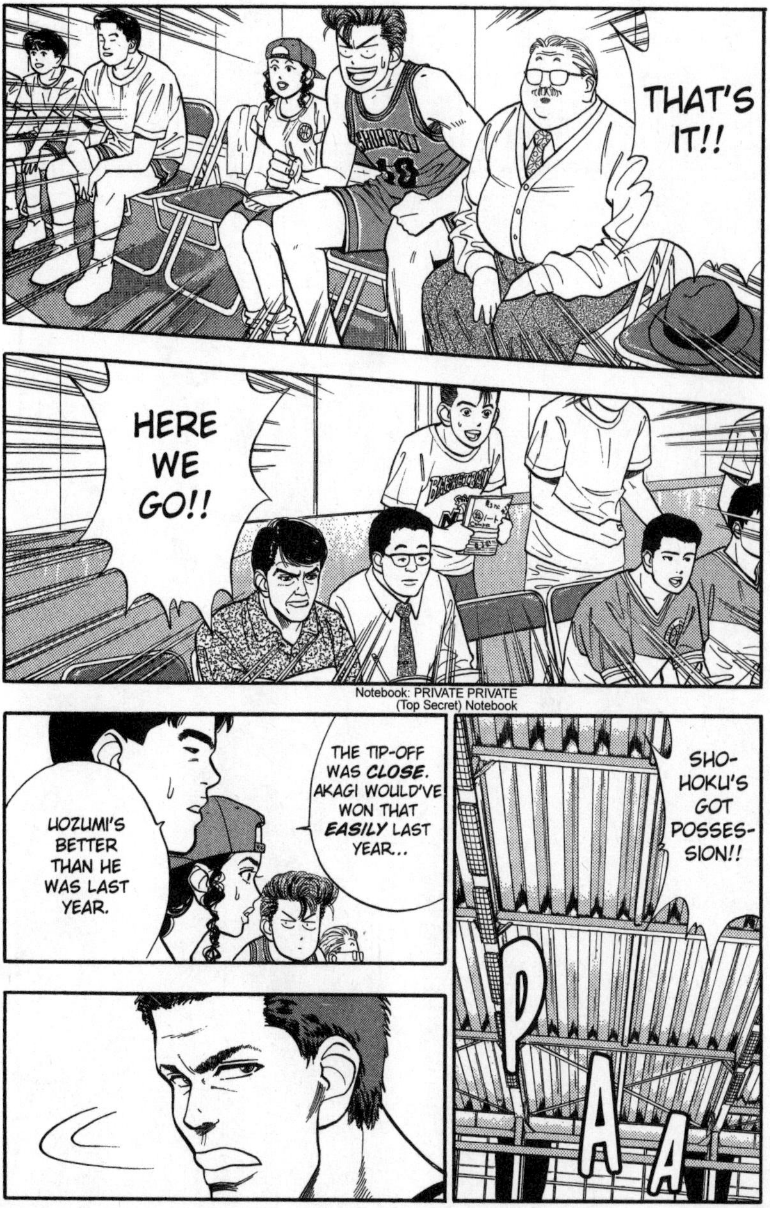
THAT'S IT!!
HERE WE GO!!
Notebook: PRIVATE PRIVATE (Top Secret) Notebook
SHO-HOKU'S GOT POSSES-SION!!
PAA
THE TIP-OFF WAS *CLOSE*. AKAGI WOULD'VE WON THAT *EASILY* LAST YEAR...
UOZUMI'S BETTER THAN HE WAS LAST YEAR.

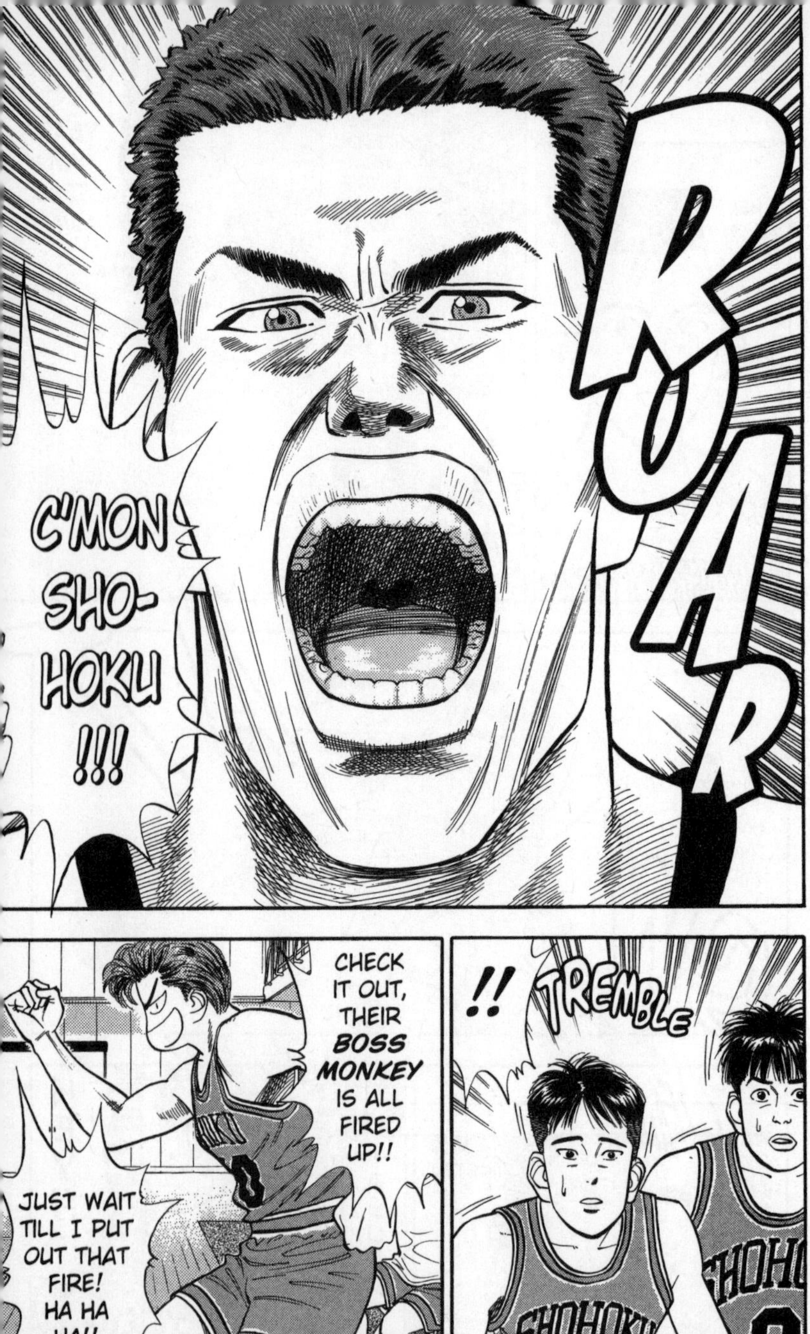
ROAR
C'MON SHO-HOKU!!!
TREMBLE
!!
CHECK IT OUT, THEIR BOSS MONKEY IS ALL FIRED UP!!
JUST WAIT TILL I PUT OUT THAT FIRE! HA HA HA!!
SHOHOKU
SHOHO

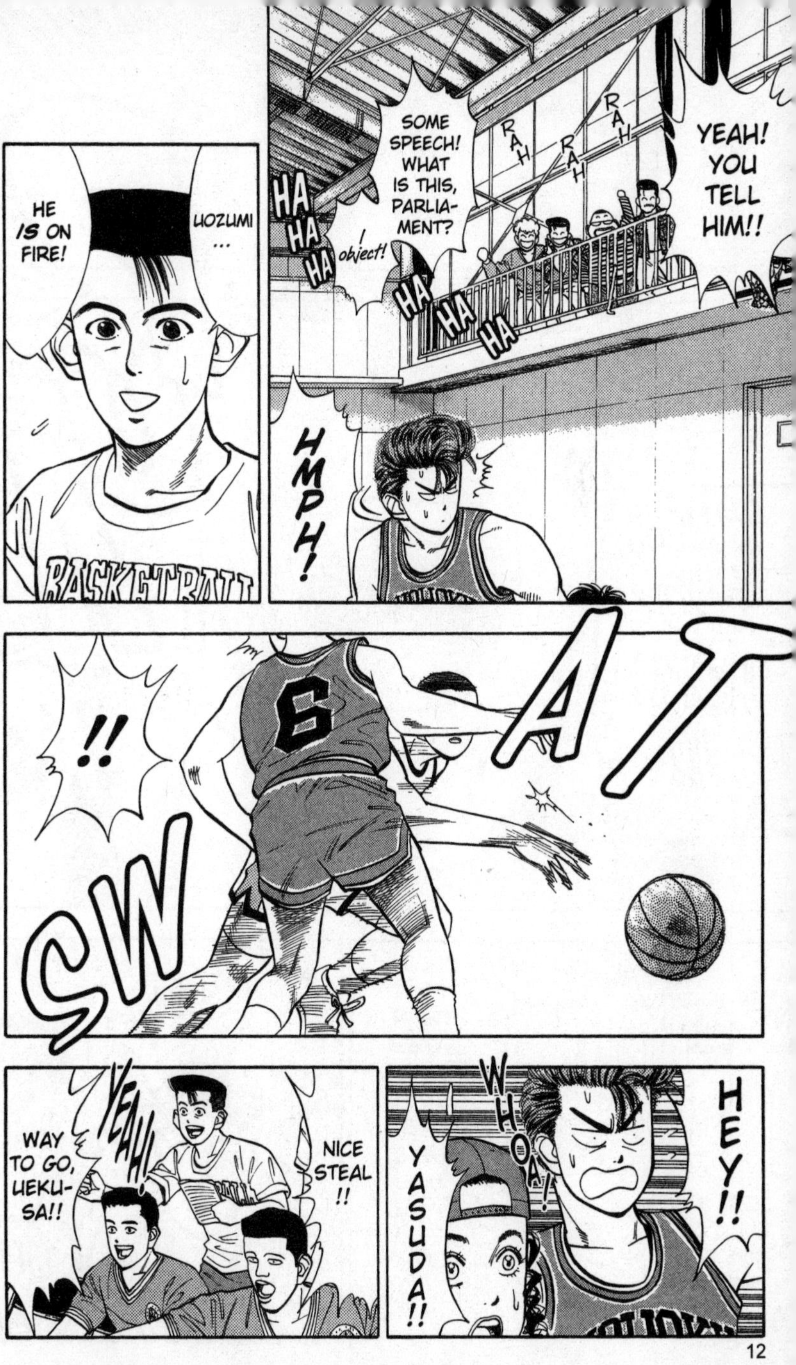
YEAH! YOU TELL HIM!!
RAH
RAH
RAH
SOME SPEECH! WHAT IS THIS, PARLIAMENT?
HA HA HA
I object!
HA HA HA
HMPH!
UOZUMI ...
HE *IS* ON FIRE!
!!
SW
AT
HEY!!
WHOA!
YASUDA!!
NICE STEAL!!
YEAH!
WAY TO GO, UEKUSA!!

READ THIS WAY

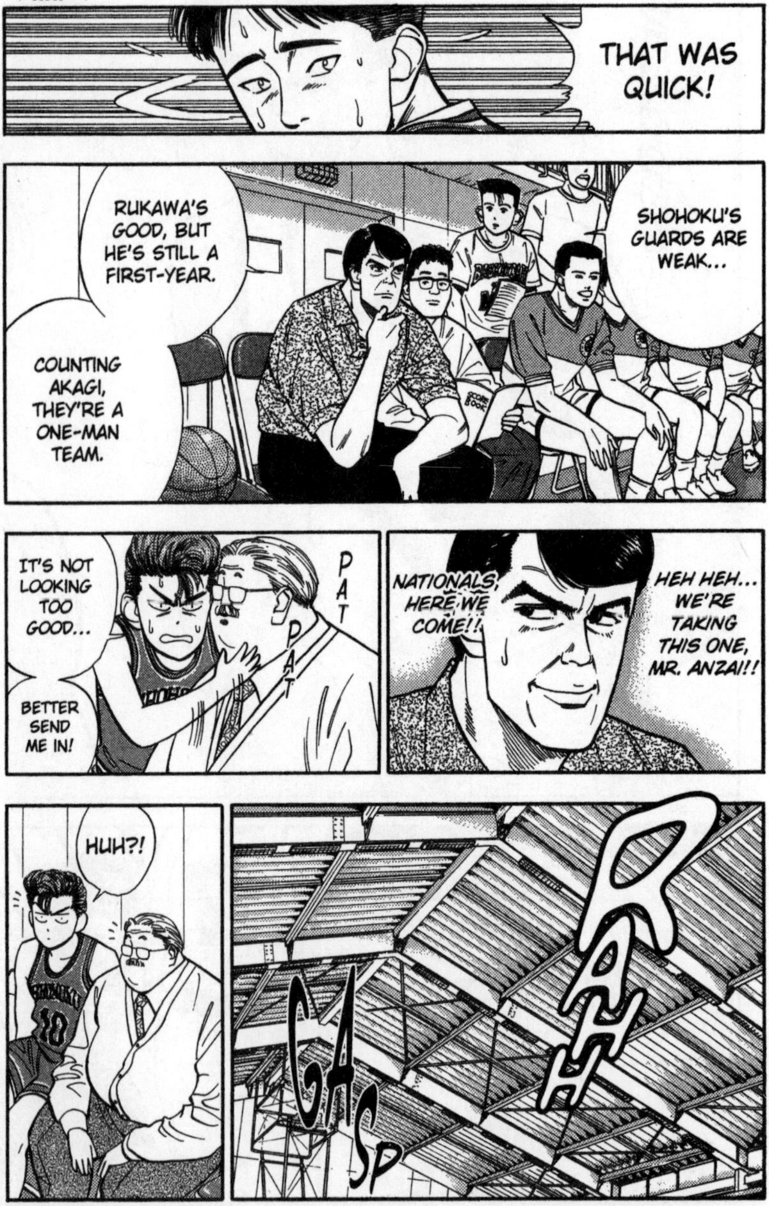
THAT WAS QUICK!
SHOHOKU'S GUARDS ARE WEAK...
RUKAWA'S GOOD, BUT HE'S STILL A FIRST-YEAR.
COUNTING AKAGI, THEY'RE A ONE-MAN TEAM.
HEH HEH... WE'RE TAKING THIS ONE, MR. ANZAI!!
NATIONALS, HERE WE COME!!
PAT
PAT
IT'S NOT LOOKING TOO GOOD...
BETTER SEND ME IN!
RAHH
GASP
HUH?!

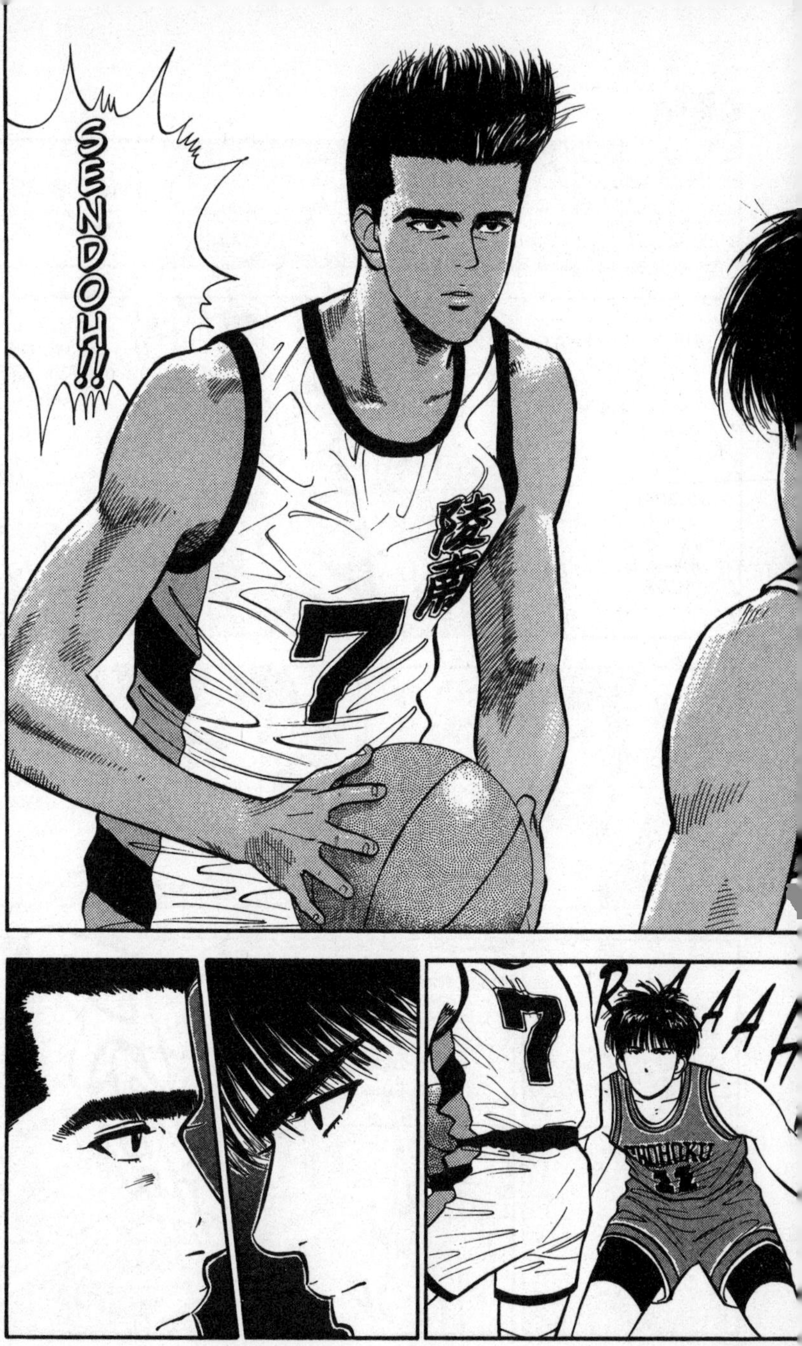
SENDOH!!
RAAAH

READ THIS WAY

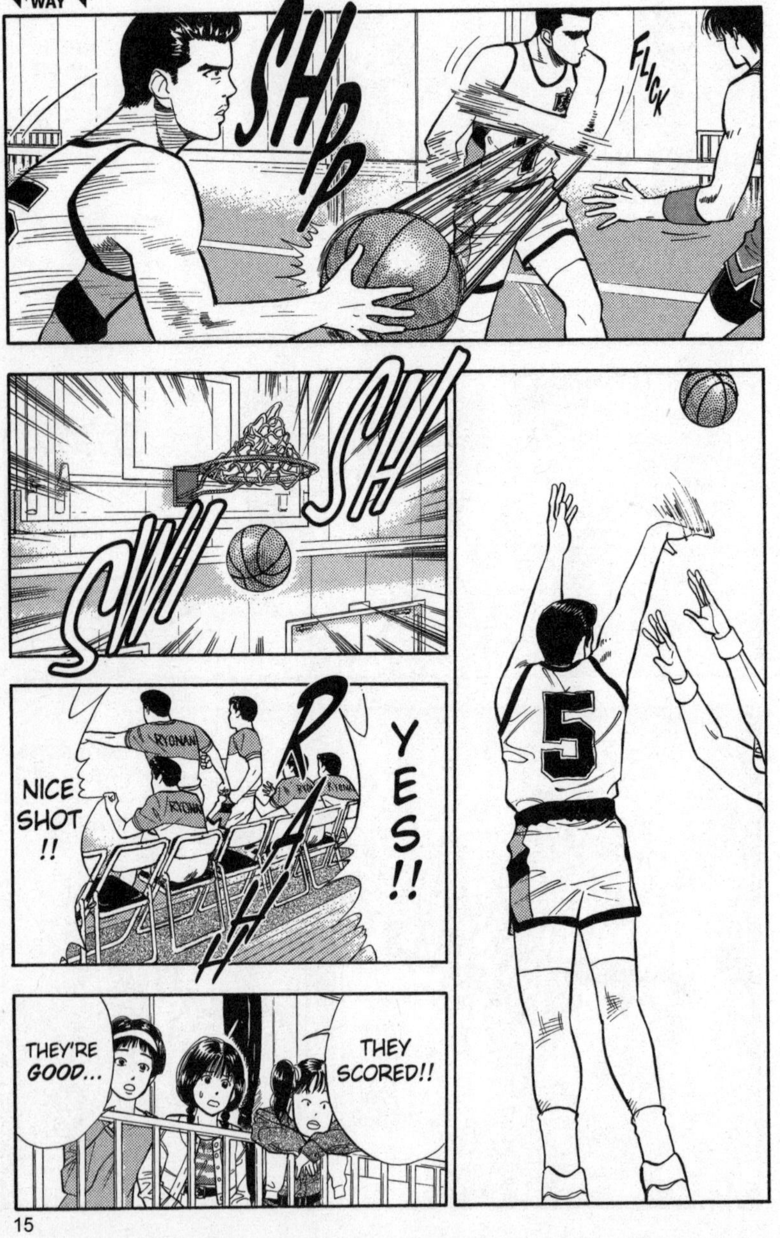

SHPP
FLICK
SW
SH
YES!!
RAAHH
NICE SHOT!!
THEY SCORED!!
THEY'RE GOOD...

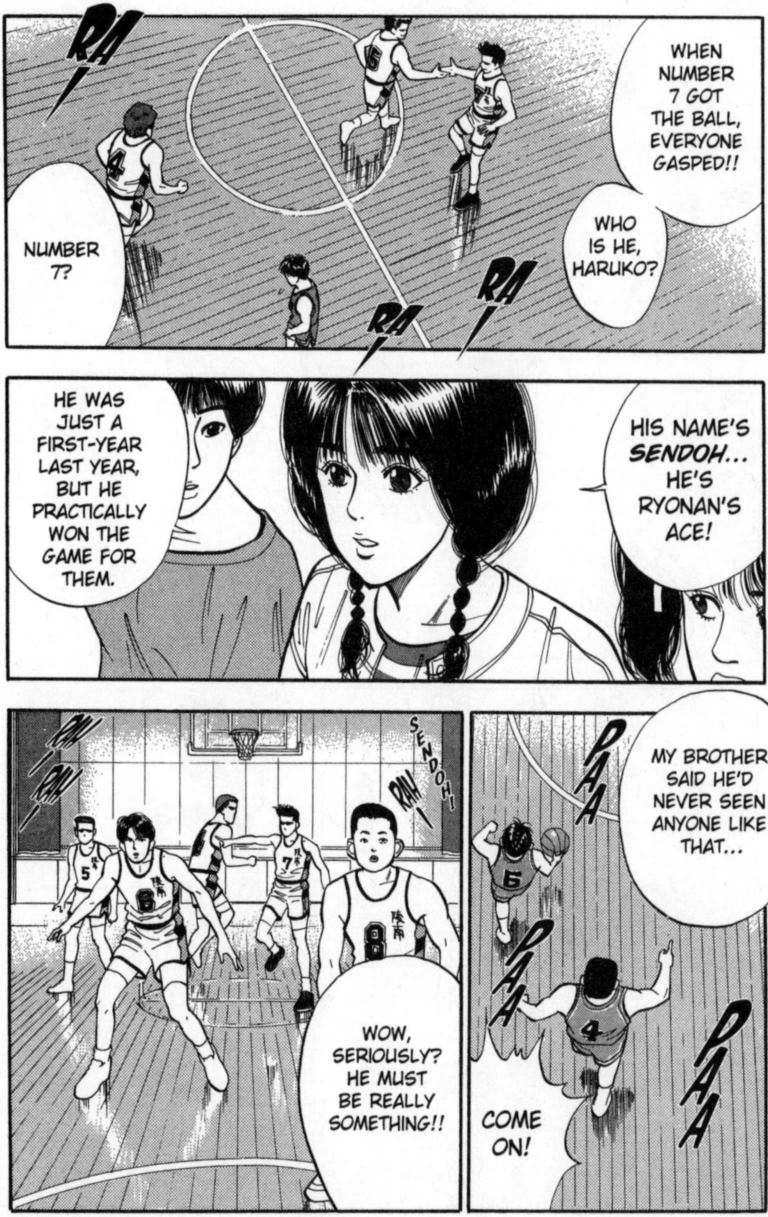
WHEN NUMBER 7 GOT THE BALL, EVERYONE GASPED!!
RA
WHO IS HE, HARUKO?
RA
RA
NUMBER 7?
HIS NAME'S SENDOH... HE'S RYONAN'S ACE!
HE WAS JUST A FIRST-YEAR LAST YEAR, BUT HE PRACTICALLY WON THE GAME FOR THEM.
MY BROTHER SAID HE'D NEVER SEEN ANYONE LIKE THAT...
PAA
PAA
PAA
COME ON!
SENDOH!
RAH!
RAH!
RAH!
WOW, SERIOUSLY? HE MUST BE REALLY SOMETHING!!

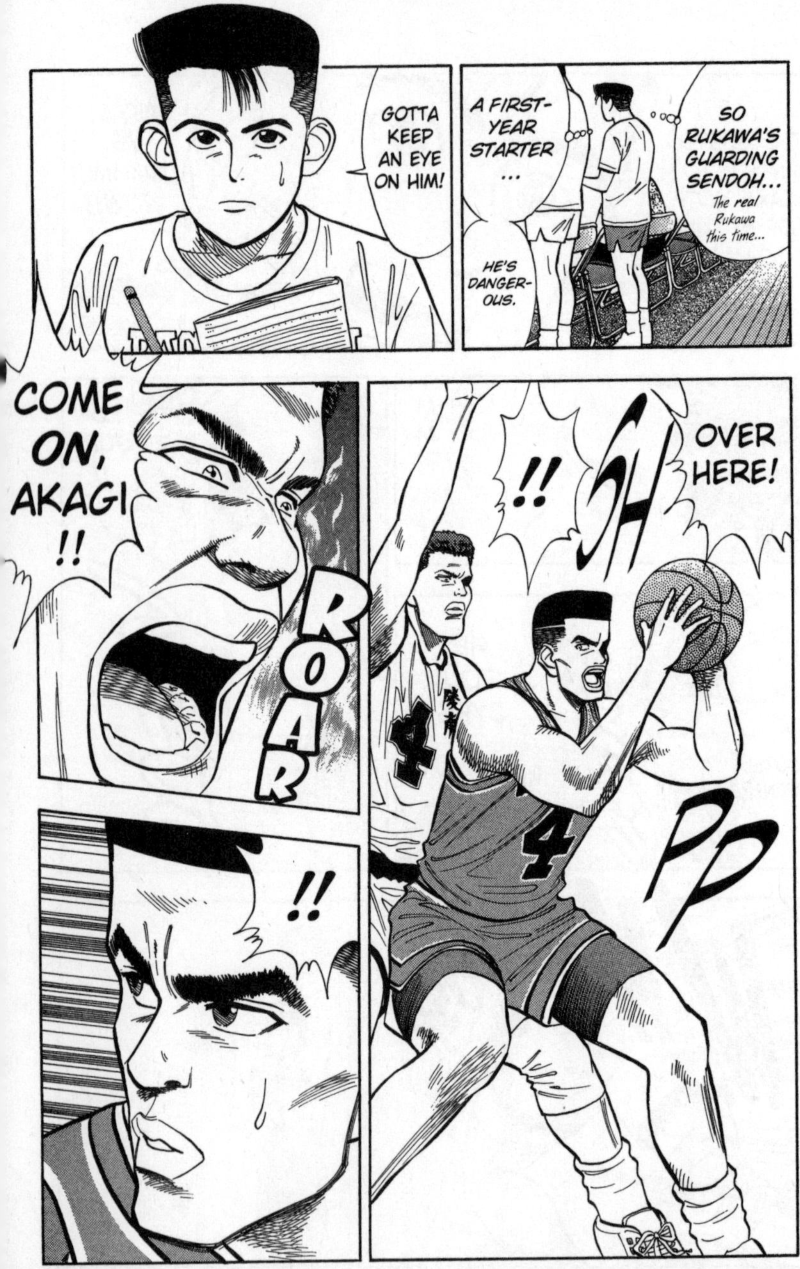
SO RUKAWA'S GUARDING SENDOH...
The real Rukawa this time...
A FIRST-YEAR STARTER ...
HE'S DANGER-OUS.
GOTTA KEEP AN EYE ON HIM!
OVER HERE!
SH
!!
PP
COME ON, AKAGI !!
ROAR
!!

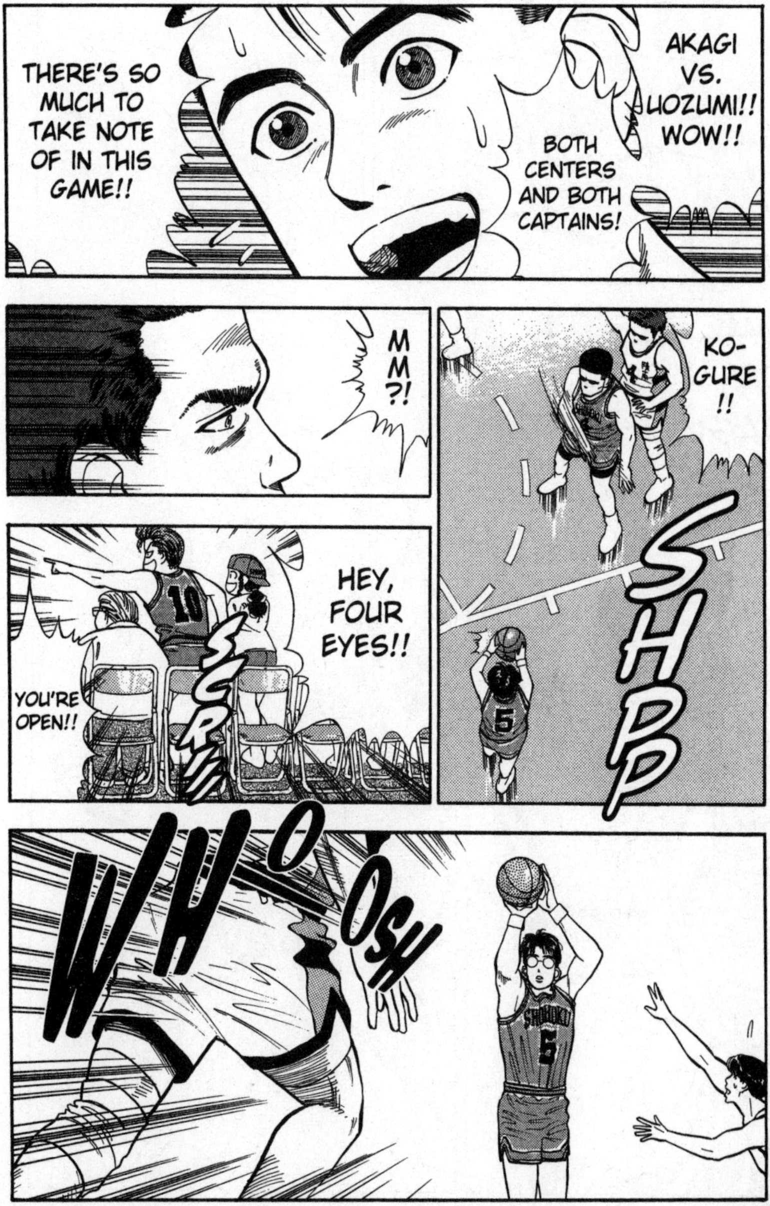
AKAGI VS. UOZUMI!! WOW!!
BOTH CENTERS AND BOTH CAPTAINS!
THERE'S SO MUCH TO TAKE NOTE OF IN THIS GAME!!
KO-GURE!!
SHPP
MM?!
HEY, FOUR EYES!!
SCRII
YOU'RE OPEN!!
WHOOSH

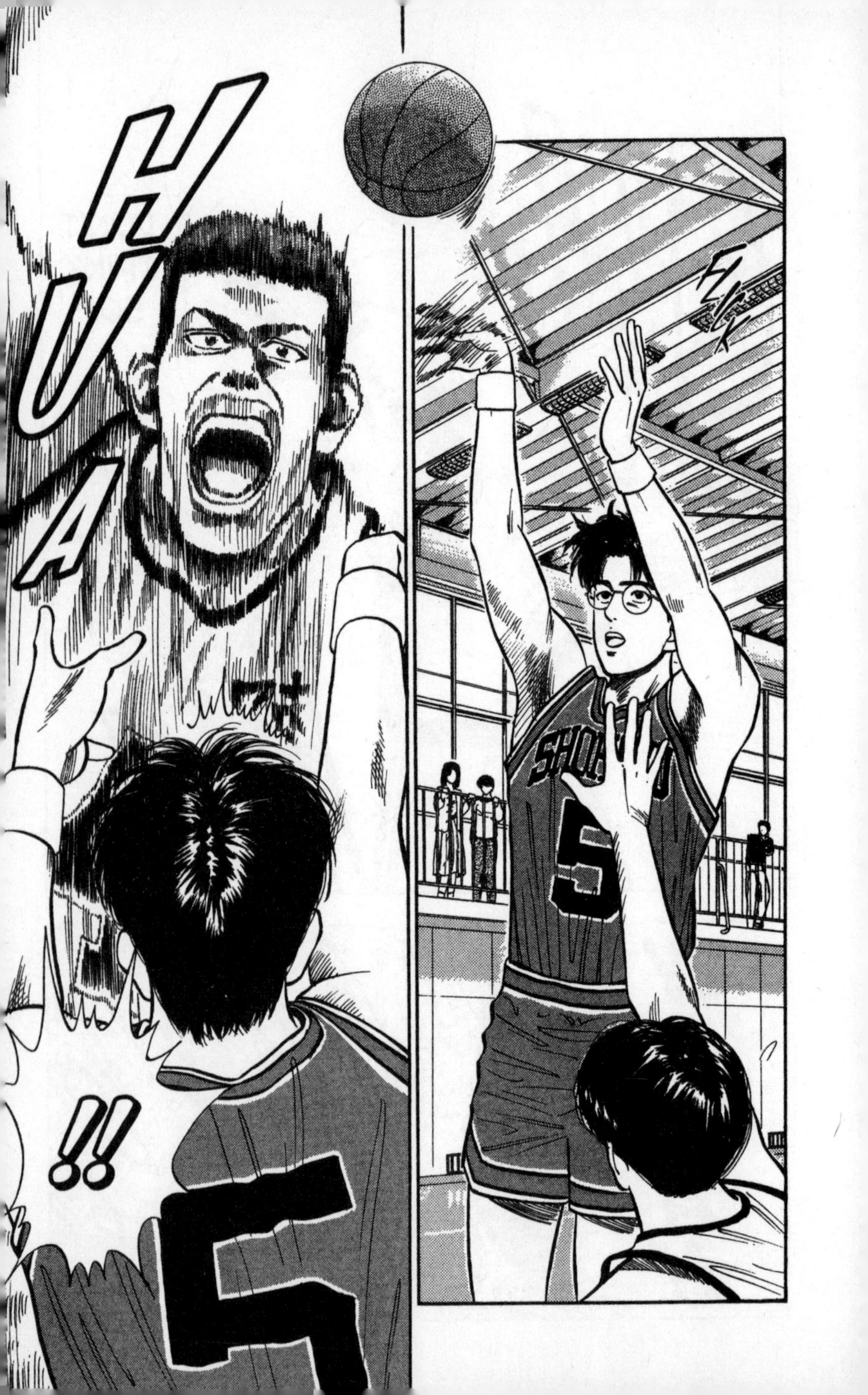
FLICK
HUA
!!

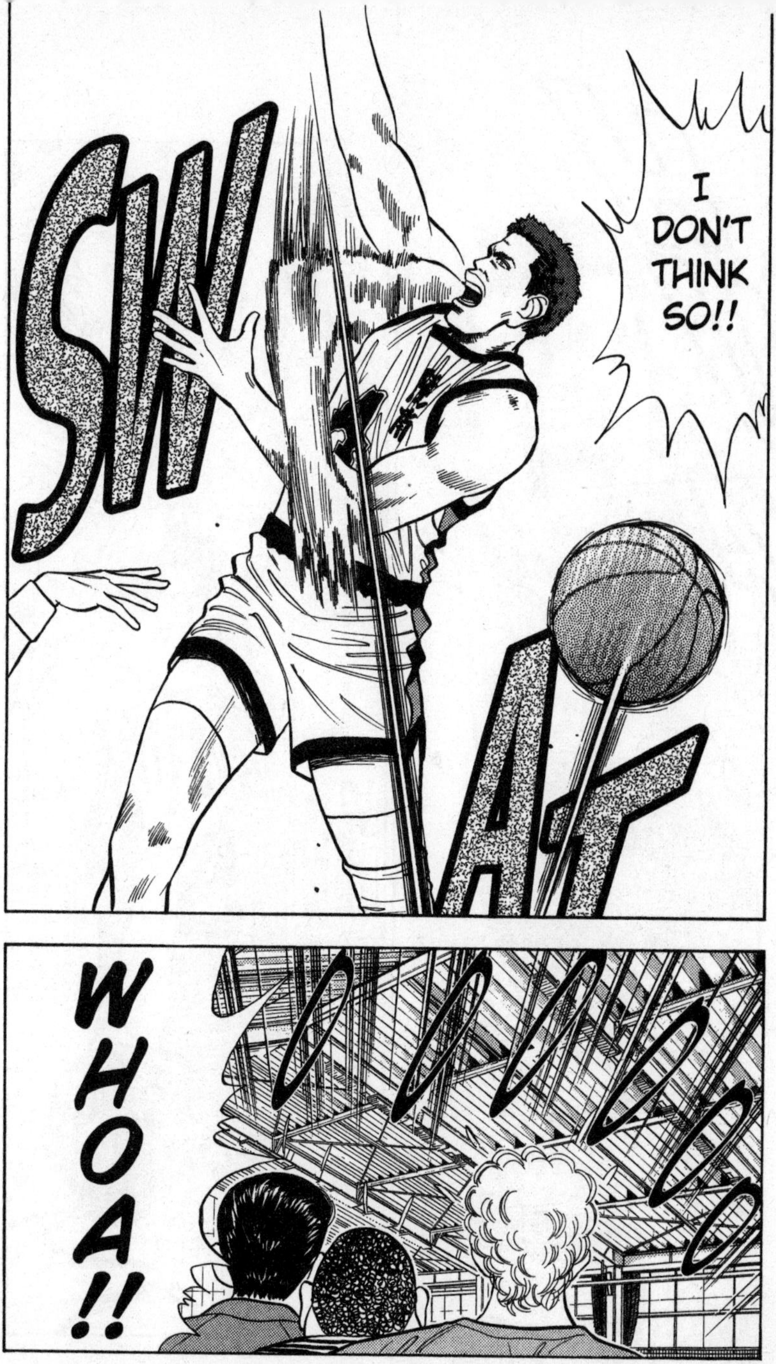
I DON'T THINK SO!!
SWAT
WHOA!!
OOOOOO

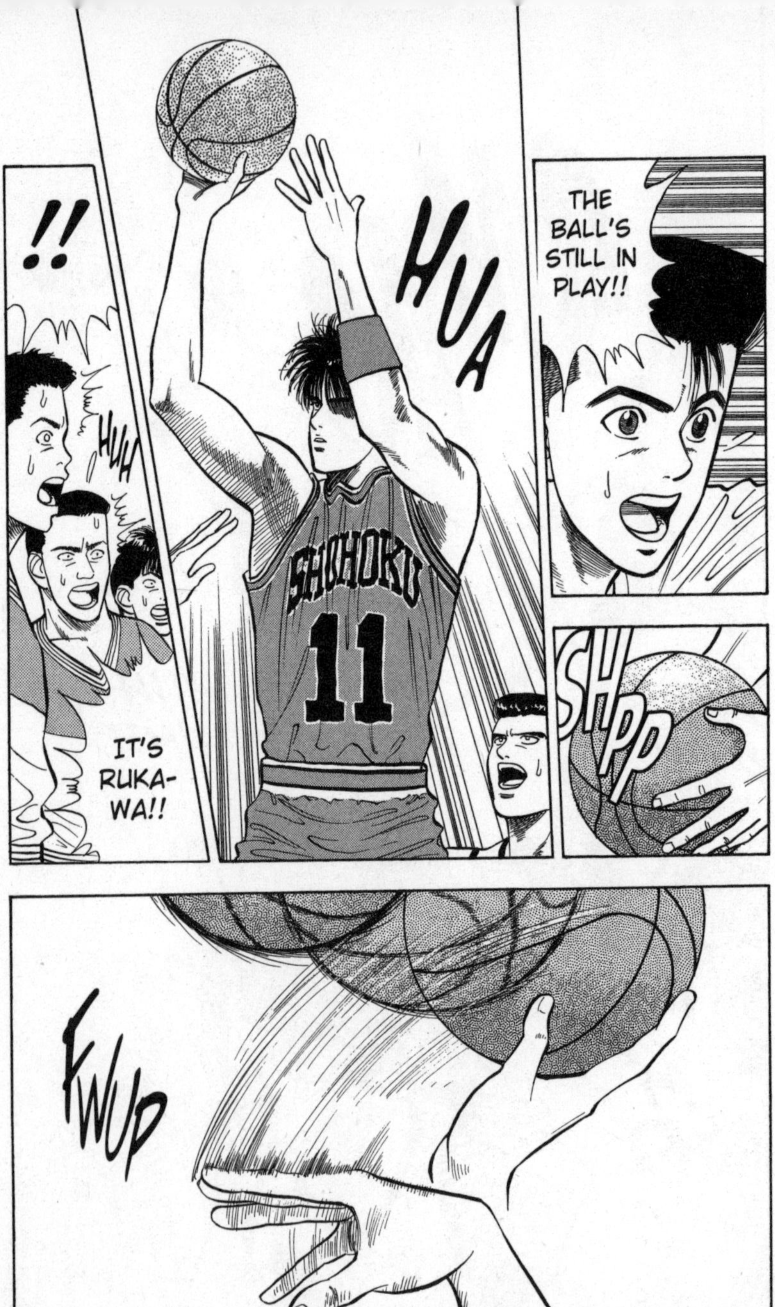
THE BALL'S STILL IN PLAY!!
SHPP
HUA
SHOHOKU 11
!!
HUH
IT'S RUKAWA!!
FWUP

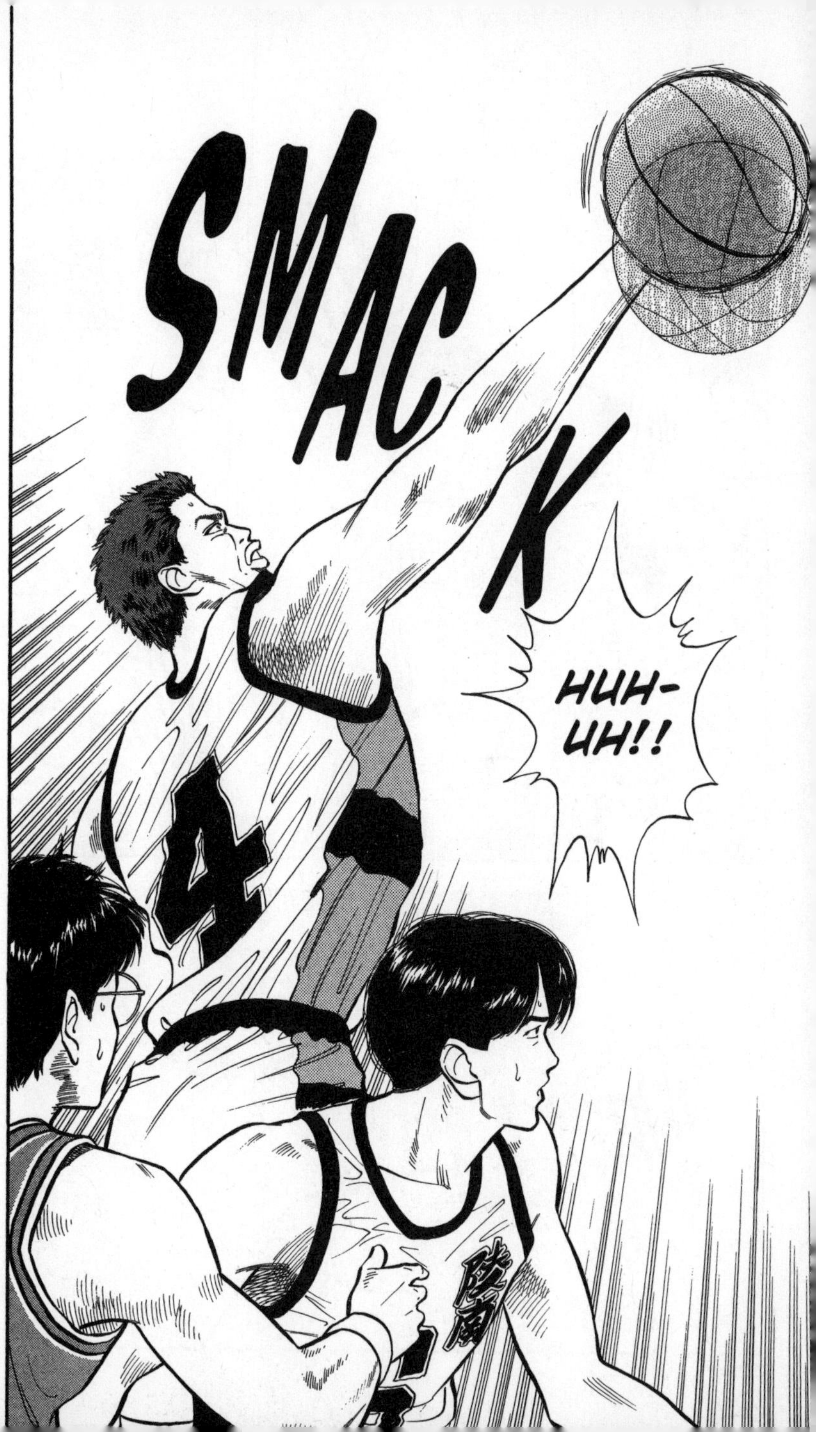
SMACK
HUH-UH!!

READ THIS WAY

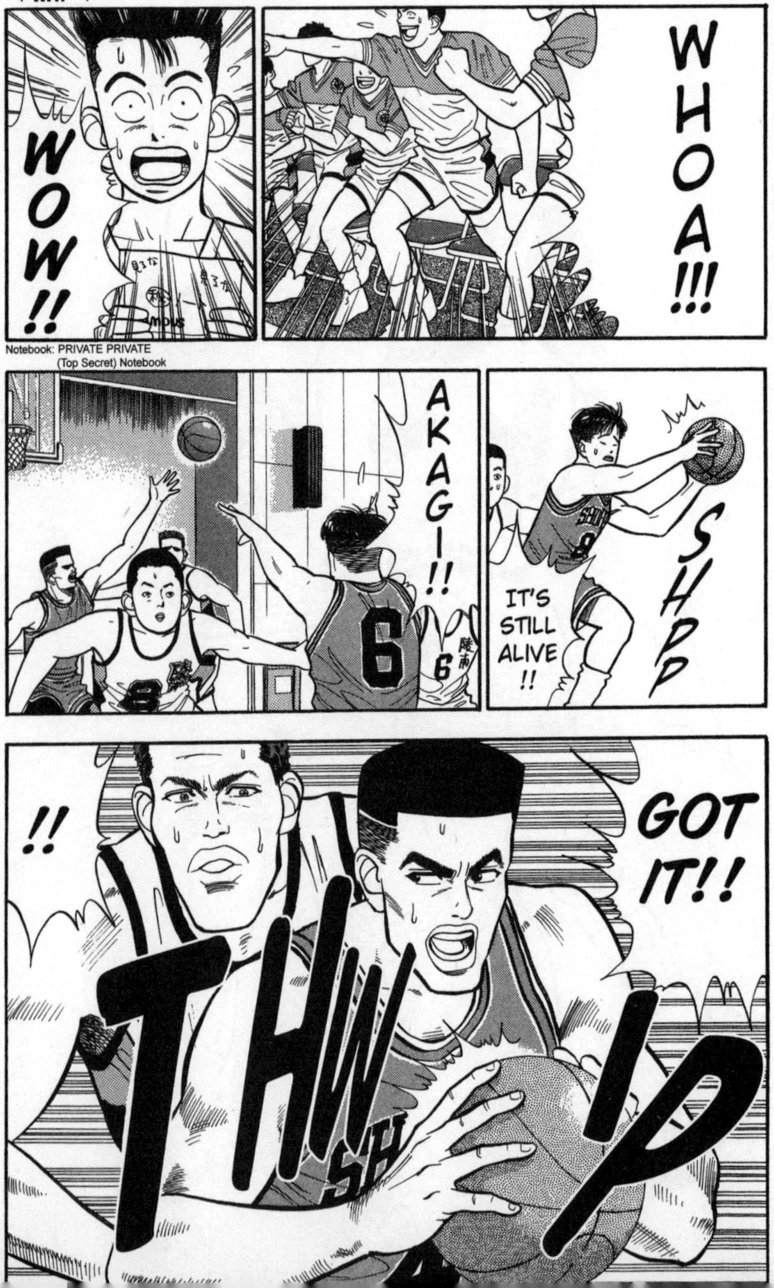
WHOA!!!
WOW!!
SHPP
IT'S STILL ALIVE!!
AKAGI!!
GOT IT!!
!!
THWIP

Notebook: PRIVATE PRIVATE (Top Secret) Notebook

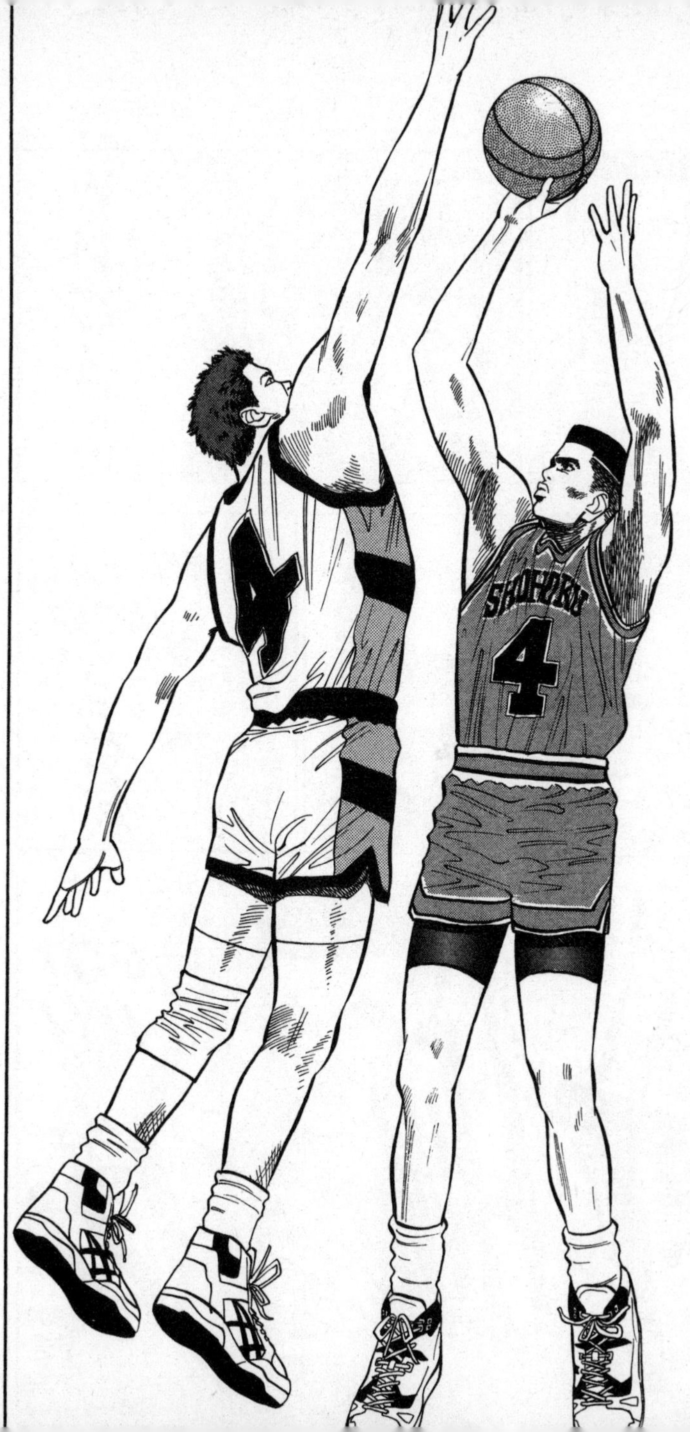
SHOHOKU
4

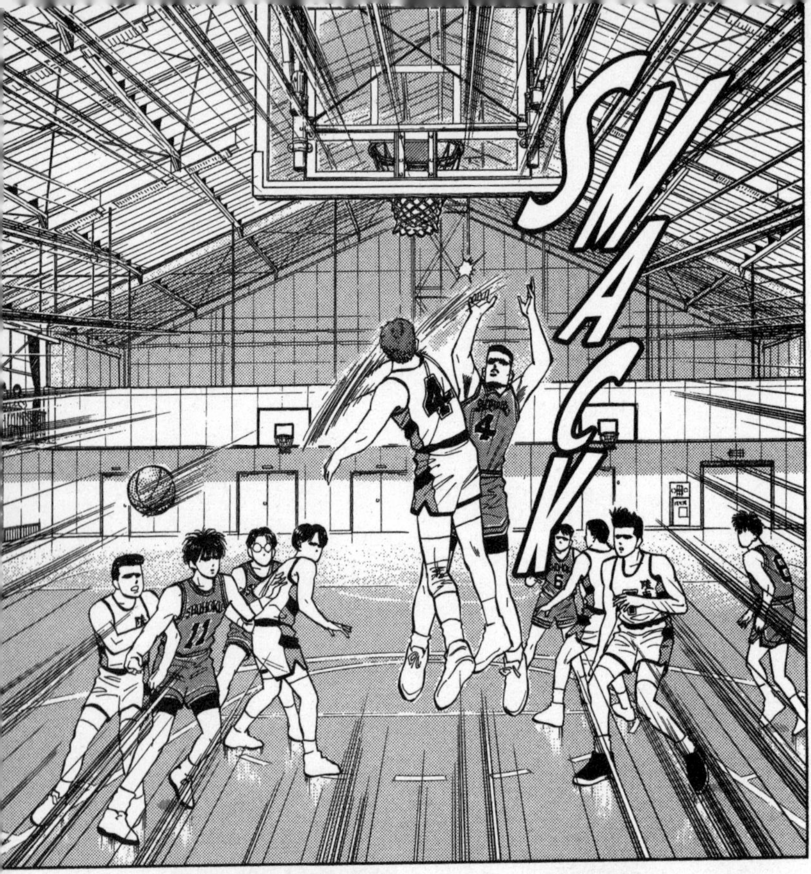
SMACK

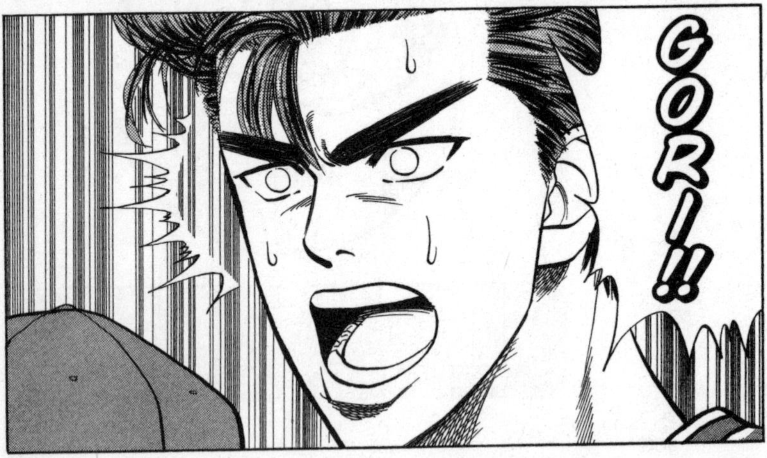
GORI!!

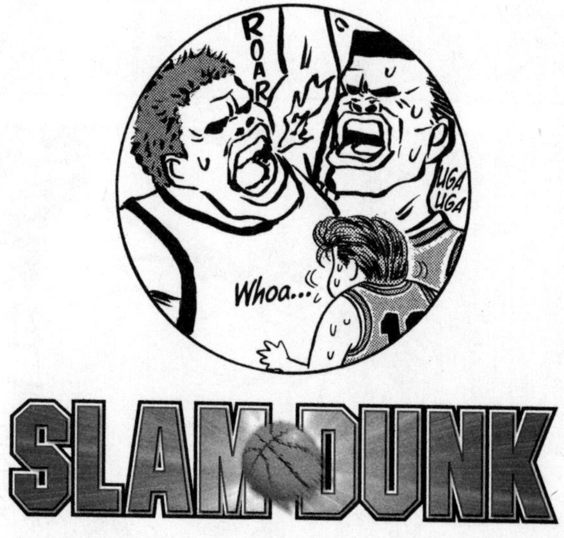
ROAR
UGA UGA
Whoa...

SLAM DUNK

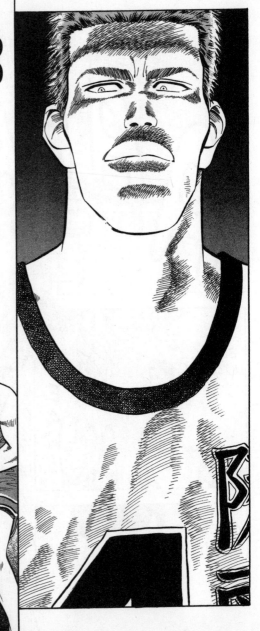

#28
RAGING RYONAN

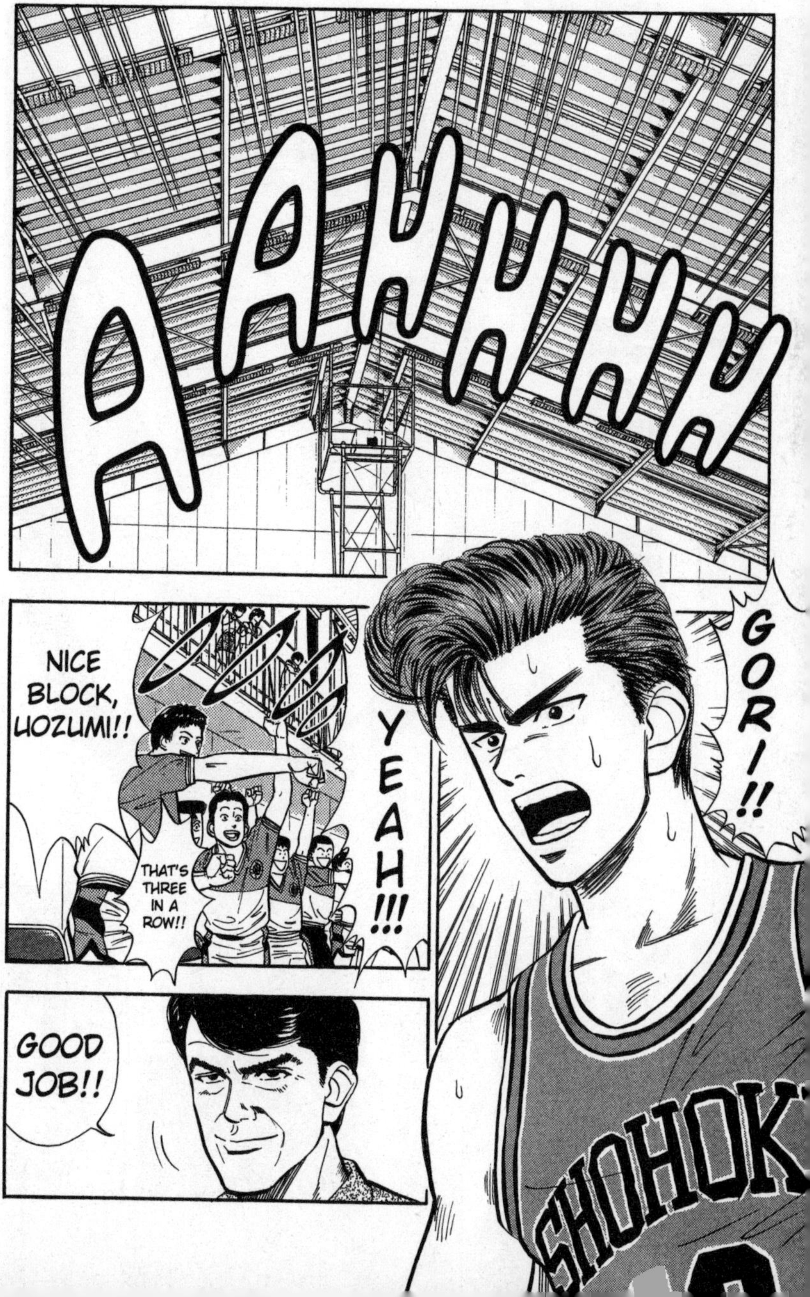
AAHHHHH
GORI!!
YEAH!!!
NICE BLOCK, UOZUMI!!
THAT'S THREE IN A ROW!!
GOOD JOB!!
SHOHOKU

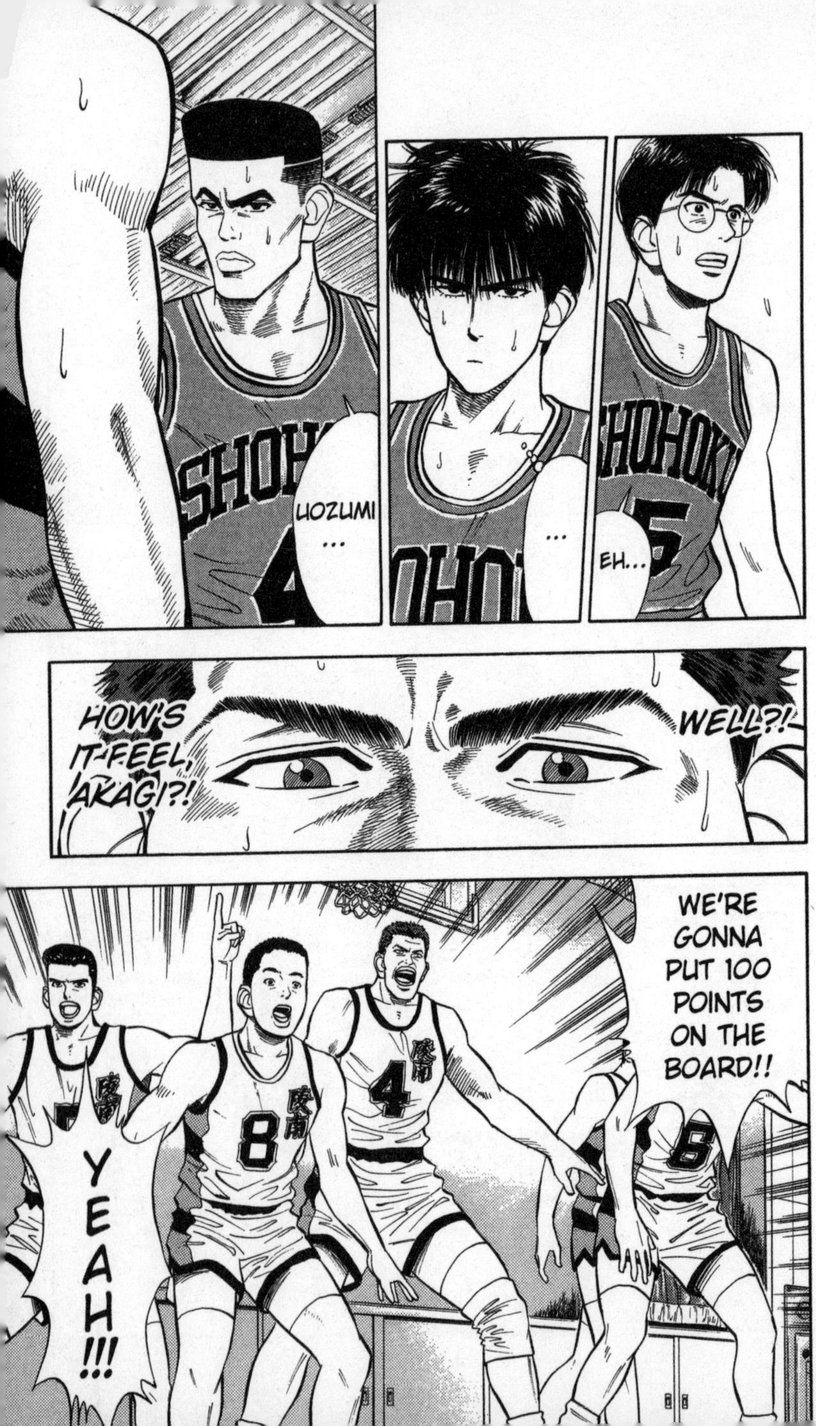
EH...
...
UOZUMI ...
WELL?!
HOW'S IT FEEL, AKAGI?!
WE'RE GONNA PUT 100 POINTS ON THE BOARD!!
YEAH!!!

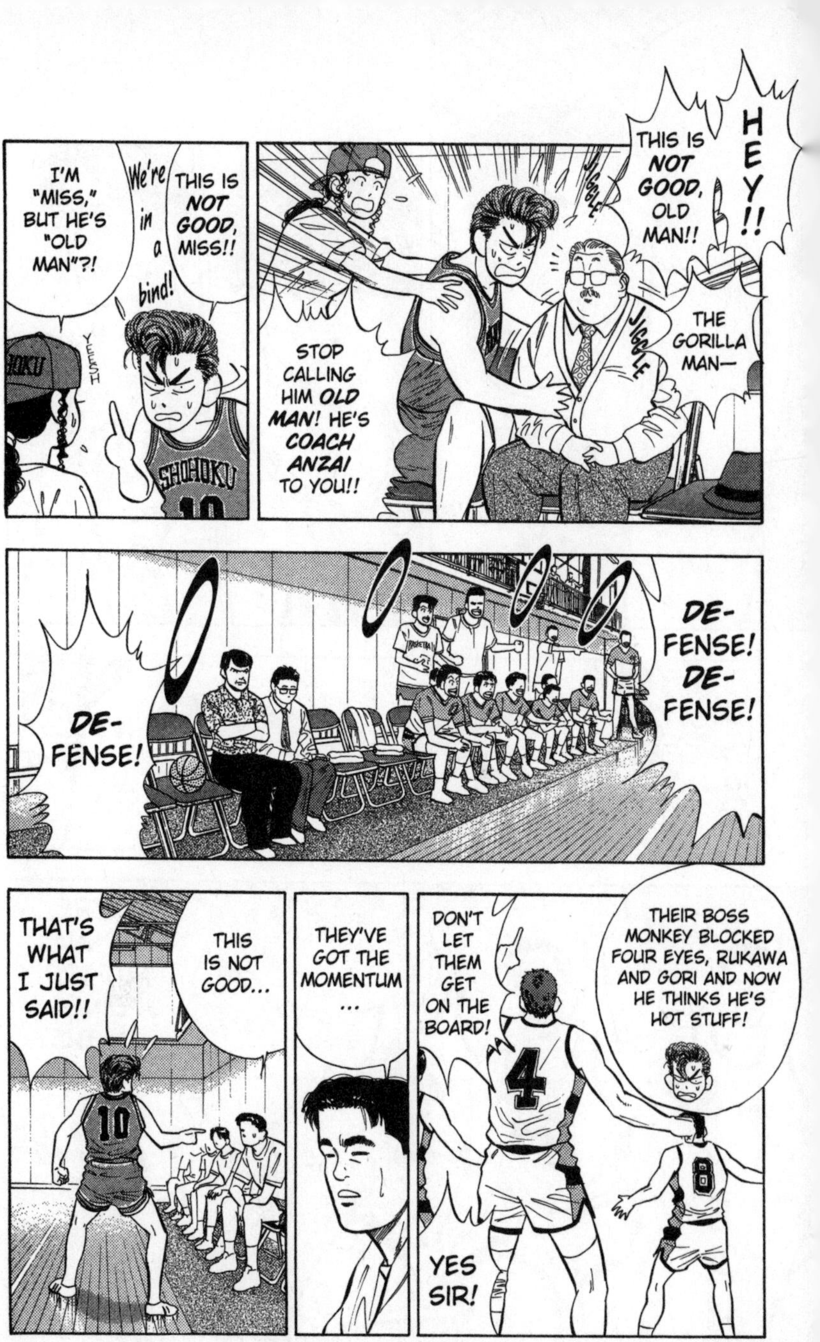
HEY!!
THIS IS NOT GOOD, OLD MAN!!
JIGGLE
JIGGLE
THE GORILLA MAN—
STOP CALLING HIM OLD MAN! HE'S COACH ANZAI TO YOU!!
THIS IS NOT GOOD, MISS!!
We're in a bind!
I'M "MISS," BUT HE'S "OLD MAN"?!
YEESH
DE-FENSE! DE-FENSE!
DE-FENSE!
THEIR BOSS MONKEY BLOCKED FOUR EYES, RUKAWA AND GORI AND NOW HE THINKS HE'S HOT STUFF!
DON'T LET THEM GET ON THE BOARD!
YES SIR!
THEY'VE GOT THE MOMENTUM ...
THIS IS NOT GOOD...
THAT'S WHAT I JUST SAID!!

READ THIS WAY

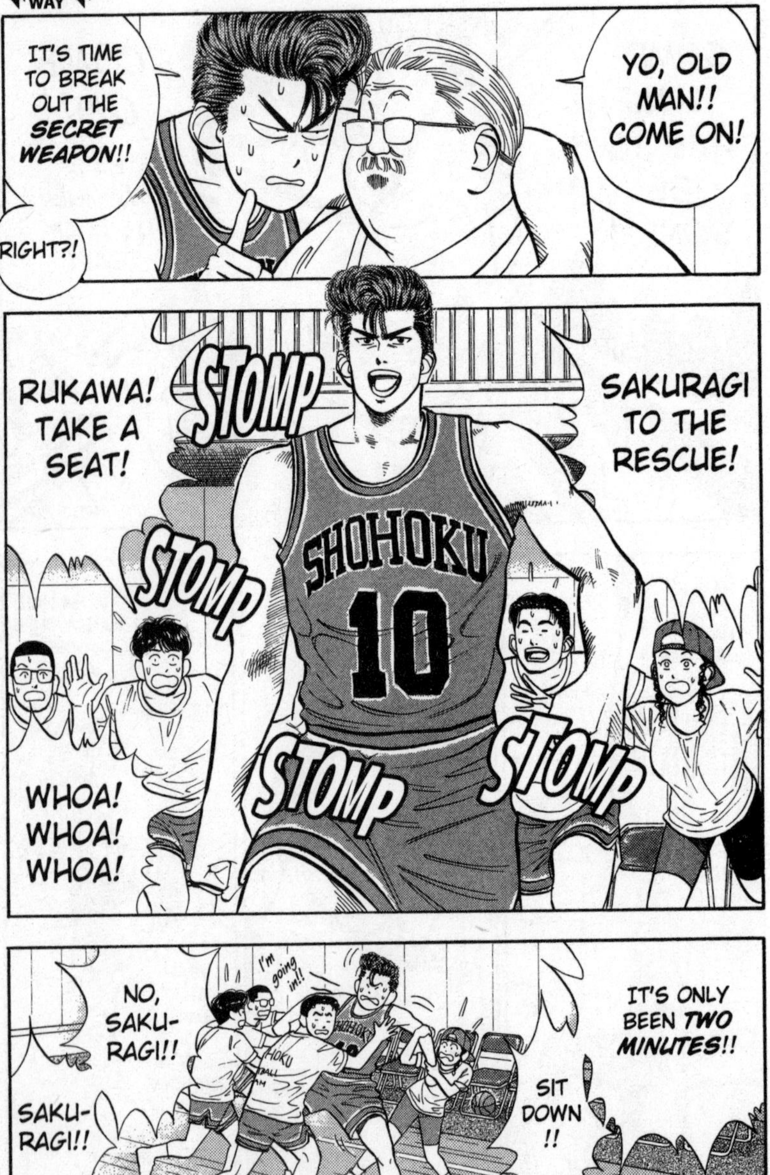
YO, OLD MAN!! COME ON!
IT'S TIME TO BREAK OUT THE SECRET WEAPON!!
RIGHT?!
SAKURAGI TO THE RESCUE!
STOMP
RUKAWA! TAKE A SEAT!
STOMP
STOMP
STOMP
WHOA! WHOA! WHOA!
IT'S ONLY BEEN TWO MINUTES!!
SIT DOWN!!
I'm going in!!
NO, SAKURAGI!!
SAKURAGI!!

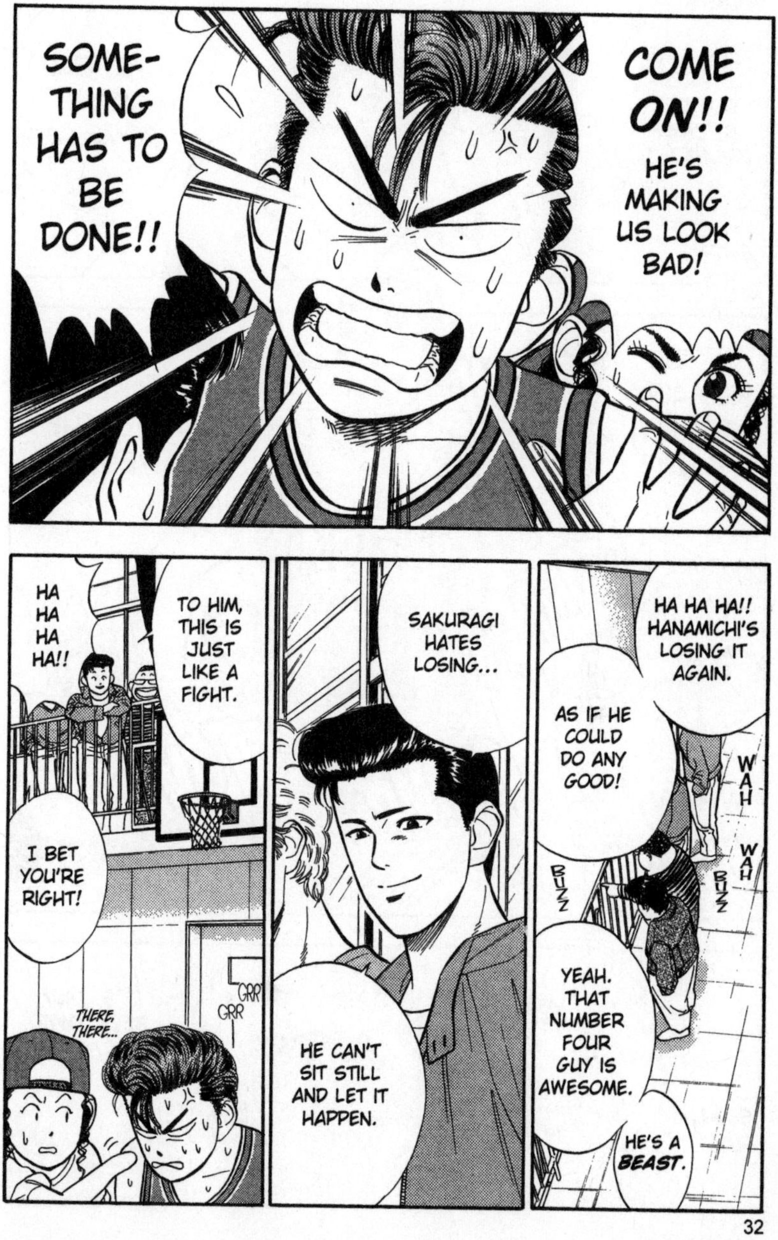
COME ON!!
HE'S MAKING US LOOK BAD!
SOME-THING HAS TO BE DONE!!
HA HA HA!! HANAMICHI'S LOSING IT AGAIN.
AS IF HE COULD DO ANY GOOD!
WAH WAH
BUZZ BUZZ
YEAH. THAT NUMBER FOUR GUY IS AWESOME.
HE'S A BEAST.
SAKURAGI HATES LOSING...
HE CAN'T SIT STILL AND LET IT HAPPEN.
TO HIM, THIS IS JUST LIKE A FIGHT.
HA HA HA HA!!
I BET YOU'RE RIGHT!
GRR GRR
THERE, THERE...

READ THIS WAY

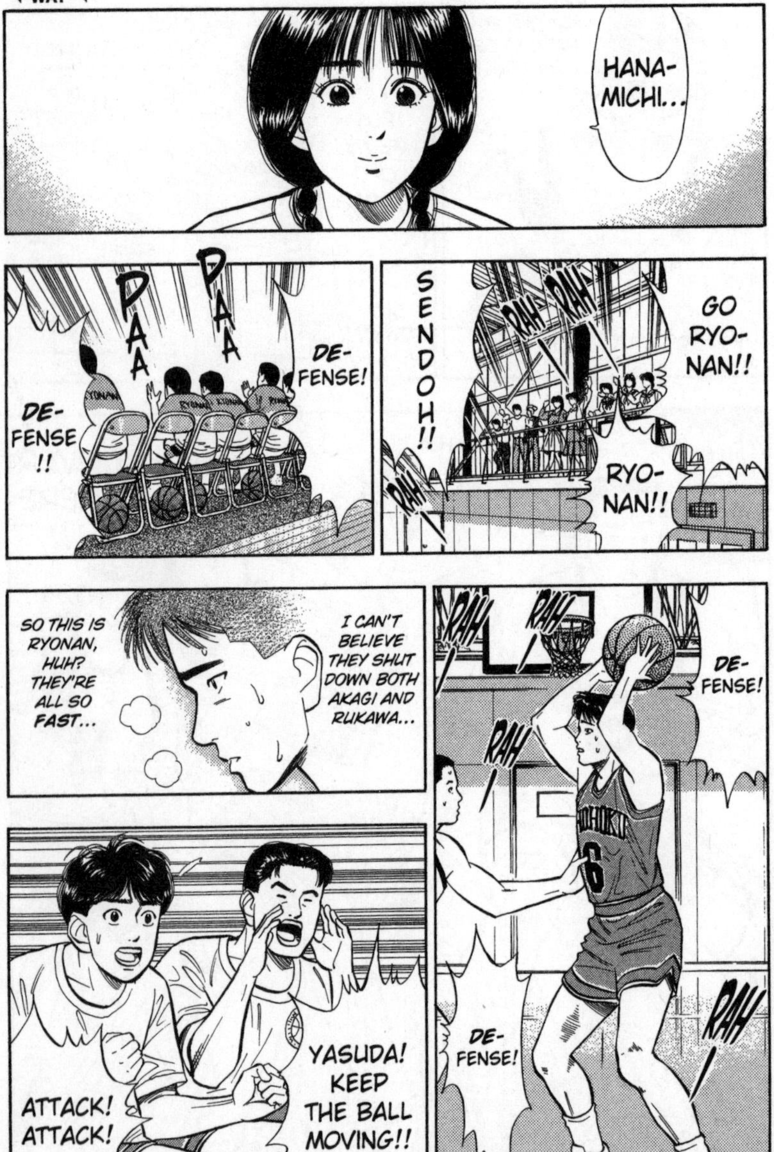

HANA-MICHI...
GO RYO-NAN!!
RAH RAH
SENDOH!!
RYO-NAN!!
RAH
PAA PAA
DE-FENSE!
DE-FENSE!!
RAH RAH
DE-FENSE!
RAH
DE-FENSE!
RAH
I CAN'T BELIEVE THEY SHUT DOWN BOTH AKAGI AND RUKAWA...
SO THIS IS RYONAN, HUH? THEY'RE ALL SO FAST...
YASUDA! KEEP THE BALL MOVING!!
ATTACK! ATTACK!

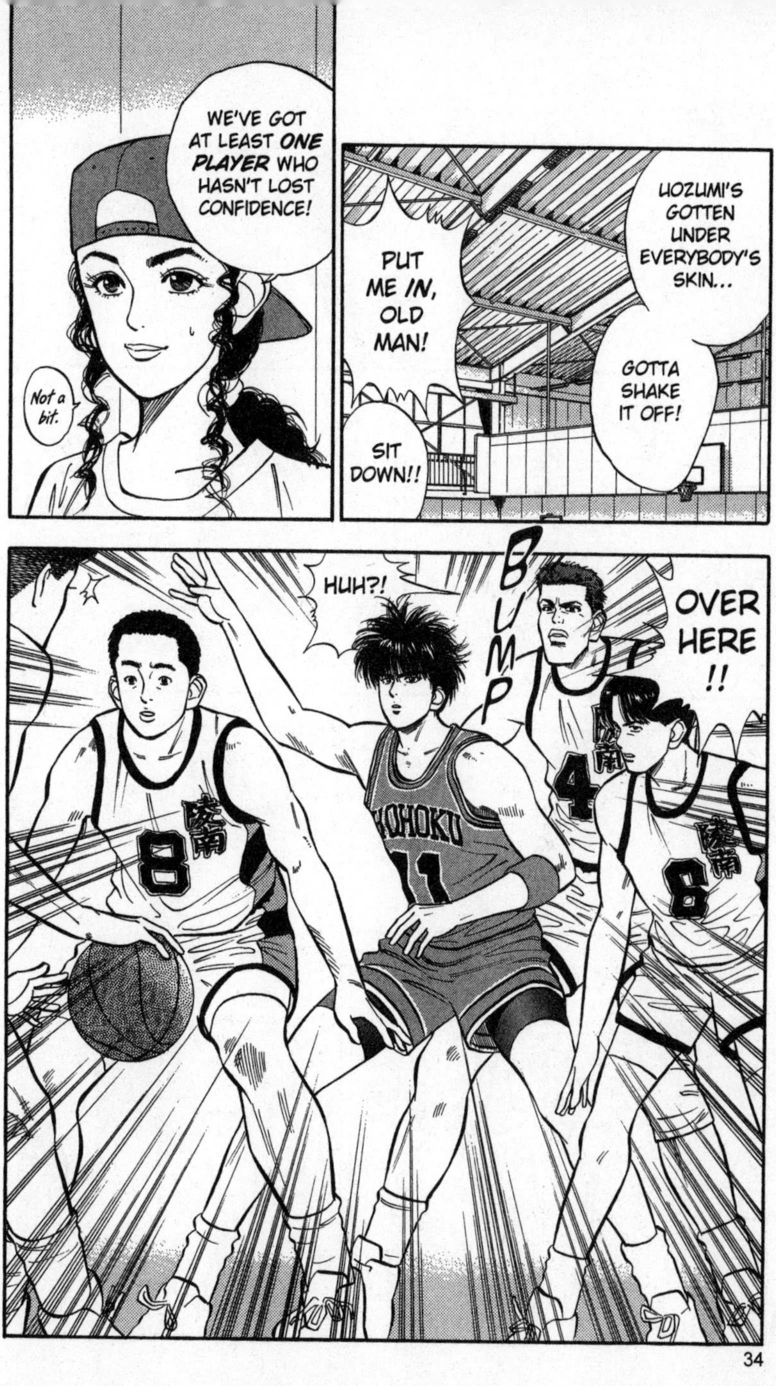
UOZUMI'S GOTTEN UNDER EVERYBODY'S SKIN...
PUT ME IN, OLD MAN!
GOTTA SHAKE IT OFF!
SIT DOWN!!
WE'VE GOT AT LEAST **ONE PLAYER** WHO HASN'T LOST CONFIDENCE!
Not a bit.
OVER HERE!!
BUMP
HUH?!
SHOHOKU
11
8
4
6

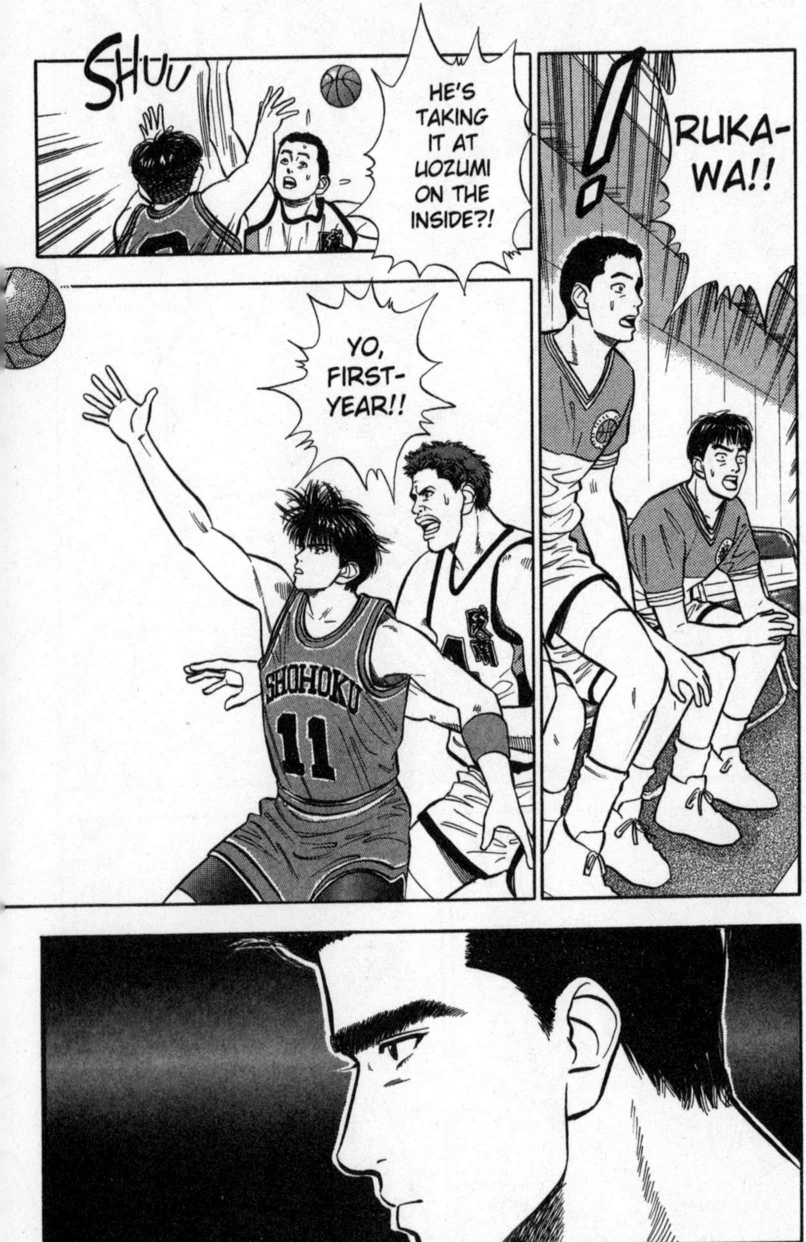
!
RUKAWA!!
SHUU
HE'S TAKING IT AT UOZUMI ON THE INSIDE?!
YO, FIRST-YEAR!!

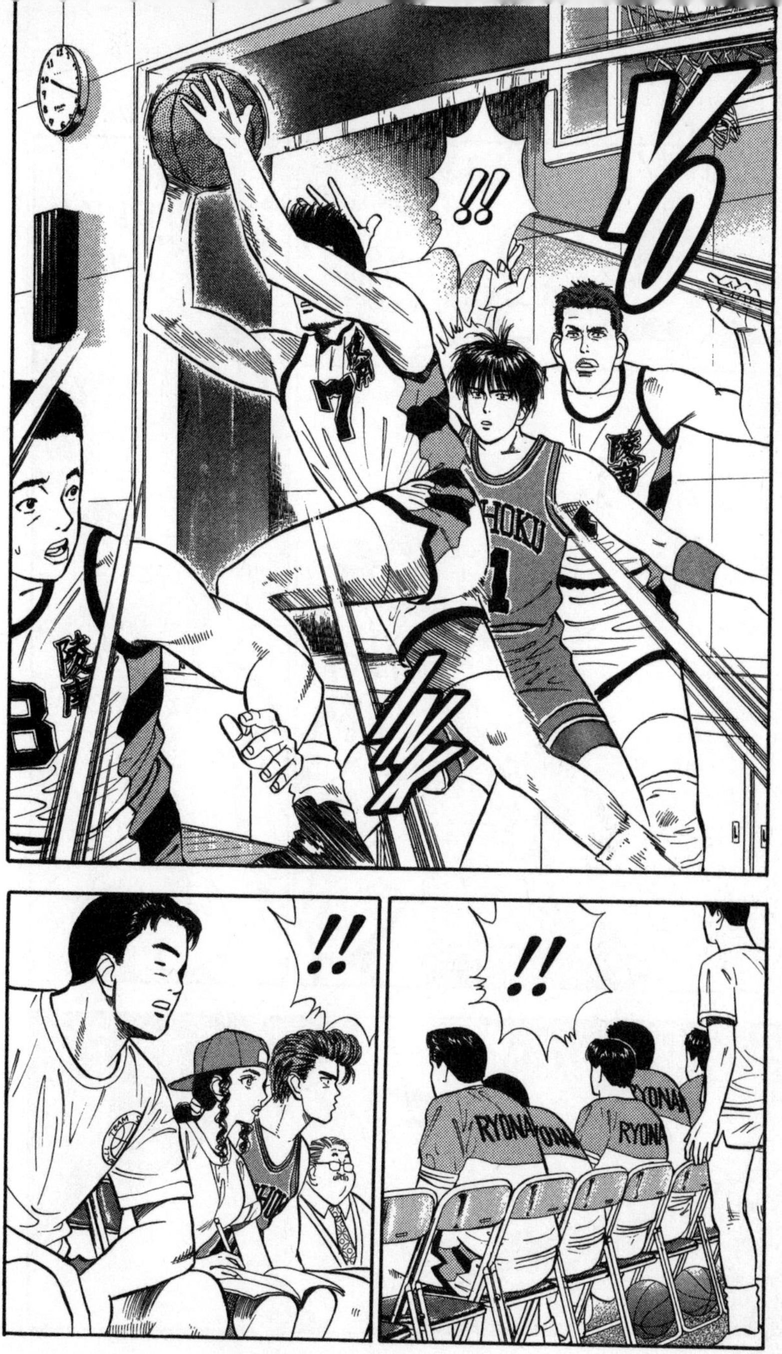
!!
YO
INK
!!
!!

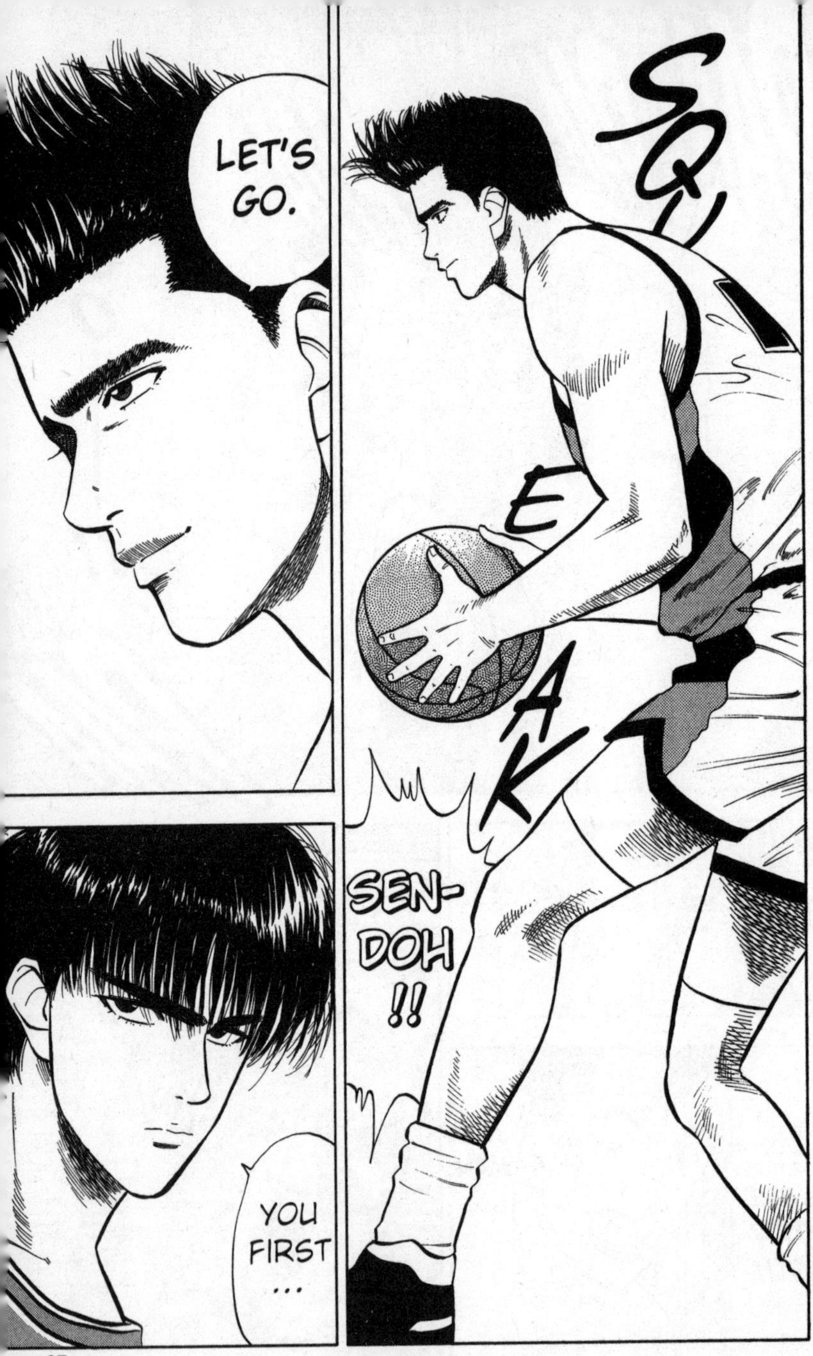
SQUEAK
SEN-DOH!!
LET'S GO.
YOU FIRST ...

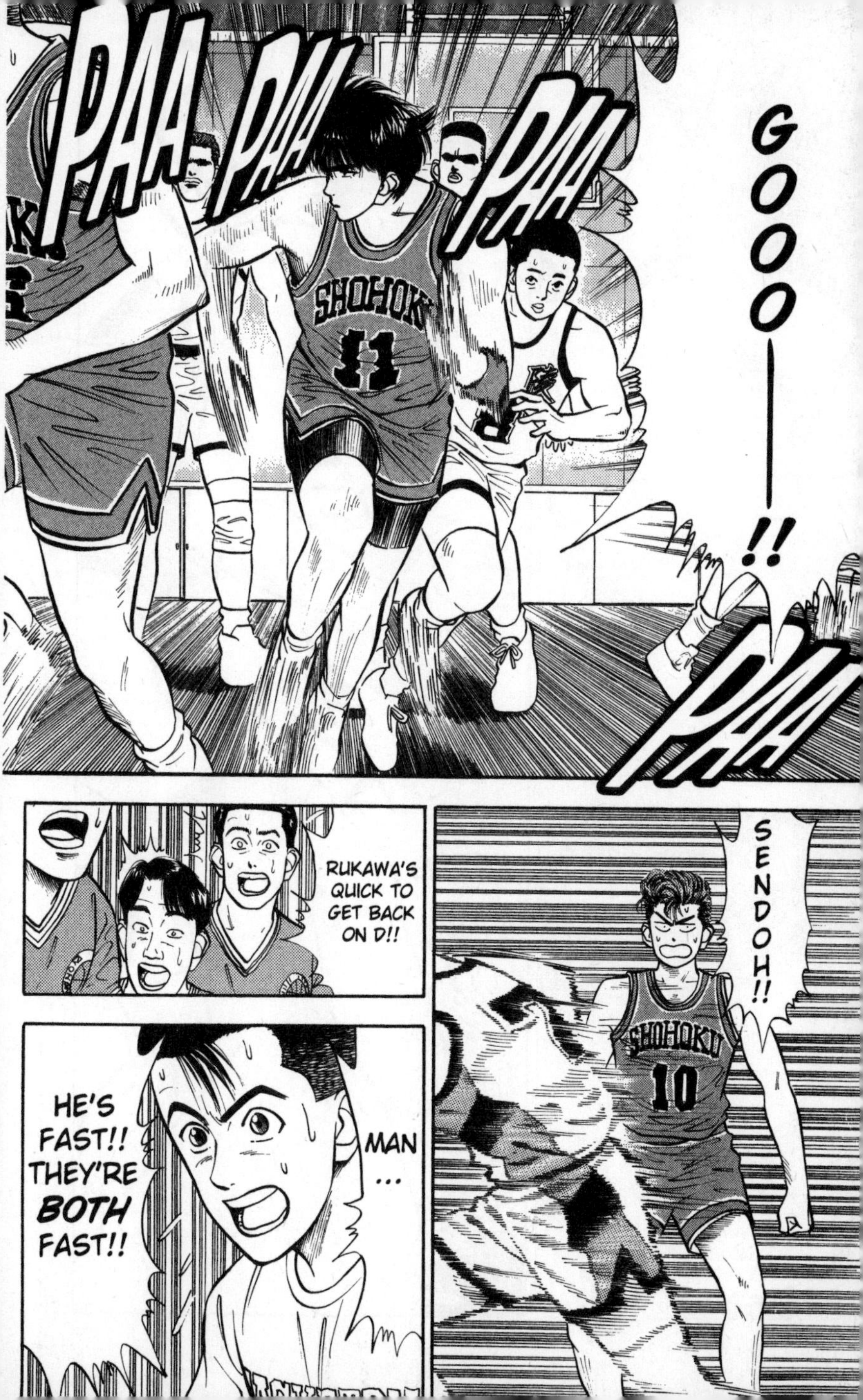
GOOO—!!
PAA
PA
PA
PA
SENDOH!!
RUKAWA'S QUICK TO GET BACK ON D!!
MAN ...
HE'S FAST!! THEY'RE BOTH FAST!!

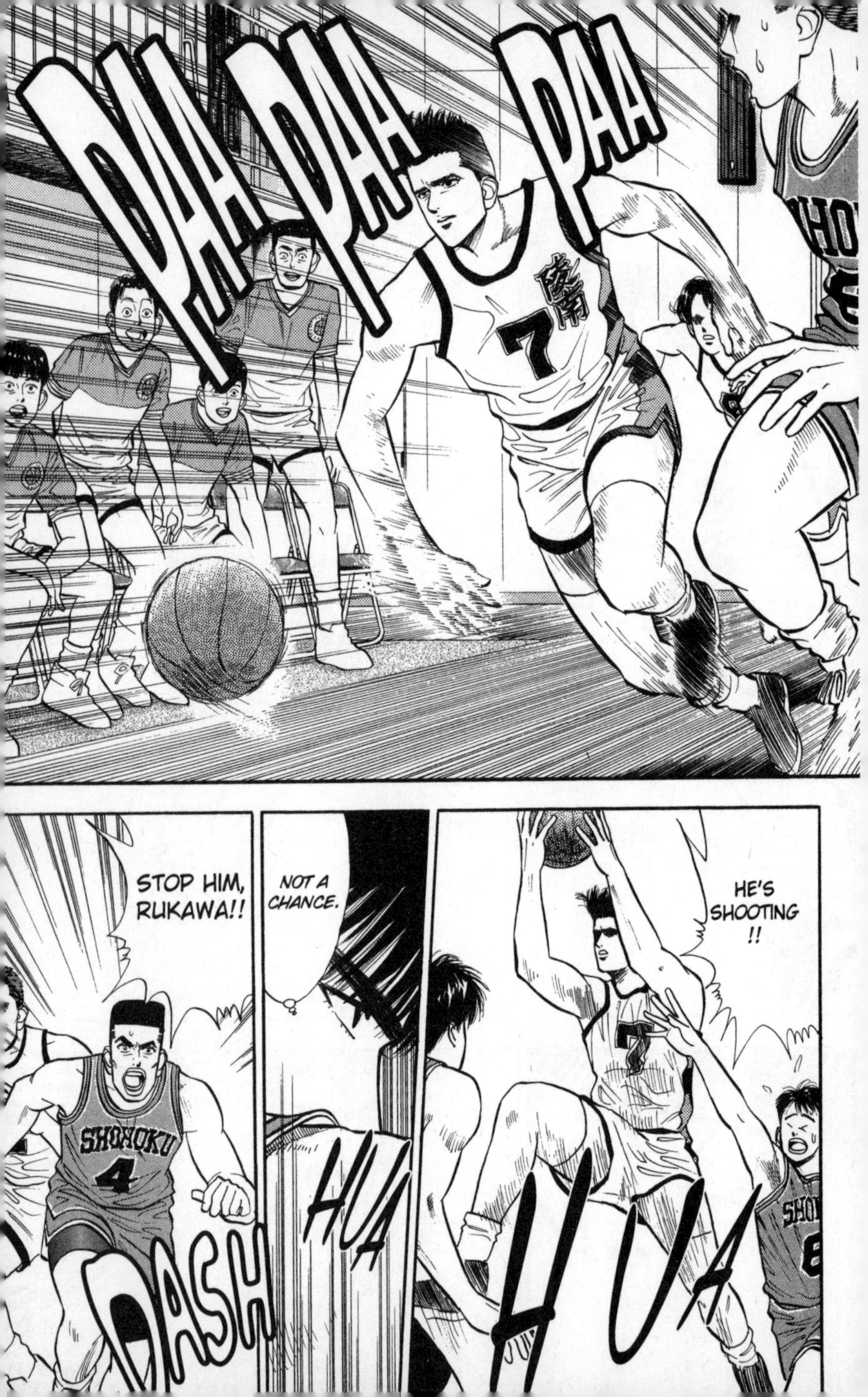
DAPA DAPA
PAA
HE'S SHOOTING !!
NOT A CHANCE.
HUA
STOP HIM, RUKAWA!!
DASH
HUA

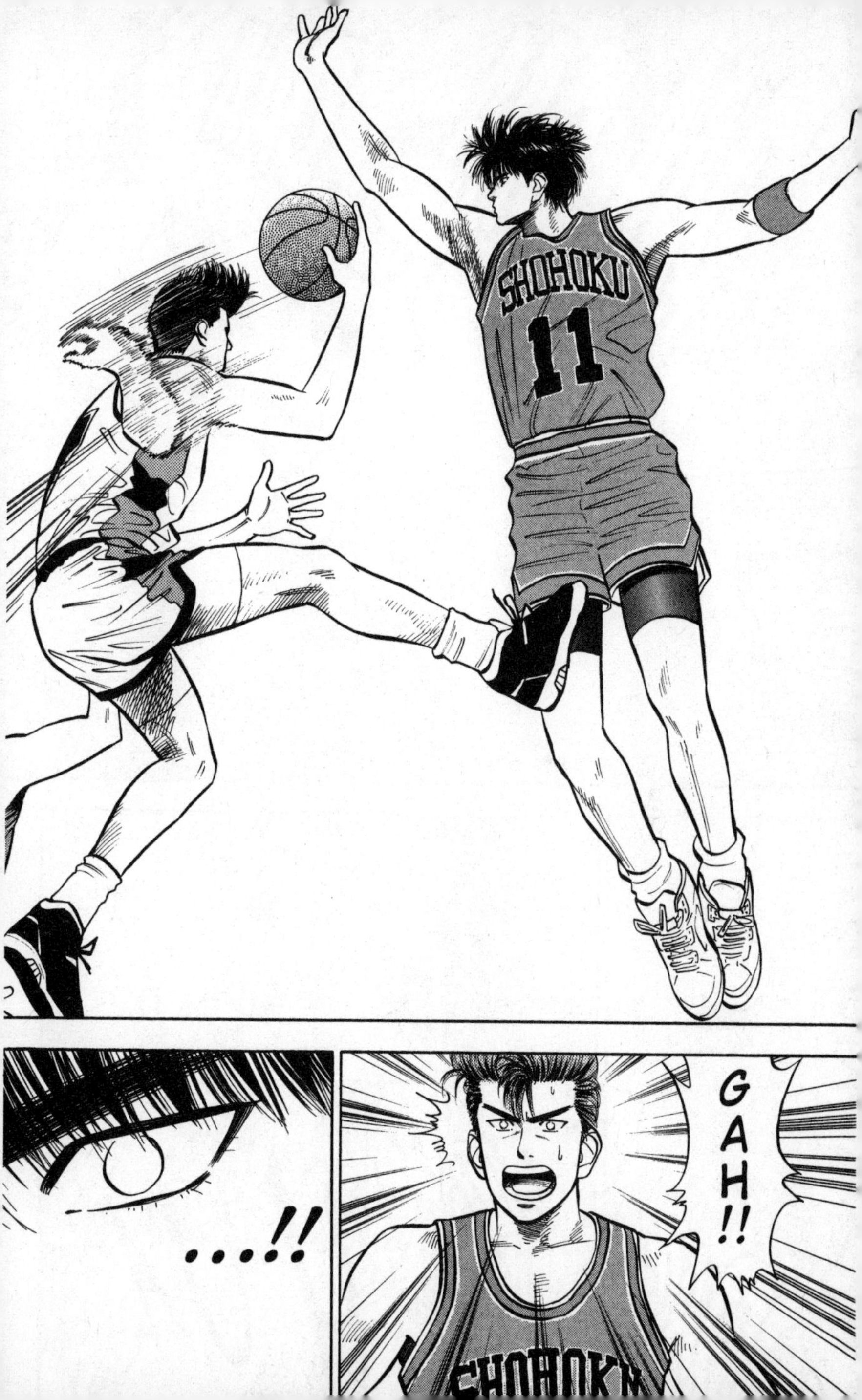
SHOHOKU
11
GAH!!
...!!

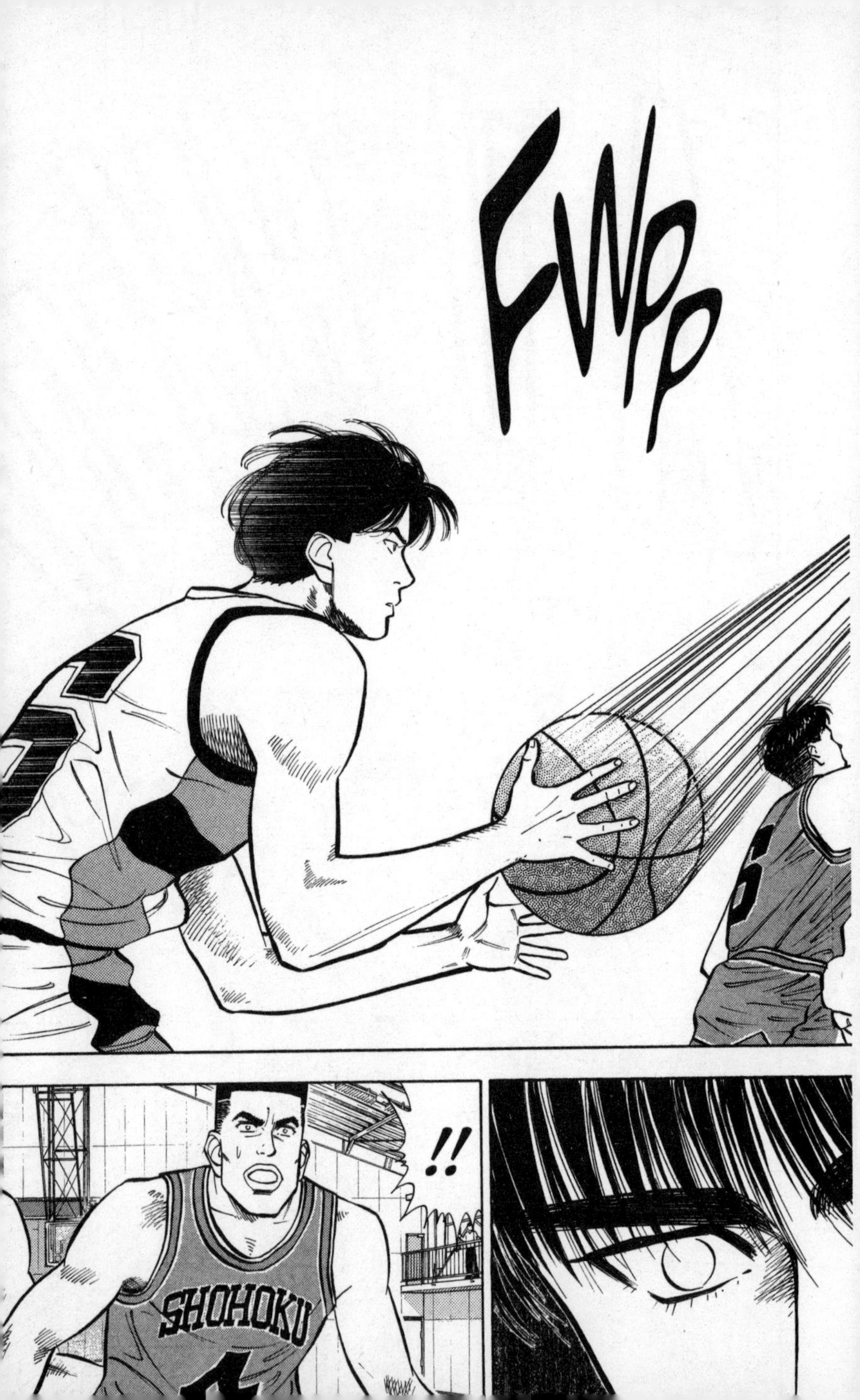
FWPP
!!
SHOHOKU

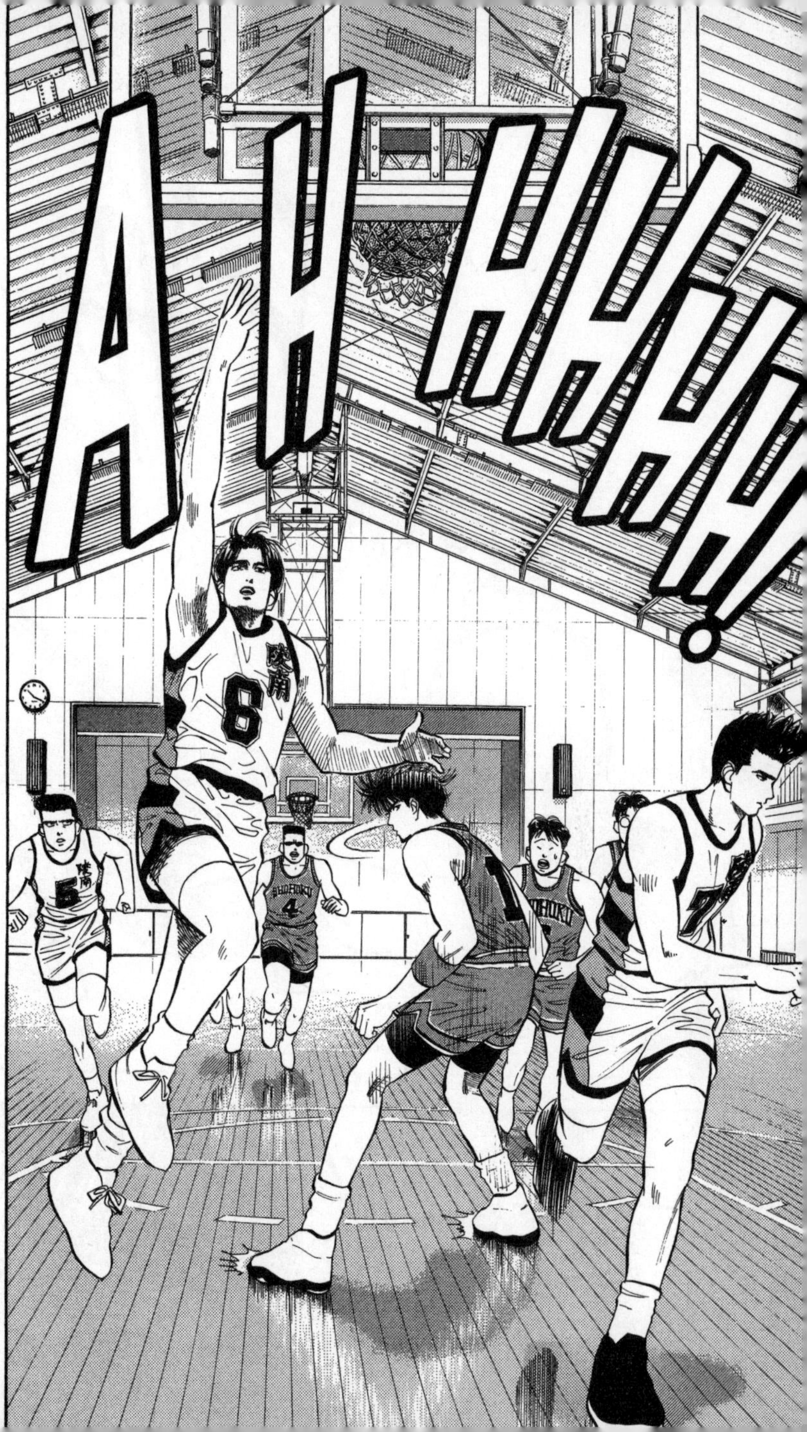
AHHHHH!

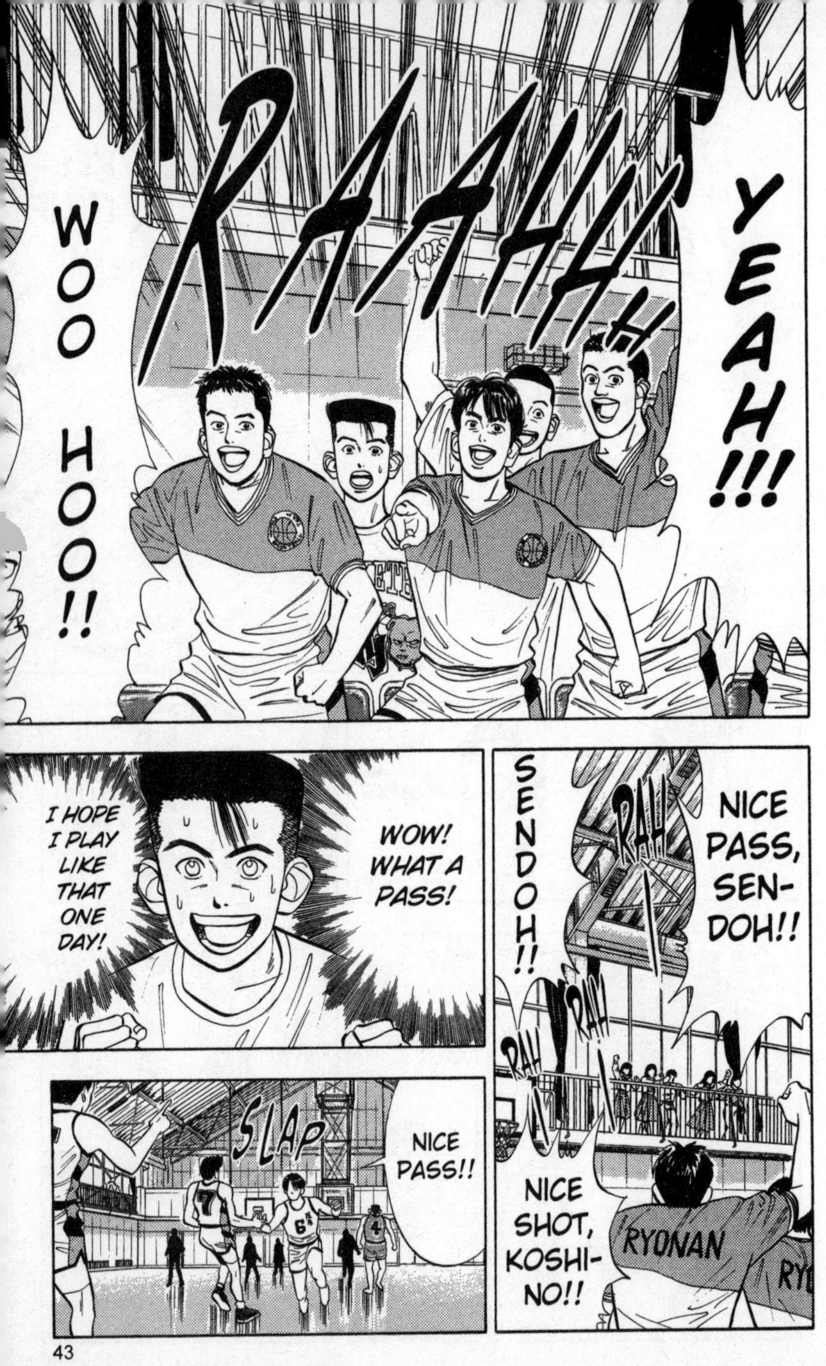
YEAH!!!
RAAHH
WOO HOO!!
NICE PASS, SEN-DOH!!
SENDOH!!
RAH
RAH
RAH
RAH
NICE SHOT, KOSHI-NO!!
RYONAN
WOW! WHAT A PASS!
I HOPE I PLAY LIKE THAT ONE DAY!
NICE PASS!!
SLAP

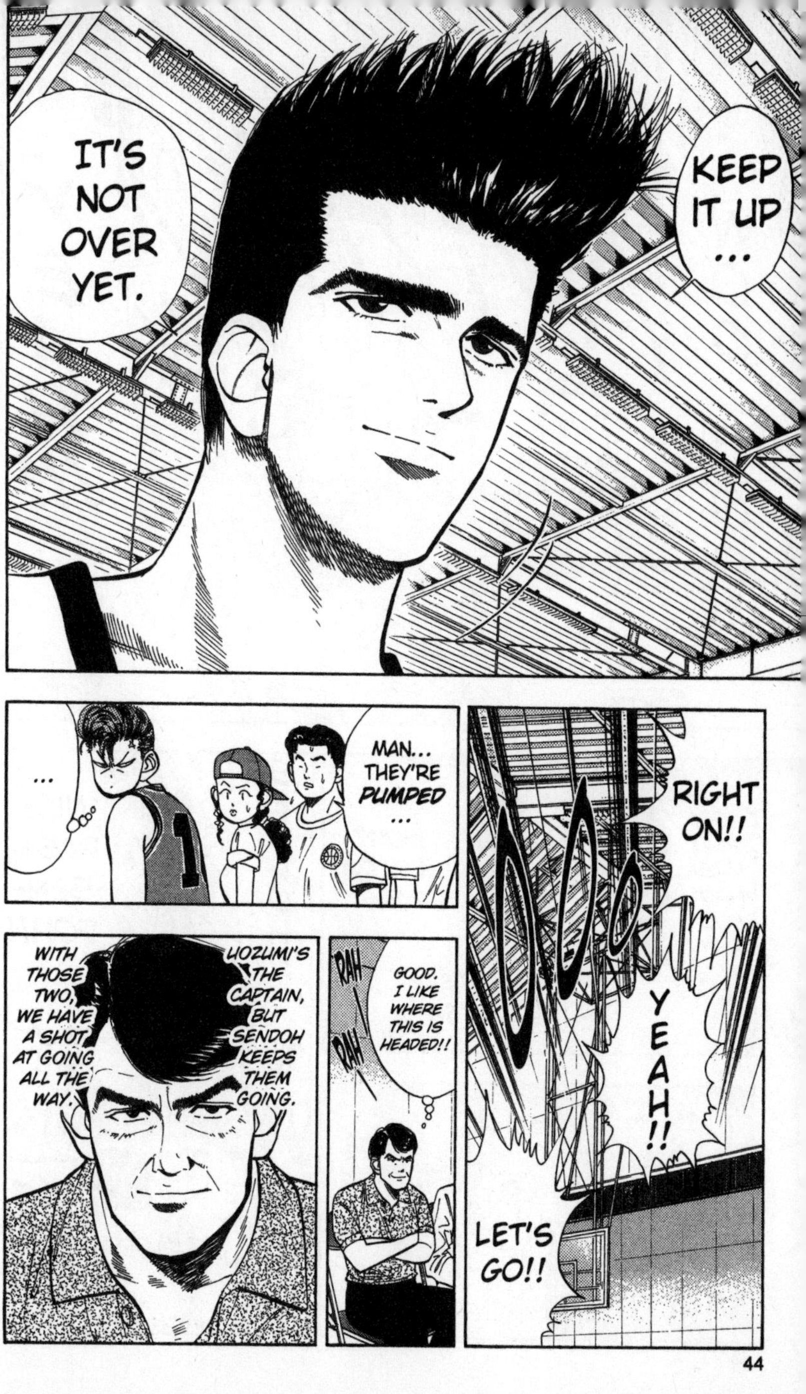
KEEP IT UP ...
IT'S NOT OVER YET.
RIGHT ON!!
YEAH!!
LET'S GO!!
MAN... THEY'RE *PUMPED* ...
...
RAH
RAH
GOOD. I LIKE WHERE THIS IS HEADED!!
UOZUMI'S THE CAPTAIN, BUT SENDOH KEEPS THEM GOING.
WITH THOSE TWO, WE HAVE A SHOT AT GOING ALL THE WAY.

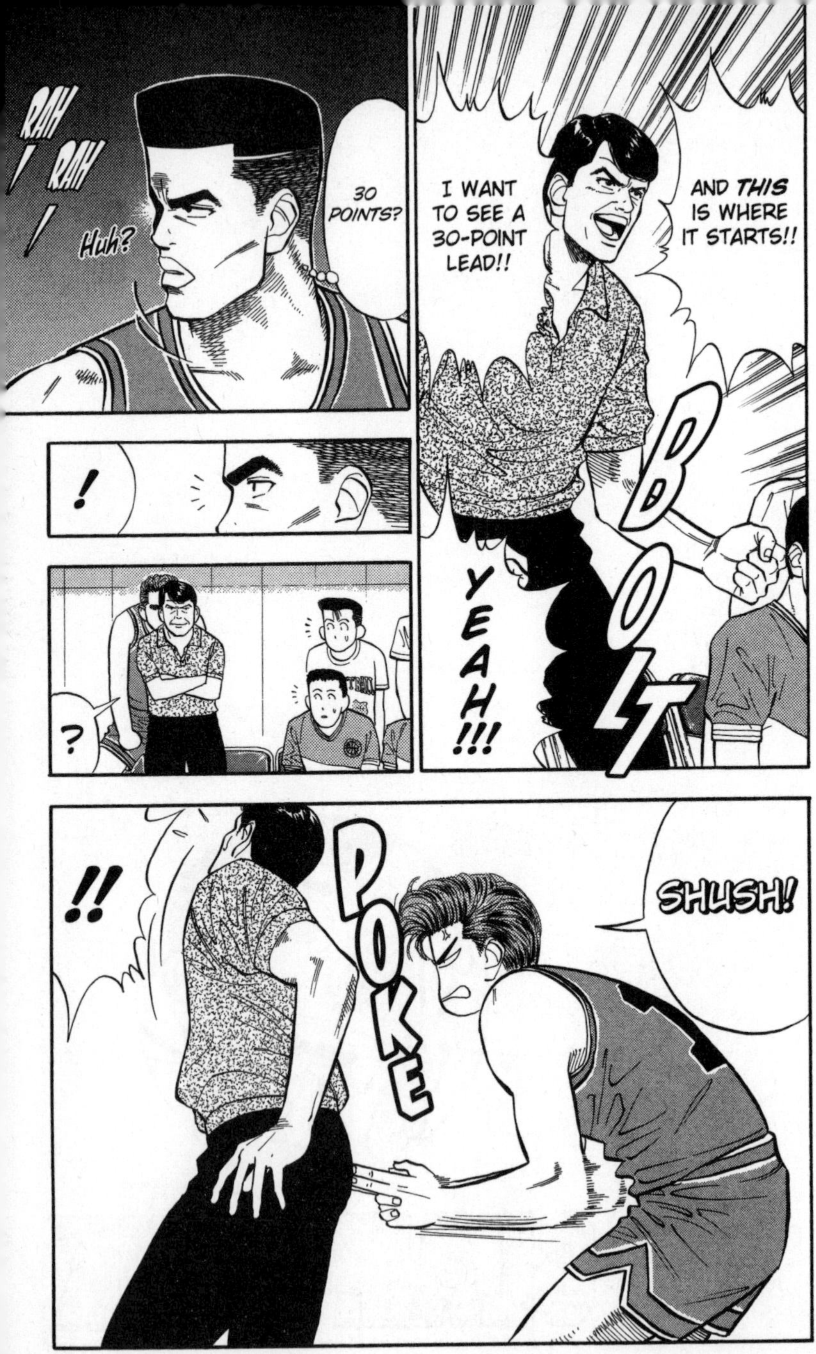
I WANT TO SEE A 30-POINT LEAD!!
AND *THIS* IS WHERE IT STARTS!!
YEAH!!!
BOLT
30 POINTS?
RAH! RAH!
Huh?
!
?
SHUSH!
POKE
!!

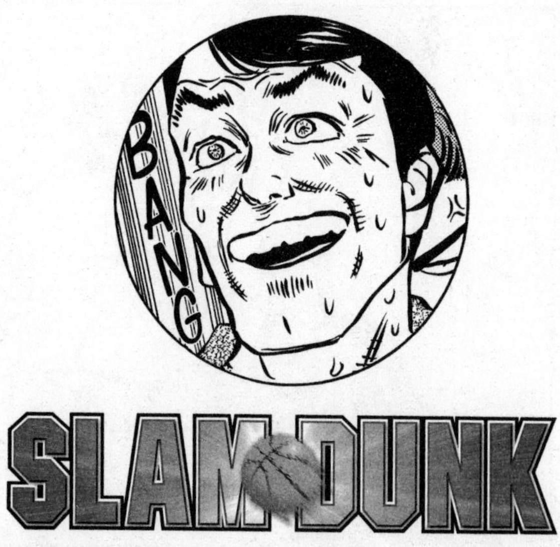
BANG

SLAM DUNK

#29 HIGH SCHOOL HIGH CLASS

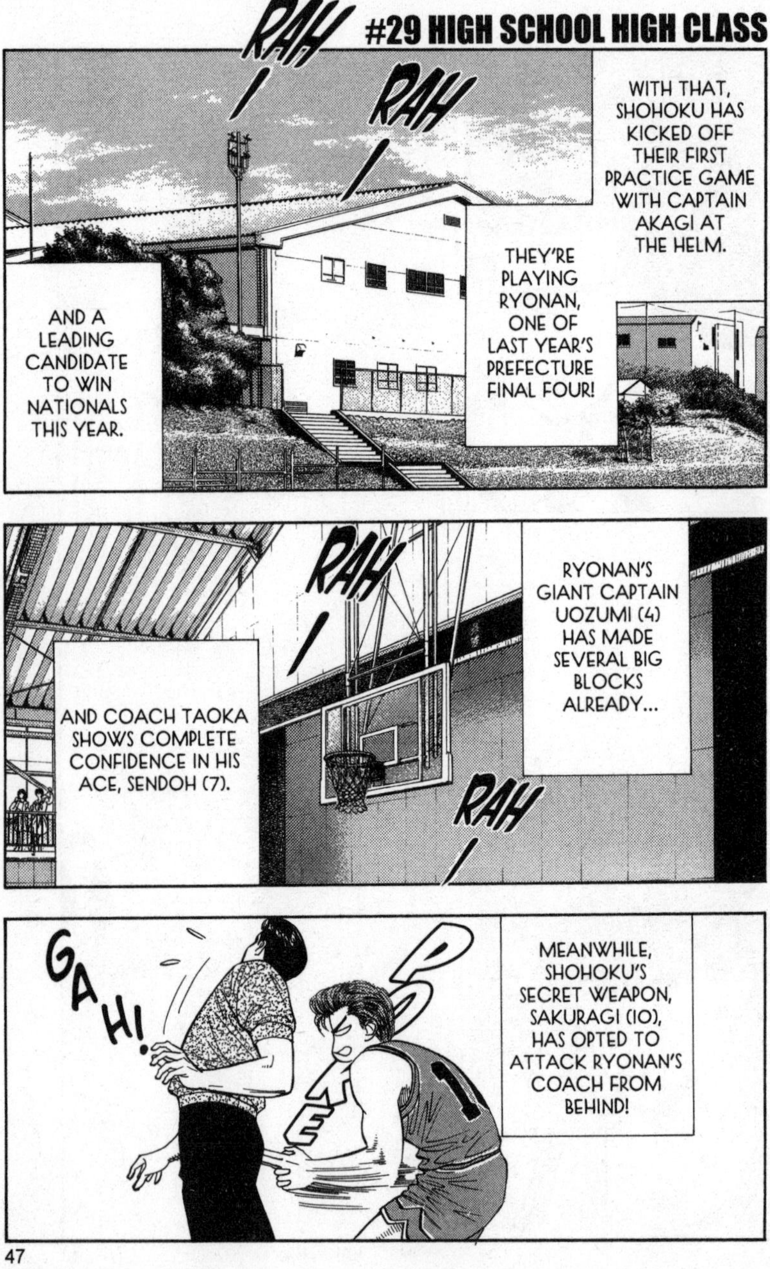
RAH
RAH
WITH THAT, SHOHOKU HAS KICKED OFF THEIR FIRST PRACTICE GAME WITH CAPTAIN AKAGI AT THE HELM.
THEY'RE PLAYING RYONAN, ONE OF LAST YEAR'S PREFECTURE FINAL FOUR!
AND A LEADING CANDIDATE TO WIN NATIONALS THIS YEAR.
RAH
RYONAN'S GIANT CAPTAIN UOZUMI (4) HAS MADE SEVERAL BIG BLOCKS ALREADY...
AND COACH TAOKA SHOWS COMPLETE CONFIDENCE IN HIS ACE, SENDOH (7).
RAH
MEANWHILE, SHOHOKU'S SECRET WEAPON, SAKURAGI (10), HAS OPTED TO ATTACK RYONAN'S COACH FROM BEHIND!
GAH!

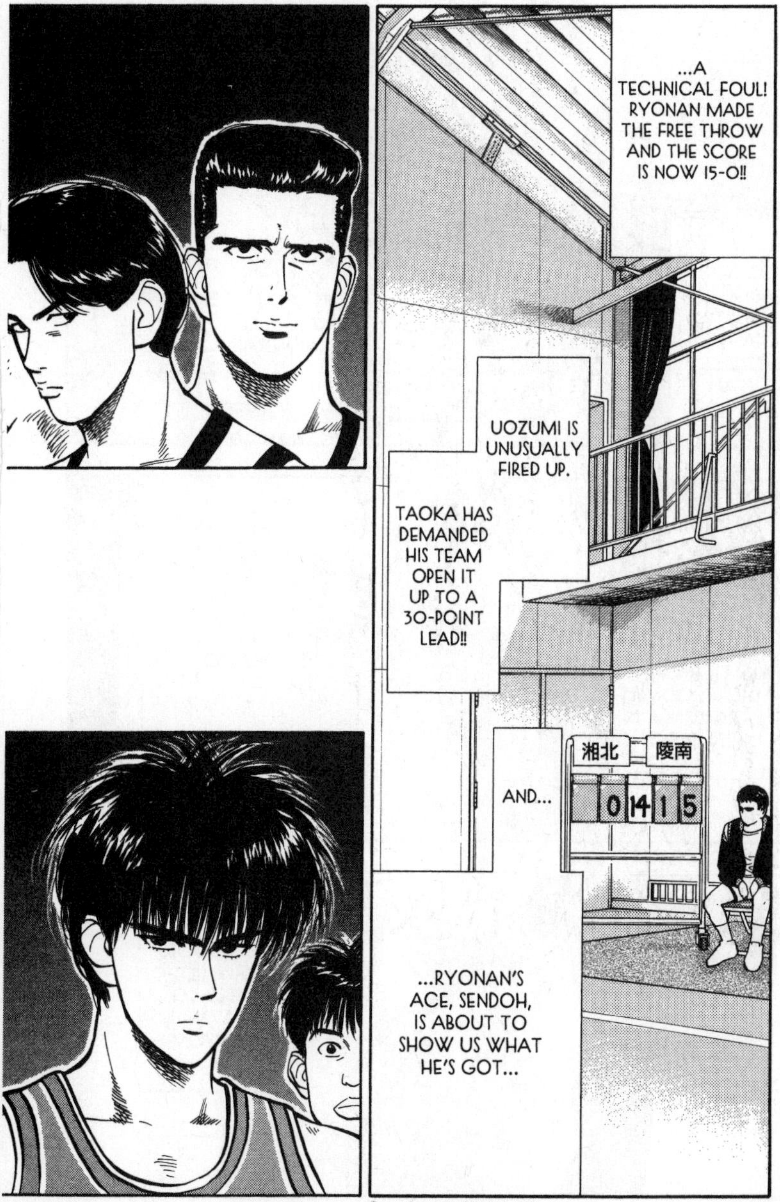
...A TECHNICAL FOUL! RYONAN MADE THE FREE THROW AND THE SCORE IS NOW 15-0!!
UOZUMI IS UNUSUALLY FIRED UP.
TAOKA HAS DEMANDED HIS TEAM OPEN IT UP TO A 30-POINT LEAD!!
湘北
陵南
AND...
...RYONAN'S ACE, SENDOH, IS ABOUT TO SHOW US WHAT HE'S GOT...
Scoreboard: Shohoku Ryonan

READ THIS WAY

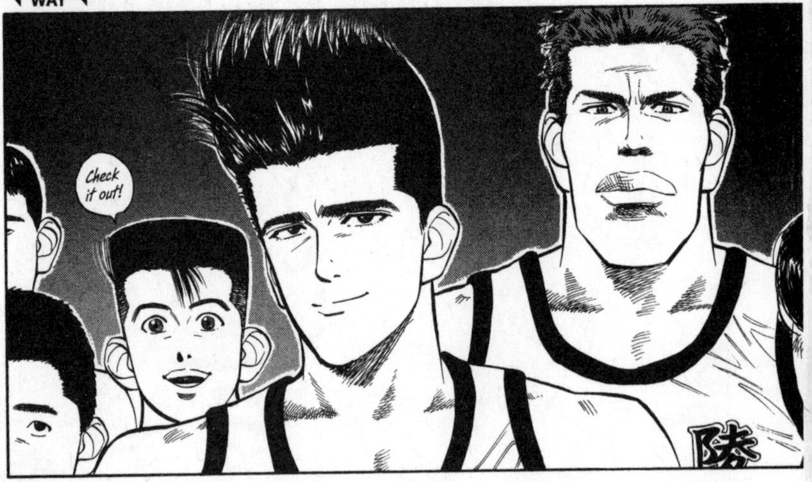
Check it out!

#29 HIGH SCHOOL HIGH CLASS

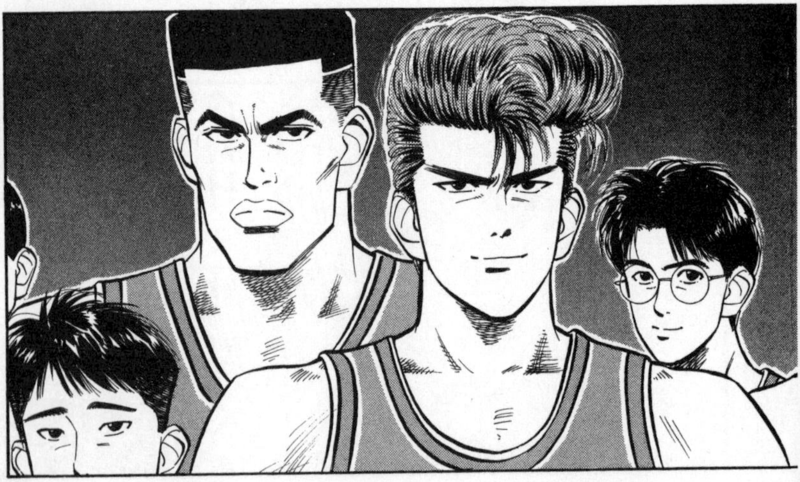

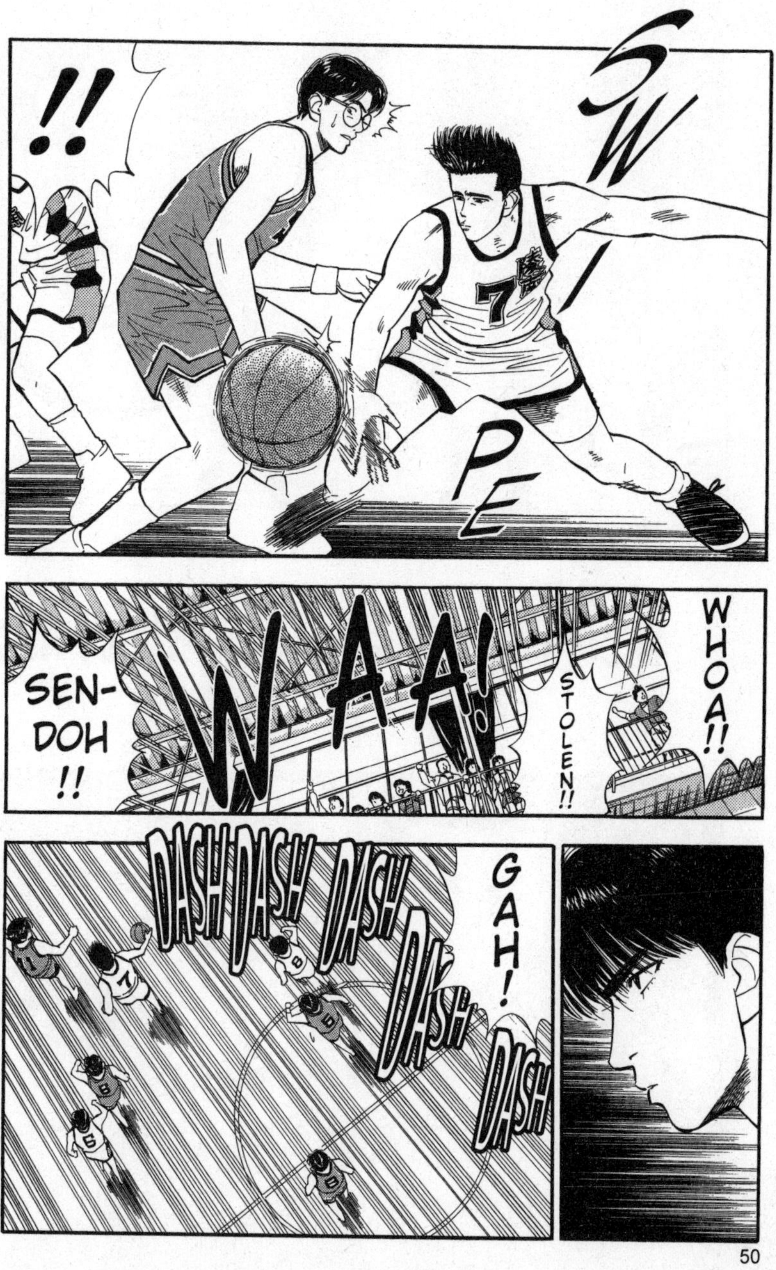
SWIPE
!!
WHOA!!
STOLEN!!
WAA!
SEN-DOH!!
GAH!
DASH DASH DASH DASH DASH

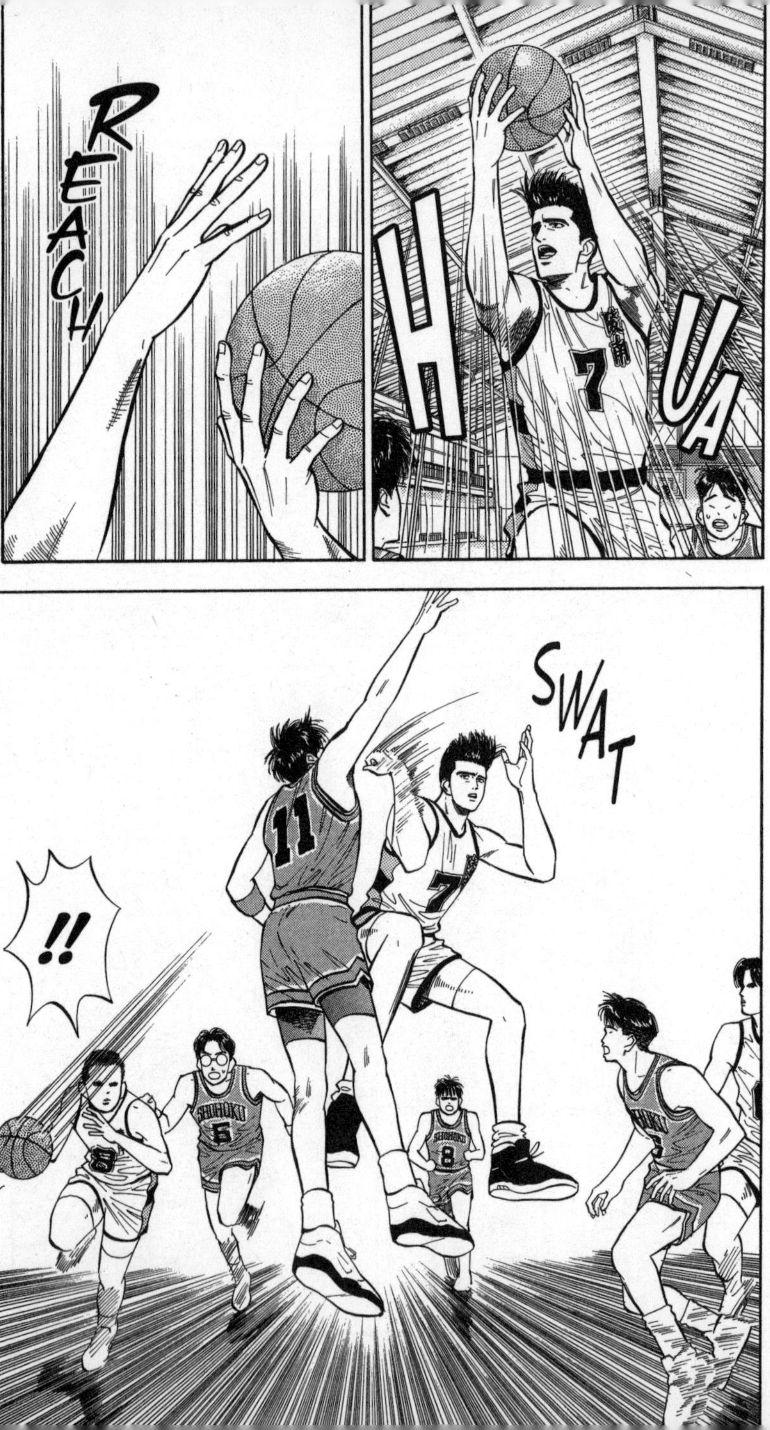
HUA
REACH
SWAT
!!

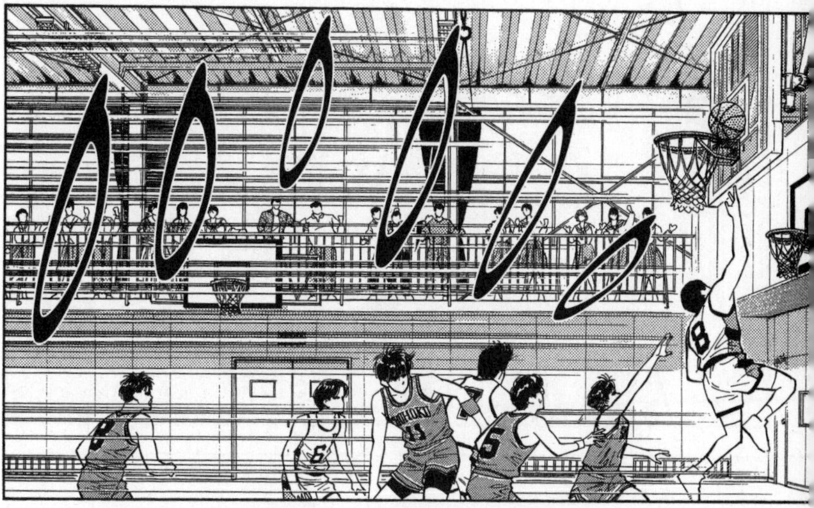

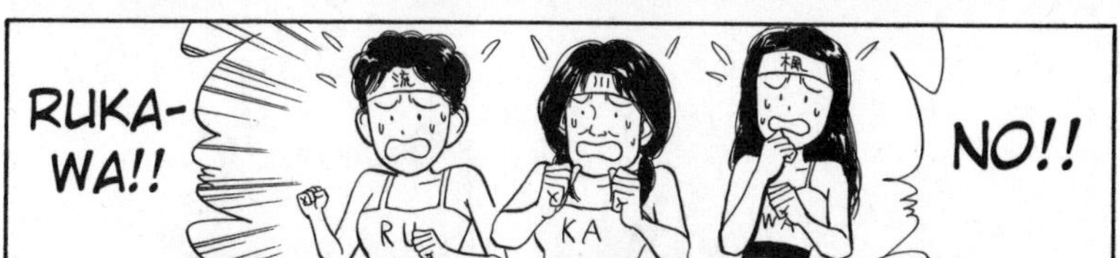
NO!!
RUKA-
WA!!
RU
KA
WA
Headbands spell "Rukawa"

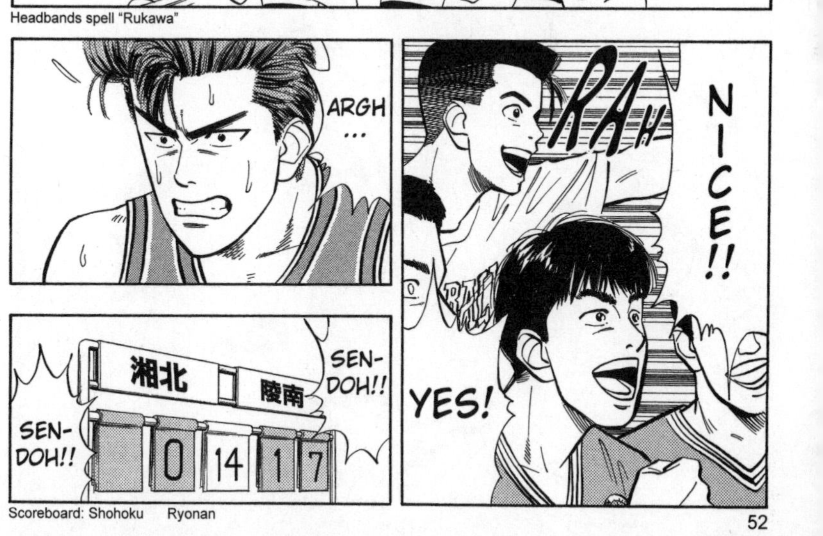
NICE!!
RAH
YES!
ARGH
...
SEN-
DOH!!
湘北
陵南
0 14 17
SEN-
DOH!!
Scoreboard: Shohoku Ryonan

READ THIS WAY

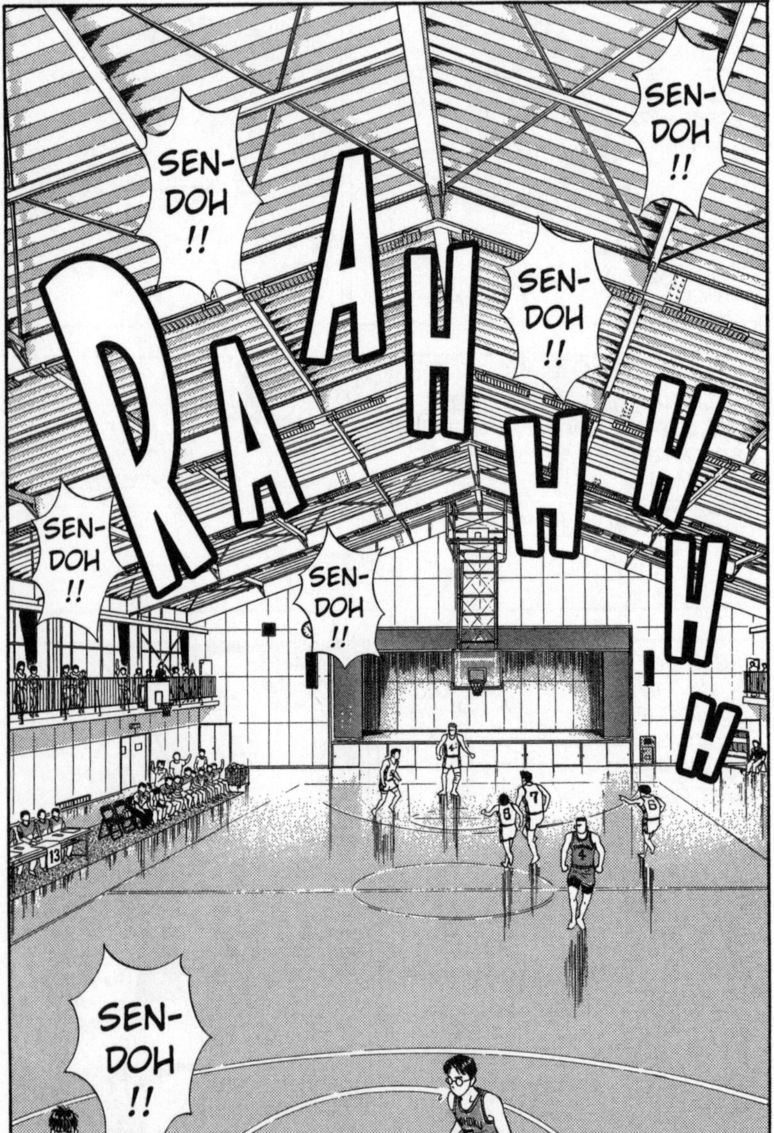
SEN-DOH!!
SEN-DOH!!
SEN-DOH!!
RAAHHHHH
SEN-DOH!!
SEN-DOH!!
SEN-DOH!!

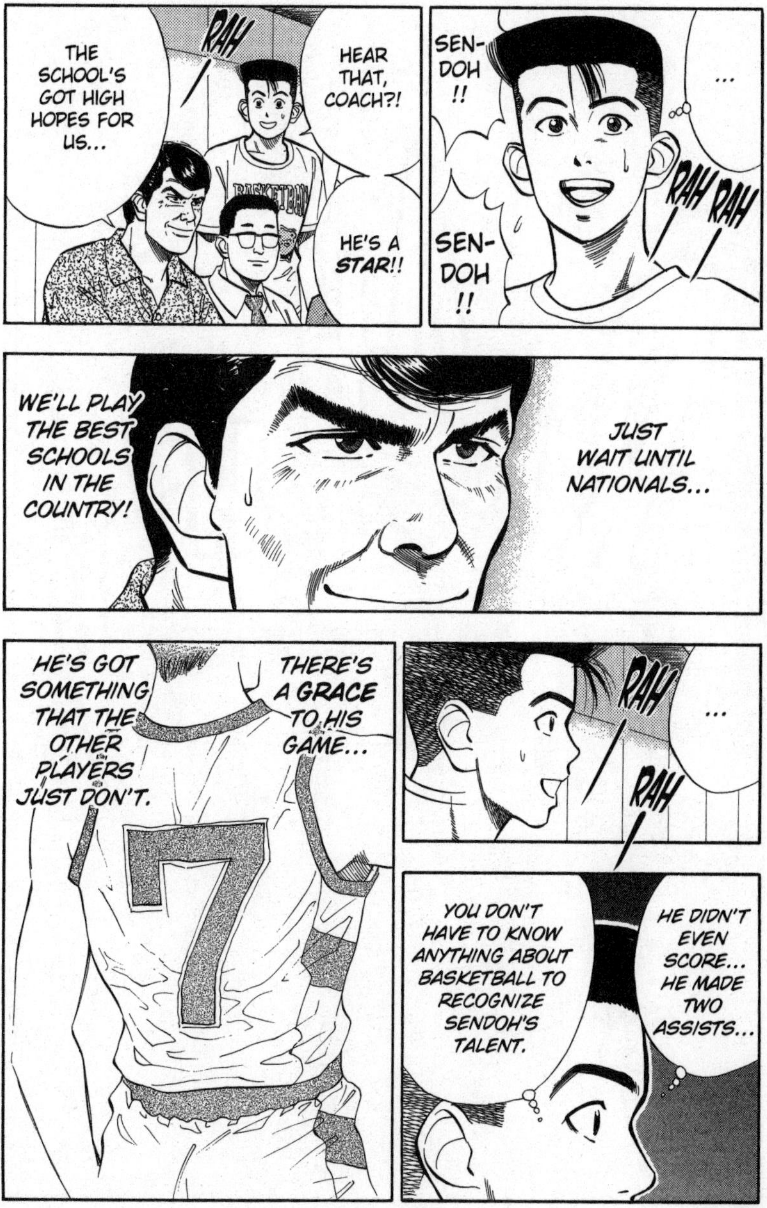
...
RAH RAH
SEN-DOH !!
SEN-DOH !!
HEAR THAT, COACH?!
RAH
THE SCHOOL'S GOT HIGH HOPES FOR US...
HE'S A STAR!!
JUST WAIT UNTIL NATIONALS...
WE'LL PLAY THE BEST SCHOOLS IN THE COUNTRY!
RAH
...
RAH
HE DIDN'T EVEN SCORE... HE MADE TWO ASSISTS...
YOU DON'T HAVE TO KNOW ANYTHING ABOUT BASKETBALL TO RECOGNIZE SENDOH'S TALENT.
THERE'S A GRACE TO HIS GAME...
HE'S GOT SOMETHING THAT THE OTHER PLAYERS JUST DON'T.

READ THIS WAY

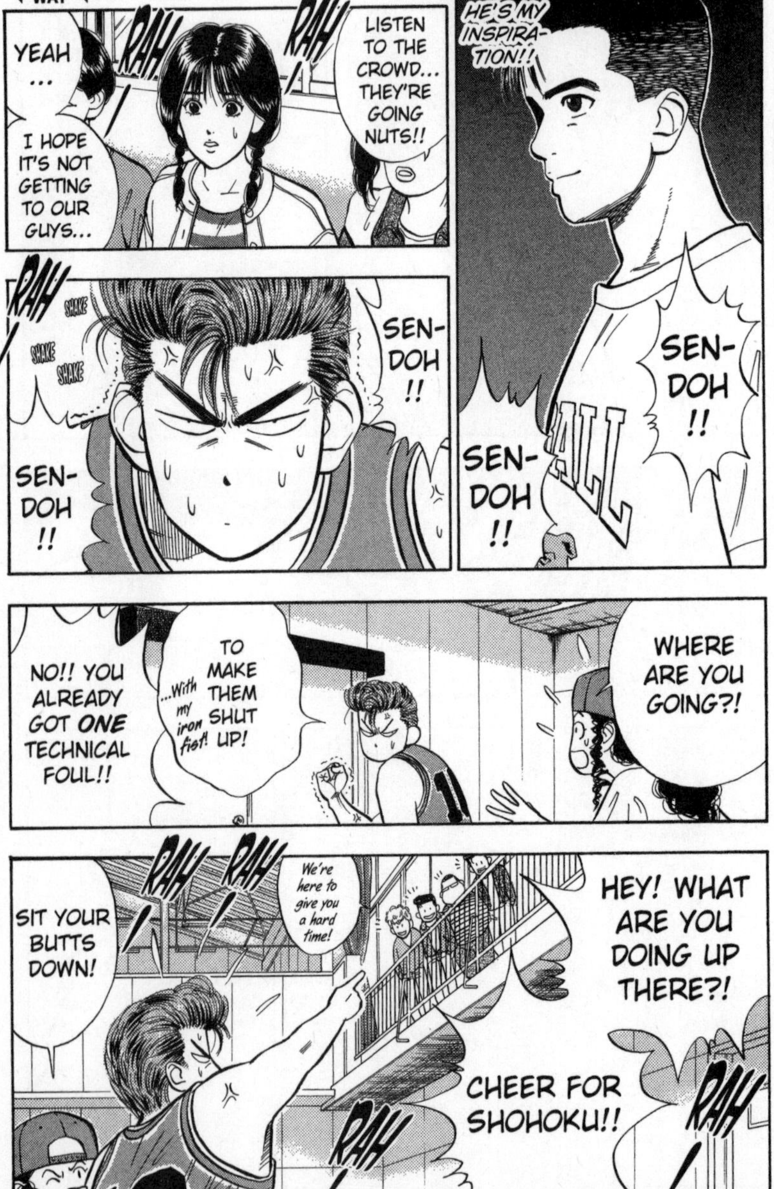
HE'S MY INSPIRATION!!
SEN-DOH!!
SEN-DOH!!
RAH!
LISTEN TO THE CROWD... THEY'RE GOING NUTS!!
RAH
YEAH ...
I HOPE IT'S NOT GETTING TO OUR GUYS...
SEN-DOH!!
SHAKE
SHAKE
SHAKE
RAH!
SEN-DOH!!
WHERE ARE YOU GOING?!
TO MAKE THEM SHUT UP!
...With my iron fist!
NO!! YOU ALREADY GOT ONE TECHNICAL FOUL!!
HEY! WHAT ARE YOU DOING UP THERE?!
CHEER FOR SHOHOKU!!
RAH!
RAH!
We're here to give you a hard time!
RAH!
RAH!
SIT YOUR BUTTS DOWN!

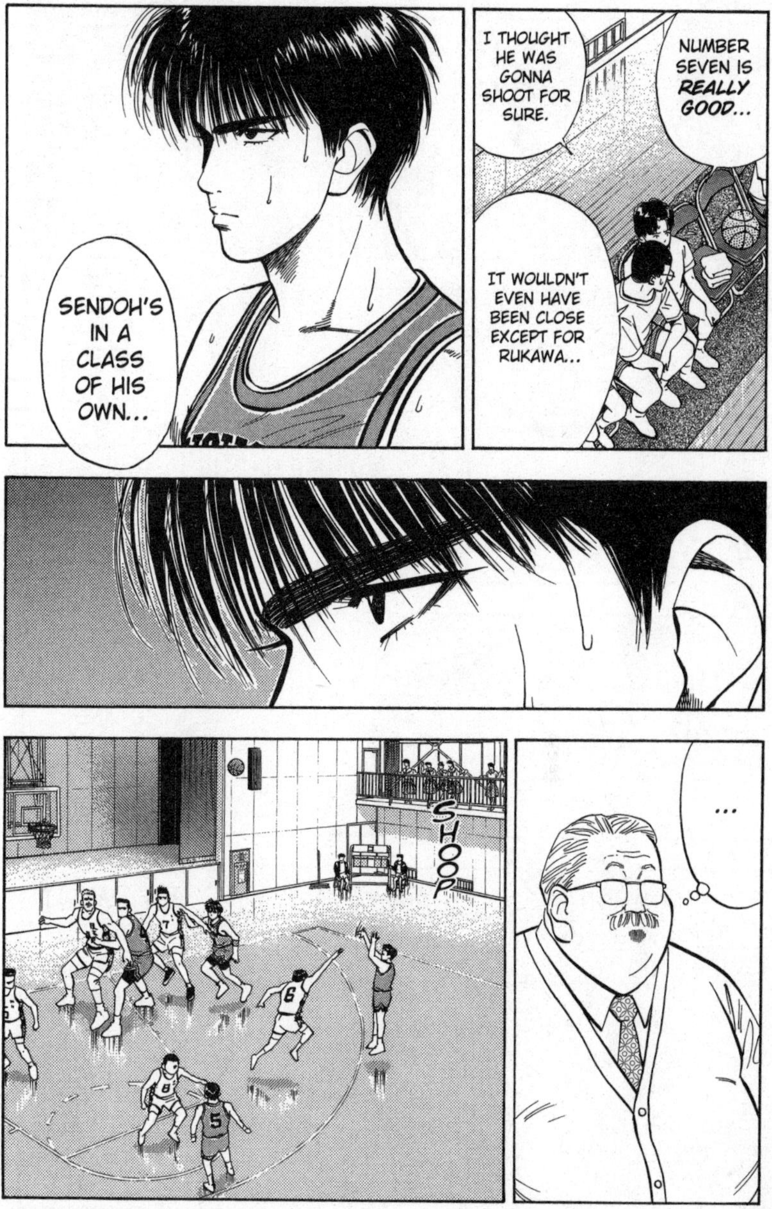
NUMBER SEVEN IS *REALLY* GOOD...
I THOUGHT HE WAS GONNA SHOOT FOR SURE.
IT WOULDN'T EVEN HAVE BEEN CLOSE EXCEPT FOR RUKAWA...
SENDOH'S IN A CLASS OF HIS OWN...
...
SHOOP

READ THIS WAY

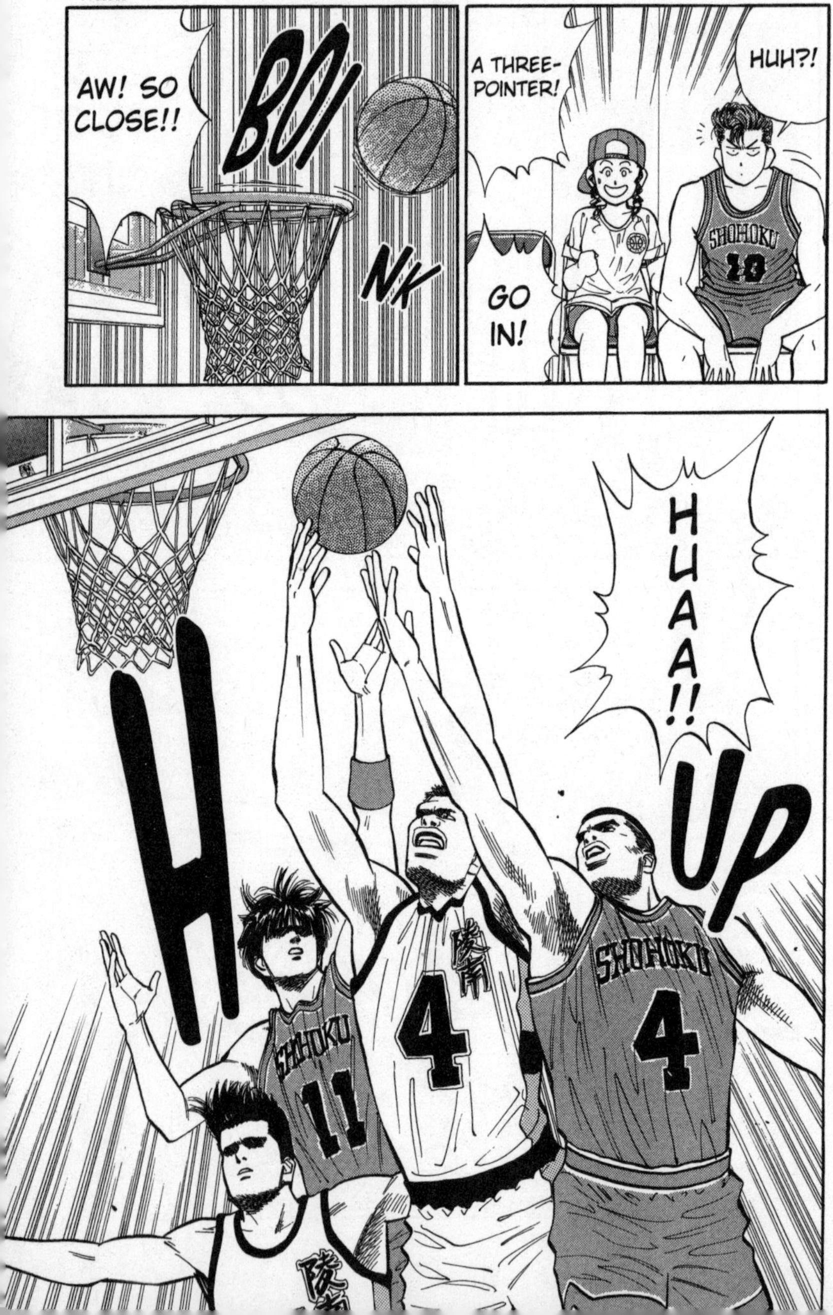
HUH?!
A THREE-POINTER!
GO IN!
AW! SO CLOSE!!
BOINK
HUAAA!!
HUP

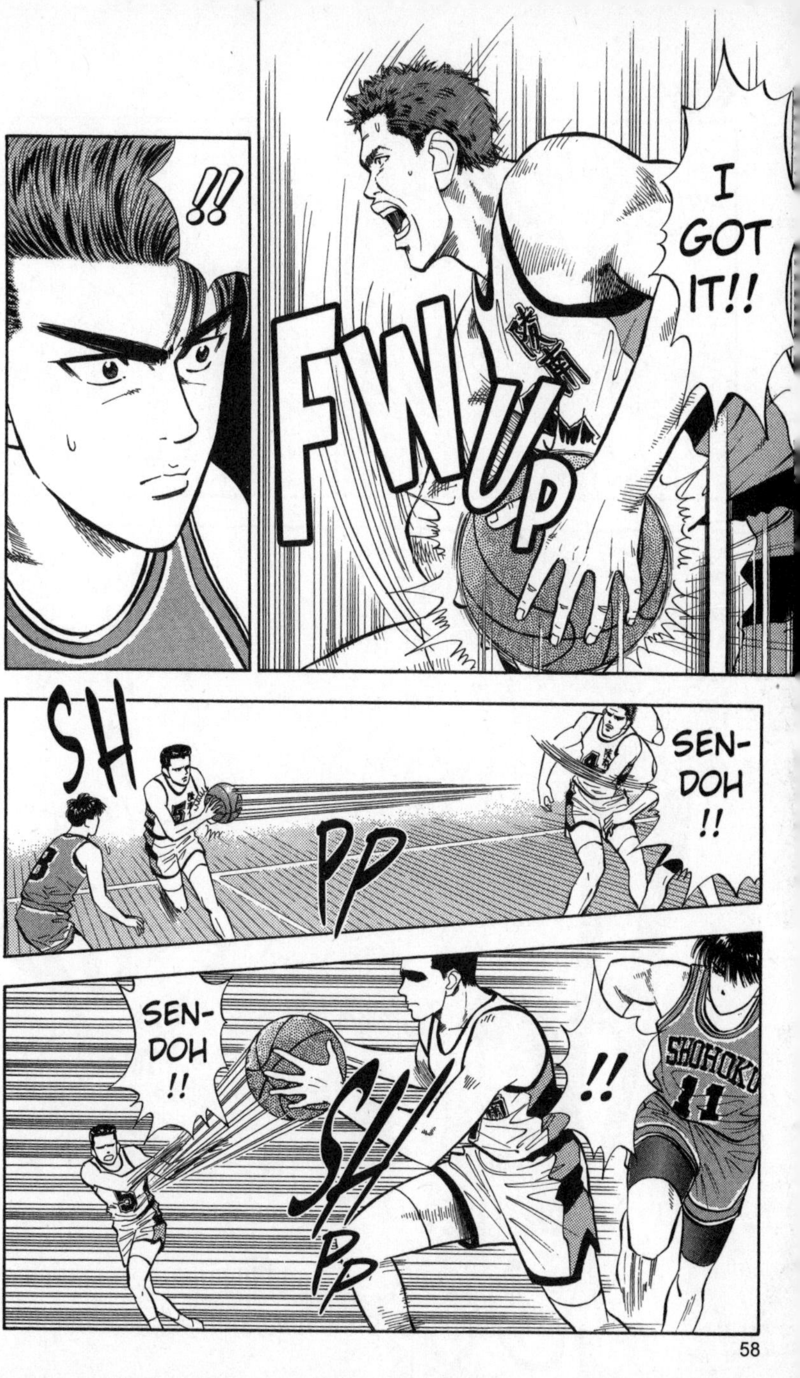
I GOT IT!!
FWUP
!!
SEN-DOH !!
PP
SH
!!
SHOHOKU 11
SEN-DOH !!
SH
PP

READ THIS WAY

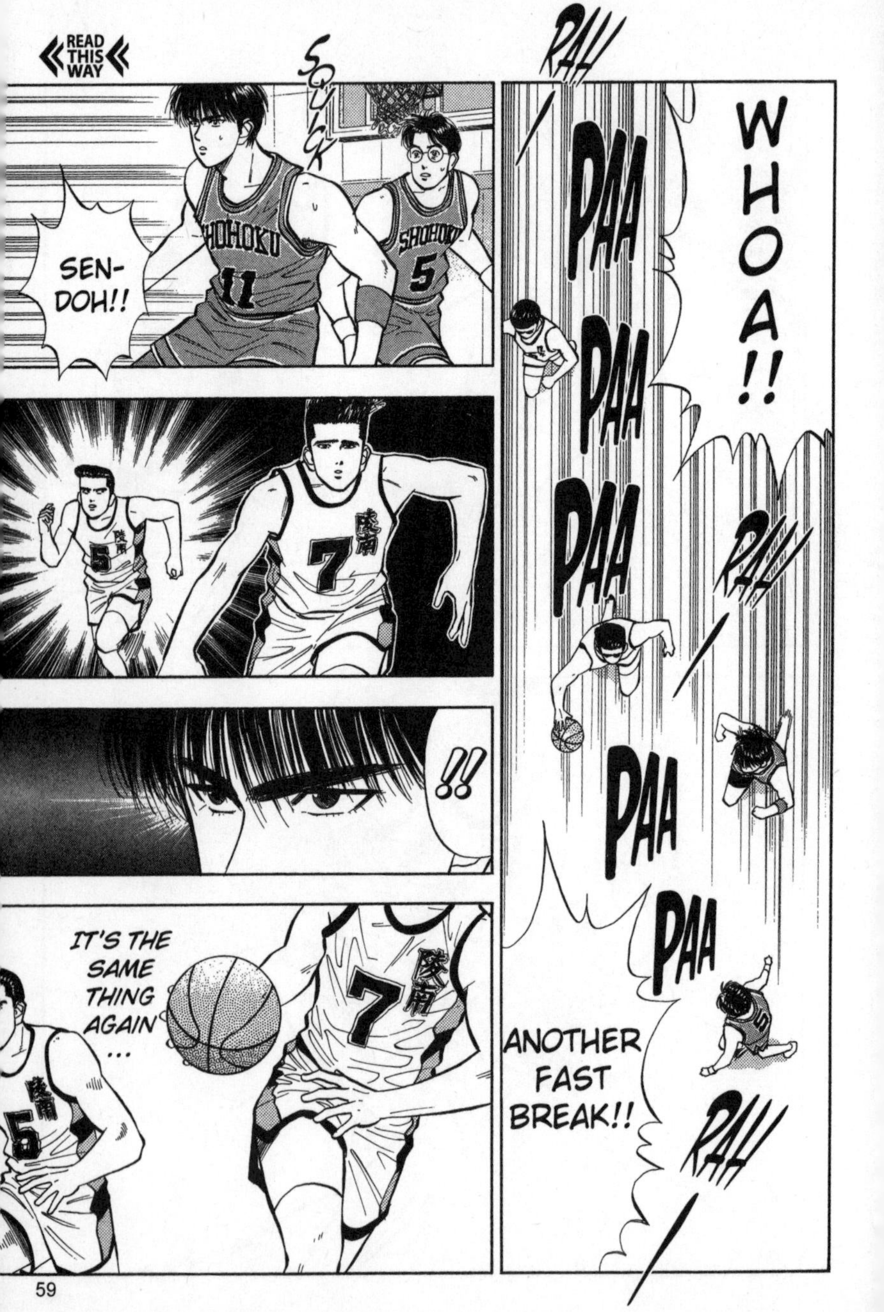

RAH
WHOA!!
PAA
PAA
PAA
RAH
PAA
PAA
ANOTHER FAST BREAK!!
RAH
SQUICK
SEN-DOH!!
!!
IT'S THE SAME THING AGAIN...

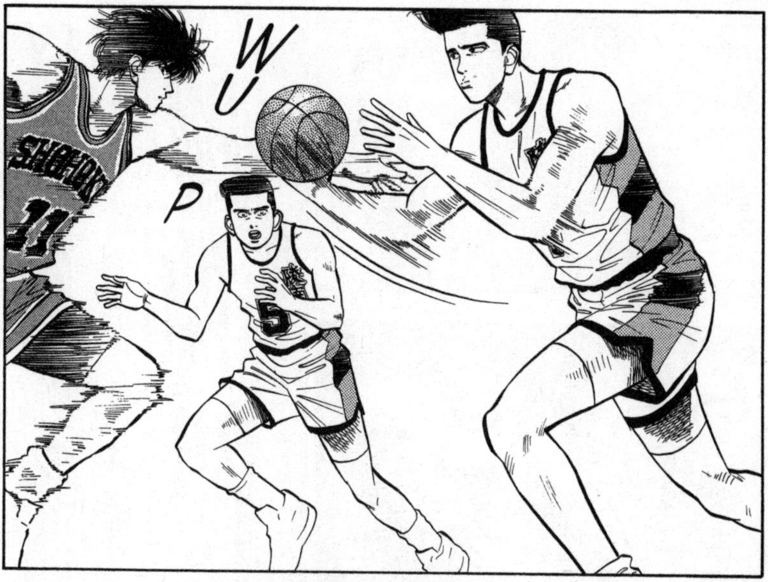
WUP
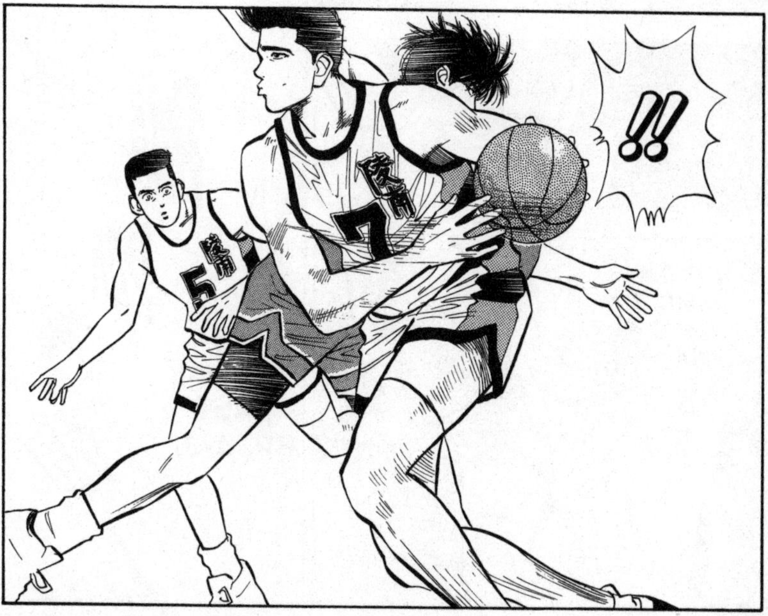
!!

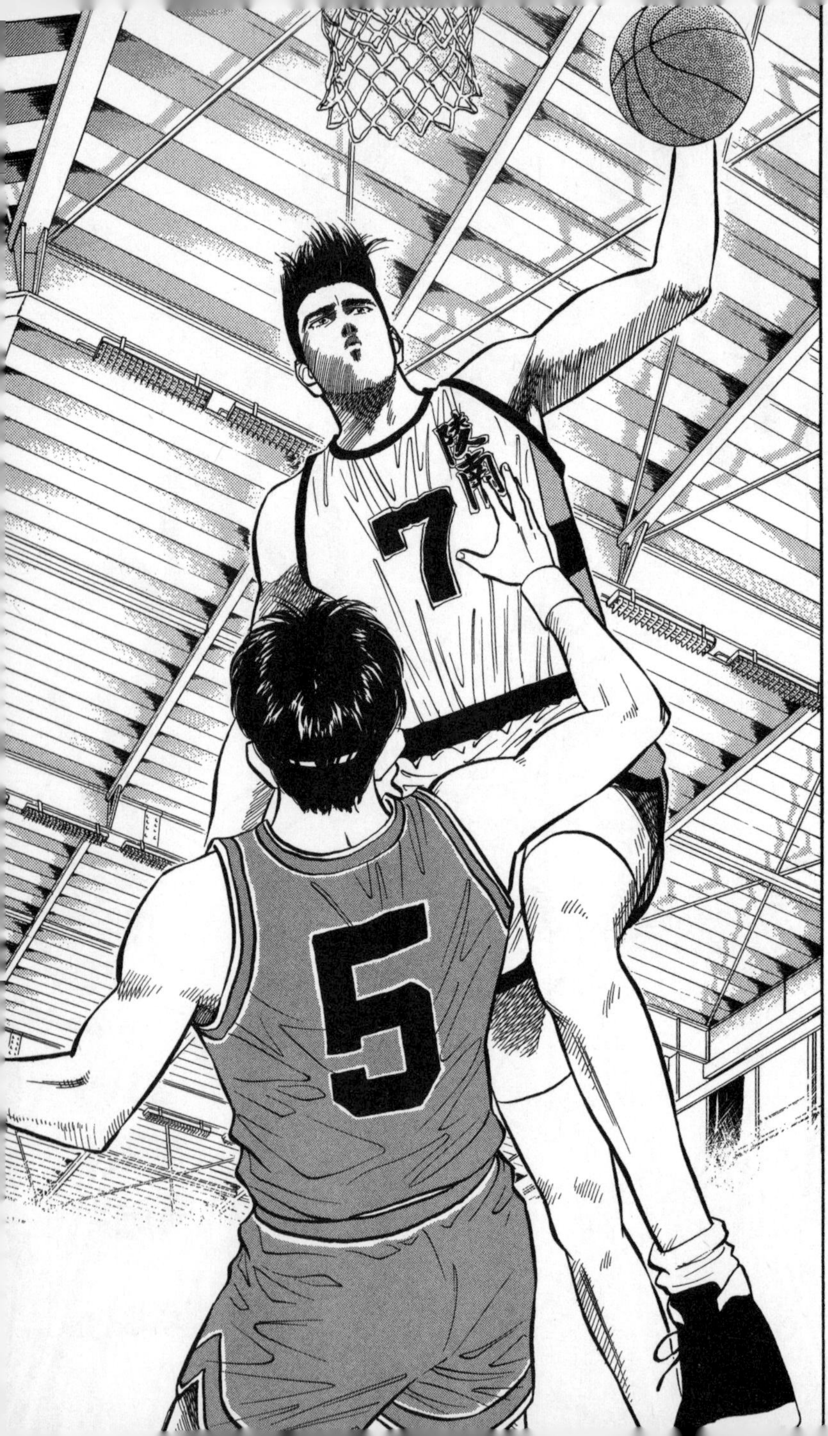
陵南

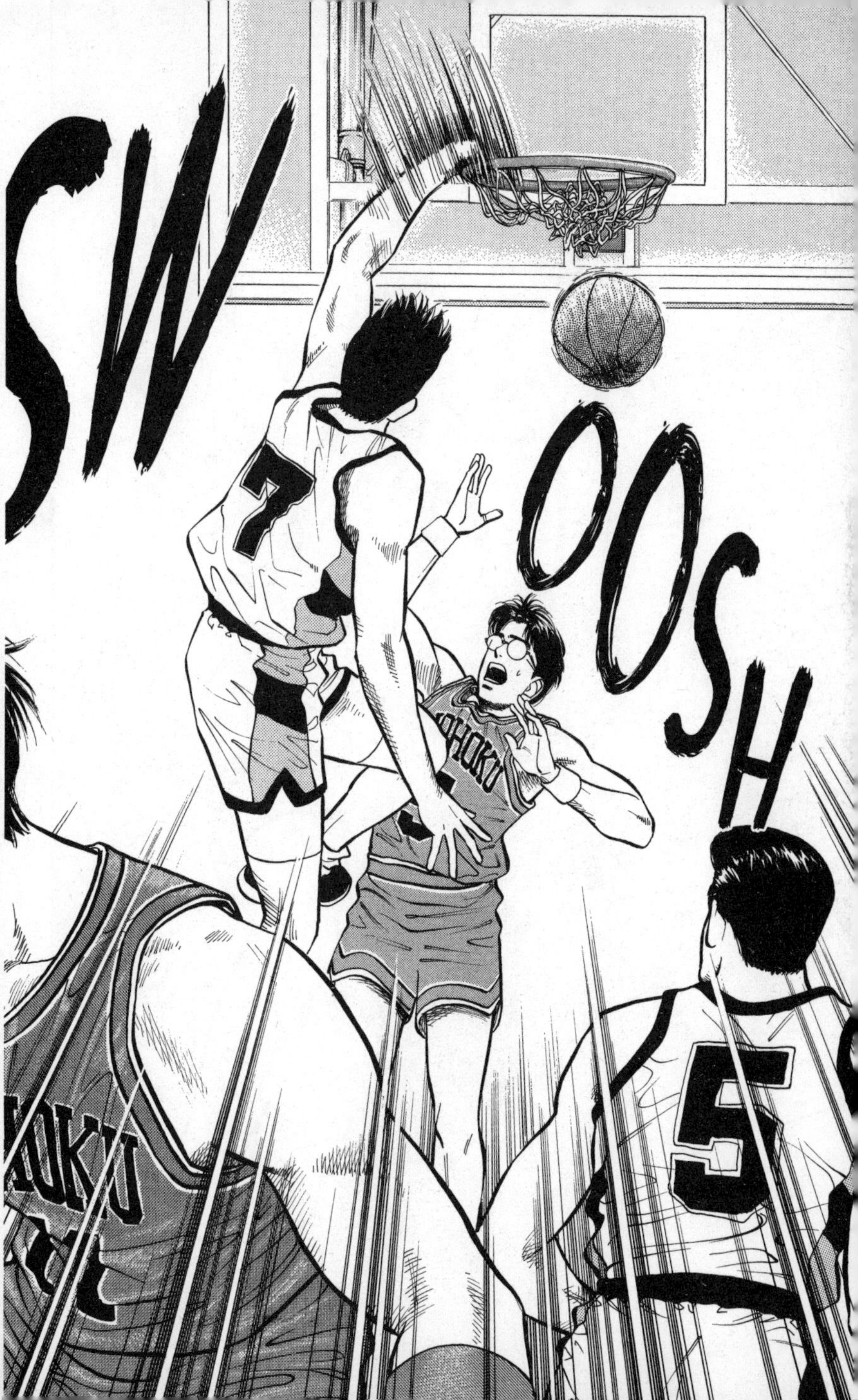
SWOOSH

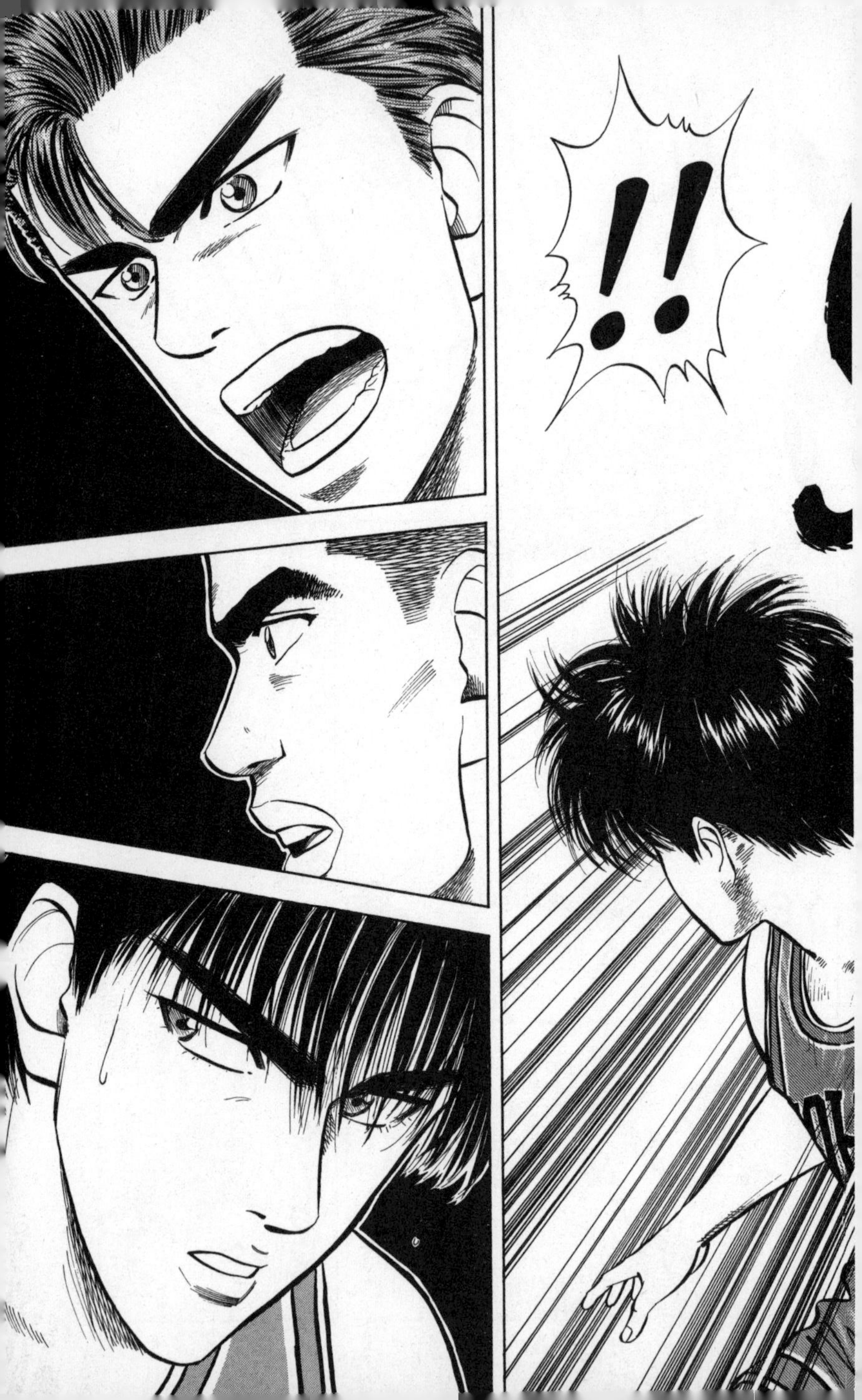
!!

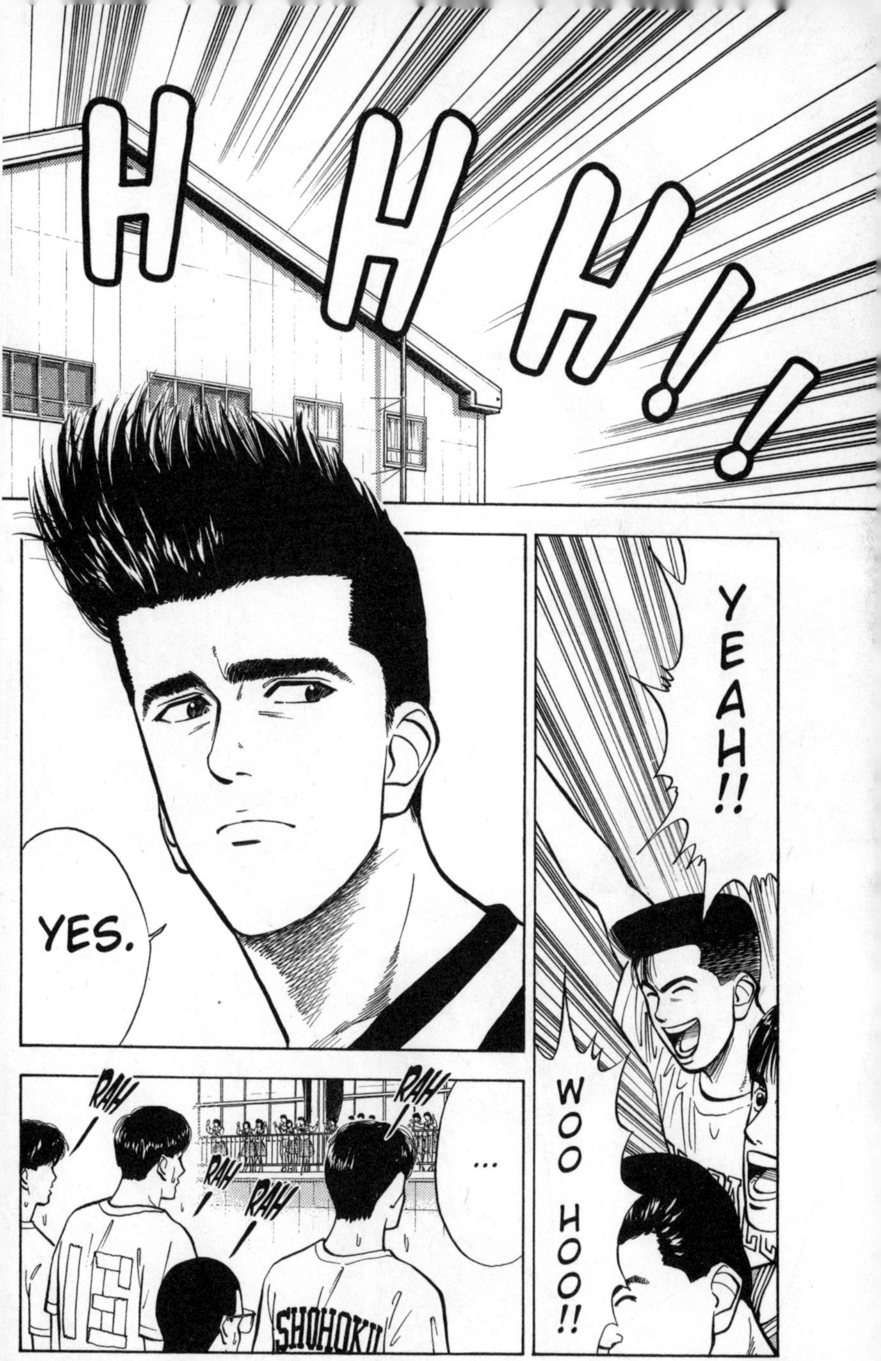
H H H!!
YEAH!!
WOO HOO!!
YES.
RAH
RAH
RAH
RAH
...

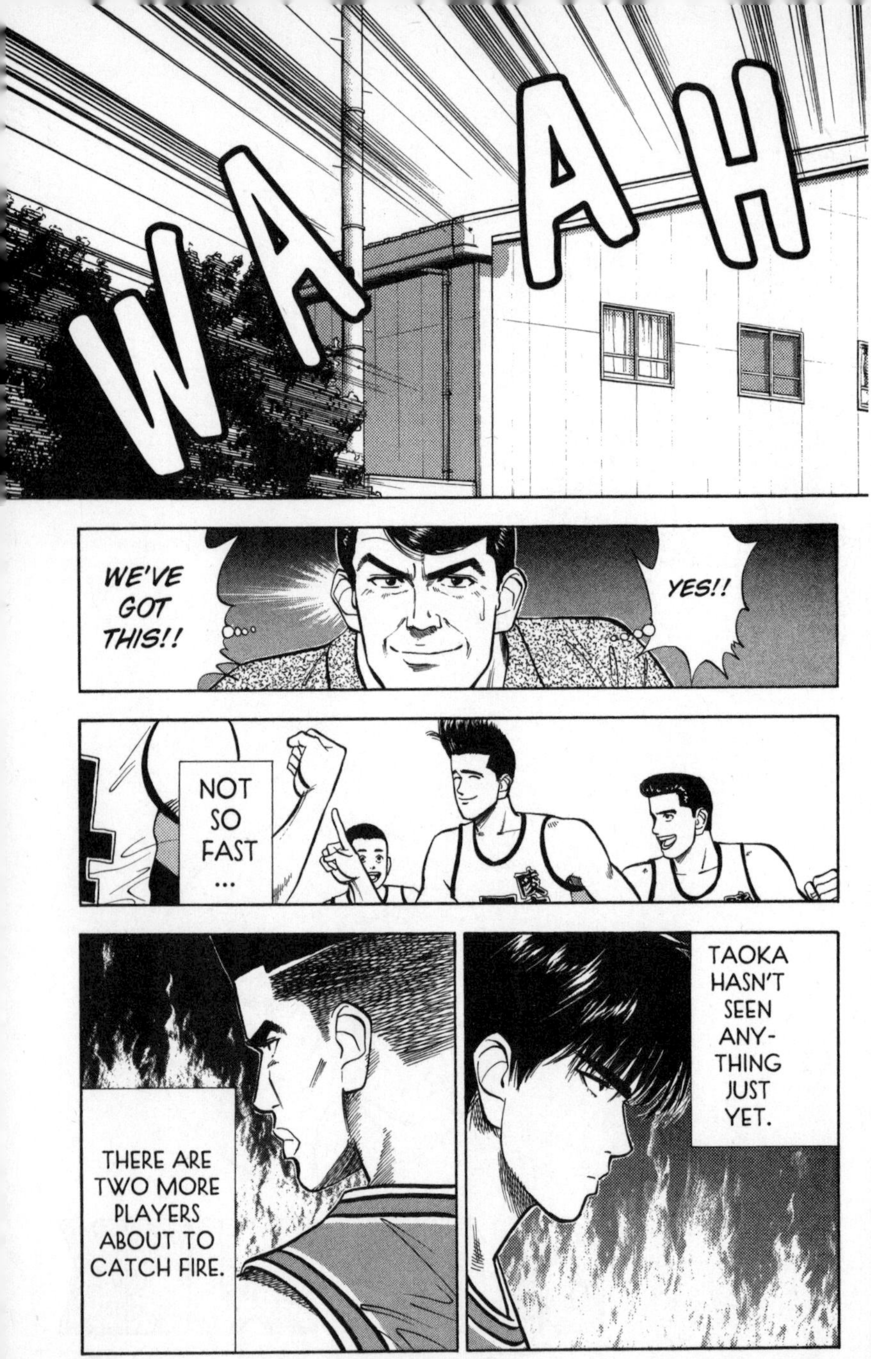
WAAH
WE'VE GOT THIS!!
YES!!
NOT SO FAST ...
TAOKA HASN'T SEEN ANY-THING JUST YET.
THERE ARE TWO MORE PLAYERS ABOUT TO CATCH FIRE.

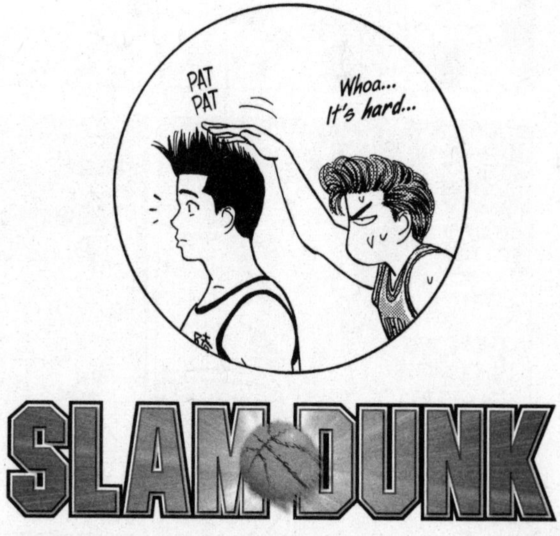
PAT
PAT
Whoa...
It's hard...

SLAM DUNK

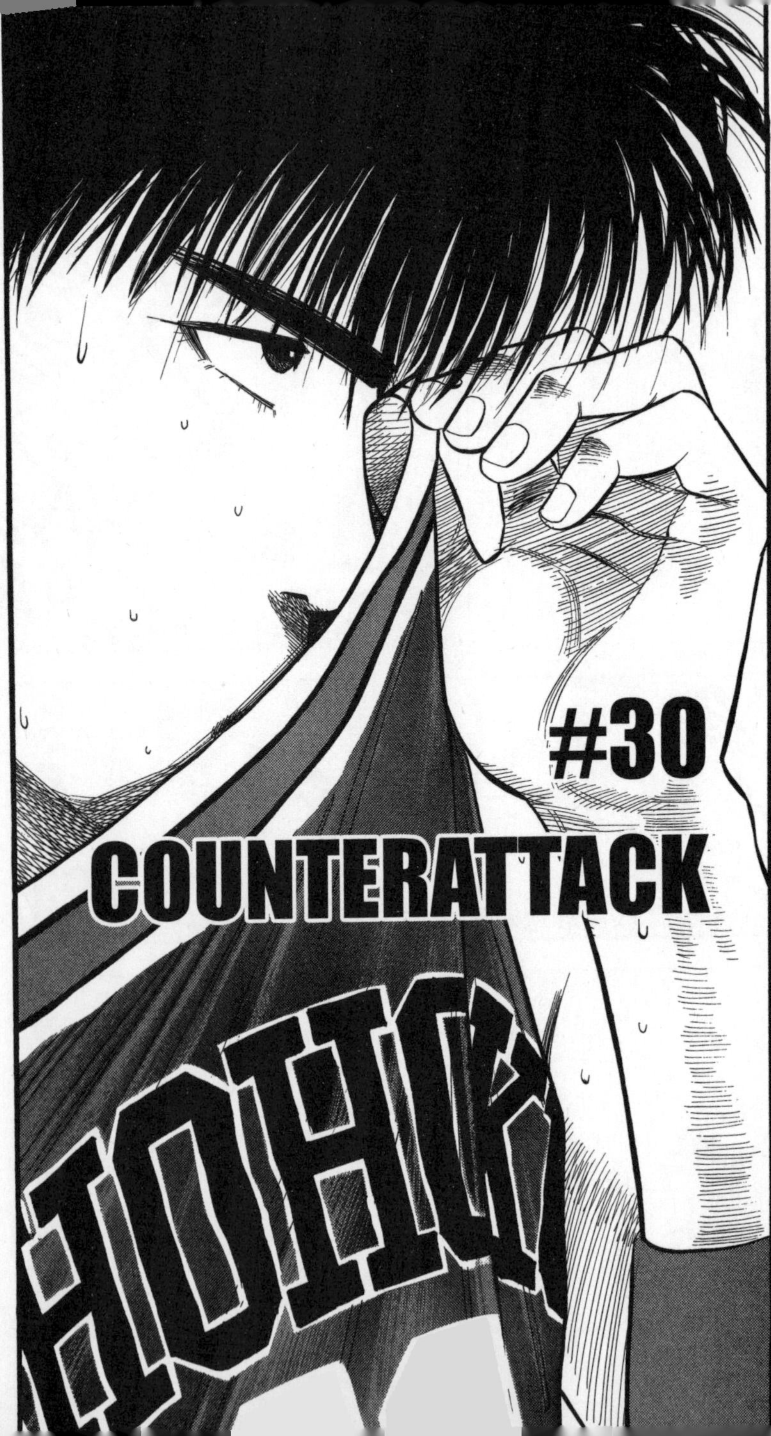

#30
COUNTERATTACK

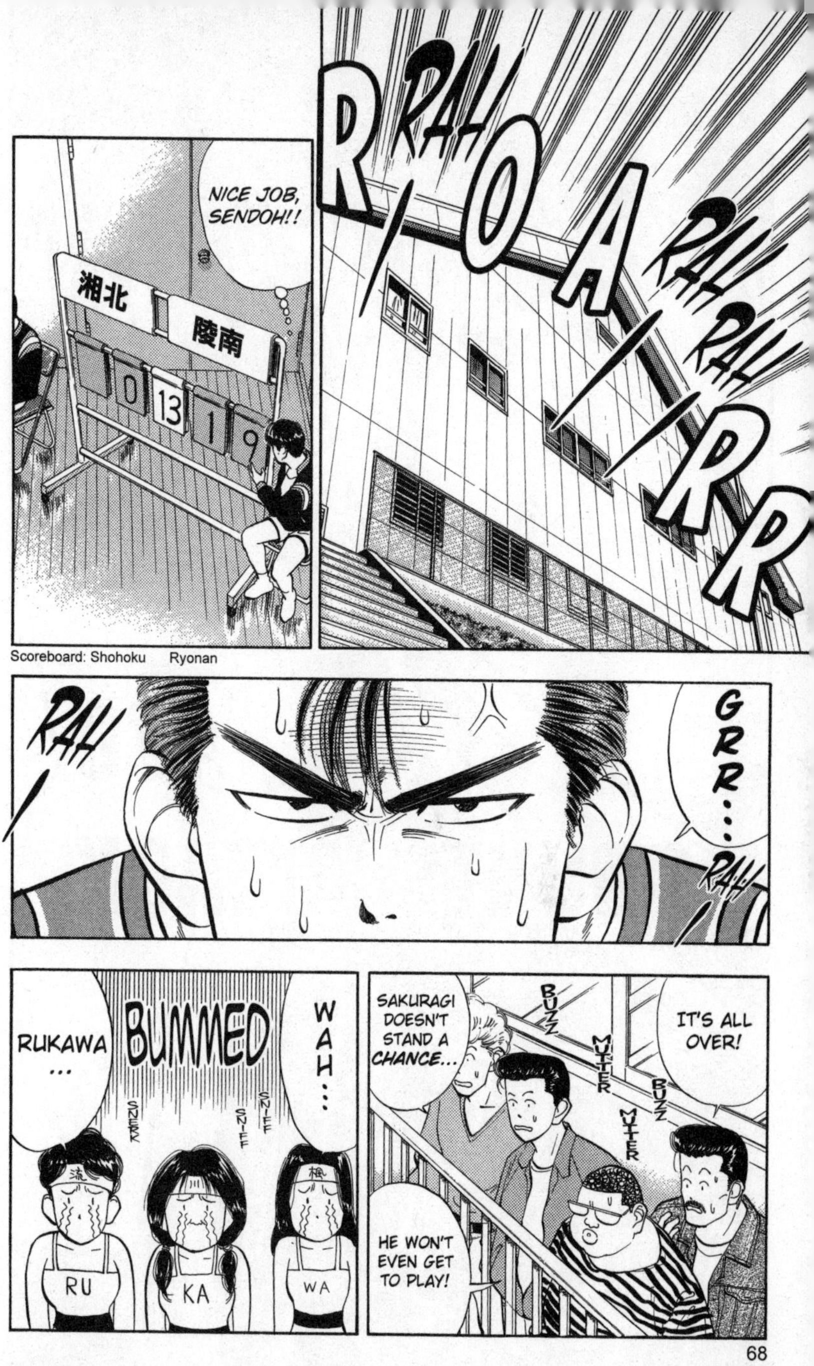
ROAARRR
RAH!
RAH!
RAH!
NICE JOB, SENDOH!!
湘北
陵南
RAH!
GRR... RAH!
IT'S ALL OVER!
BUZZ
MUTTER
MUTTER
BUZZ
SAKURAGI DOESN'T STAND A CHANCE...
HE WON'T EVEN GET TO PLAY!
WAH...
SNIFF
SNIFF
SNERK
BUMMED
RUKAWA...
RU
KA
WA
Scoreboard: Shohoku Ryonan

READ THIS WAY

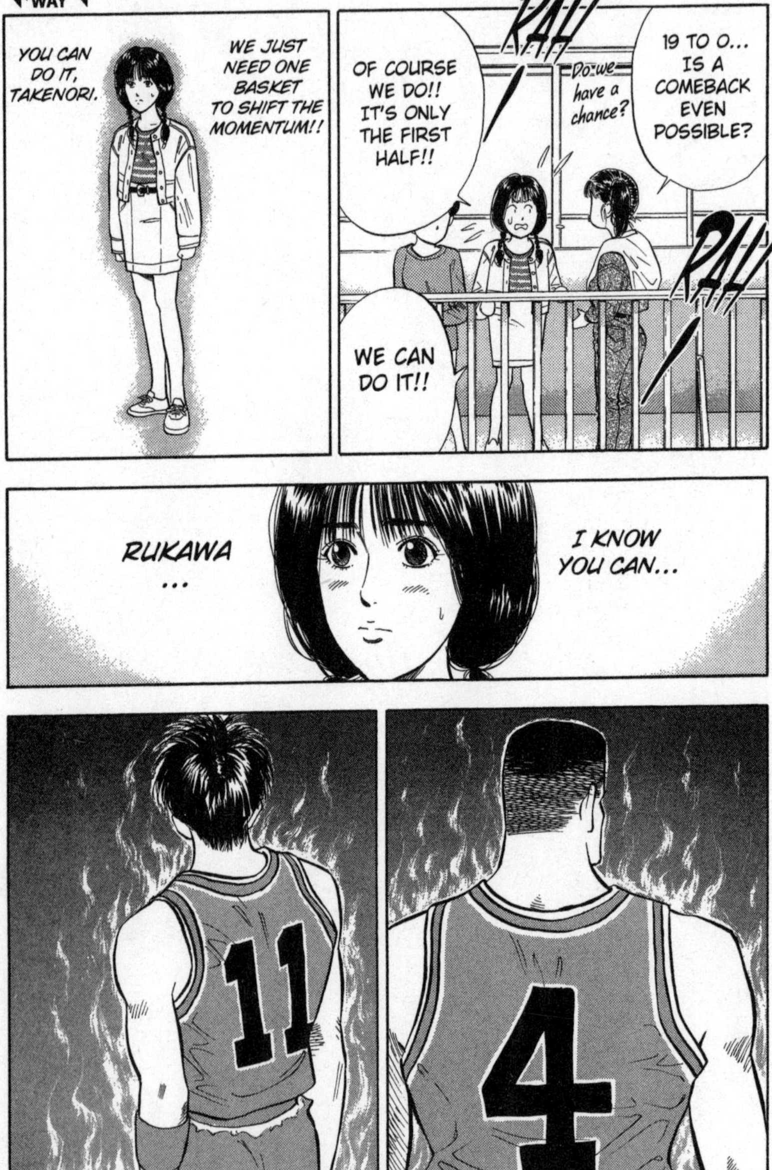

19 TO 0... IS A COMEBACK EVEN POSSIBLE?
RAH
Do we have a chance?
RAH
OF COURSE WE DO!! IT'S ONLY THE FIRST HALF!!
WE CAN DO IT!!
WE JUST NEED ONE BASKET TO SHIFT THE MOMENTUM!!
YOU CAN DO IT, TAKENORI.
I KNOW YOU CAN...
RUKAWA ...

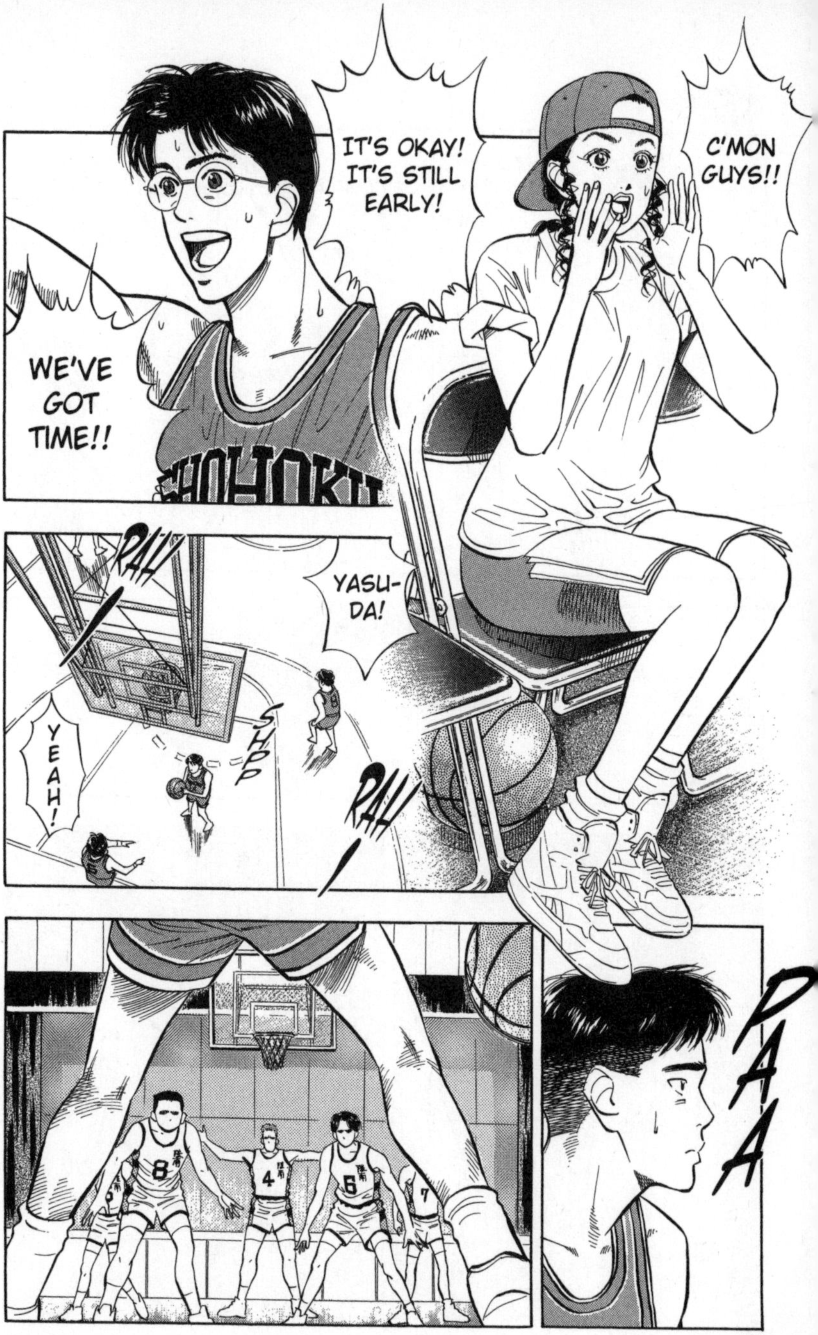
C'MON GUYS!!
IT'S OKAY! IT'S STILL EARLY!
WE'VE GOT TIME!!
YASU-DA!
RAH
SHPP
YEAH!
RAH
PAAA

READ THIS WAY

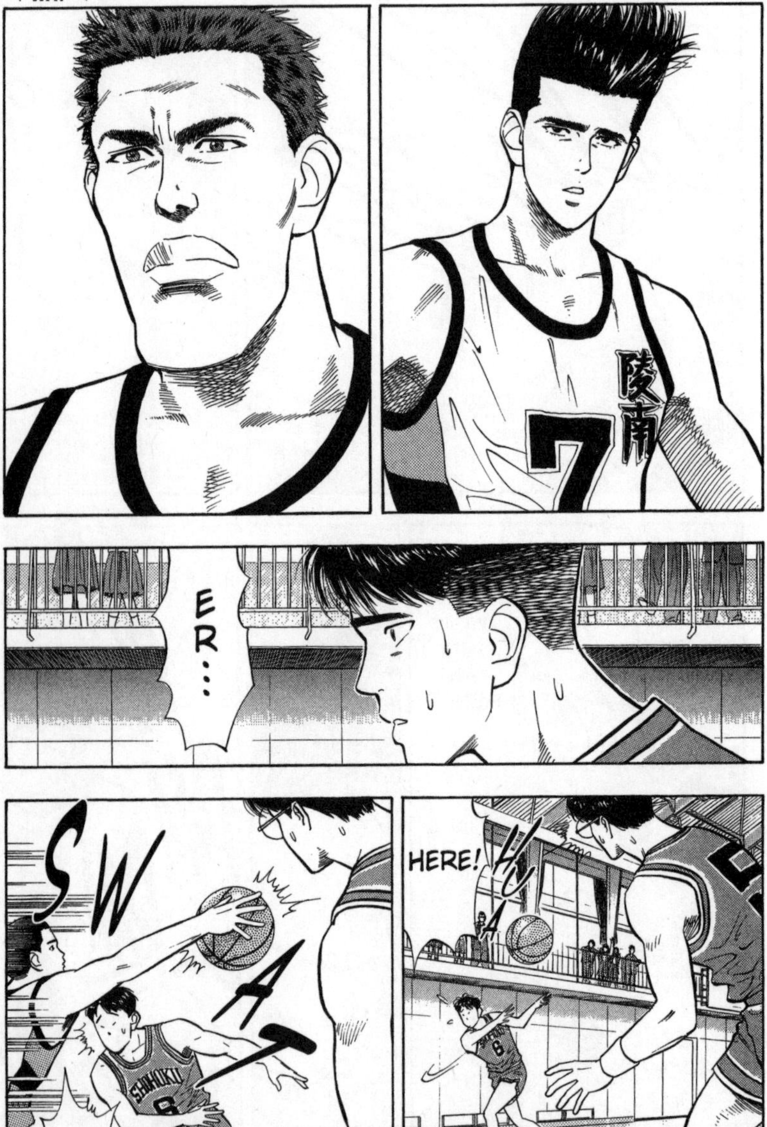

陵南
ER...
HERE!
SWAT
!!

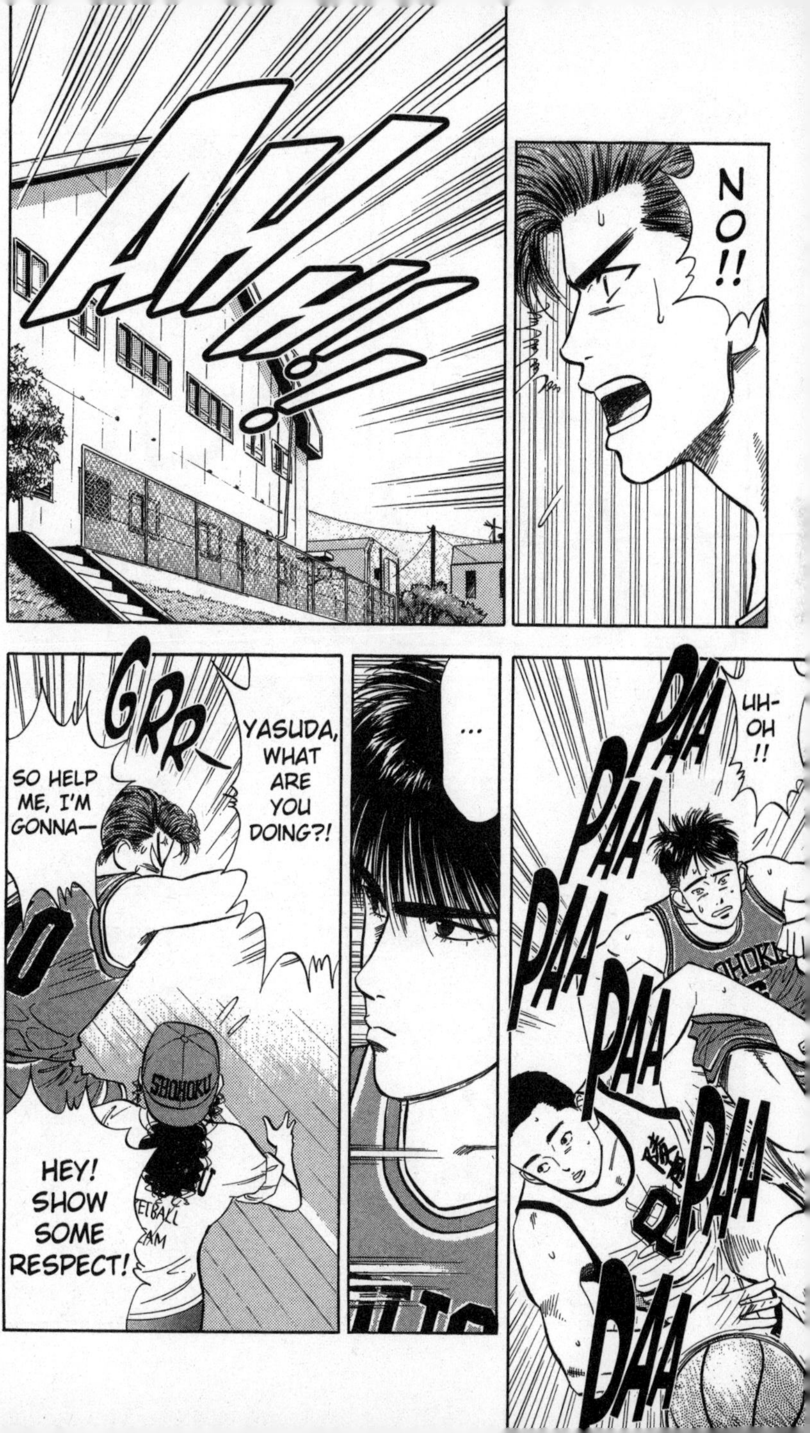
NO!!
UH-OH !!
PAA PAA PAA PAA PAA PAA PAA DAA
...
YASUDA, WHAT ARE YOU DOING?!
GRR—
SO HELP ME, I'M GONNA—
HEY! SHOW SOME RESPECT!

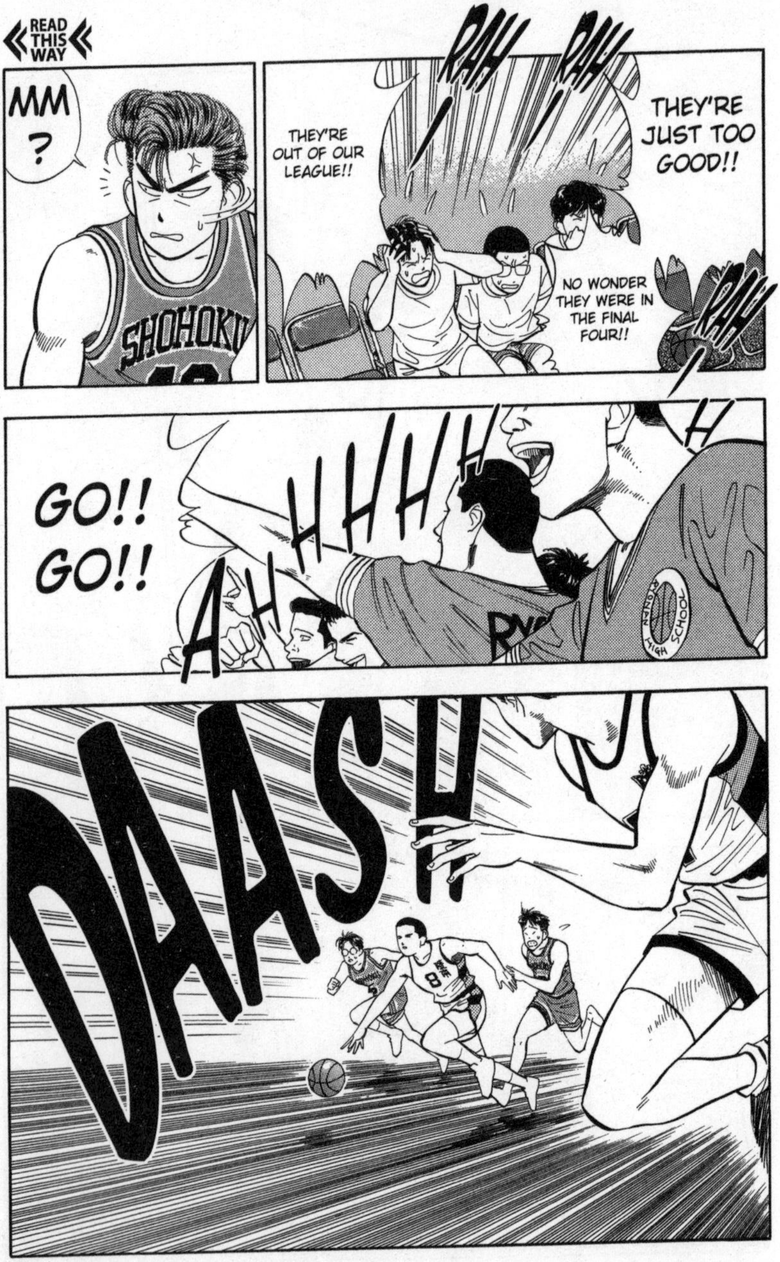
READ THIS WAY
RAH
RAH
THEY'RE JUST TOO GOOD!!
THEY'RE OUT OF OUR LEAGUE!!
NO WONDER THEY WERE IN THE FINAL FOUR!!
RAH
MM ?
AHHHHHHHH
GO!! GO!!
DAASH

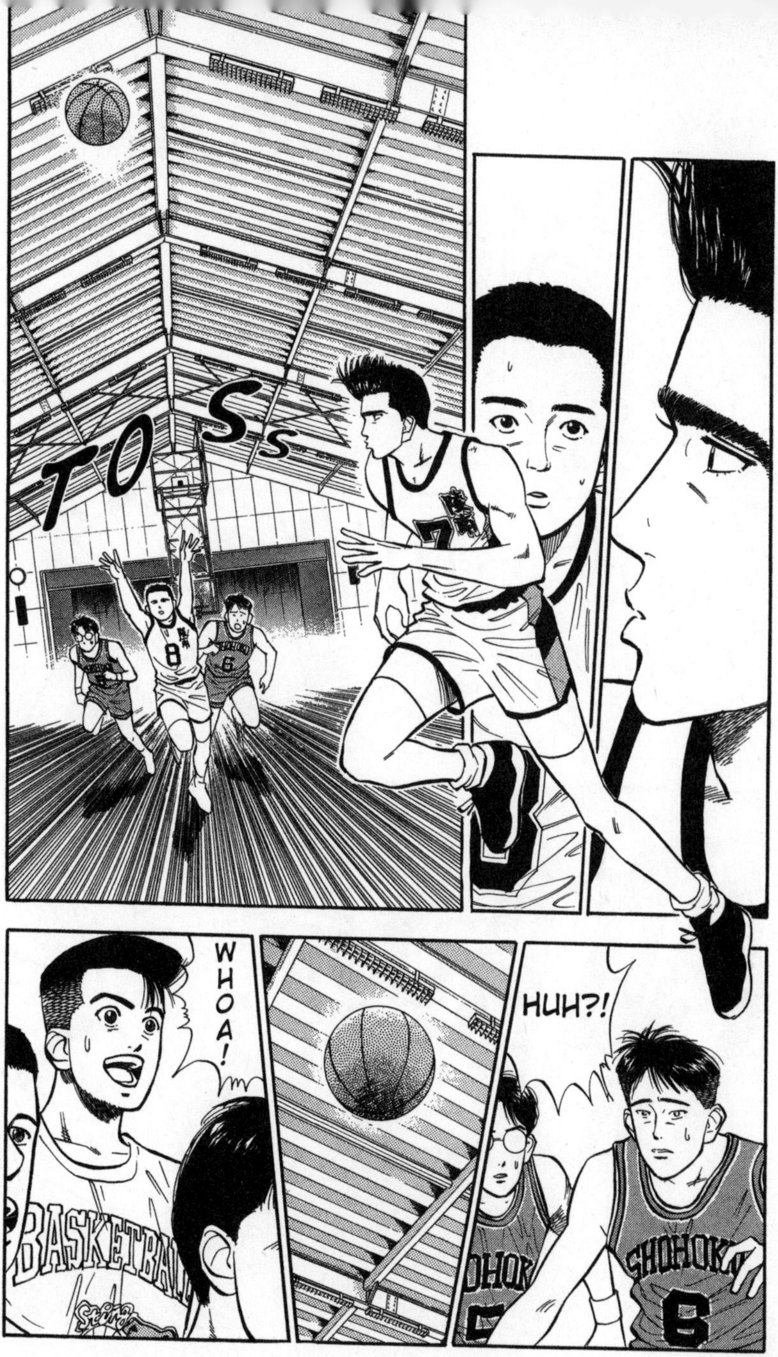
TOSS
HUH?!
WHOA!
SHOHOKU
BASKETBALL

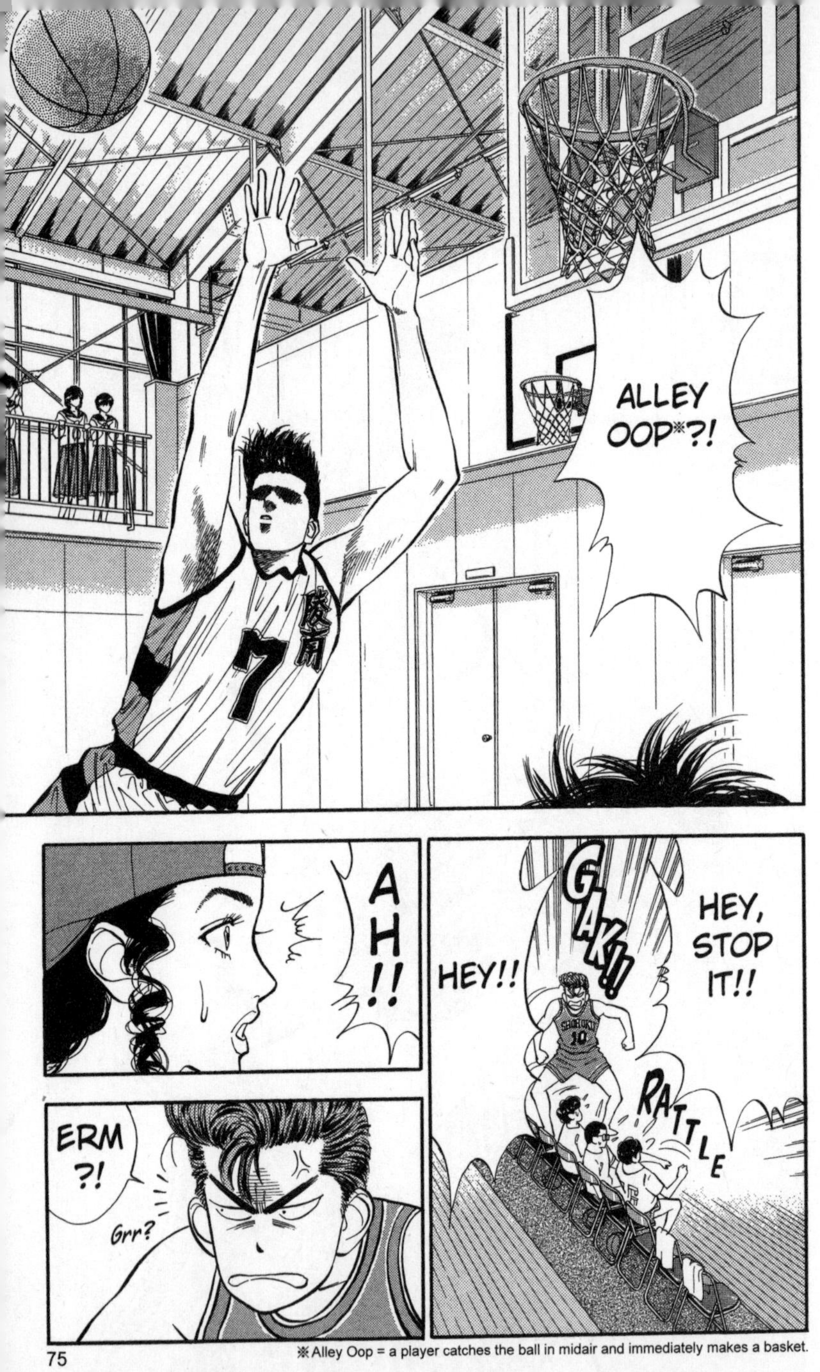
ALLEY OOP※?!
HEY, STOP IT!!
GAK!!
HEY!!
RATTLE
AH!!
ERM ?!
Grr?

※Alley Oop = a player catches the ball in midair and immediately makes a basket.

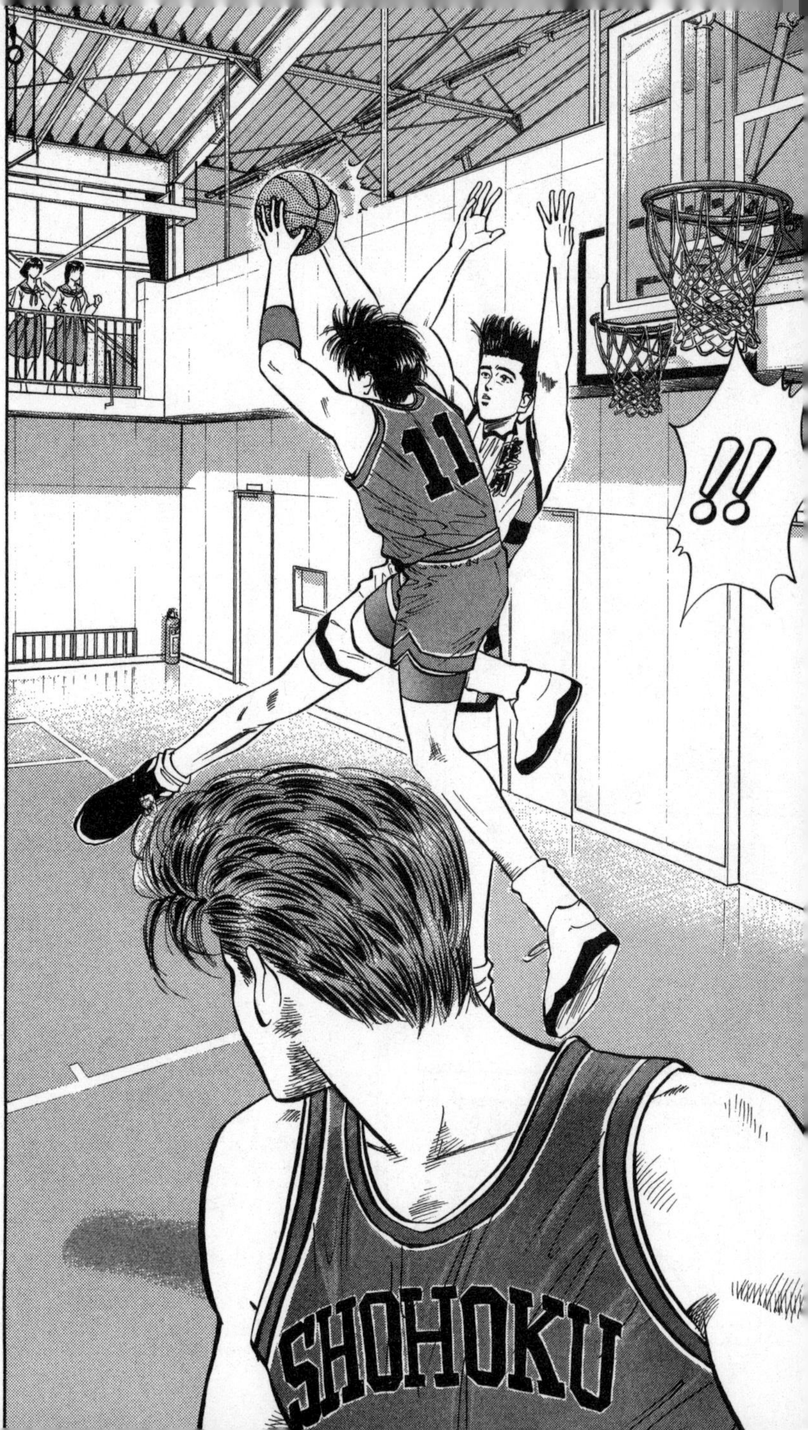
!!
SHOHOKU

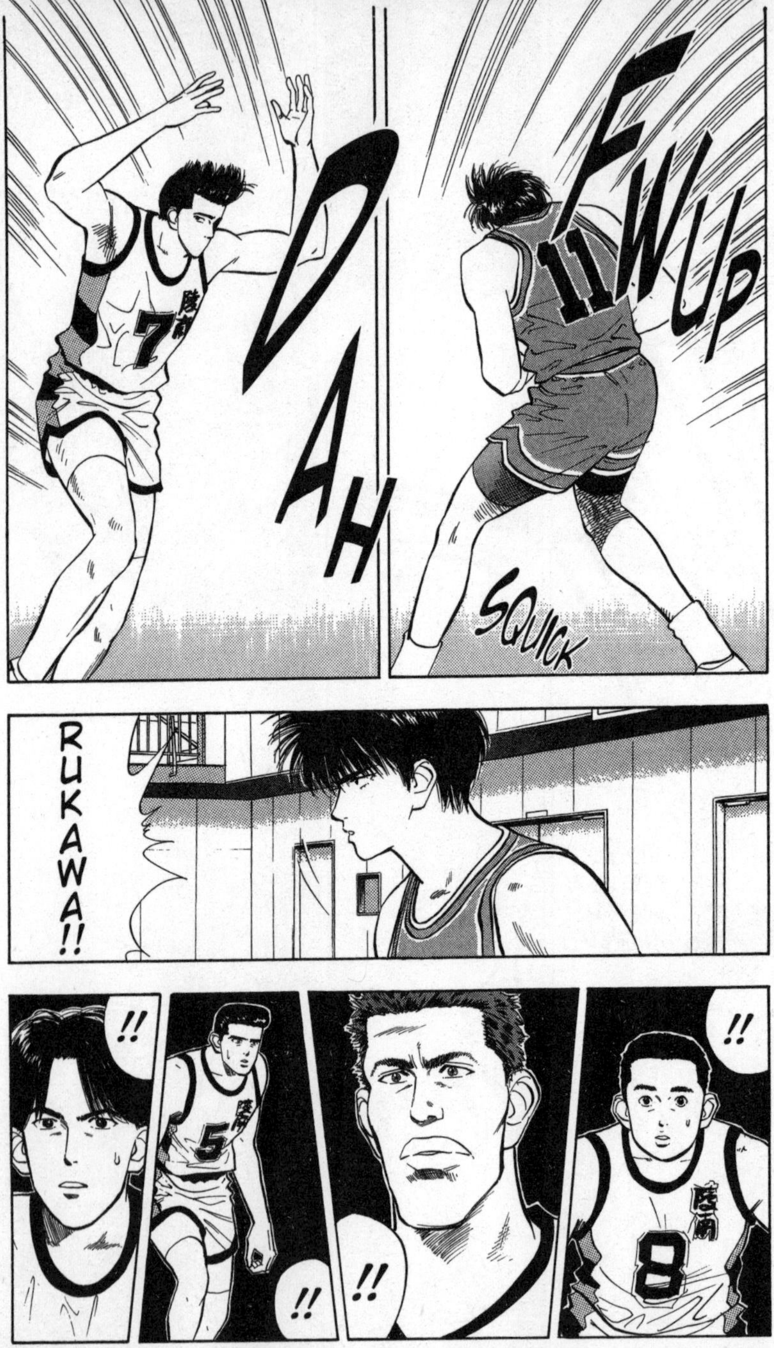
FWUP
SQUICK
DAH
RUKAWA!!
!!
!!
!!
!!

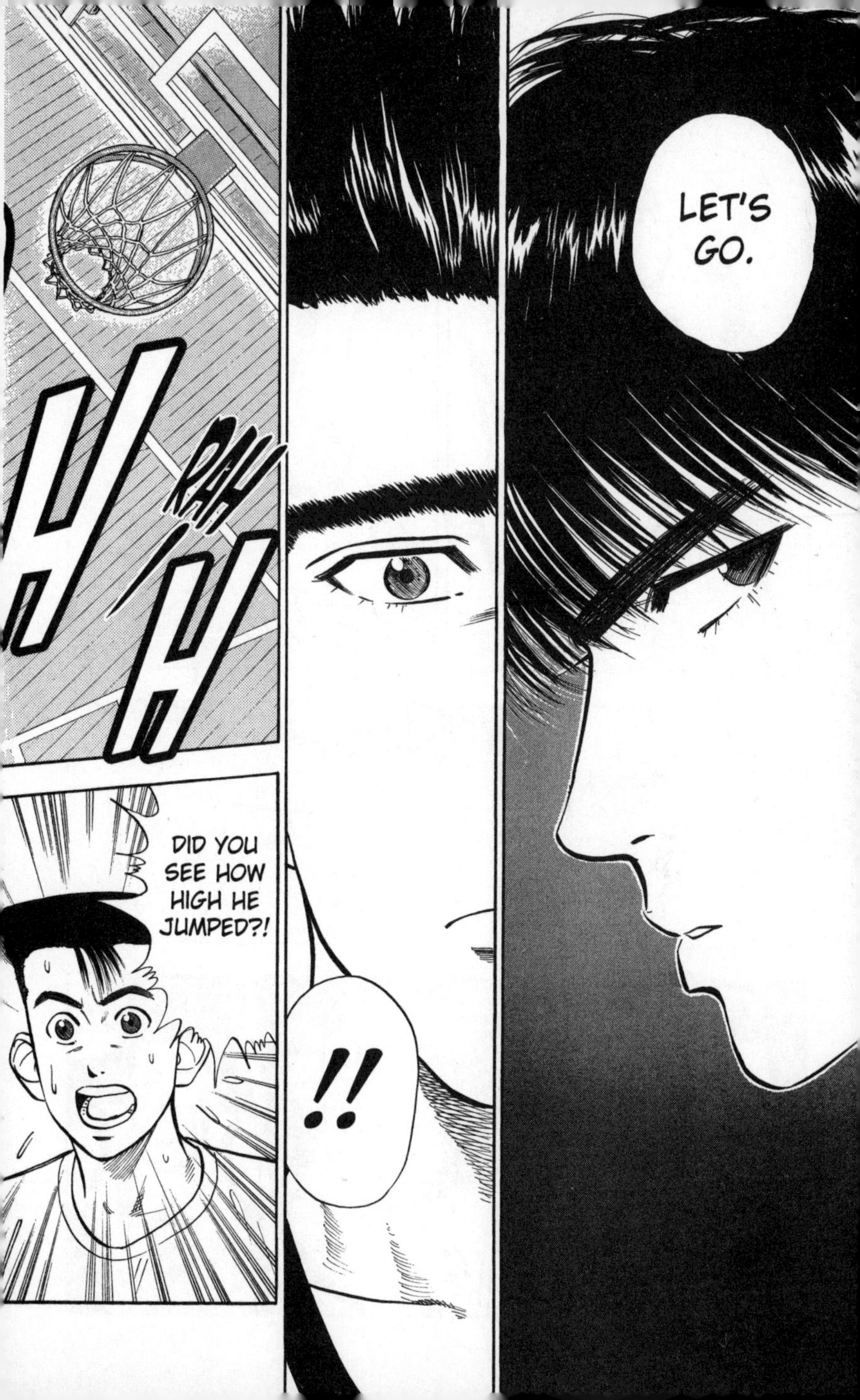
LET'S GO.
!!
RAH
DID YOU SEE HOW HIGH HE JUMPED?!

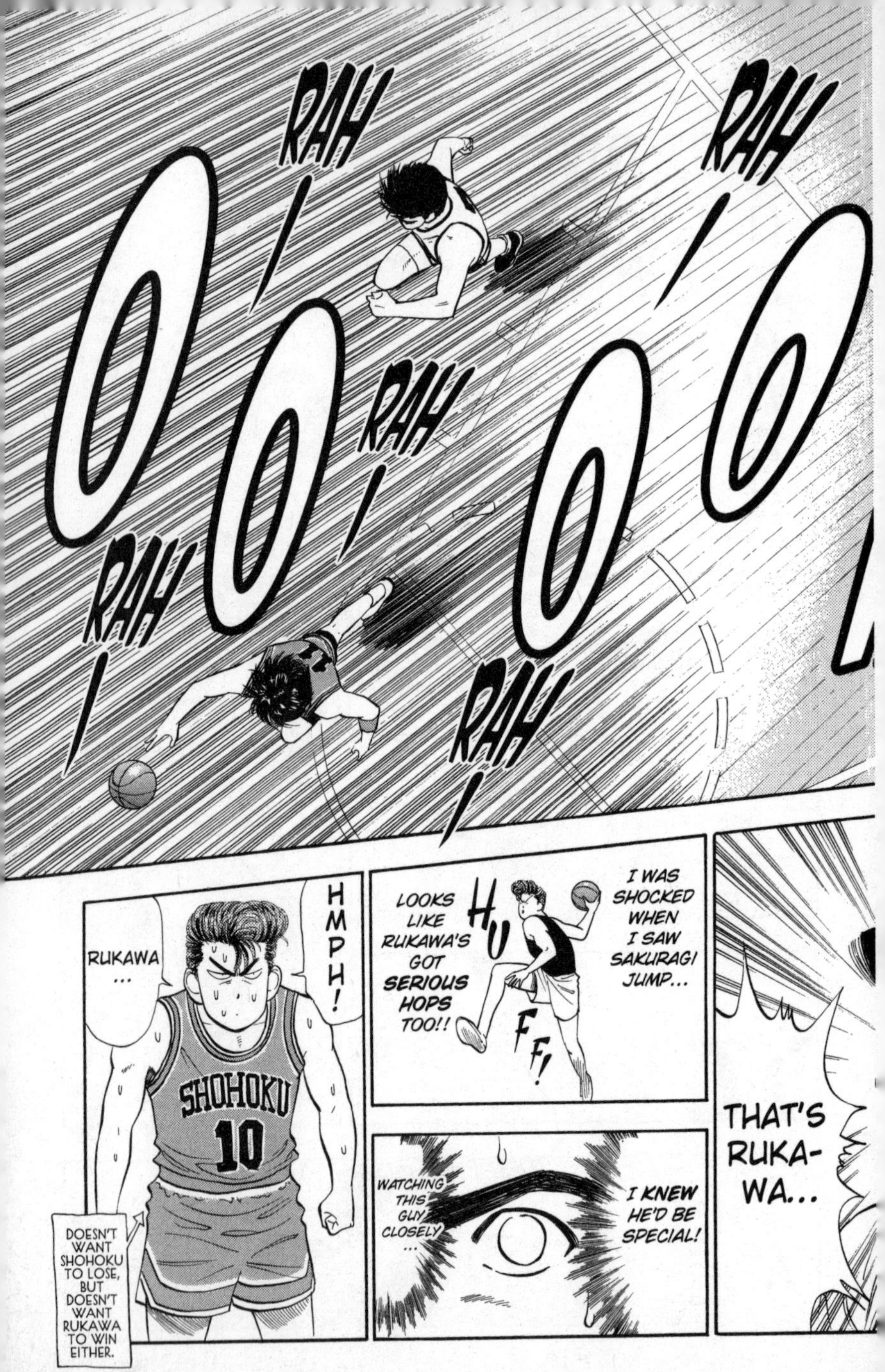
RAH!
RAH!
RAH!
RAH!
RAH!
THAT'S RUKA-WA...
I WAS SHOCKED WHEN I SAW SAKURAGI JUMP...
LOOKS LIKE RUKAWA'S GOT SERIOUS HOPS TOO!!
HUFF!
I KNEW HE'D BE SPECIAL!
WATCHING THIS GUY CLOSELY...
HMPH!
RUKAWA...
DOESN'T WANT SHOHOKU TO LOSE, BUT DOESN'T WANT RUKAWA TO WIN EITHER.

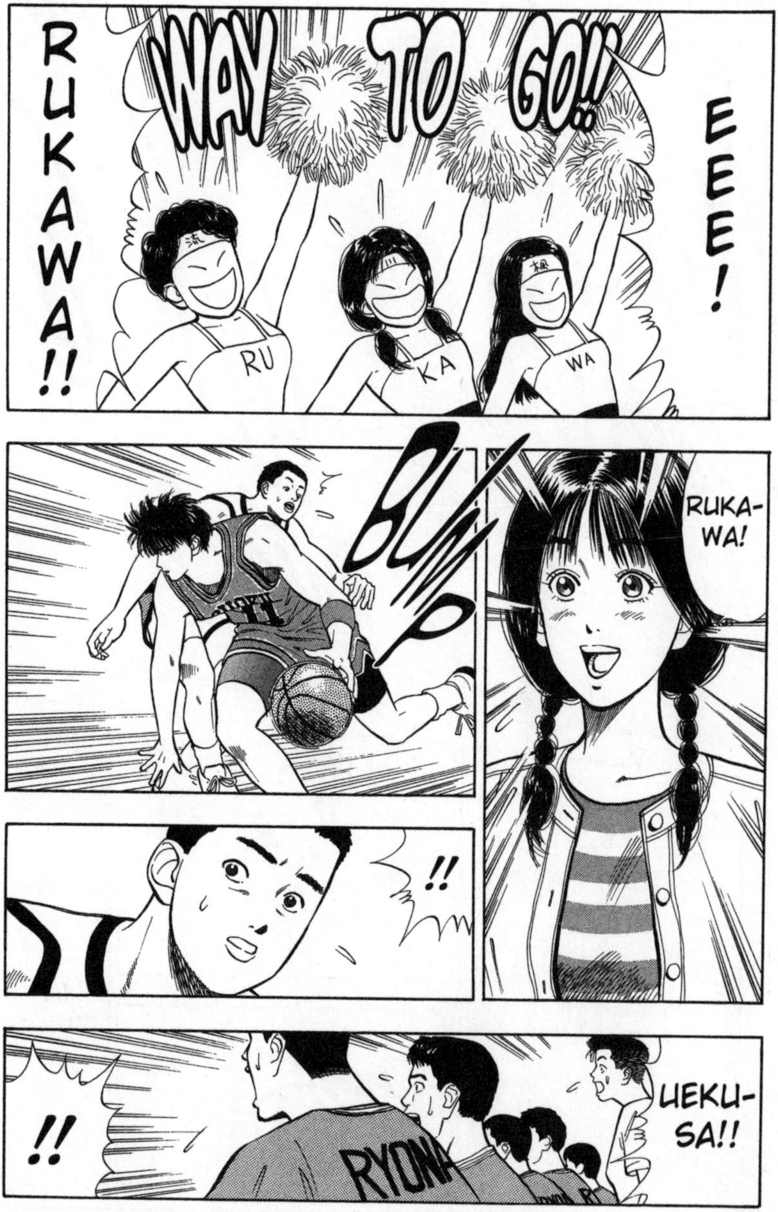
EEEE!
WAY TO GO!!
WA
KA
RU
RUKAWA!!
RUKA-WA!
BUMP
!!
UEKU-SA!!
!!
RYONAN

READ THIS WAY

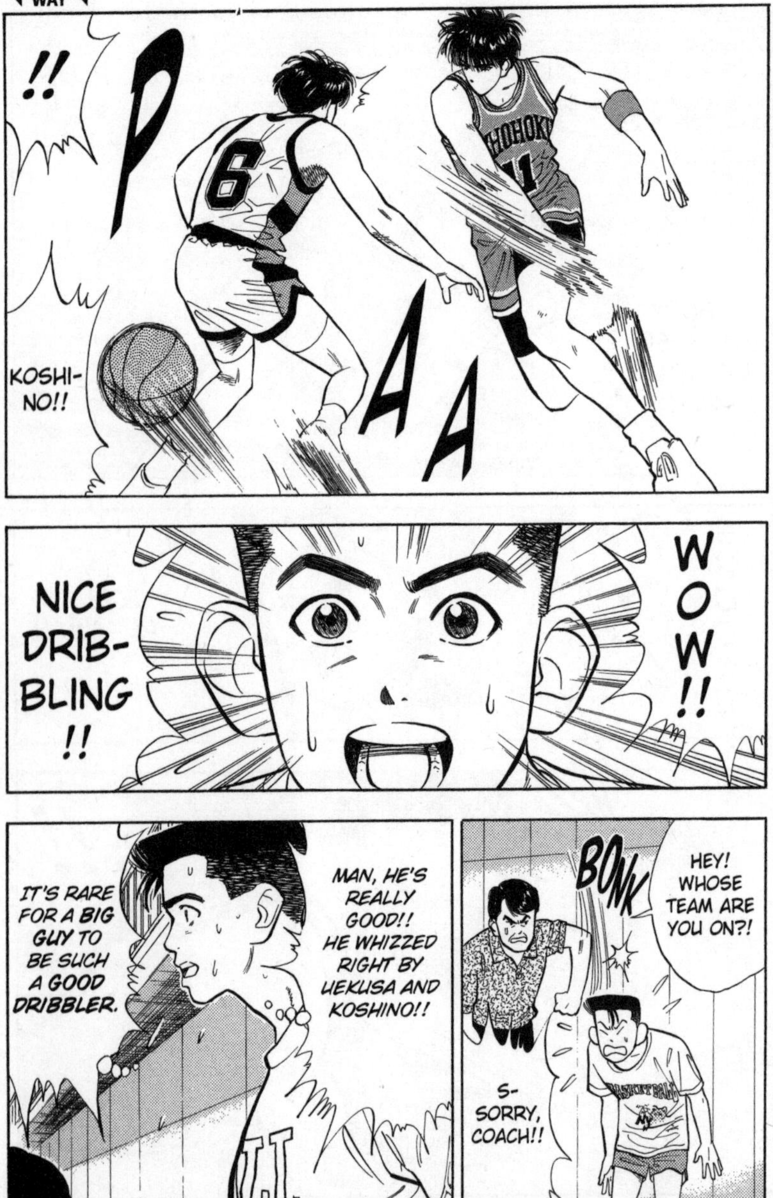

PAAA
!!
KOSHINO!!
WOW!!
NICE DRIBBLING!!
HEY! WHOSE TEAM ARE YOU ON?!
BONK
S-SORRY, COACH!!
MAN, HE'S REALLY GOOD!! HE WHIZZED RIGHT BY UEKUSA AND KOSHINO!!
IT'S RARE FOR A BIG GUY TO BE SUCH A GOOD DRIBBLER.

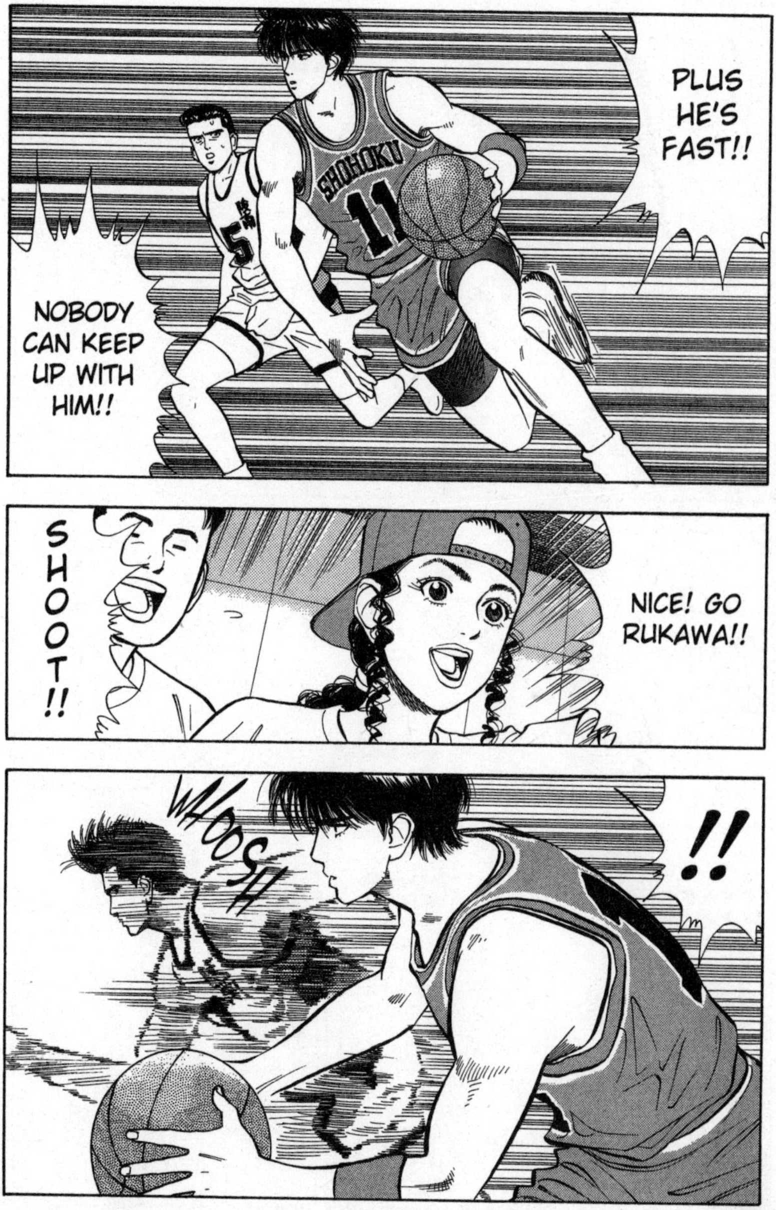
PLUS HE'S FAST!!
NOBODY CAN KEEP UP WITH HIM!!
NICE! GO RUKAWA!!
SHOOOT!!
!!
WHOOSH

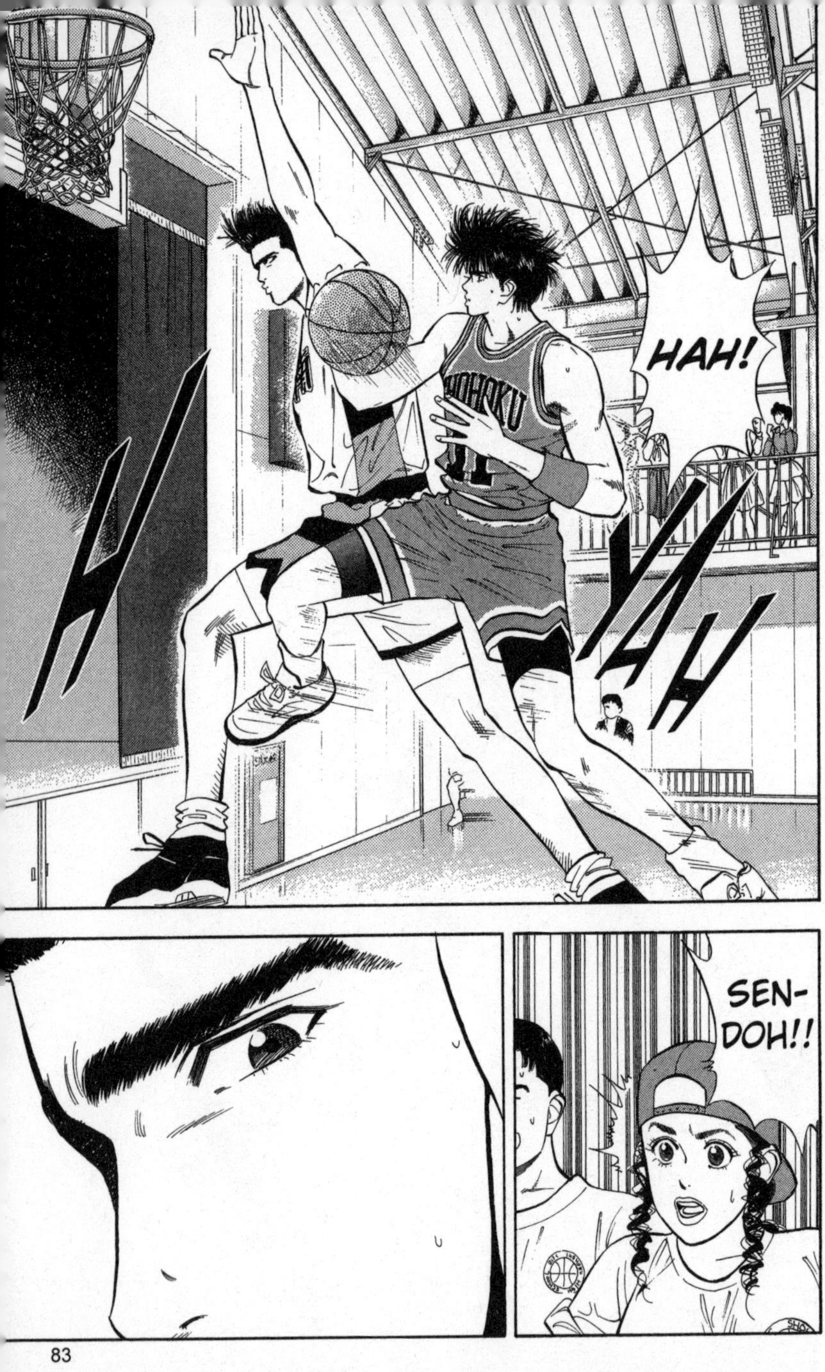
HAH!
SEN-DOH!!

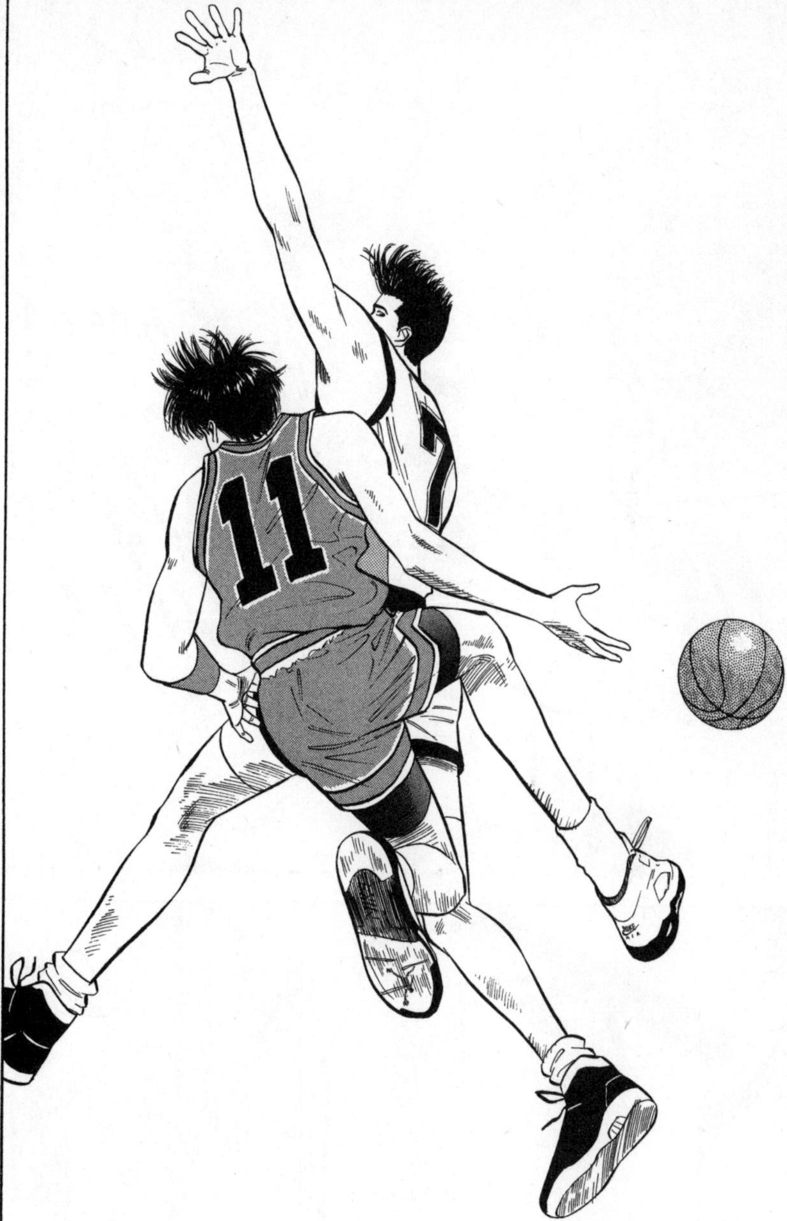

READ THIS WAY

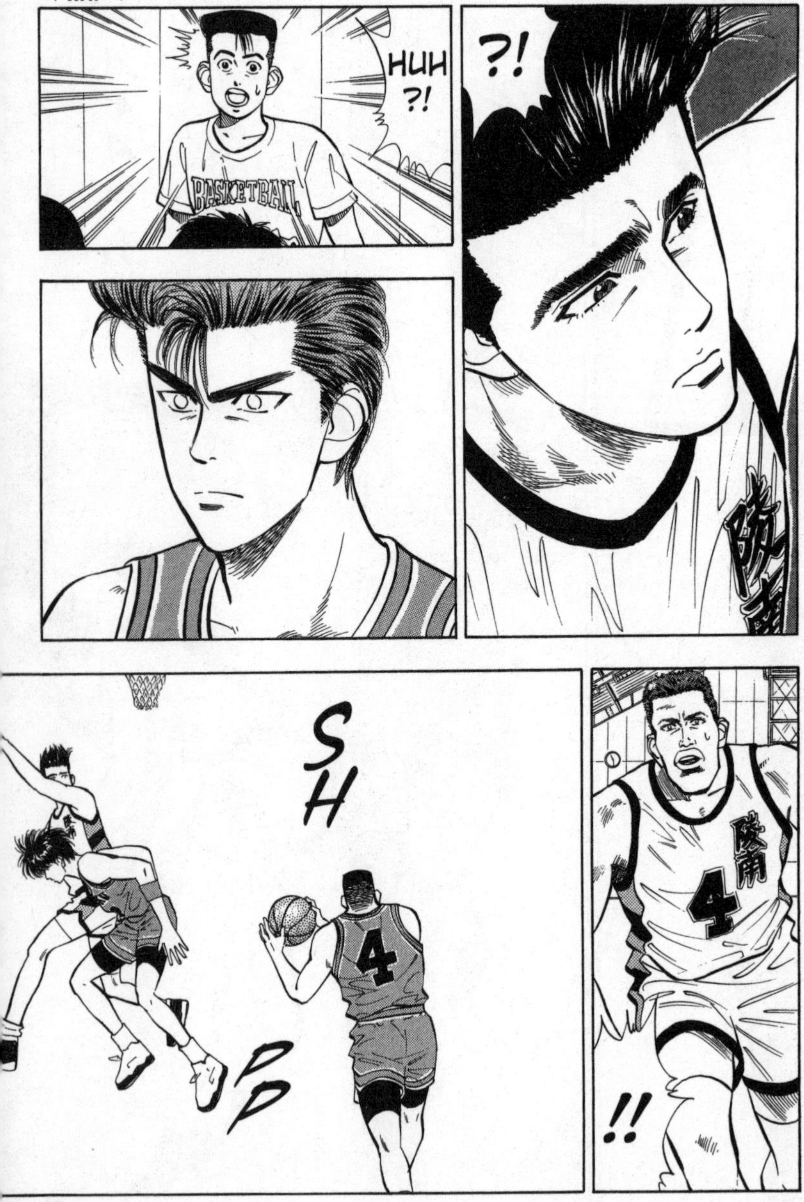
?!
HUH ?!
BASKETBALL
!!
SH
PP

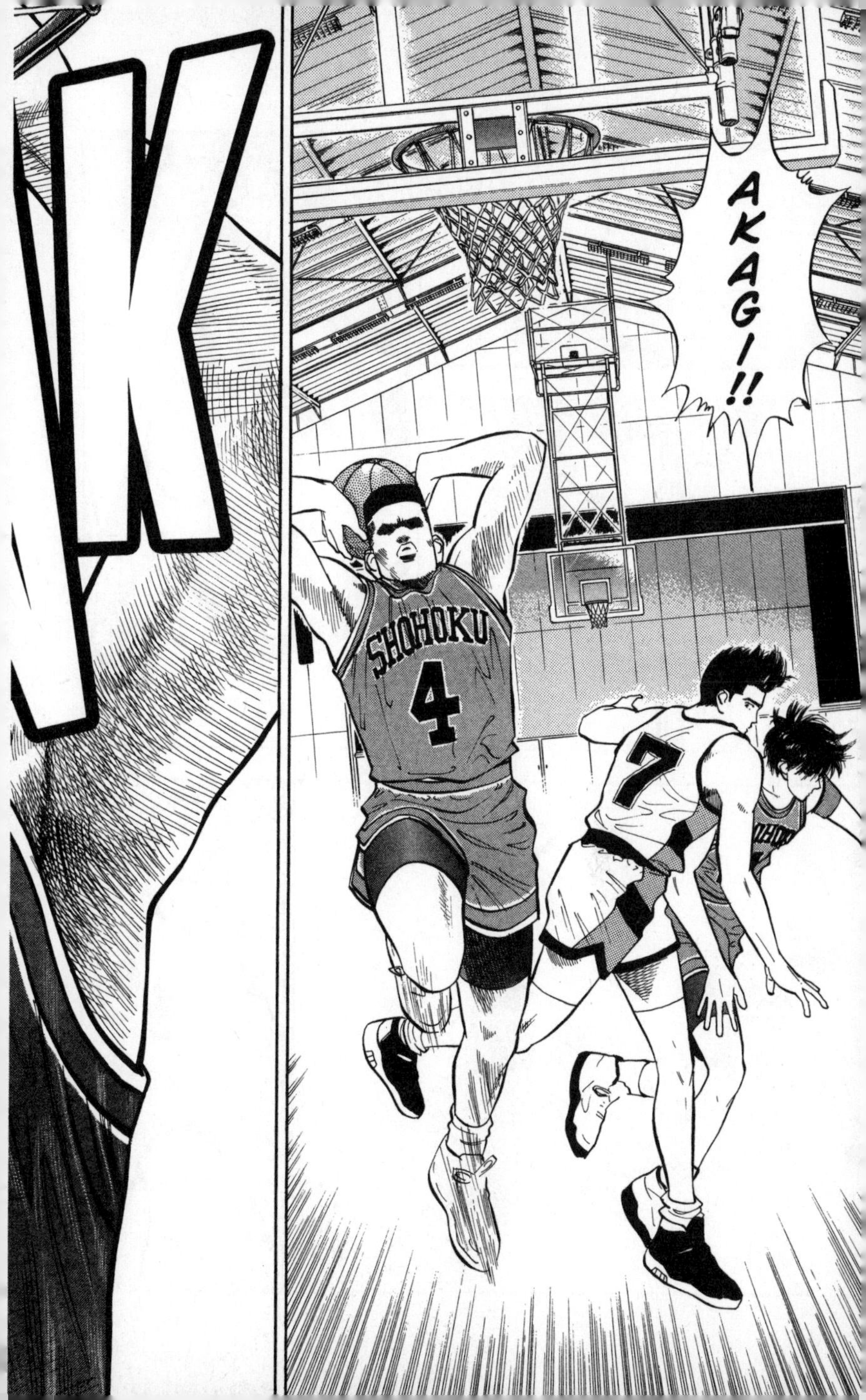
AKAGI!!
SHOHOKU
4
7
K

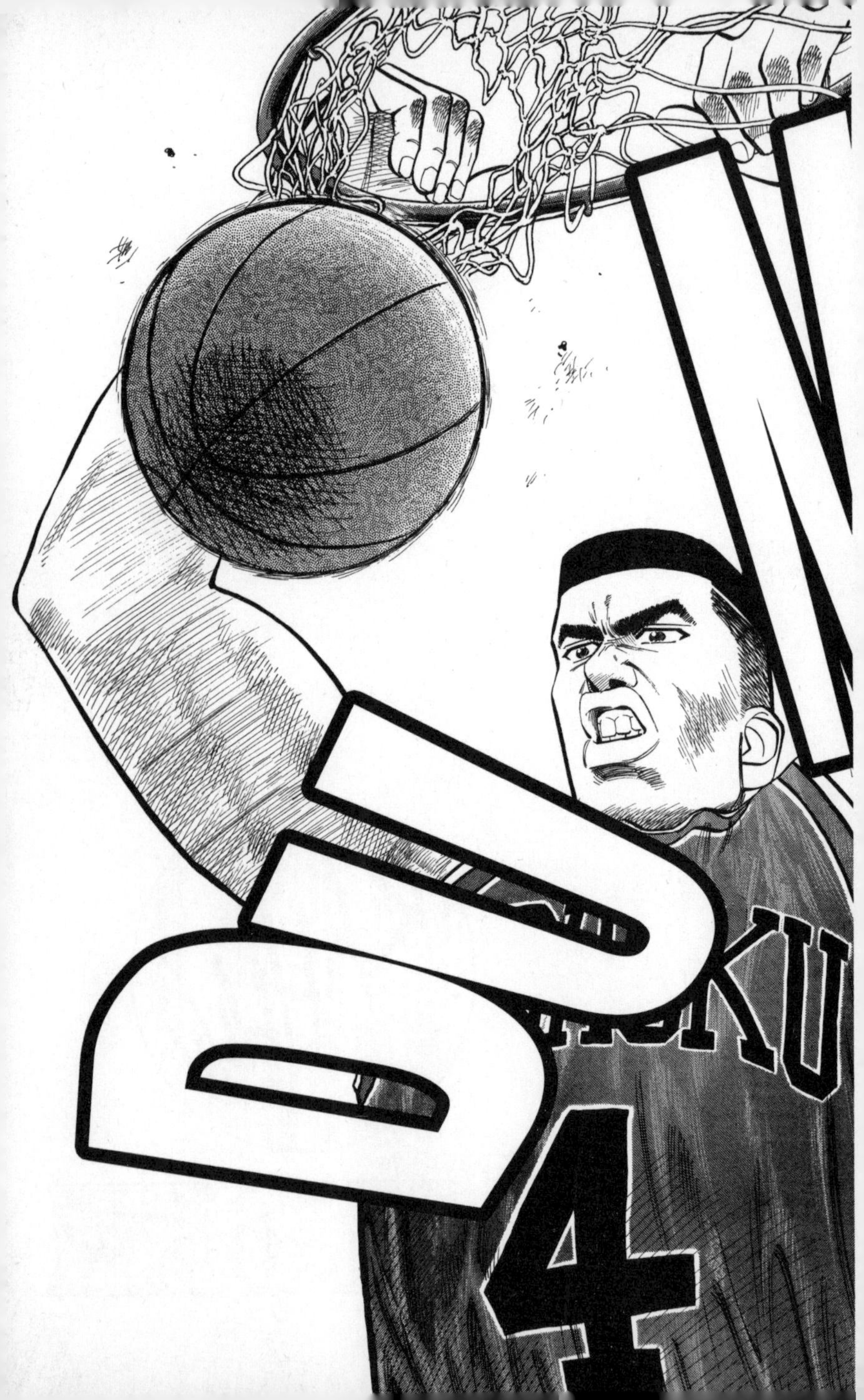
DUN

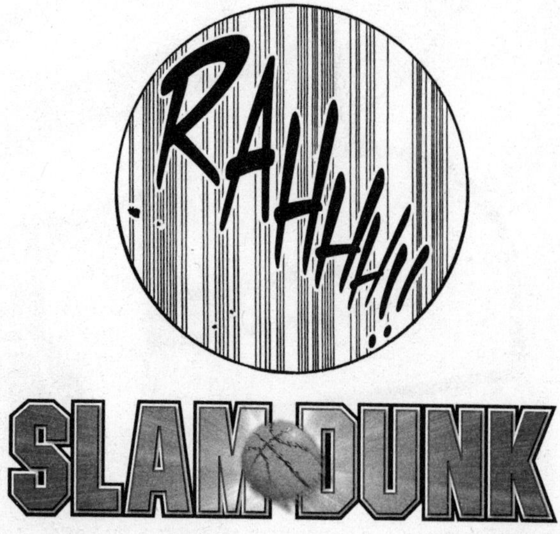
RAHHH!!

SLAM DUNK

#31 ANTICIPATION

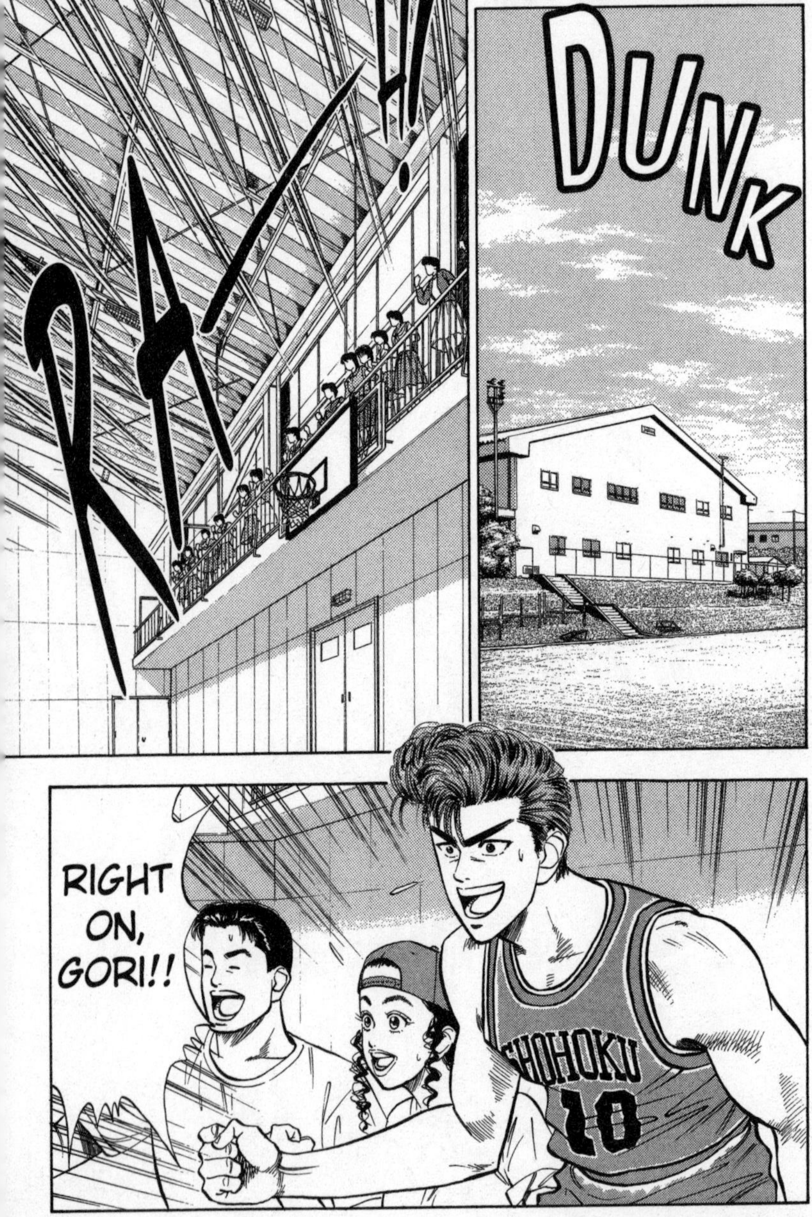
DUNK
RA—H!!
RIGHT ON, GORI!!
SHOHOKU
10

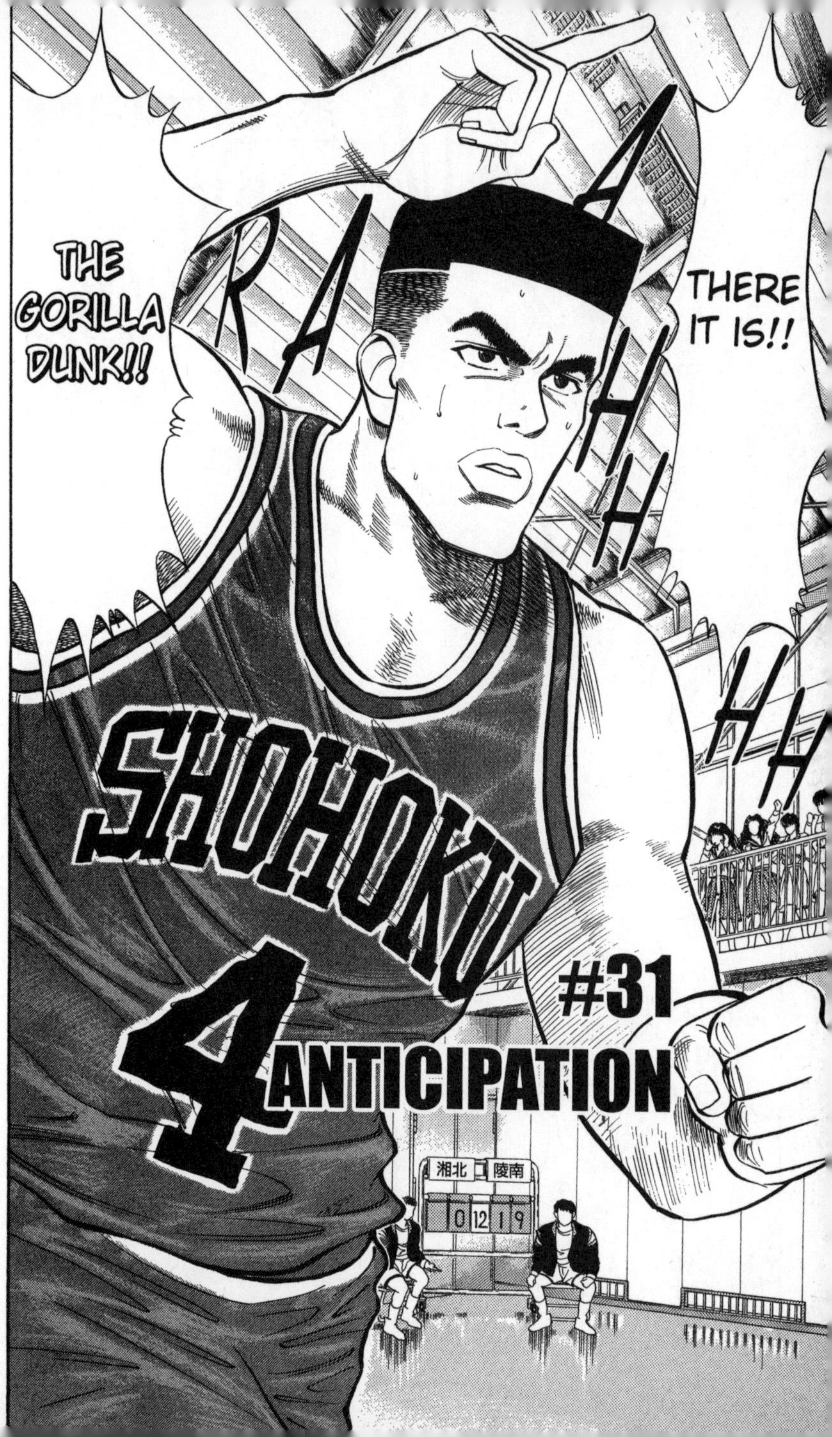
THERE IT IS!!
THE GORILLA DUNK!!
RAAHHHHH
SHOHOKU
4
#31
ANTICIPATION
湘北
陵南

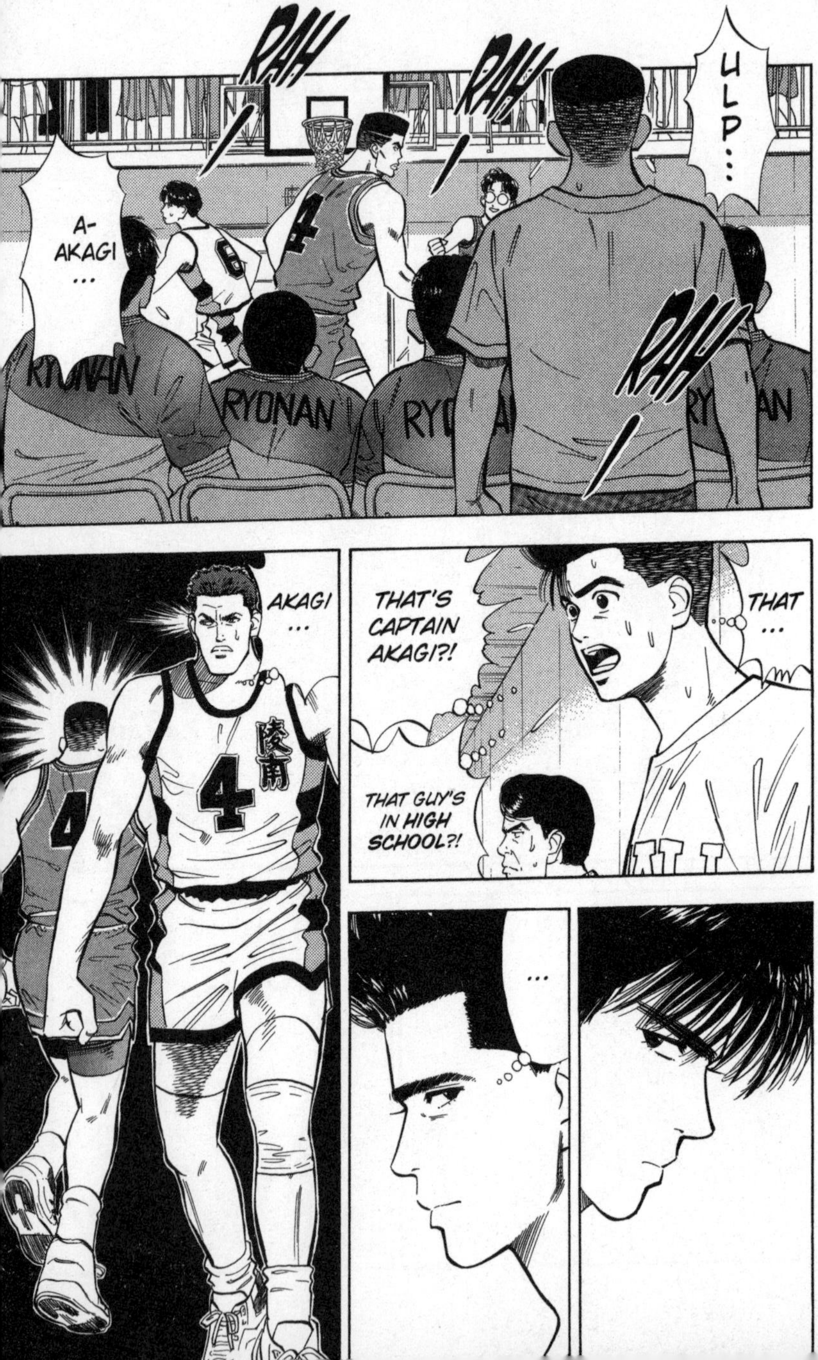
ULP...
RAH
RAH
RAH
A-AKAGI...
THAT...
THAT'S CAPTAIN AKAGI?!
THAT GUY'S IN HIGH SCHOOL?!
...
AKAGI...

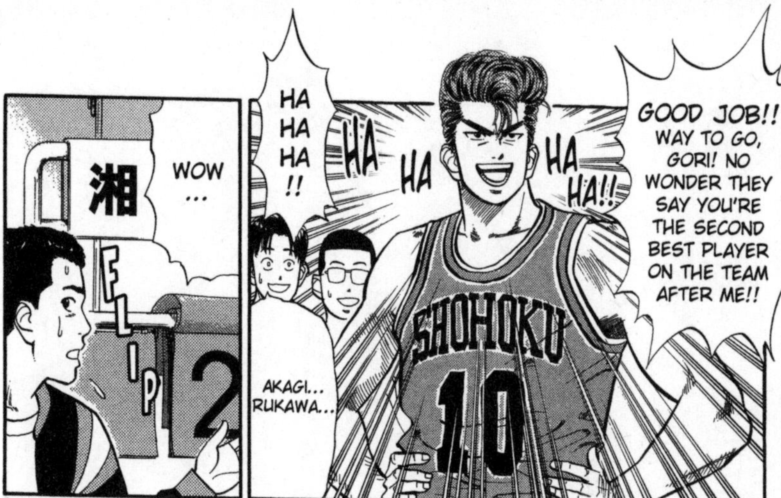
GOOD JOB!! WAY TO GO, GORI! NO WONDER THEY SAY YOU'RE THE SECOND BEST PLAYER ON THE TEAM AFTER ME!!
HA HA HA HA!!
HA HA HA !!
AKAGI... RUKAWA...
WOW ...
湘
FLIP

Scoreboard: Shohoku

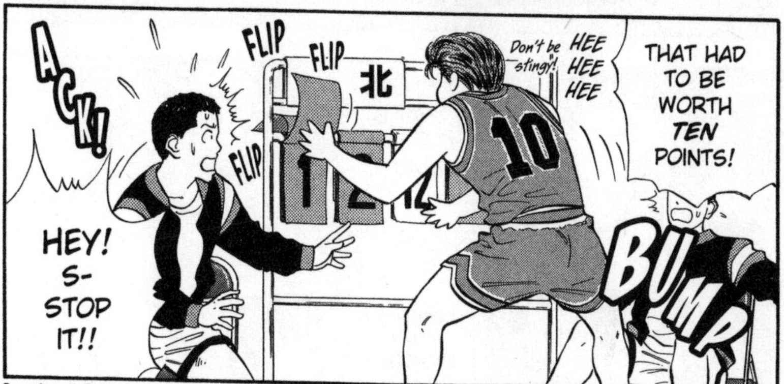
THAT HAD TO BE WORTH TEN POINTS!
HEE HEE HEE
Don't be stingy!
BUMP
北
FLIP
FLIP
FLIP
ACK!
HEY! S-STOP IT!!

Scoreboard: Shohoku

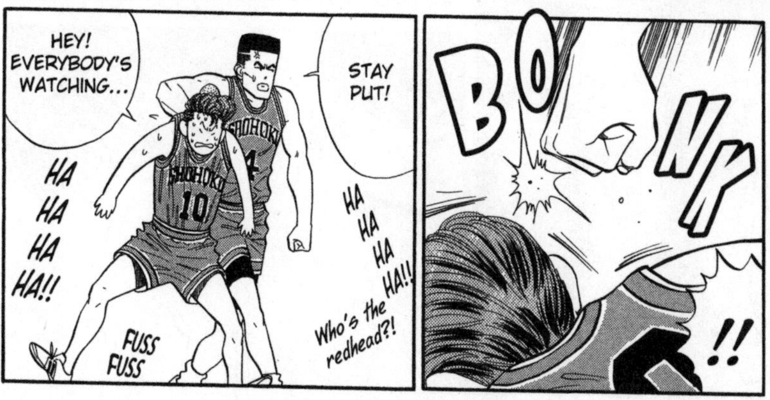
BONK
!!
STAY PUT!
HA HA HA HA!!
Who's the redhead?!
HEY! EVERYBODY'S WATCHING...
HA HA HA HA!!
FUSS FUSS

READ THIS WAY

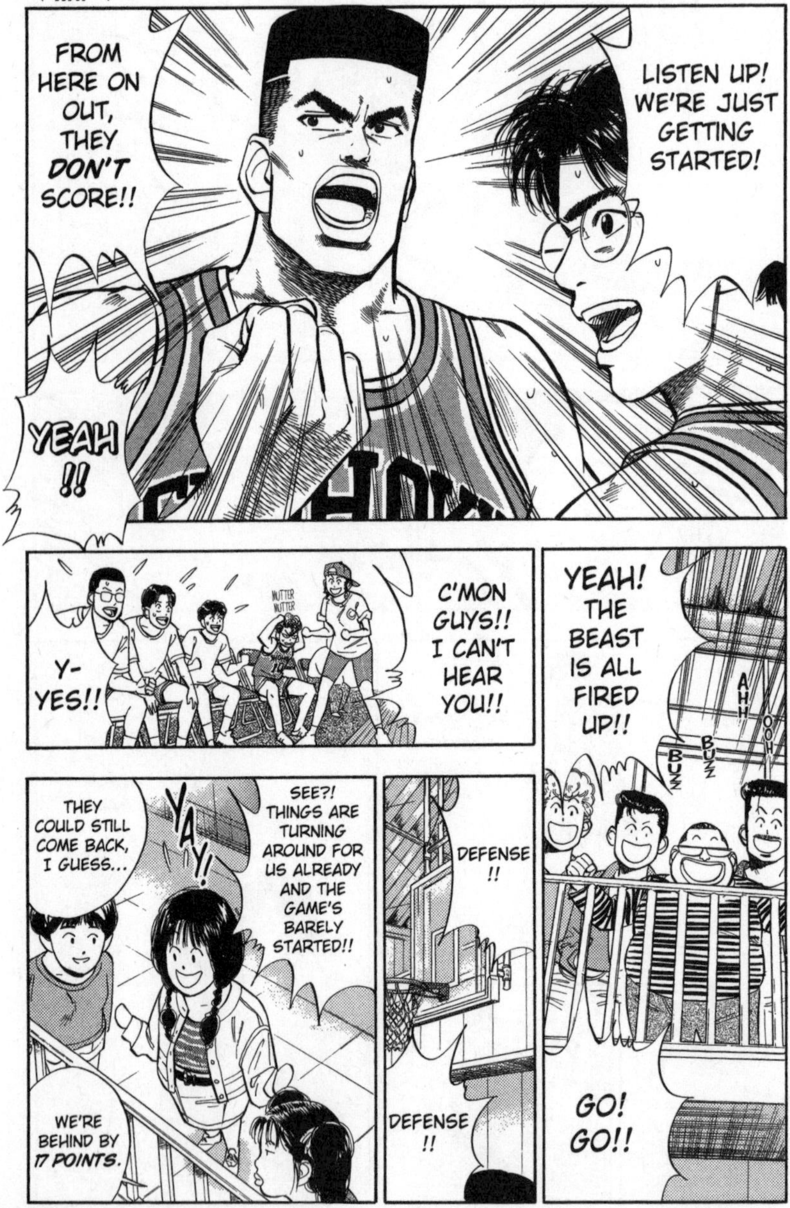

LISTEN UP! WE'RE JUST GETTING STARTED!
FROM HERE ON OUT, THEY DON'T SCORE!!
YEAH!!
YEAH! THE BEAST IS ALL FIRED UP!!
AHH
OOH
BUZZ
BUZZ
GO! GO!!
C'MON GUYS!! I CAN'T HEAR YOU!!
MUTTER MUTTER
Y- YES!!
DEFENSE!!
DEFENSE!!
SEE?! THINGS ARE TURNING AROUND FOR US ALREADY AND THE GAME'S BARELY STARTED!!
YAY!
THEY COULD STILL COME BACK, I GUESS...
WE'RE BEHIND BY 17 POINTS.

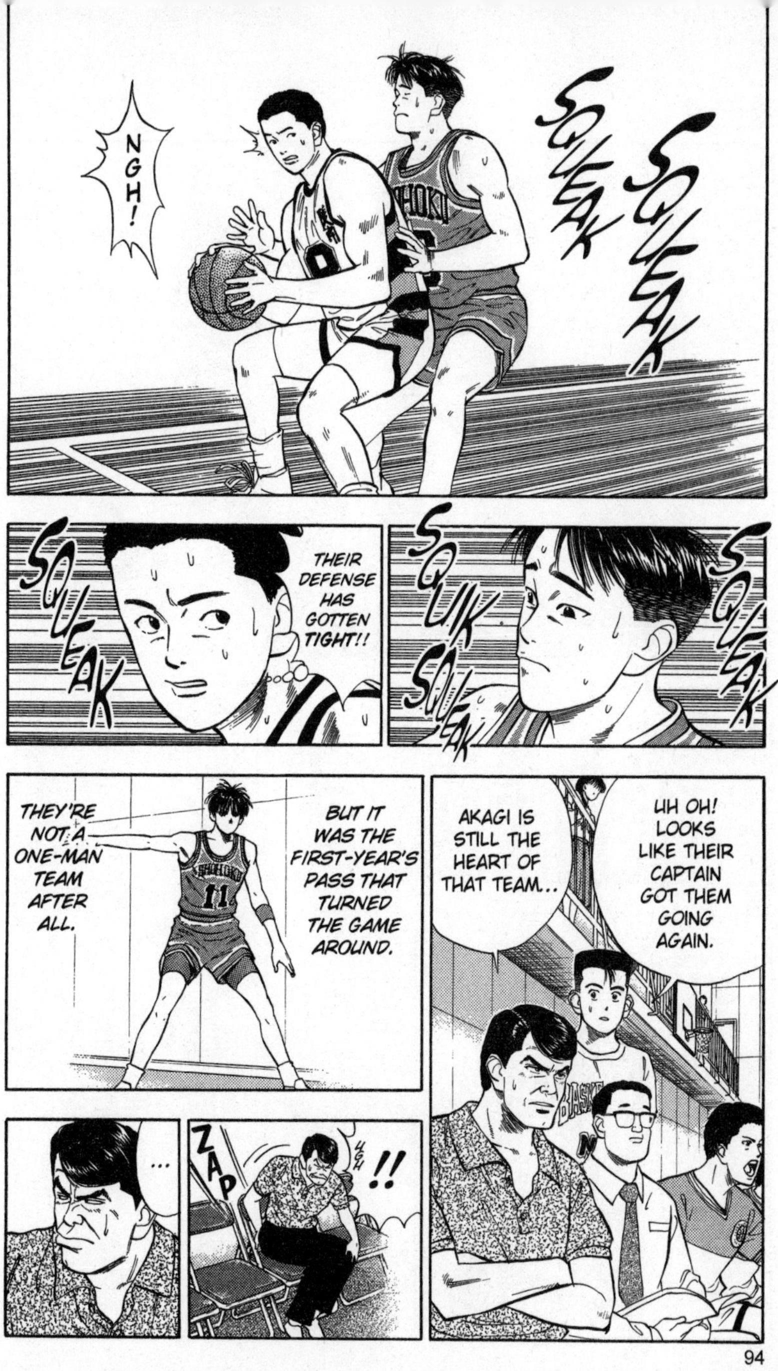
SQUEAK
SQUEAK
NGH!
SQUEAK
SQUIK SQUEAK
SQUEAK
THEIR DEFENSE HAS GOTTEN TIGHT!!
UH OH! LOOKS LIKE THEIR CAPTAIN GOT THEM GOING AGAIN.
AKAGI IS STILL THE HEART OF THAT TEAM...
BUT IT WAS THE FIRST-YEAR'S PASS THAT TURNED THE GAME AROUND.
THEY'RE NOT A ONE-MAN TEAM AFTER ALL.
ZAP
UGH
!!
...

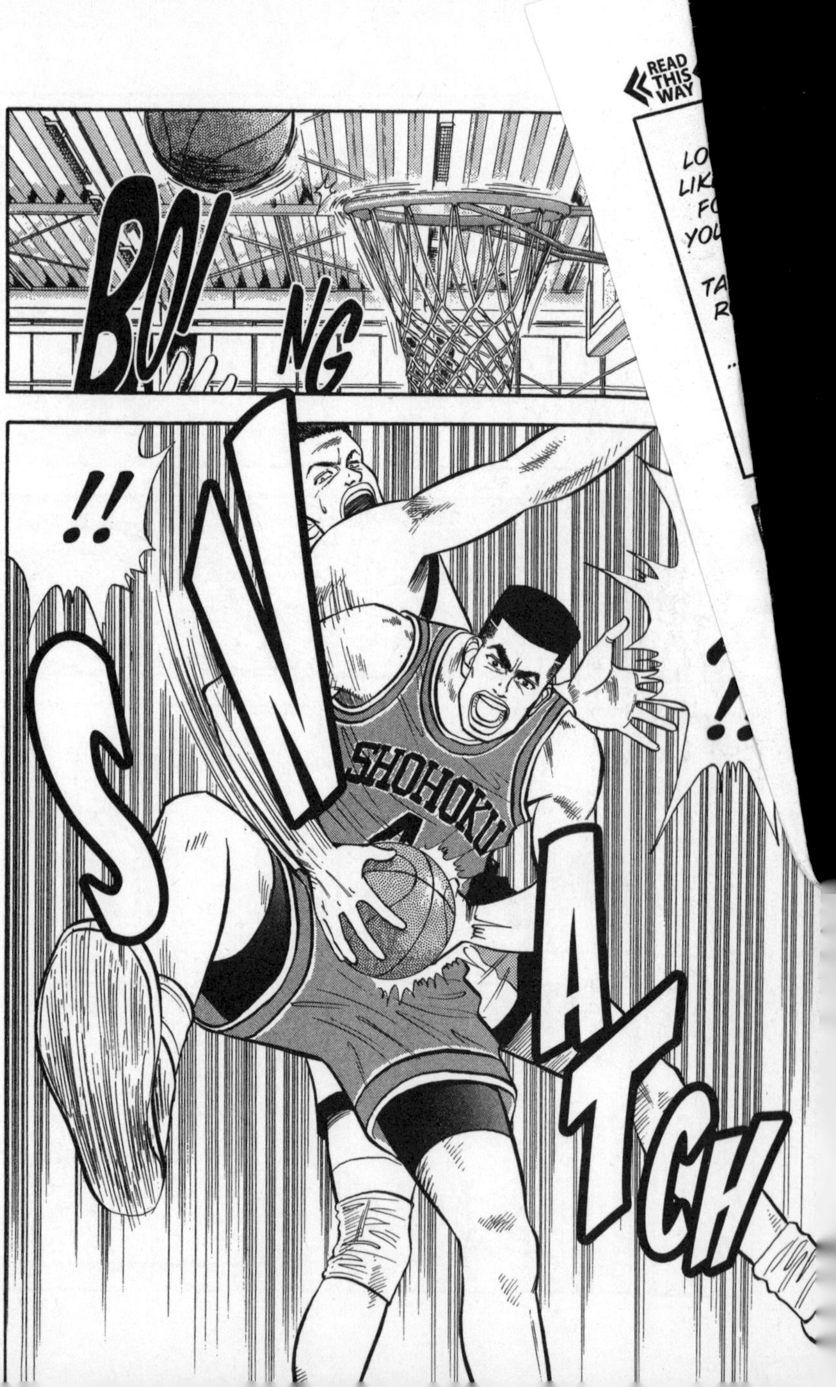
READ THIS WAY
BOING
!!
!?
SNATCH
SHOHOKU

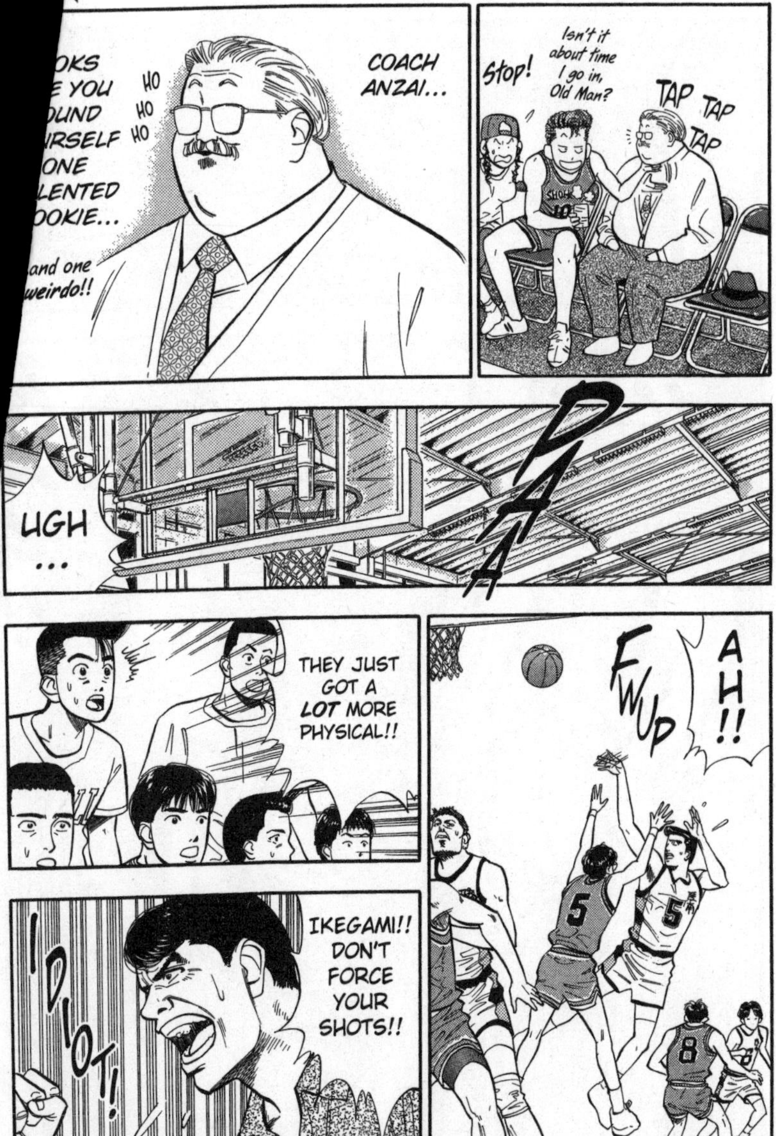
Isn't it about time I go in, Old Man?
Stop!
TAP TAP TAP
COACH ANZAI...
HO HO HO
OKS
E YOU
OUND
URSELF
ONE
LENTED
OOKIE...
and one weirdo!!
DAAA
UGH ...
AH!!
FWUP
THEY JUST GOT A LOT MORE PHYSICAL!!
IKEGAMI!! DON'T FORCE YOUR SHOTS!!
IDIOT!

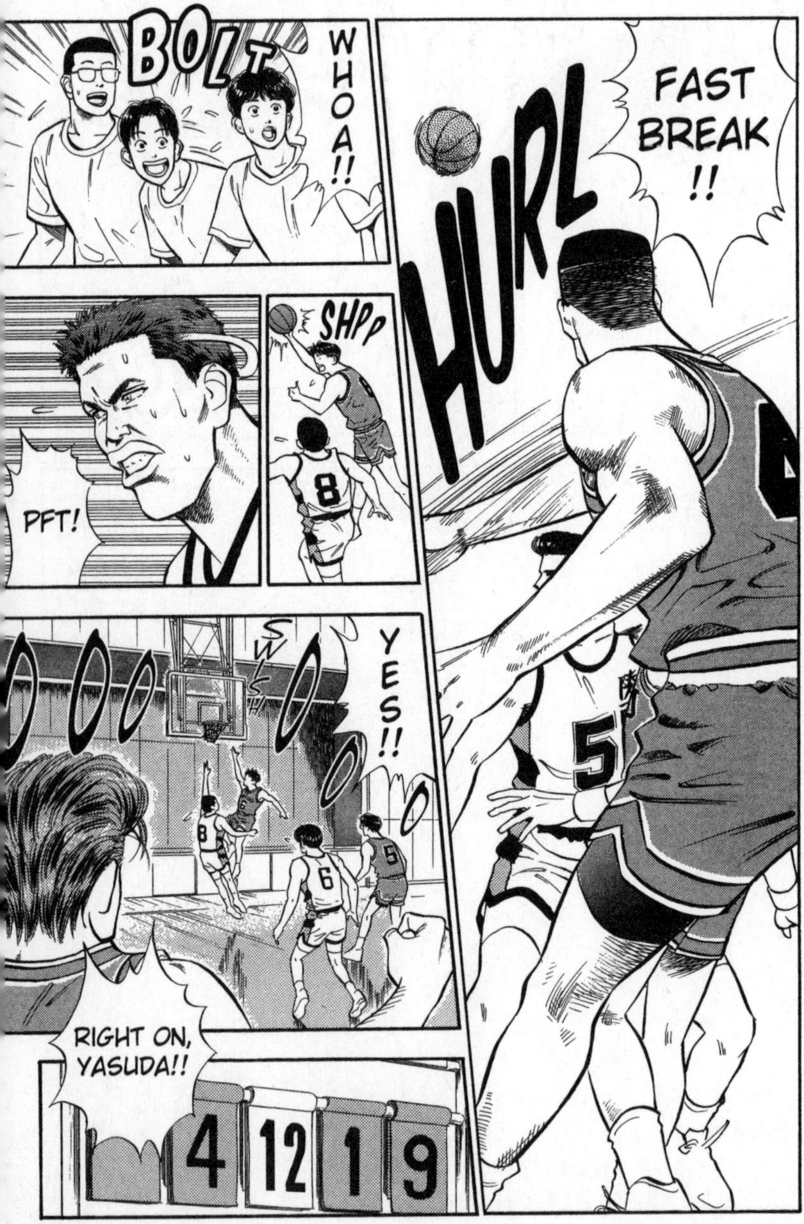
HURL
FAST BREAK!!
BOLT
WHOA!!
SHPP
PFT!
SWISH
YES!!
OOOOOOOO
RIGHT ON, YASUDA!!
4 12 19 9

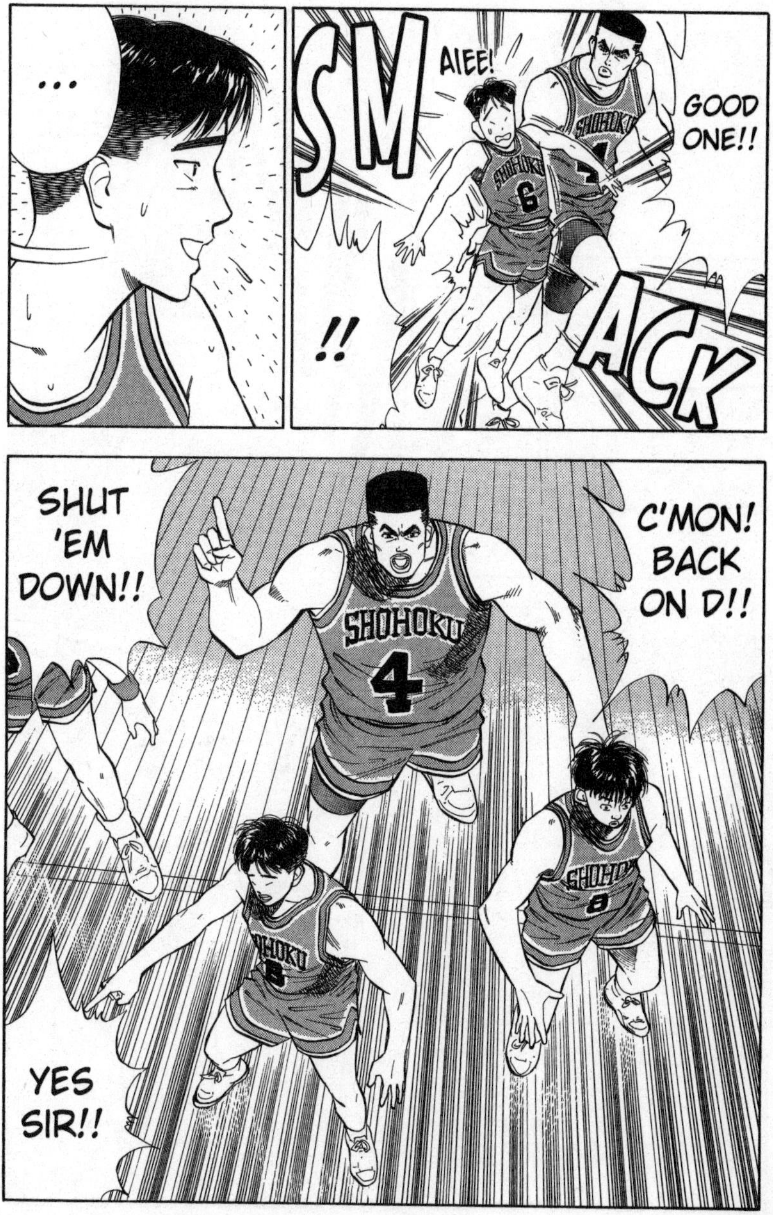
GOOD ONE!!
AIEE!
SM
ACK
!!
...
C'MON! BACK ON D!!
SHUT 'EM DOWN!!
YES SIR!!

READ THIS WAY

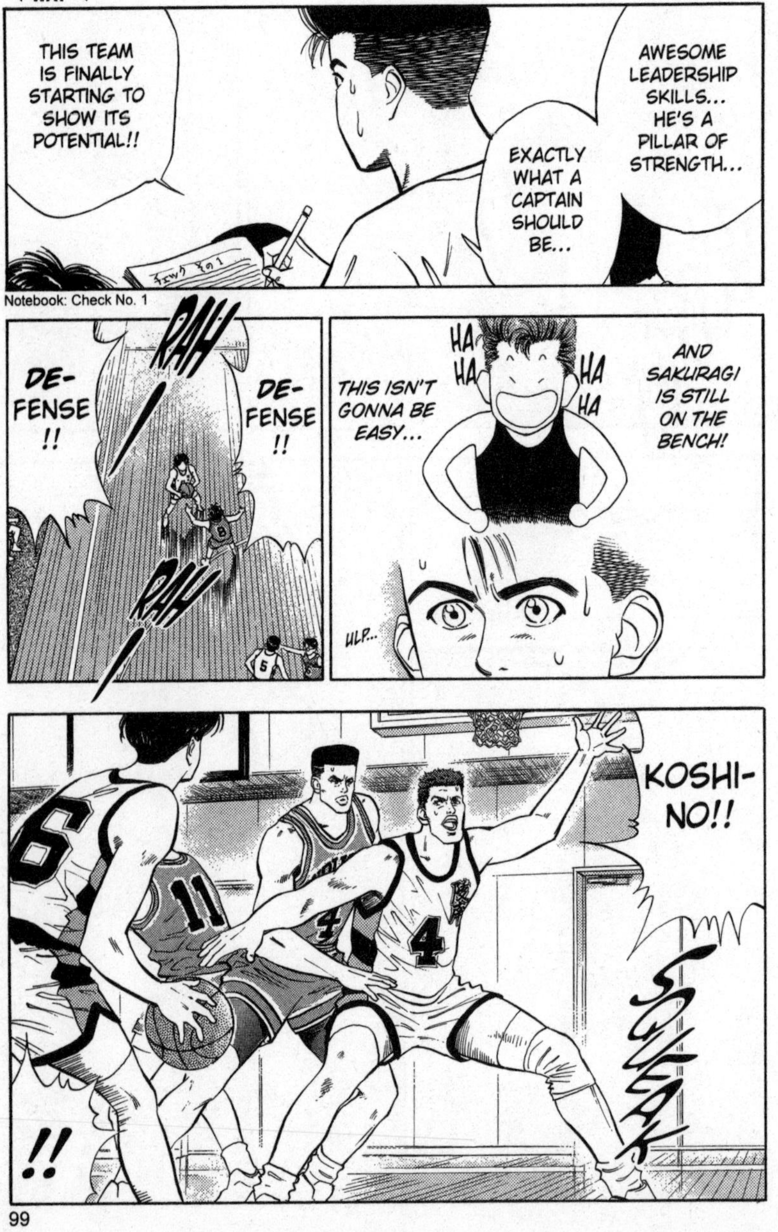
AWESOME LEADERSHIP SKILLS... HE'S A PILLAR OF STRENGTH...
EXACTLY WHAT A CAPTAIN SHOULD BE...
THIS TEAM IS FINALLY STARTING TO SHOW ITS POTENTIAL!!
Notebook: Check No. 1
AND SAKURAGI IS STILL ON THE BENCH!
HA HA
HA HA
THIS ISN'T GONNA BE EASY...
ULP...
DE-FENSE!!
RAH
DE-FENSE!!
RAH
KOSHI-NO!!
SQUEAK
!!

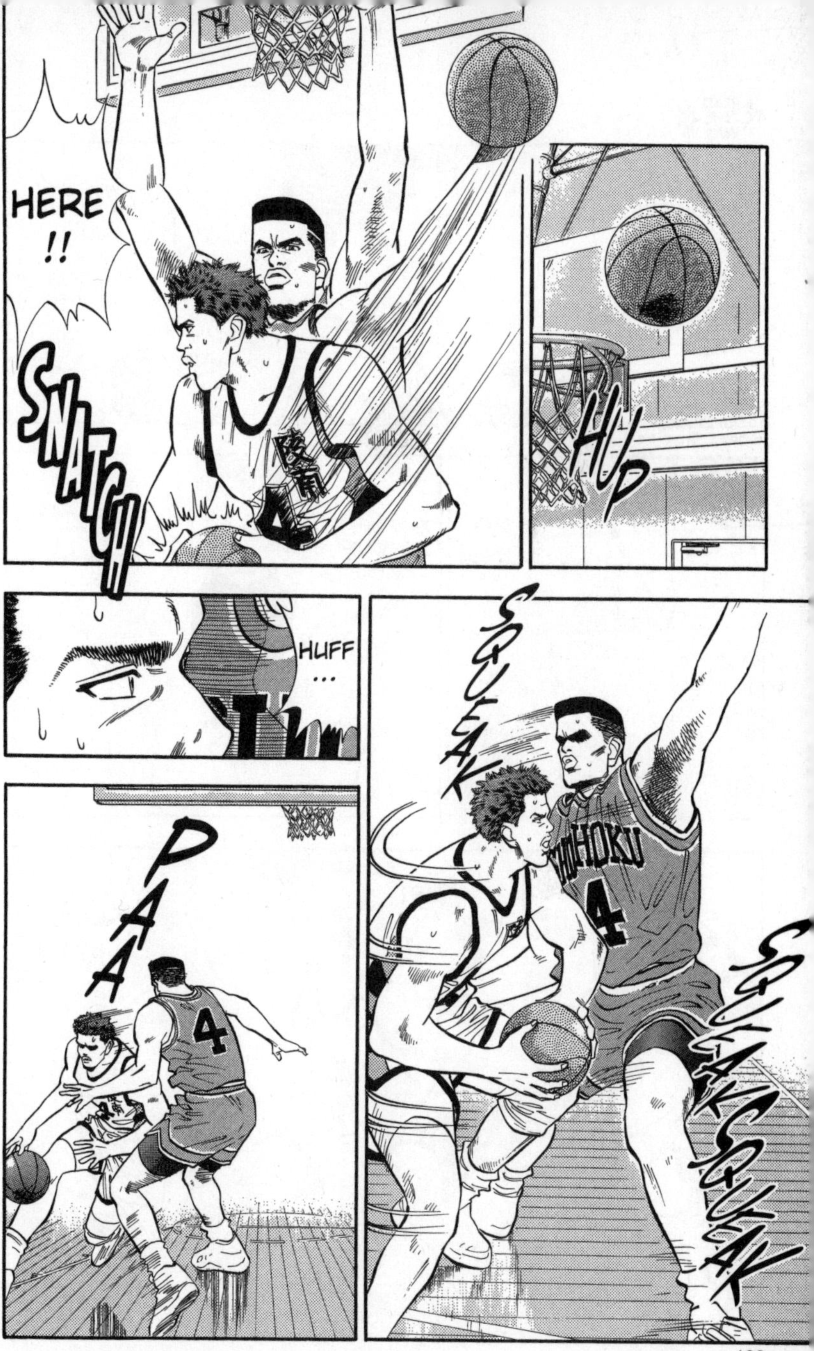
HUP
HERE !!
SNATCH
SQUEAK
SQUEAKSQUEAK
HUFF ...
PAAA

LOOK AT THAT!! UOZUMI CAN'T PUT UP A SHOT!!

EVEN UOZUMI?!

GAH!!

GO AT HIM, UOZU-MI!!

MAKE YOUR PLAY! MAKE YOUR PLAY!!

THREE SECONDS! THREE SECONDS!

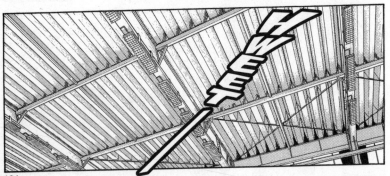

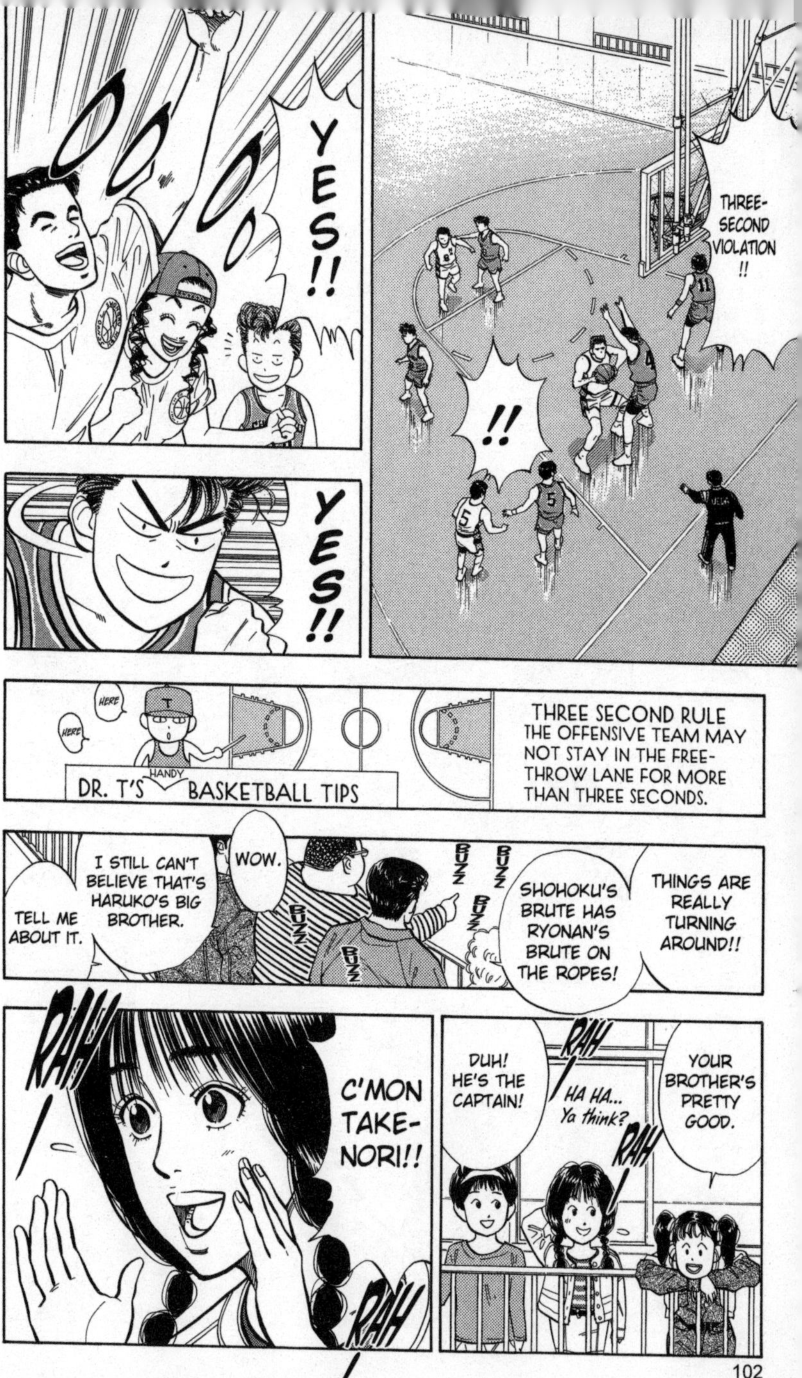
THREE-SECOND VIOLATION !!
!!
YES!!
YES!!
THREE SECOND RULE
THE OFFENSIVE TEAM MAY NOT STAY IN THE FREE-THROW LANE FOR MORE THAN THREE SECONDS.
HERE
HERE
DR. T'S HANDY BASKETBALL TIPS
THINGS ARE REALLY TURNING AROUND!!
SHOHOKU'S BRUTE HAS RYONAN'S BRUTE ON THE ROPES!
BUZZ BUZZ BUZZ BUZZ BUZZ
WOW.
I STILL CAN'T BELIEVE THAT'S HARUKO'S BIG BROTHER.
TELL ME ABOUT IT.
YOUR BROTHER'S PRETTY GOOD.
RAH
HA HA... Ya think?
RAH
DUH! HE'S THE CAPTAIN!
C'MON TAKE-NORI!!
RAH
RAH

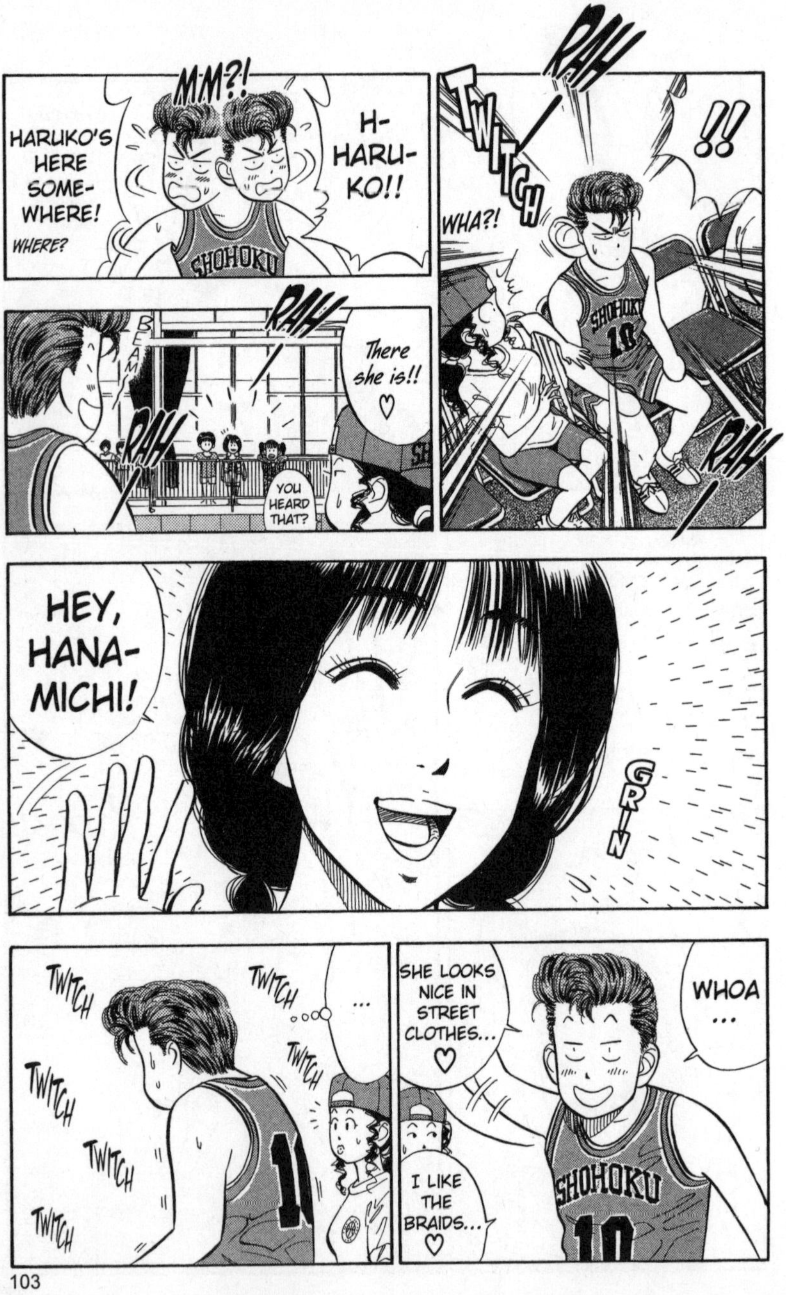
RAH
TWITCH
!!
WHA?!
RAH
H-HARUKO!!
MM?!
HARUKO'S HERE SOMEWHERE!
WHERE?
There she is!! ♡
RAH
BEAM
RAH
YOU HEARD THAT?
HEY, HANAMICHI!
GRIN
WHOA ...
SHE LOOKS NICE IN STREET CLOTHES... ♡
I LIKE THE BRAIDS... ♡
...
TWITCH
TWITCH
TWITCH
TWITCH
TWITCH
TWITCH

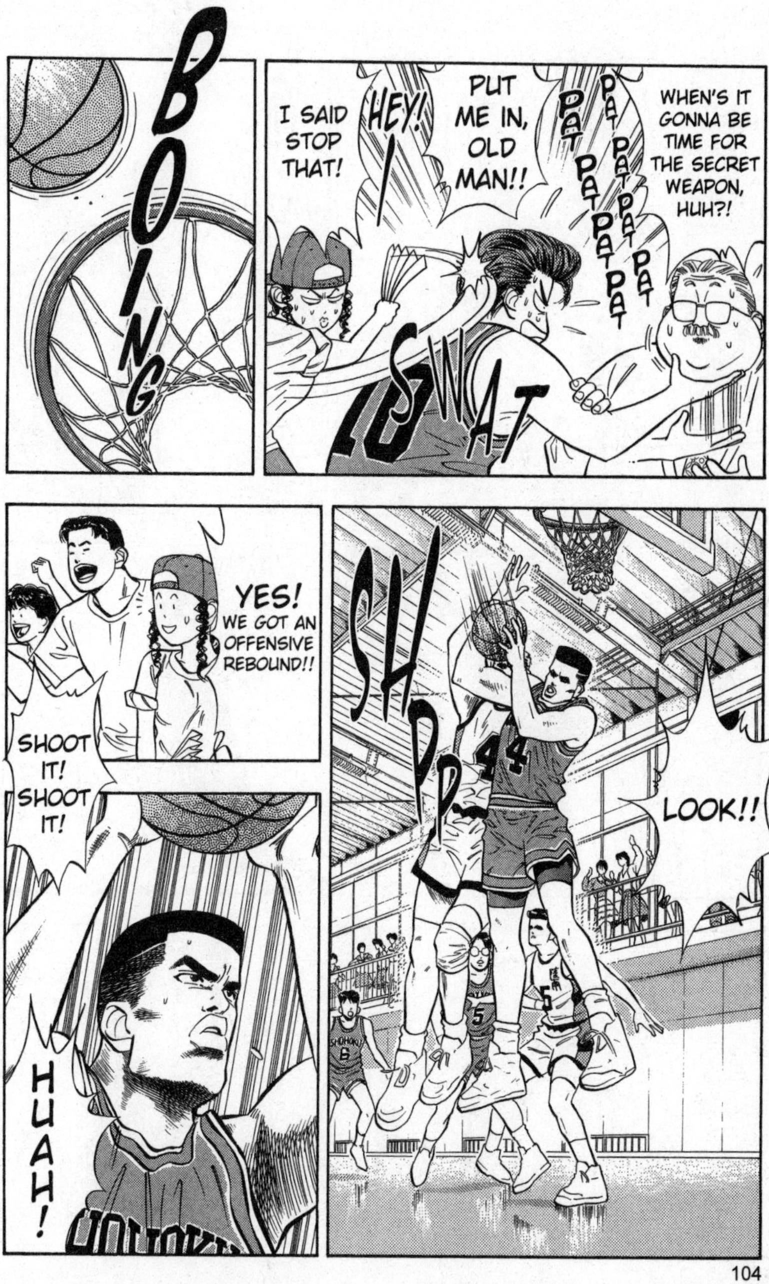
WHEN'S IT GONNA BE TIME FOR THE SECRET WEAPON, HUH?!
PAT PAT PAT PAT PAT PAT PAT PAT
PUT ME IN, OLD MAN!!
HEY!
I SAID STOP THAT!
SWAT
BOING
LOOK!!
SHPP
YES! WE GOT AN OFFENSIVE REBOUND!!
SHOOT IT! SHOOT IT!
HUAH!

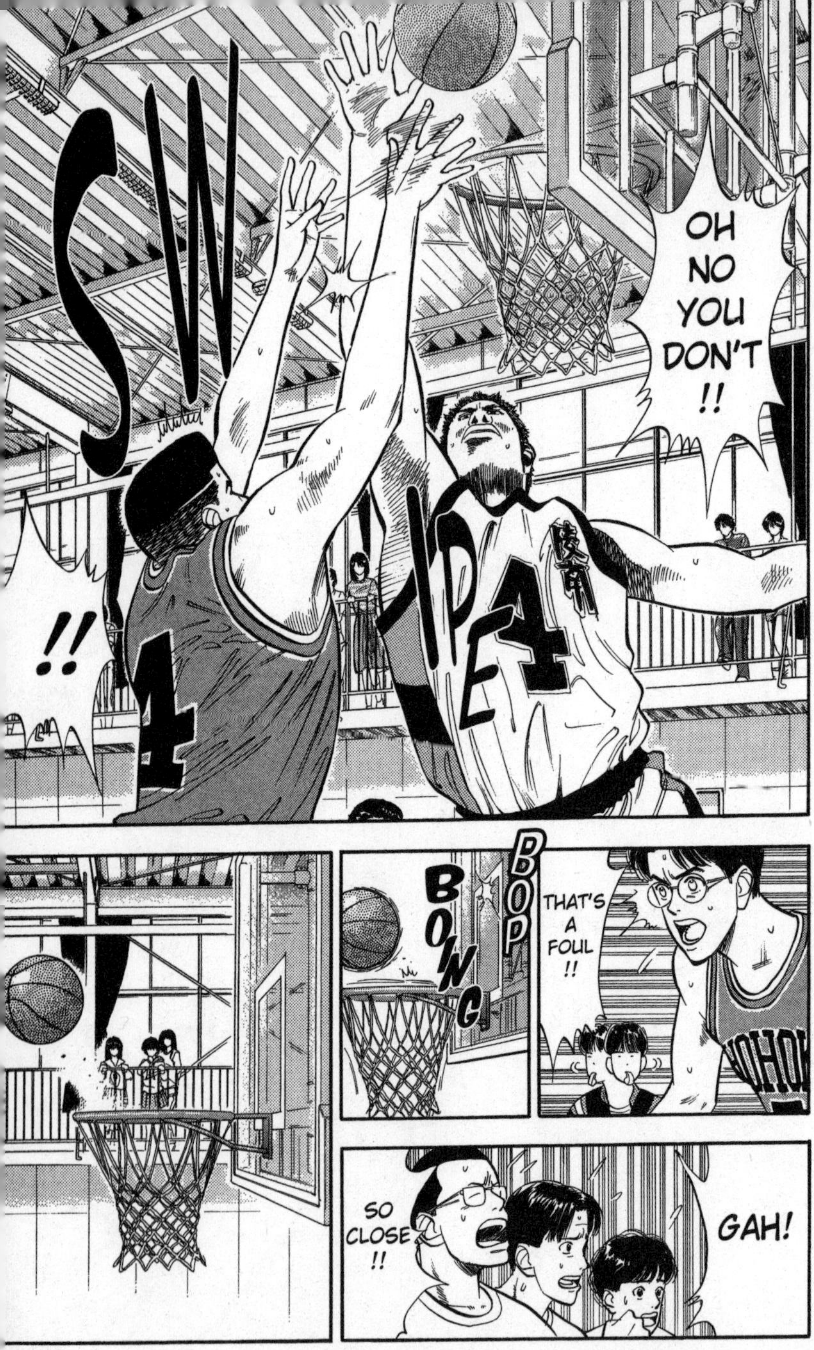
OH NO YOU DON'T !!
SWIPE
!!
THAT'S A FOUL !!
BOP
BOING
GAH!
SO CLOSE !!

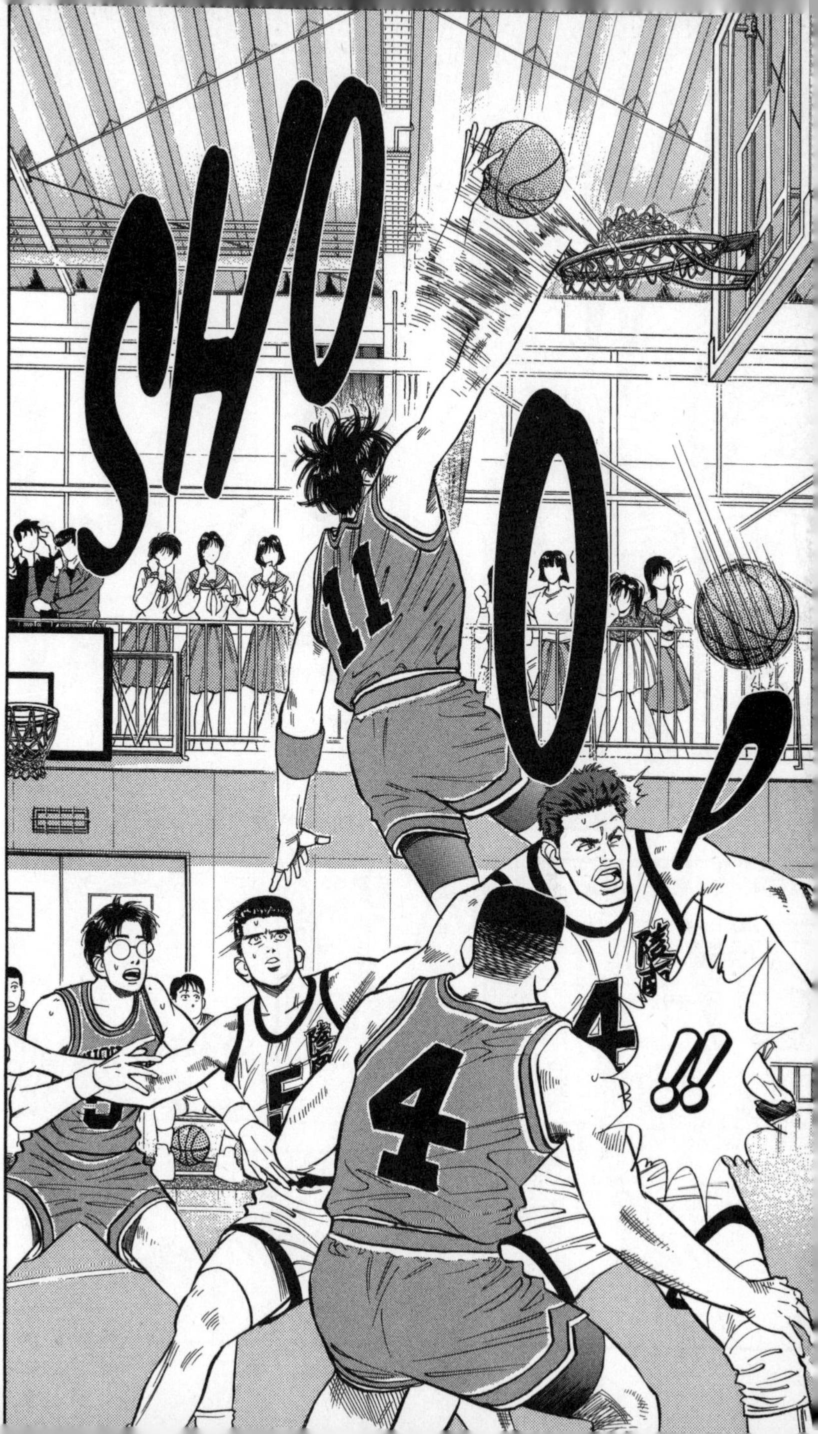
SHOOP
!!

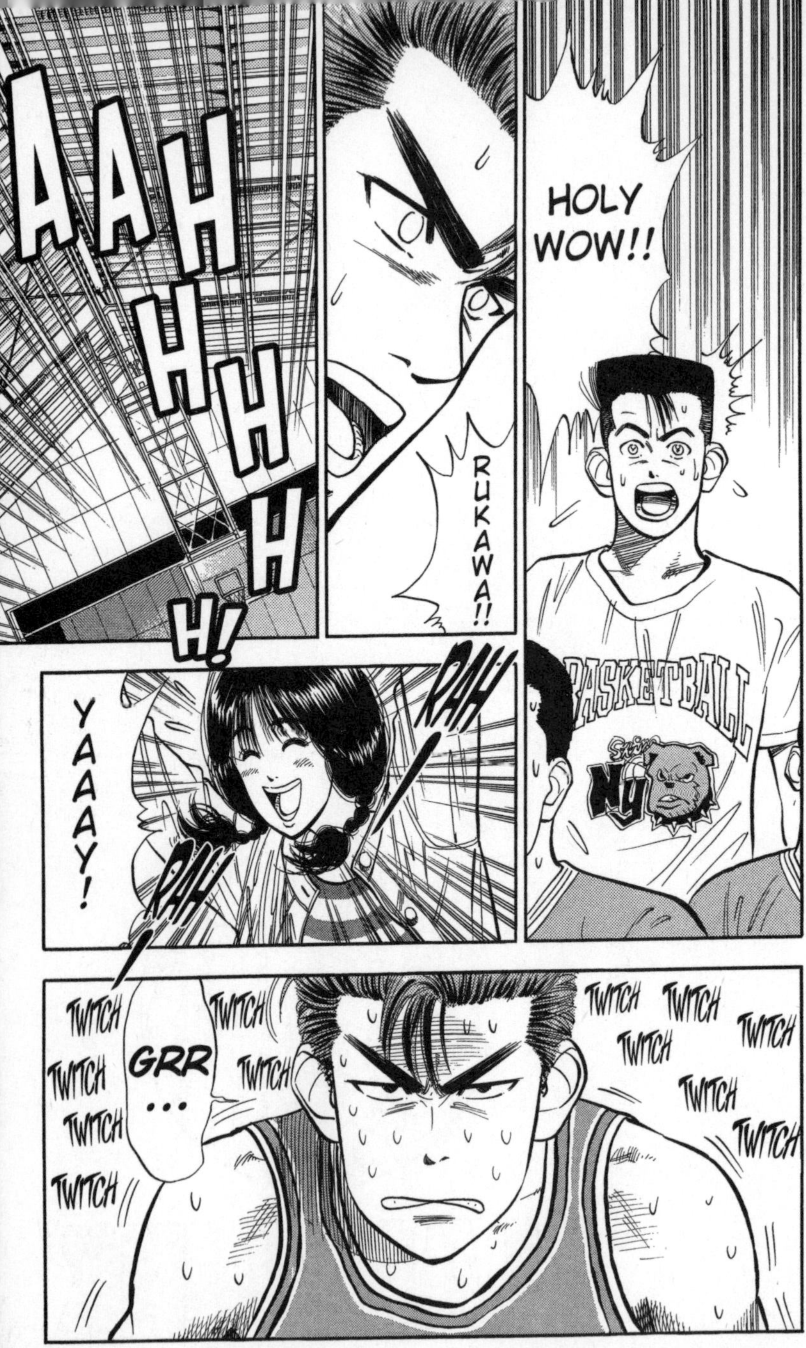
HOLY WOW!!
RUKAWA!!
AAHHHHH!
RAH
RAH
YAAAAY!
TWITCH TWITCH TWITCH TWITCH TWITCH TWITCH
GRR...
TWITCH TWITCH TWITCH TWITCH TWITCH

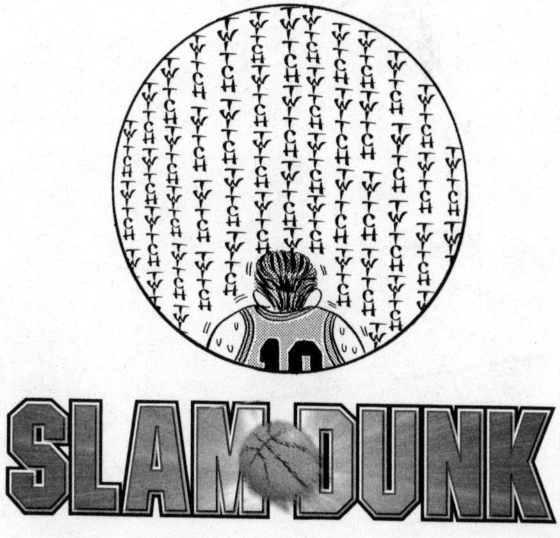
TWITCH

SLAM DUNK

#32 LOOSE CANNON

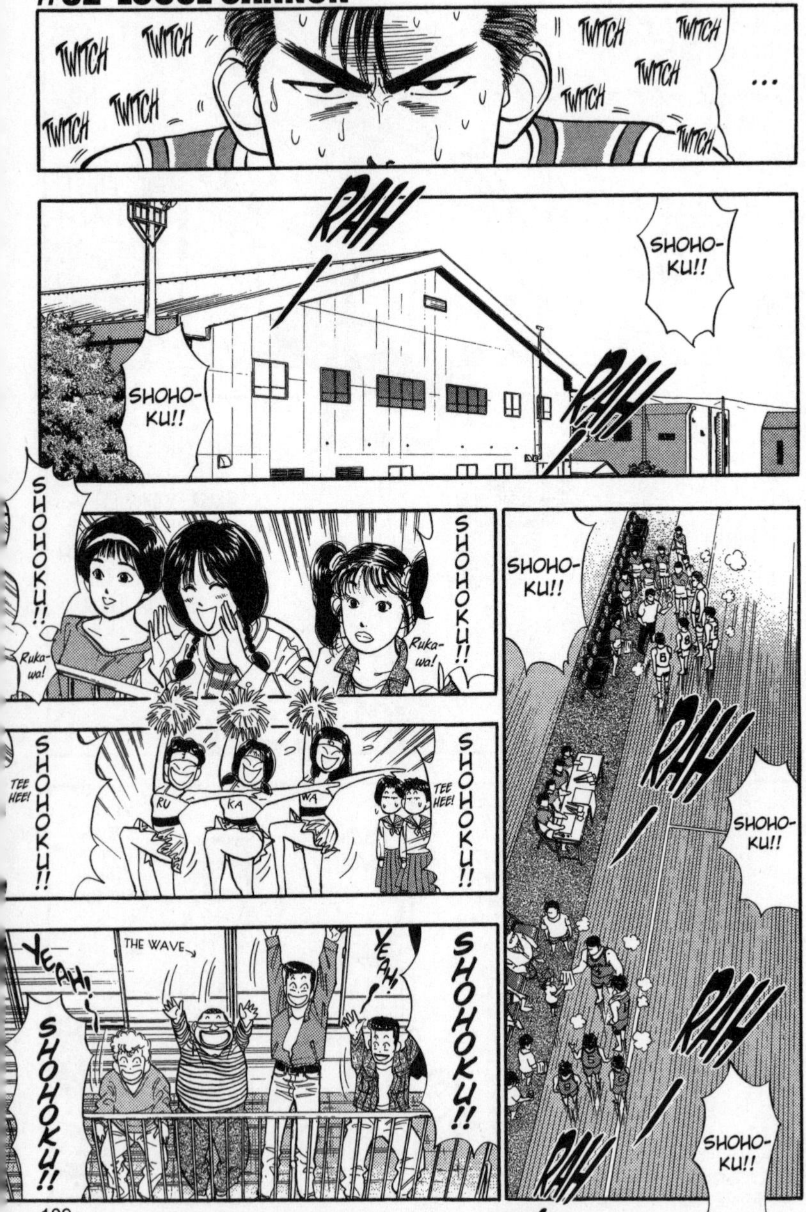
...
TWITCH
TWITCH
TWITCH
TWITCH
TWITCH
TWITCH
TWITCH
TWITCH
RAH
SHOHO-KU!!
RAH
SHOHO-KU!!
SHOHO-KU!!
RAH
SHOHO-KU!!
RAH
RAH
SHOHO-KU!!
SHOHOKU!!
Ruka-wa!
SHOHOKU!!
Ruka-wa!
SHOHOKU!!
TEE HEE!
RU
KA
WA
TEE HEE!
SHOHOKU!!
SHOHOKU!!
YEAH!
THE WAVE →
YEAH!
SHOHOKU!!

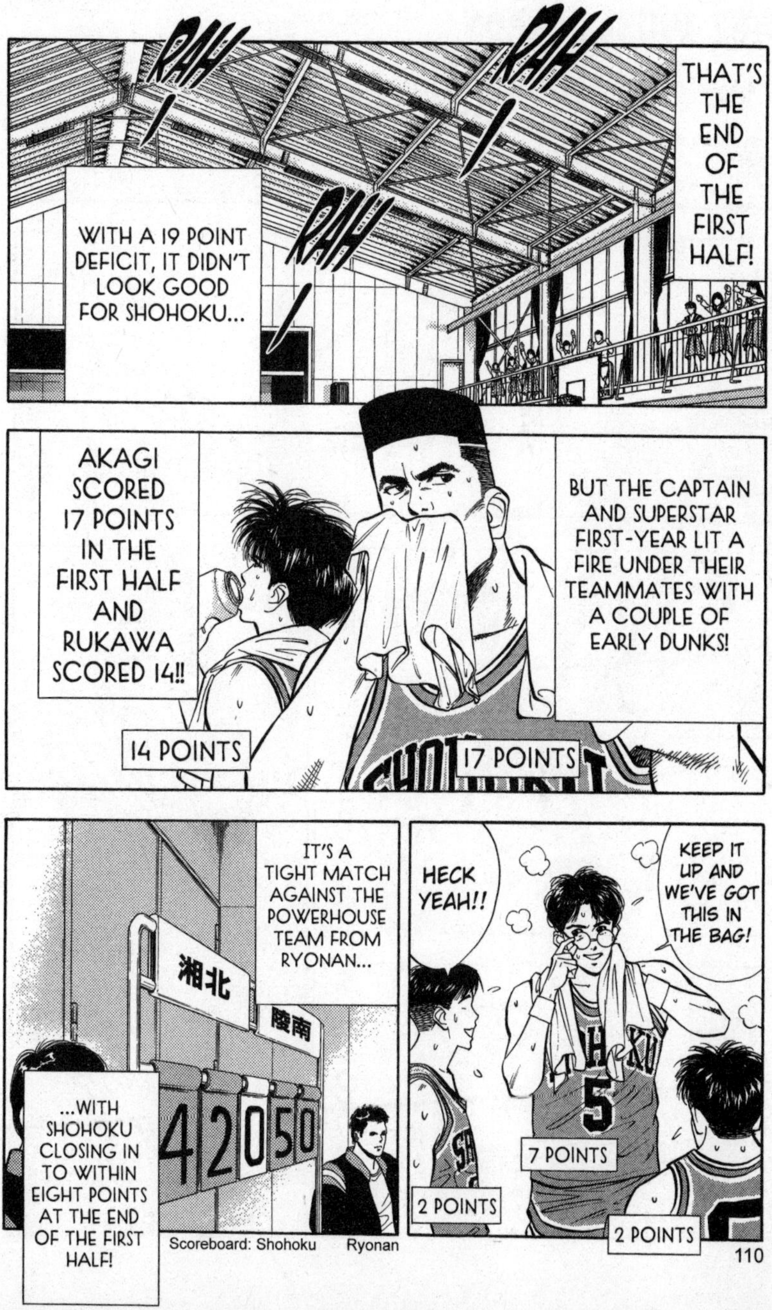
THAT'S THE END OF THE FIRST HALF!
RAH!
RAH!
RAH!
WITH A 19 POINT DEFICIT, IT DIDN'T LOOK GOOD FOR SHOHOKU...
BUT THE CAPTAIN AND SUPERSTAR FIRST-YEAR LIT A FIRE UNDER THEIR TEAMMATES WITH A COUPLE OF EARLY DUNKS!
AKAGI SCORED 17 POINTS IN THE FIRST HALF AND RUKAWA SCORED 14!!
17 POINTS
14 POINTS
KEEP IT UP AND WE'VE GOT THIS IN THE BAG!
HECK YEAH!!
7 POINTS
2 POINTS
2 POINTS
IT'S A TIGHT MATCH AGAINST THE POWERHOUSE TEAM FROM RYONAN...
湘北
陵南
42
50
...WITH SHOHOKU CLOSING IN TO WITHIN EIGHT POINTS AT THE END OF THE FIRST HALF!
Scoreboard: Shohoku Ryonan

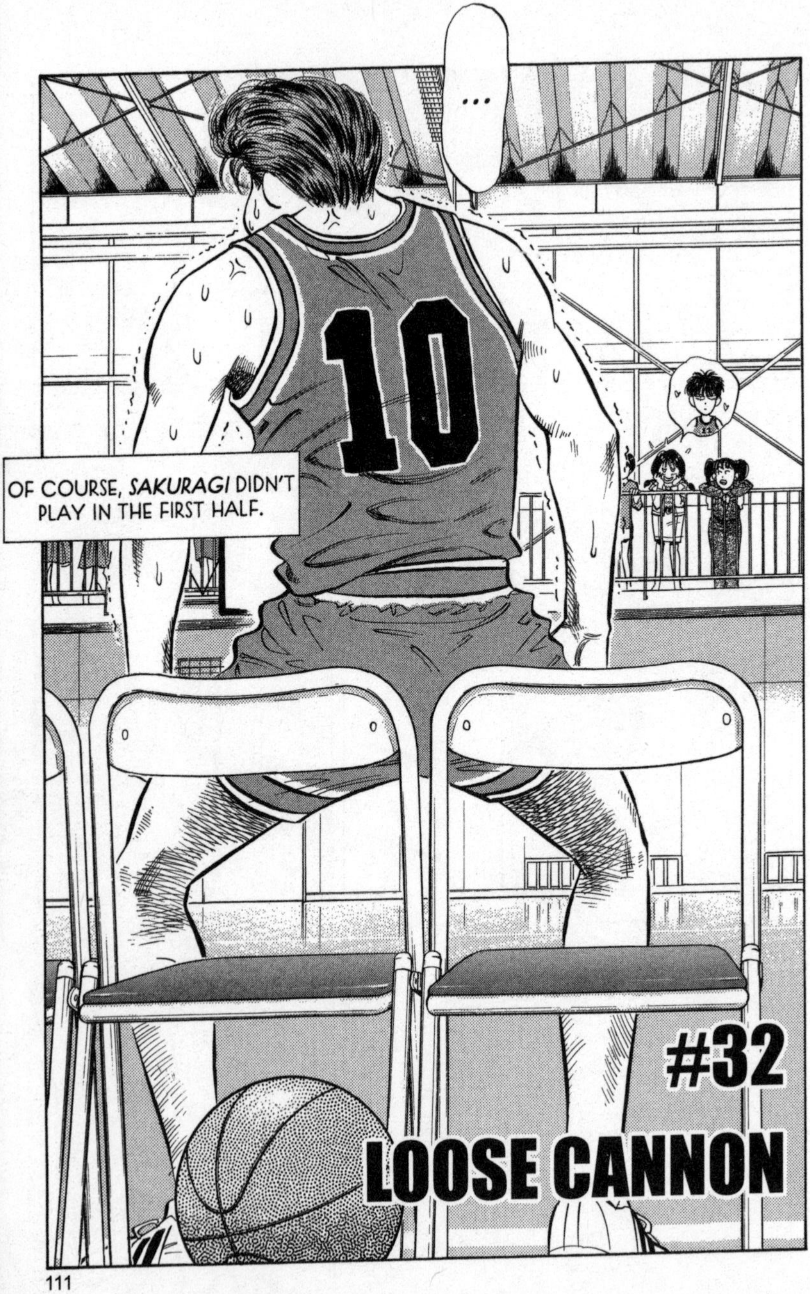
...
OF COURSE, SAKURAGI DIDN'T PLAY IN THE FIRST HALF.
#32
LOOSE CANNON

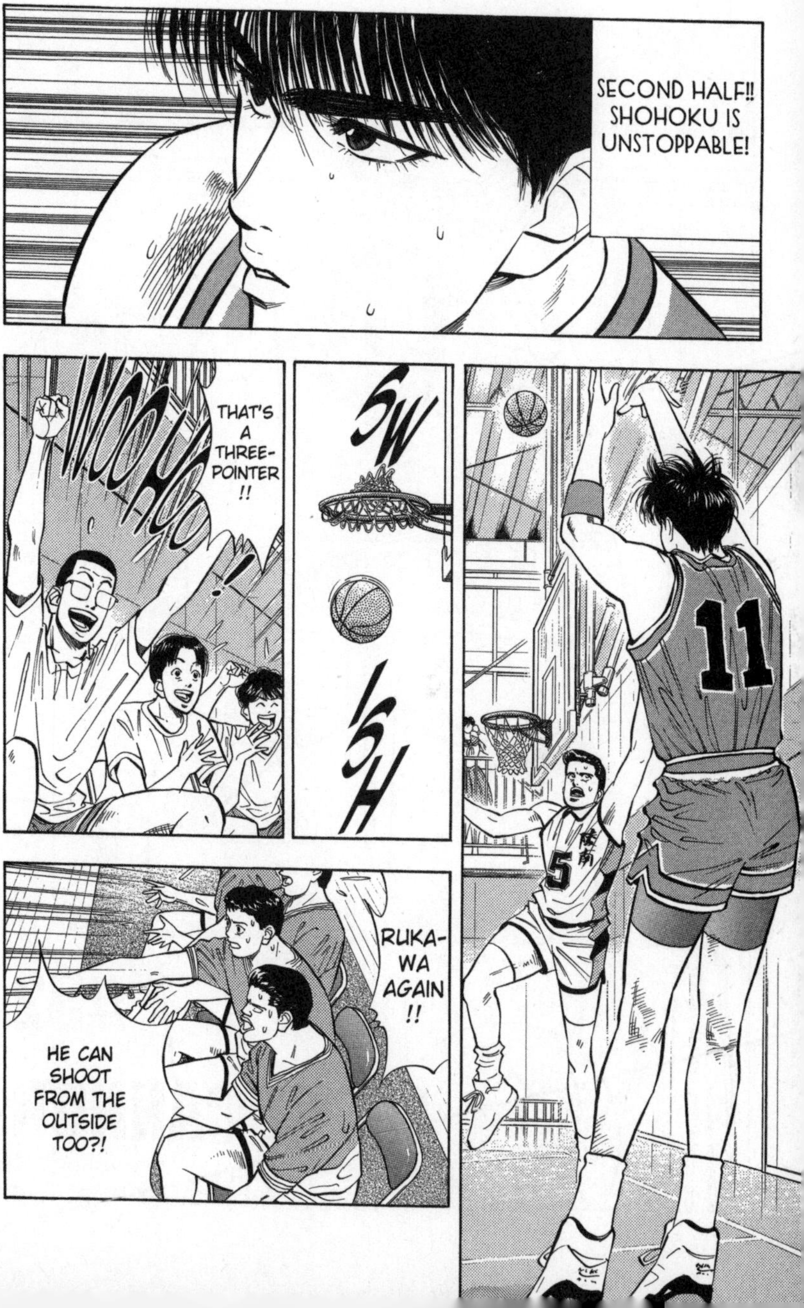
SECOND HALF!! SHOHOKU IS UNSTOPPABLE!
SWISH
WOOHOO!
THAT'S A THREE-POINTER!!
RUKAWA AGAIN!!
HE CAN SHOOT FROM THE OUTSIDE TOO?!

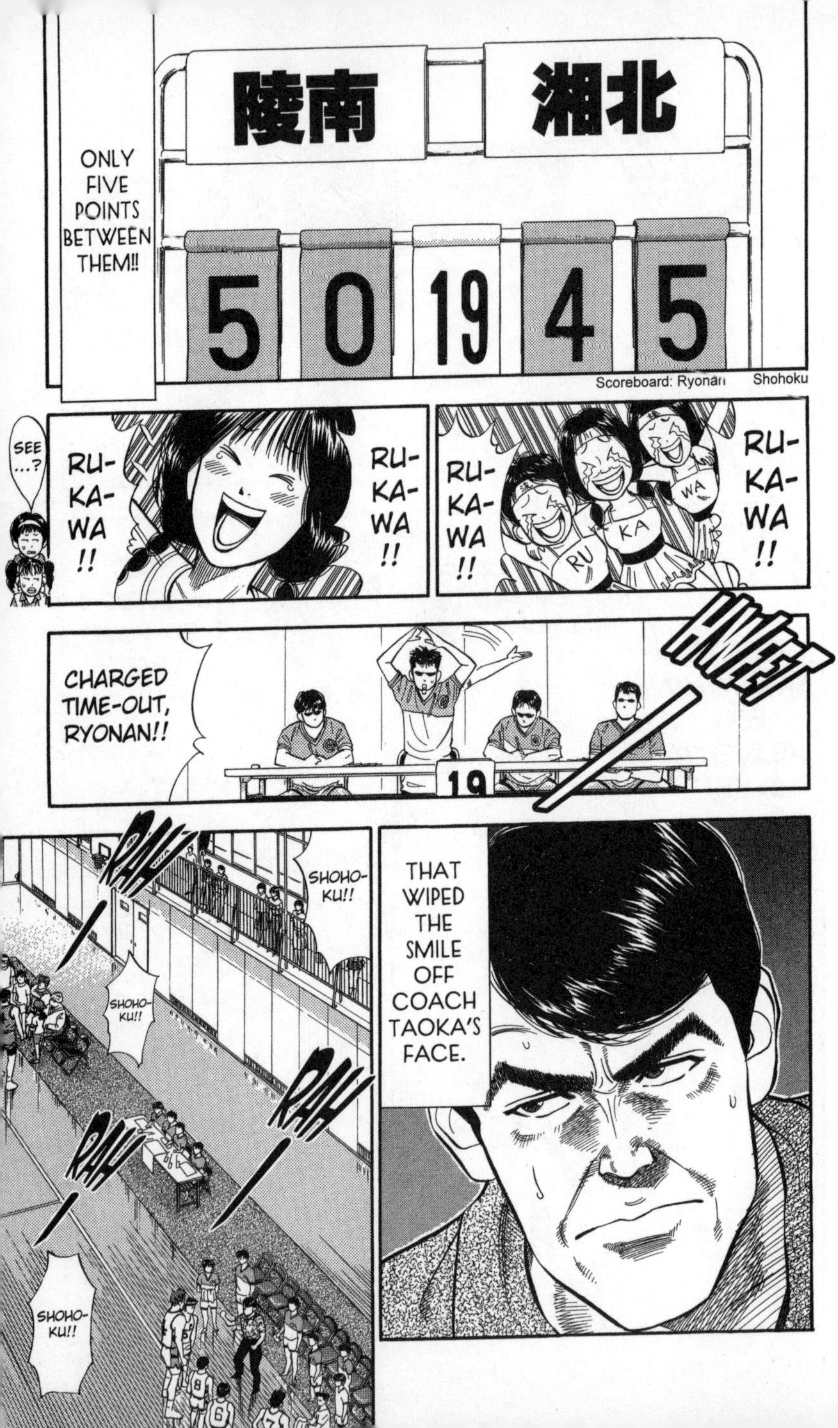
陵南
湘北
5 0 19 4 5
ONLY FIVE POINTS BETWEEN THEM!!
Scoreboard: Ryonan Shohoku
RU-KA-WA!!
RU-KA-WA!!
WA
KA
RU
RU-KA-WA!!
RU-KA-WA!!
SEE ...?
HWEET
19
CHARGED TIME-OUT, RYONAN!!
THAT WIPED THE SMILE OFF COACH TAOKA'S FACE.
RAH
SHOHO-KU!!
RAH
SHOHO-KU!!
RAH
SHOHO-KU!!

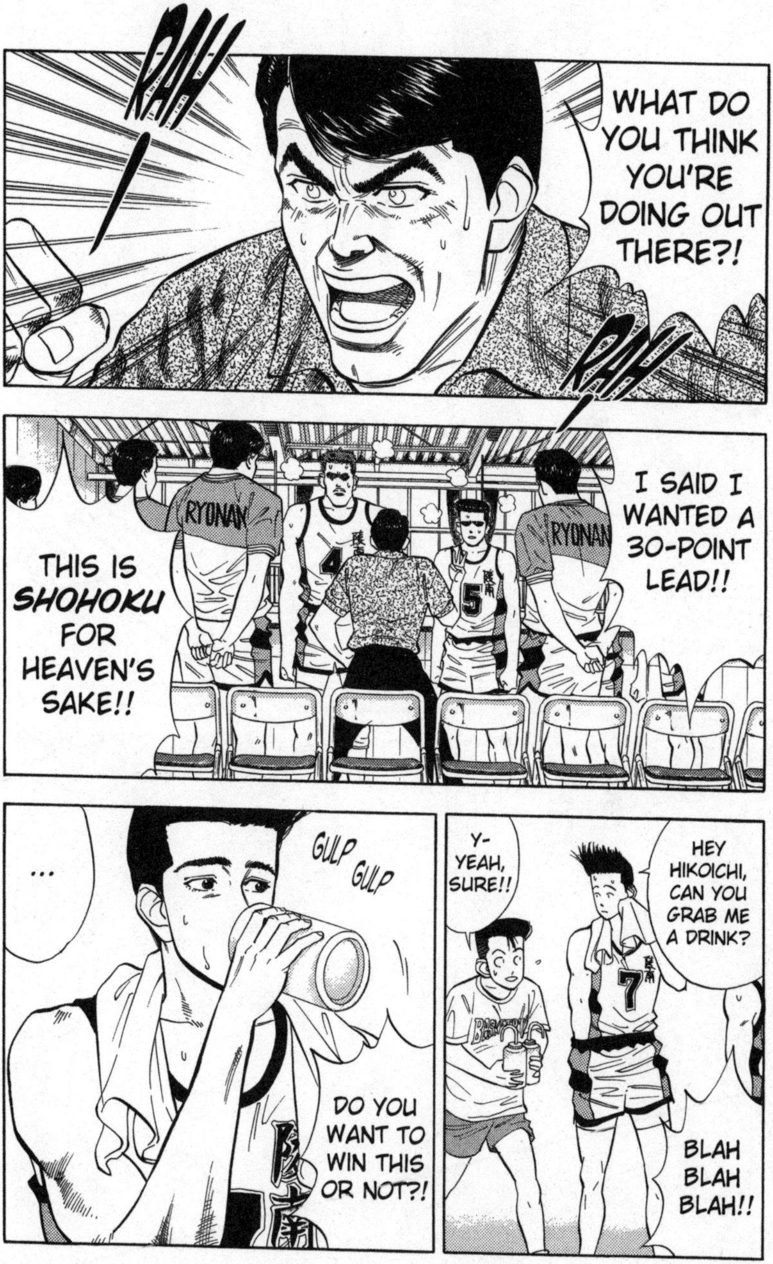
WHAT DO YOU THINK YOU'RE DOING OUT THERE?!
RAH
RAH
I SAID I WANTED A 30-POINT LEAD!!
THIS IS SHOHOKU FOR HEAVEN'S SAKE!!
HEY HIKOICHI, CAN YOU GRAB ME A DRINK?
Y-YEAH, SURE!!
BLAH BLAH BLAH!!
GULP GULP
...
DO YOU WANT TO WIN THIS OR NOT?!

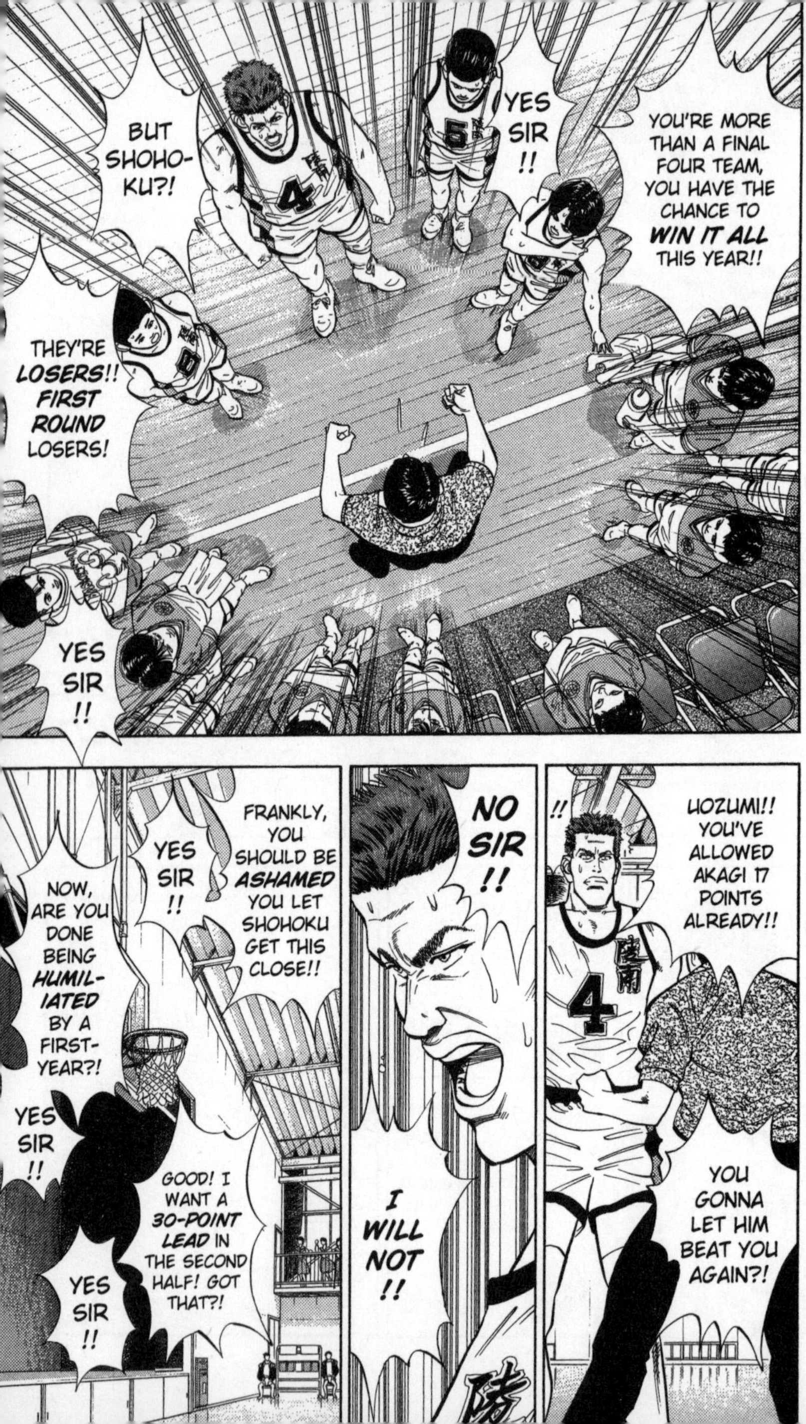
YOU'RE MORE THAN A FINAL FOUR TEAM, YOU HAVE THE CHANCE TO **WIN IT ALL** THIS YEAR!!
YES SIR!!
BUT SHOHOKU?!
THEY'RE **LOSERS!! FIRST ROUND** LOSERS!
YES SIR!!
UOZUMI!! YOU'VE ALLOWED AKAGI 17 POINTS ALREADY!!
!!
YOU GONNA LET HIM BEAT YOU AGAIN?!
NO SIR!!
I WILL NOT!!
FRANKLY, YOU SHOULD BE **ASHAMED** YOU LET SHOHOKU GET THIS CLOSE!!
YES SIR!!
NOW, ARE YOU DONE BEING **HUMILIATED** BY A FIRST-YEAR?!
GOOD! I WANT A **30-POINT LEAD** IN THE SECOND HALF! GOT THAT?!
YES SIR!!
YES SIR!!

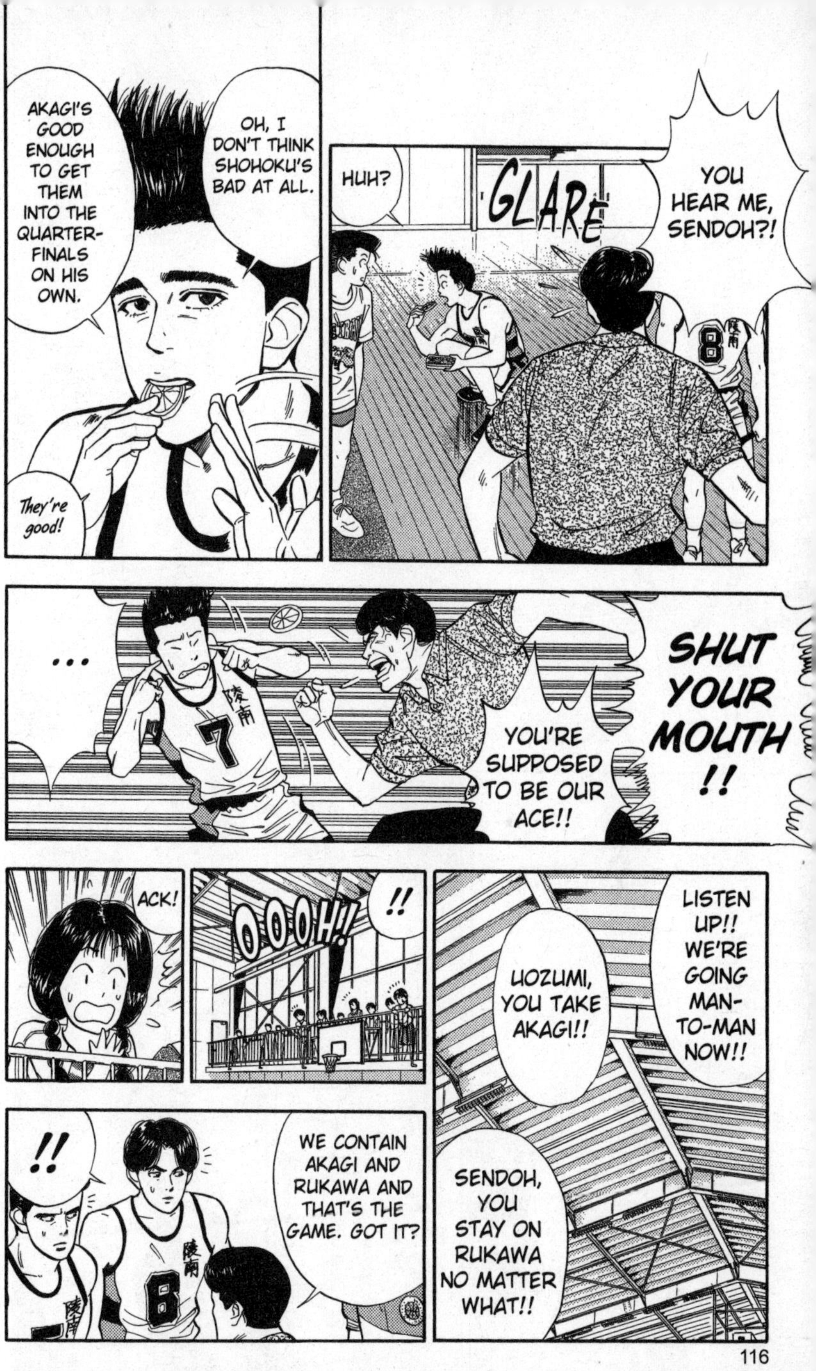
YOU HEAR ME, SENDOH?!
GLARE
HUH?
OH, I DON'T THINK SHOHOKU'S BAD AT ALL.
AKAGI'S GOOD ENOUGH TO GET THEM INTO THE QUARTER-FINALS ON HIS OWN.
They're good!
SHUT YOUR MOUTH!!
YOU'RE SUPPOSED TO BE OUR ACE!!
...
LISTEN UP!! WE'RE GOING MAN-TO-MAN NOW!!
UOZUMI, YOU TAKE AKAGI!!
SENDOH, YOU STAY ON RUKAWA NO MATTER WHAT!!
!!
OOOH!!
ACK!
WE CONTAIN AKAGI AND RUKAWA AND THAT'S THE GAME. GOT IT?
!!

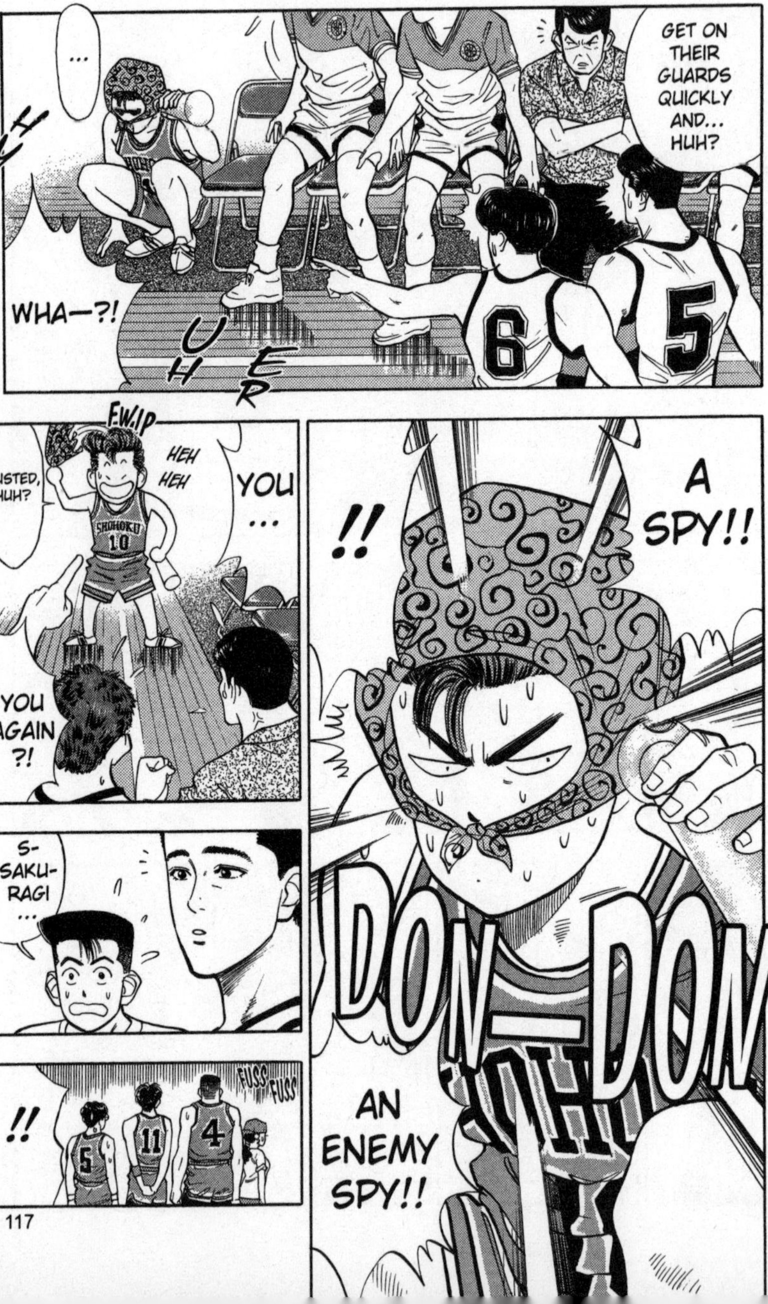
GET ON THEIR GUARDS QUICKLY AND... HUH?
...
WHA—?!
UH HER
A SPY!!
!!
DON-DON
AN ENEMY SPY!!
YOU ...
HEH HEH
F.W.IP
BUSTED, HUH?
YOU AGAIN ?!
S-SAKU-RAGI ...
FUSS FUSS
!!

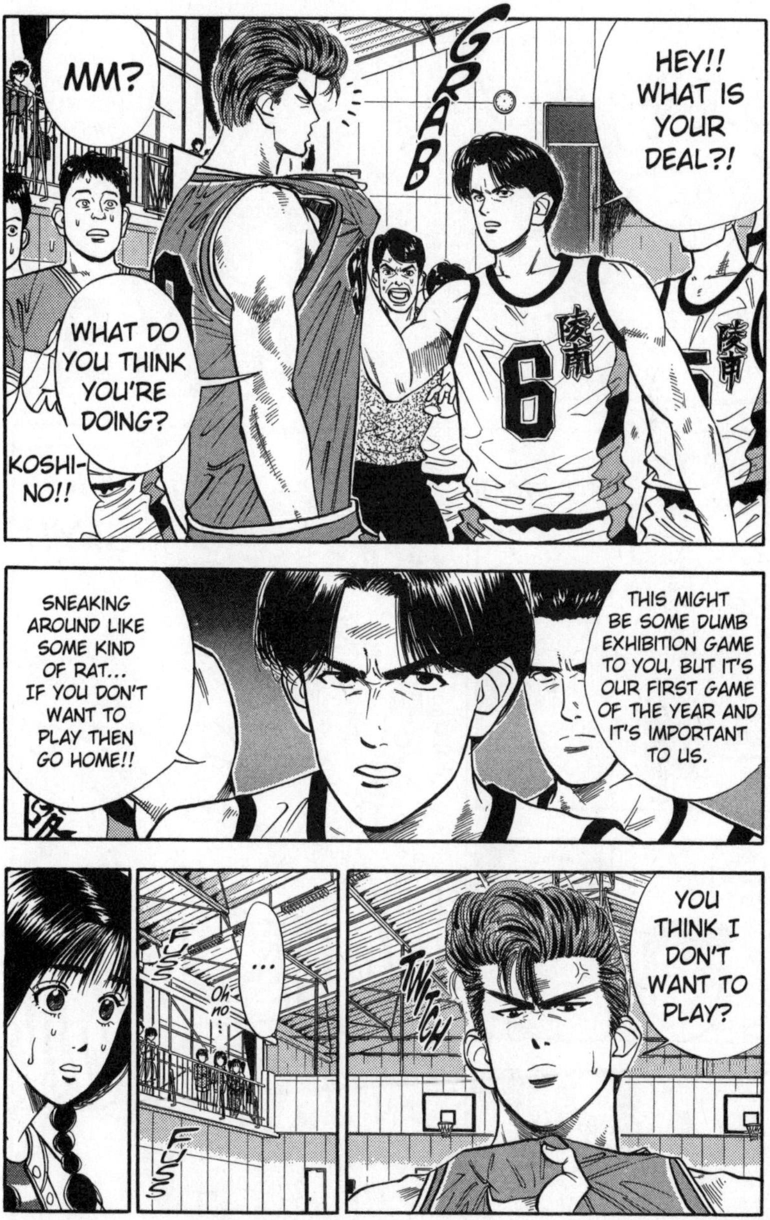
HEY!! WHAT IS YOUR DEAL?!
GRAB
MM?
WHAT DO YOU THINK YOU'RE DOING?
KOSHI-NO!!
THIS MIGHT BE SOME DUMB EXHIBITION GAME TO YOU, BUT IT'S OUR FIRST GAME OF THE YEAR AND IT'S IMPORTANT TO US.
SNEAKING AROUND LIKE SOME KIND OF RAT... IF YOU DON'T WANT TO PLAY THEN GO HOME!!
YOU THINK I DON'T WANT TO PLAY?
TWITCH
...
FUSS
Oh no...
FUSS

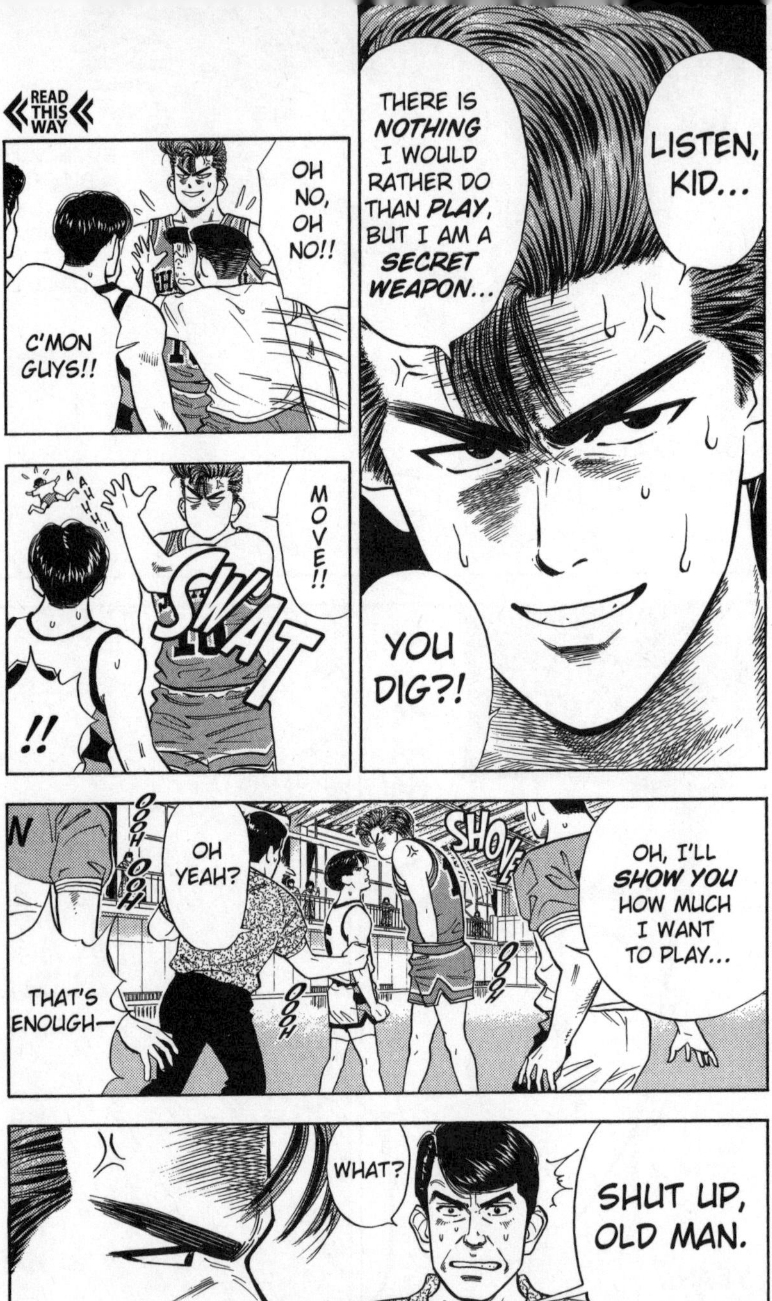
READ THIS WAY
LISTEN, KID...
THERE IS NOTHING I WOULD RATHER DO THAN PLAY, BUT I AM A SECRET WEAPON...
YOU DIG?!
OH NO, OH NO!!
C'MON GUYS!!
MOVE!!
AHHH!!
SWAT
!!
OH, I'LL SHOW YOU HOW MUCH I WANT TO PLAY...
SHOVE
OOOH
OH YEAH?
OOOH OOH
OOOH
THAT'S ENOUGH—
SHUT UP, OLD MAN.
WHAT?

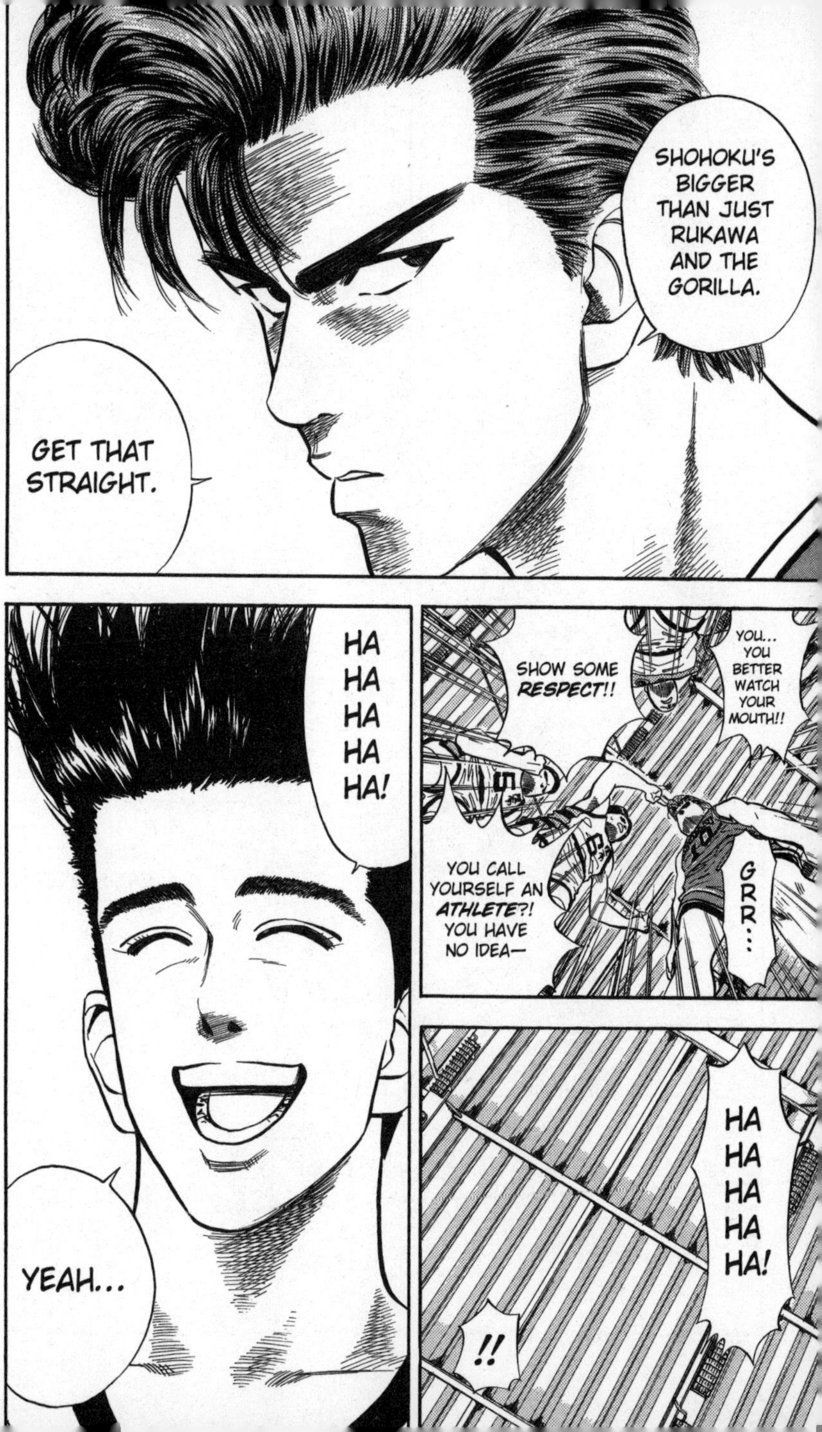

SHOHOKU'S BIGGER THAN JUST RUKAWA AND THE GORILLA.
GET THAT STRAIGHT.
YOU... YOU BETTER WATCH YOUR MOUTH!!
SHOW SOME *RESPECT*!!
GRR...
YOU CALL YOURSELF AN *ATHLETE*?! YOU HAVE NO IDEA—
HA HA HA HA HA!
!!
HA HA HA HA HA!
YEAH...

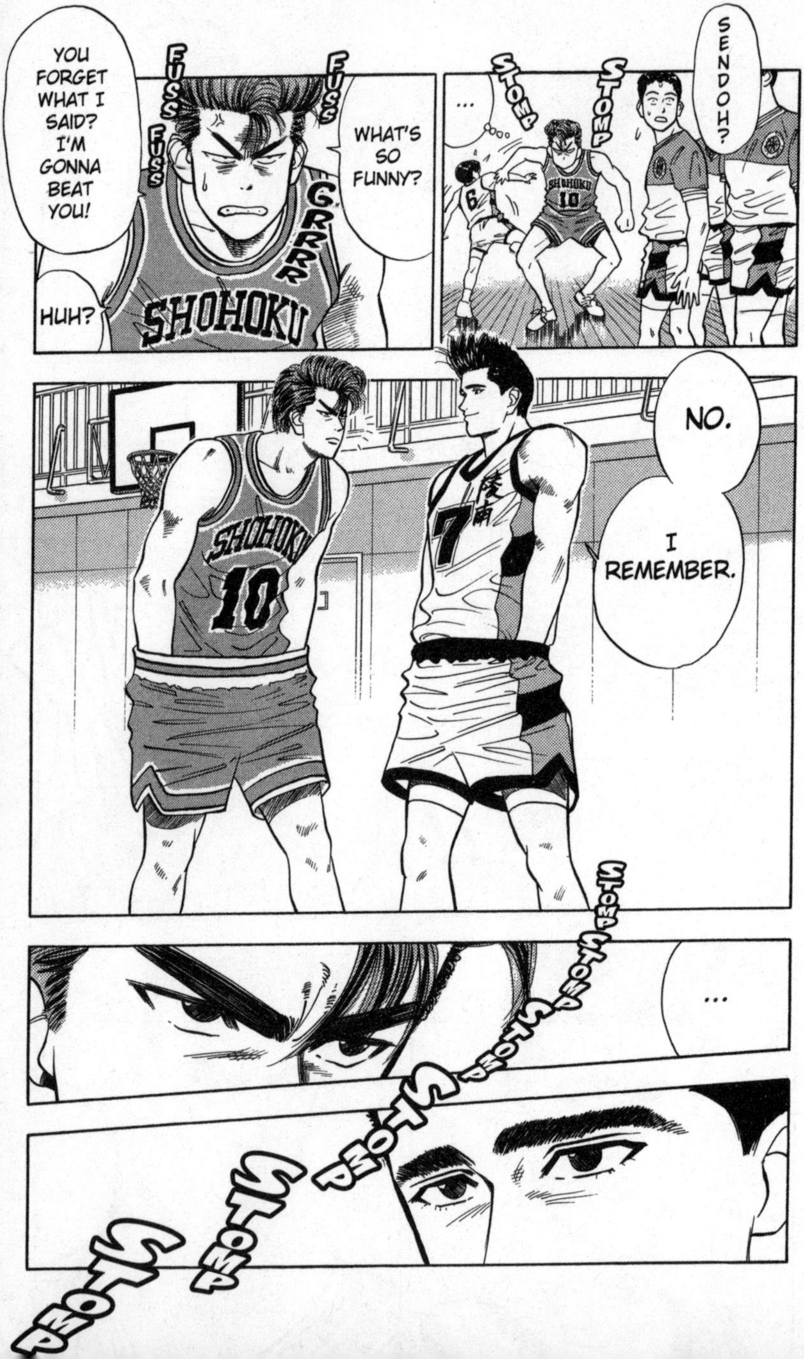
SENDOH?
STOMP
STOMP
...
FUSS
WHAT'S SO FUNNY?
GRRRR
FUSS
FUSS
YOU FORGET WHAT I SAID? I'M GONNA BEAT YOU!
HUH?
NO.
I REMEMBER.
STOMP
STOMP
STOMP
...
STOMP
STOMP
STOMP

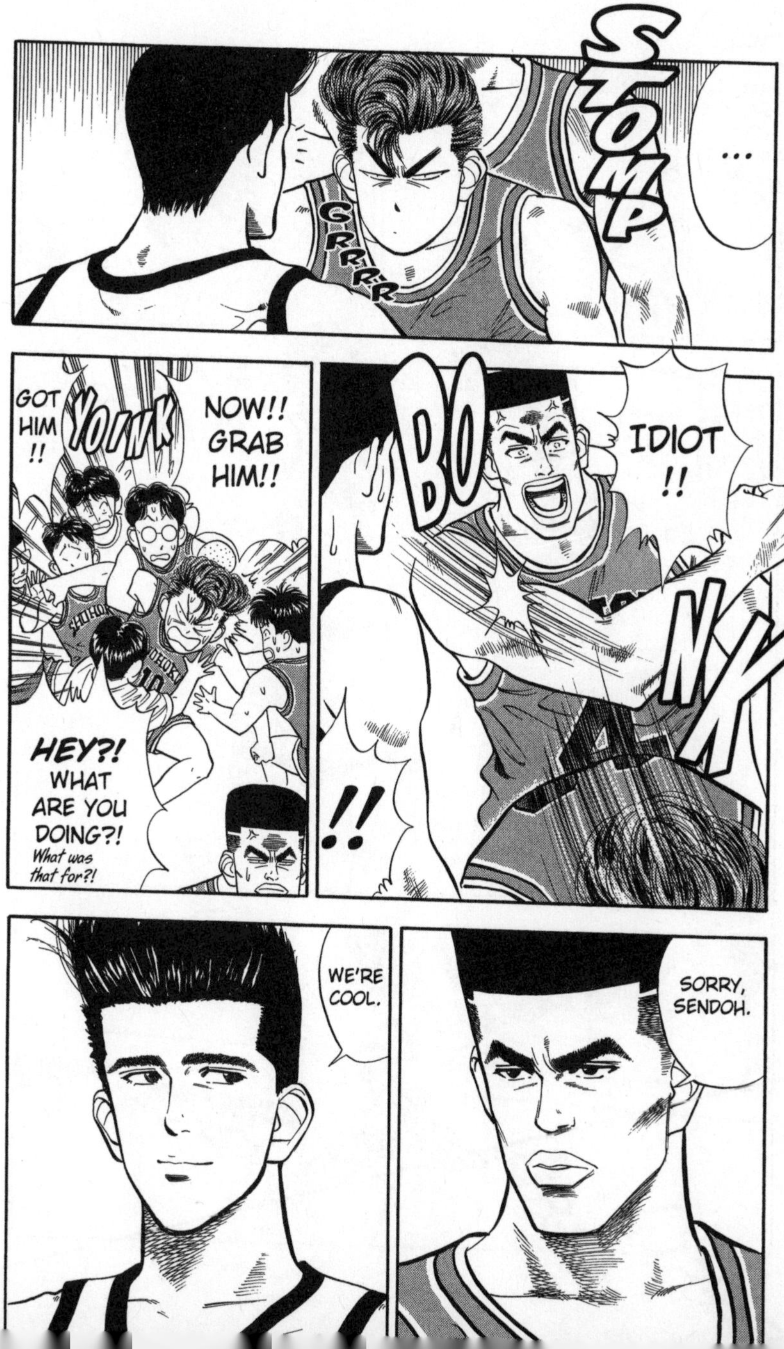

...
STOMP
GRRRR
IDIOT!!
BONK
!!
NOW!! GRAB HIM!!
YOINK
GOT HIM!!
HEY?! WHAT ARE YOU DOING?!
What was that for?!
SORRY, SENDOH.
WE'RE COOL.

READ THIS WAY

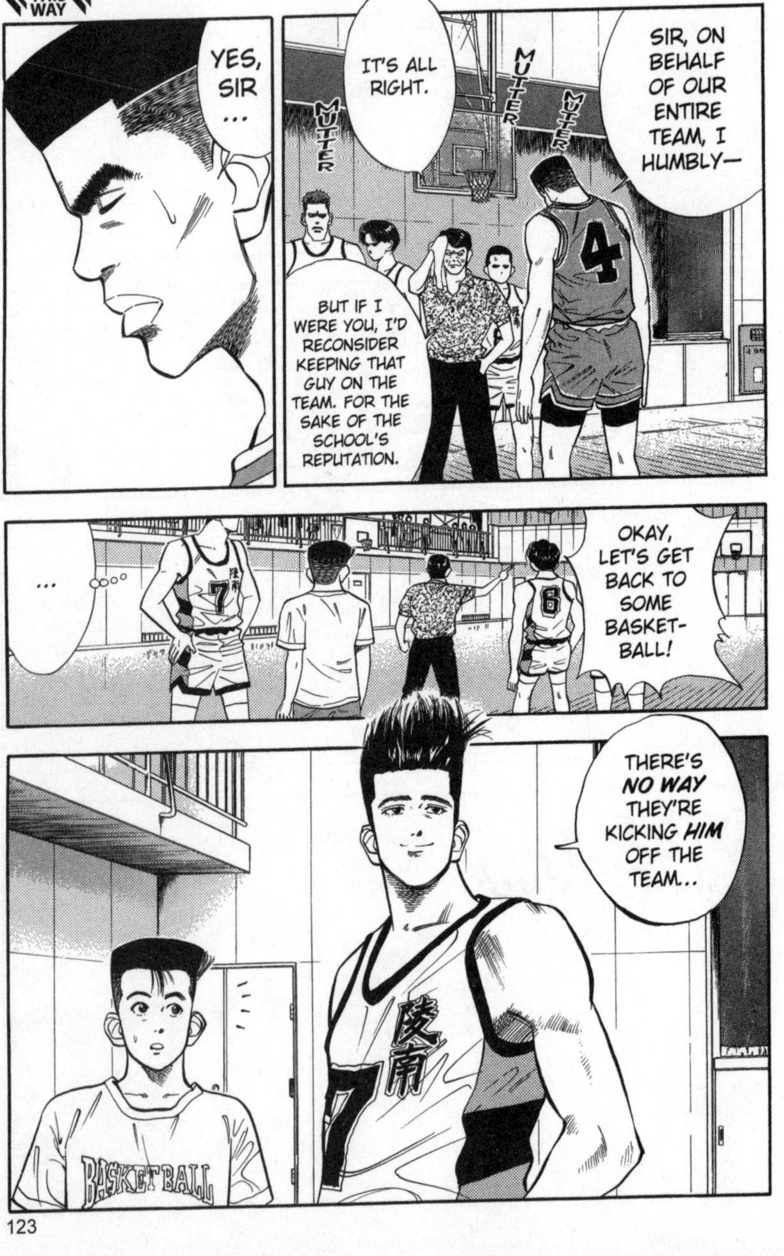

SIR, ON BEHALF OF OUR ENTIRE TEAM, I HUMBLY—
MUTTER
MUTTER
IT'S ALL RIGHT.
MUTTER
BUT IF I WERE YOU, I'D RECONSIDER KEEPING THAT GUY ON THE TEAM. FOR THE SAKE OF THE SCHOOL'S REPUTATION.
YES, SIR ...
OKAY, LET'S GET BACK TO SOME BASKET-BALL!
...
THERE'S NO WAY THEY'RE KICKING HIM OFF THE TEAM...
BASKETBALL

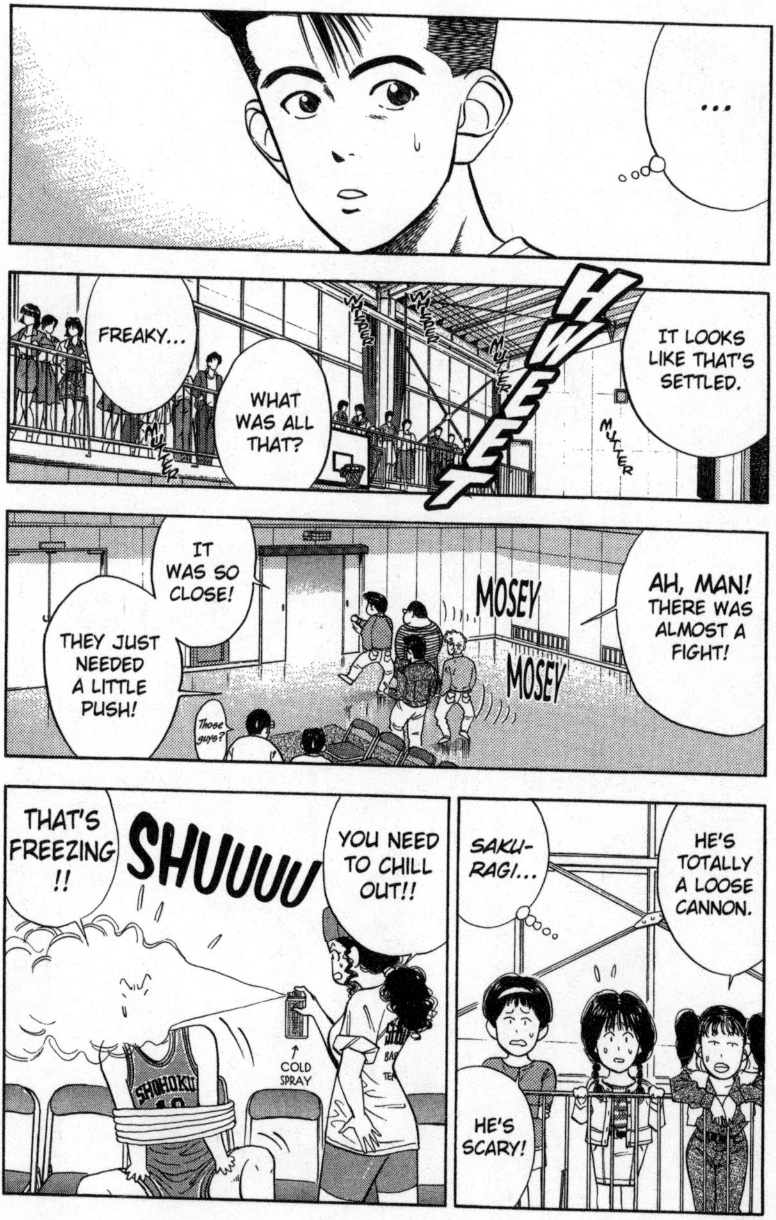
...
IT LOOKS LIKE THAT'S SETTLED.
HWEEEET
MUTTER
MUTTER
WHISPER
WHISPER
WHAT WAS ALL THAT?
FREAKY...
MUTTER
AH, MAN! THERE WAS ALMOST A FIGHT!
MOSEY
MOSEY
IT WAS SO CLOSE!
THEY JUST NEEDED A LITTLE PUSH!
Those guys?
HE'S TOTALLY A LOOSE CANNON.
SAKU-RAGI...
HE'S SCARY!
YOU NEED TO CHILL OUT!!
SHUUUUU
THAT'S FREEZING!!
COLD SPRAY
SHOHOKU

READ THIS WAY

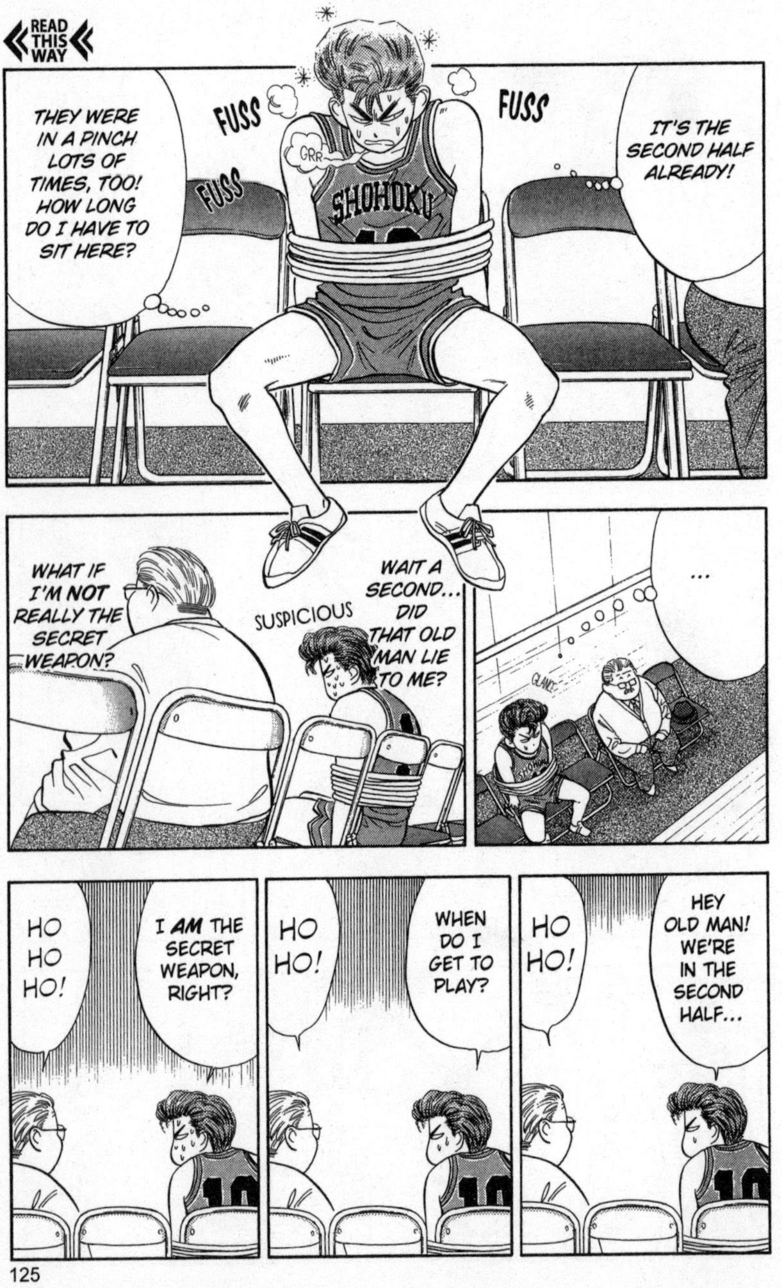

IT'S THE SECOND HALF ALREADY!
FUSS
FUSS
FUSS
GRR
THEY WERE IN A PINCH LOTS OF TIMES, TOO! HOW LONG DO I HAVE TO SIT HERE?
...
GLANCE
WAIT A SECOND... DID THAT OLD MAN LIE TO ME?
SUSPICIOUS
WHAT IF I'M NOT REALLY THE SECRET WEAPON?
HEY OLD MAN! WE'RE IN THE SECOND HALF...
HO HO!
WHEN DO I GET TO PLAY?
HO HO!
I AM THE SECRET WEAPON, RIGHT?
HO HO HO!

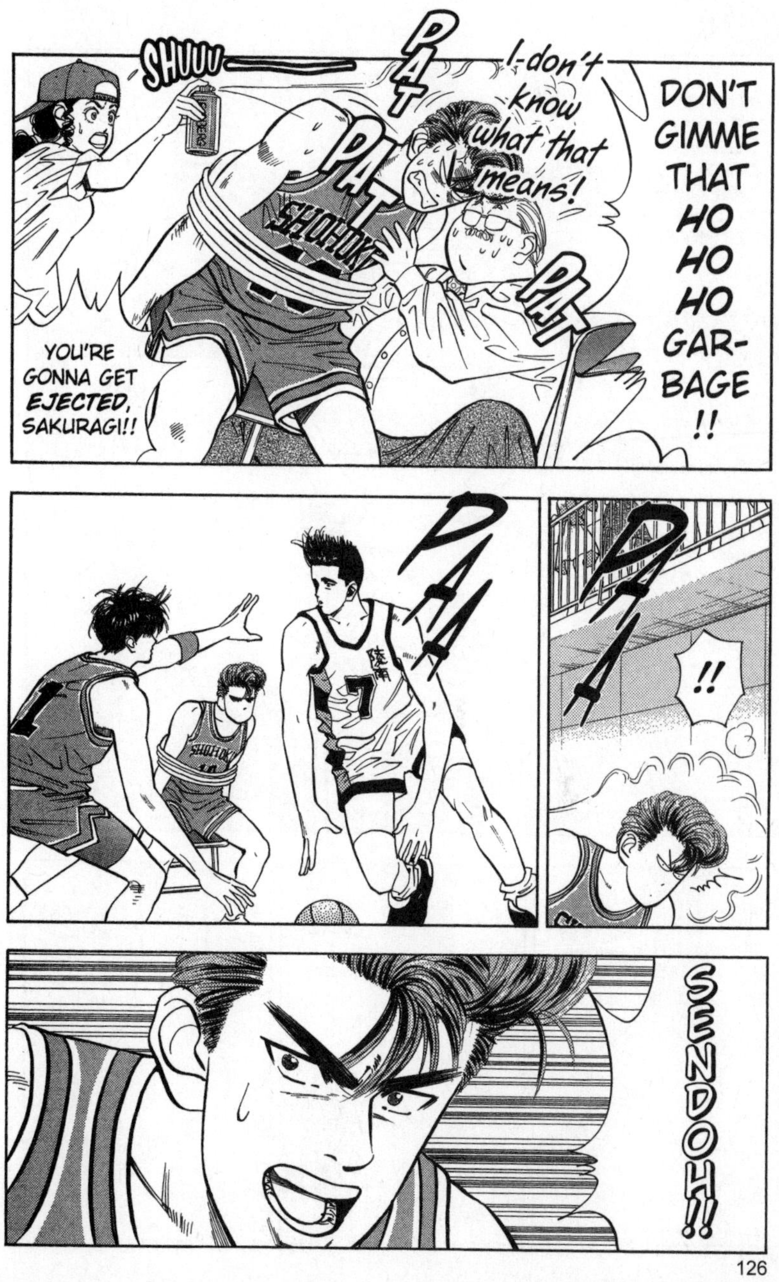
DON'T GIMME THAT HO HO HO GARBAGE!!
I-don't know what that means!
PAT
PAT
PAT
SHUUU
YOU'RE GONNA GET EJECTED, SAKURAGI!!
DAAA
!!
PAAA
SENDOH!!

READ THIS WAY

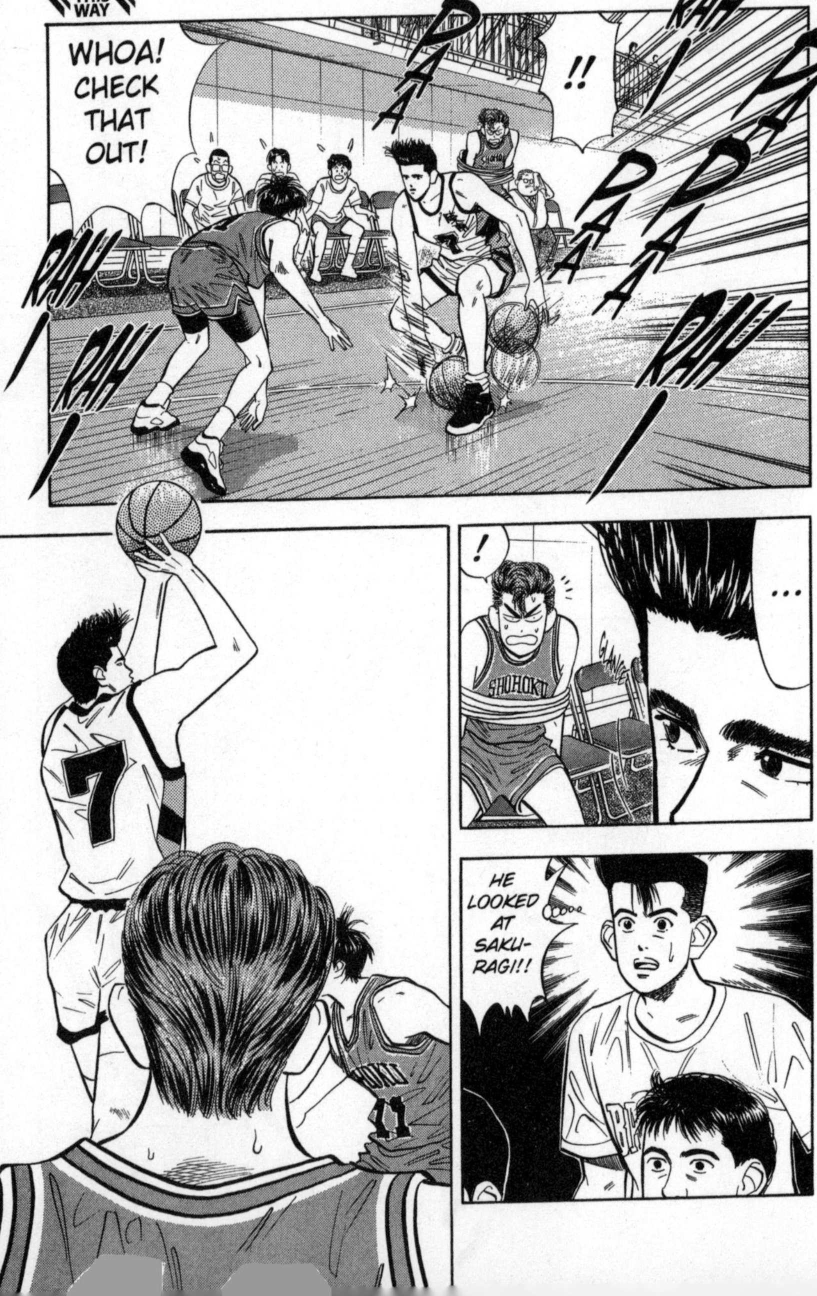

RAH RAH!
PA PA PAA
RAH RAH!
PAA
!!
WHOA! CHECK THAT OUT!
RAH RAH!
...
!
GLANCE
SHOHOKU
HE LOOKED AT SAKU-RAGI!!

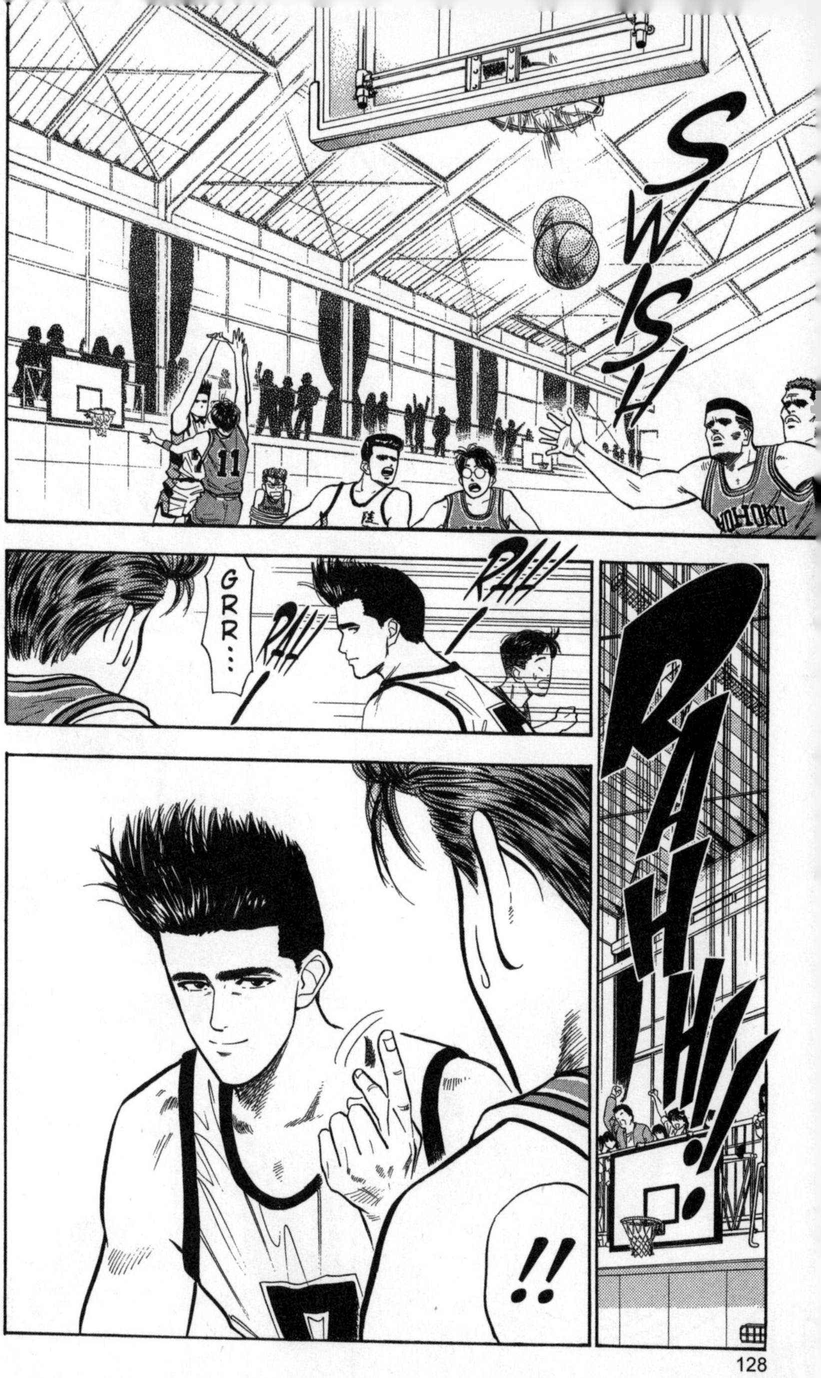
SWISH
RAAHH!!
RAH!
GRR...
RAH!
!!

READ THIS WAY

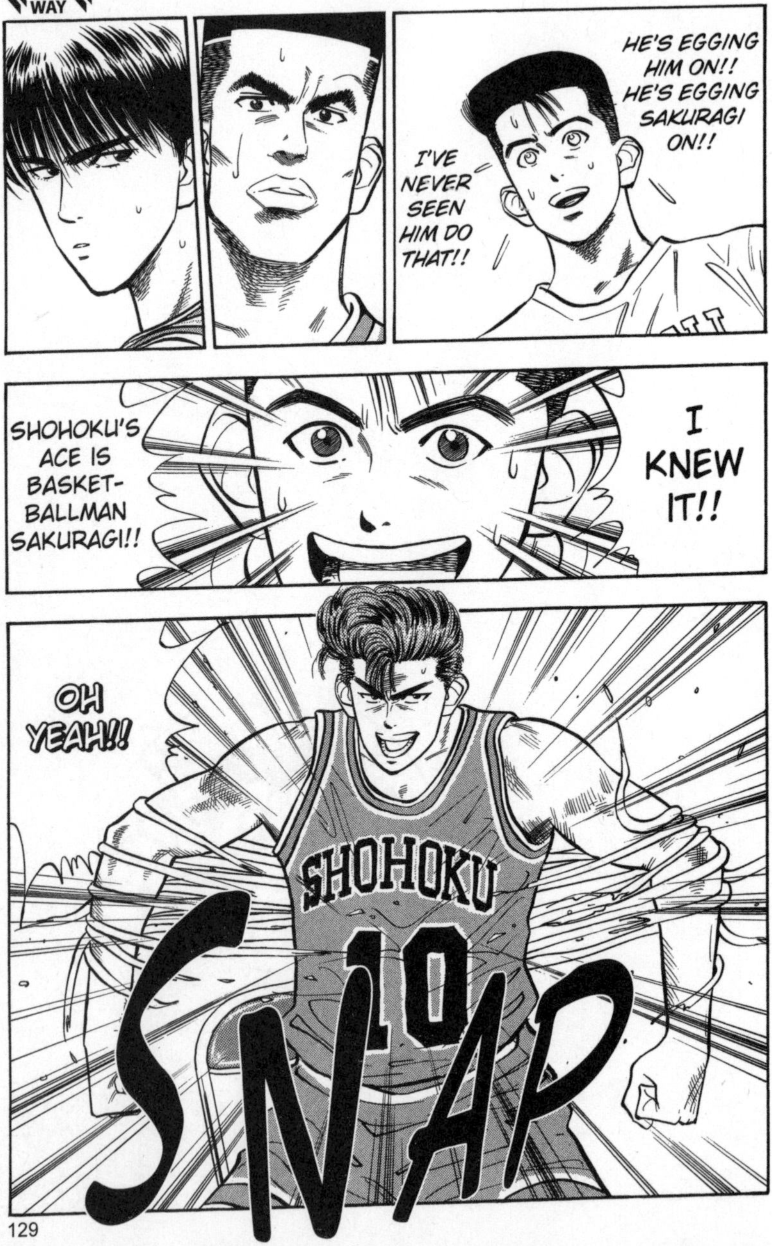
HE'S EGGING HIM ON!! HE'S EGGING SAKURAGI ON!!
I'VE NEVER SEEN HIM DO THAT!!
I KNEW IT!!
SHOHOKU'S ACE IS BASKET-BALLMAN SAKURAGI!!
OH YEAH!!
SHOHOKU
10
SNAP

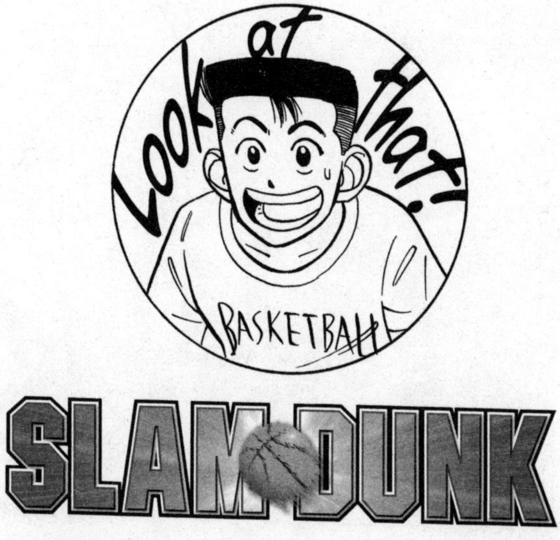
Look at that!
BASKETBALL

SLAM DUNK

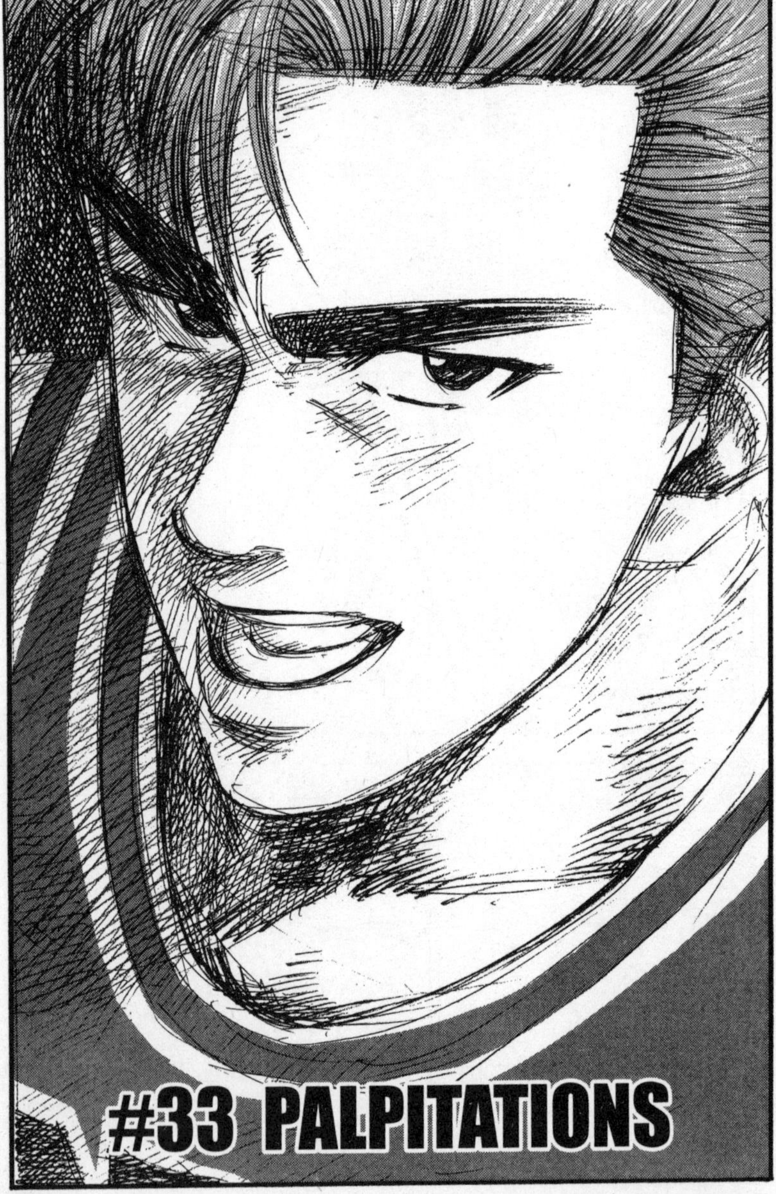
#33 PALPITATIONS

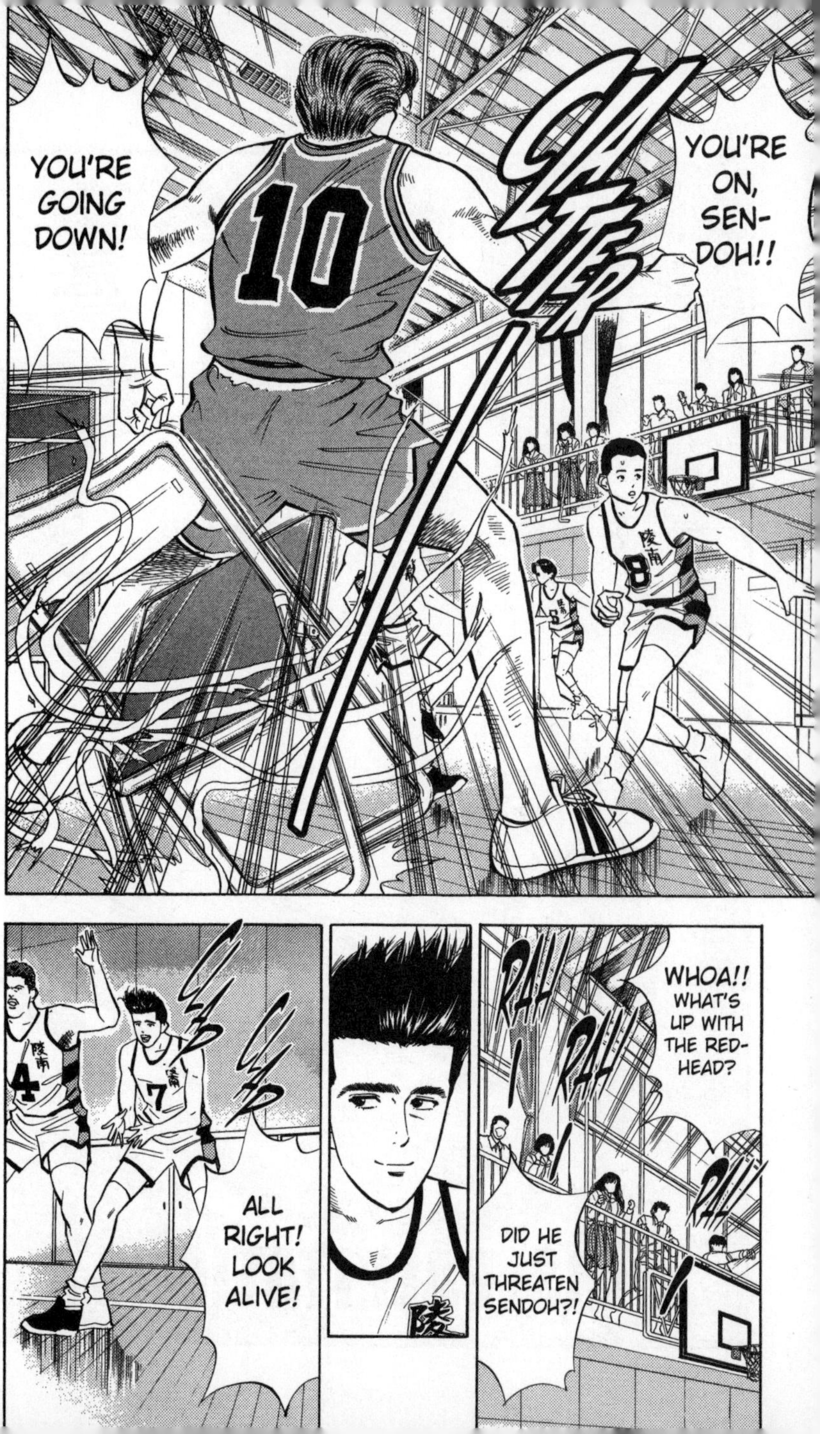
YOU'RE ON, SEN-DOH!!
CHATTER
YOU'RE GOING DOWN!
WHOA!! WHAT'S UP WITH THE RED-HEAD?
RAH RAH RAH
DID HE JUST THREATEN SENDOH?!
CLAP CLAP
ALL RIGHT! LOOK ALIVE!

READ THIS WAY

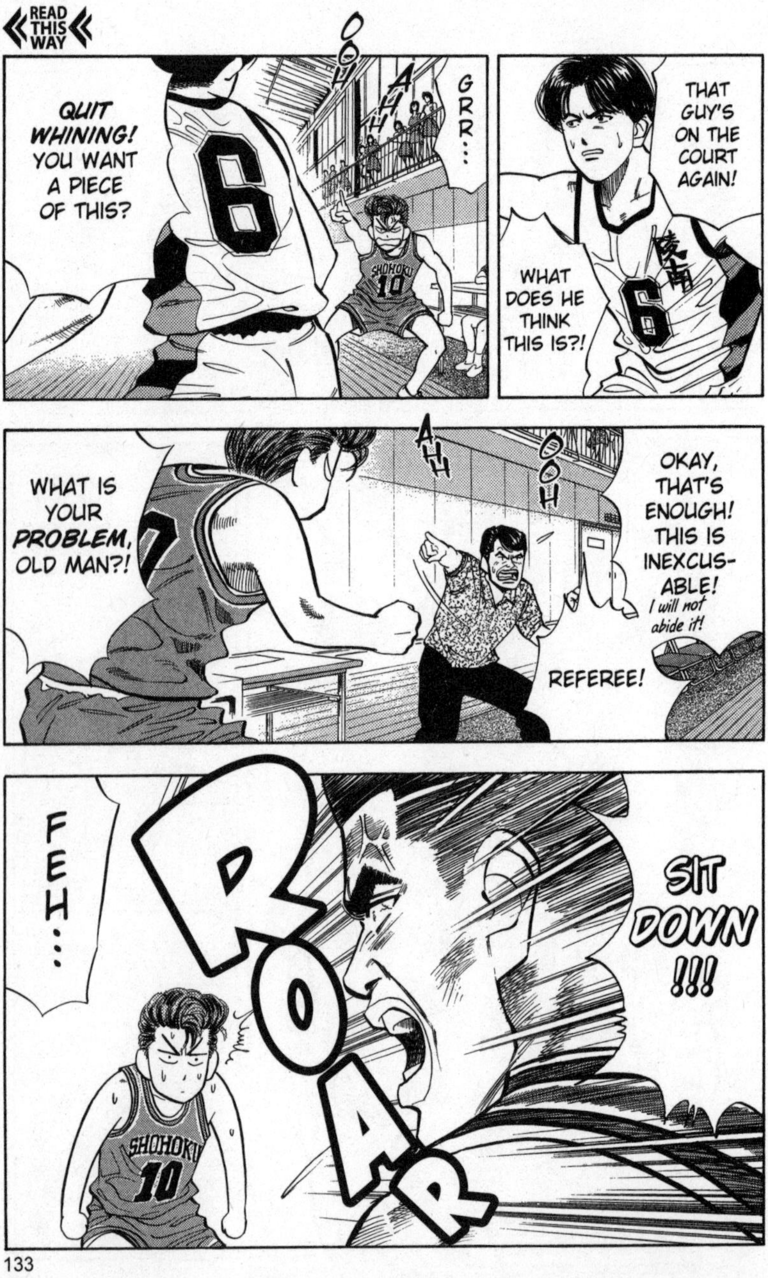
THAT GUY'S ON THE COURT AGAIN!
WHAT DOES HE THINK THIS IS?!
GRR...
AHH
OOOH
QUIT WHINING! YOU WANT A PIECE OF THIS?
OKAY, THAT'S ENOUGH! THIS IS INEXCUS-ABLE!
I will not abide it!
REFEREE!
OOOH
AHH
WHAT IS YOUR PROBLEM, OLD MAN?!
SIT DOWN!!!
ROAR
FEH...

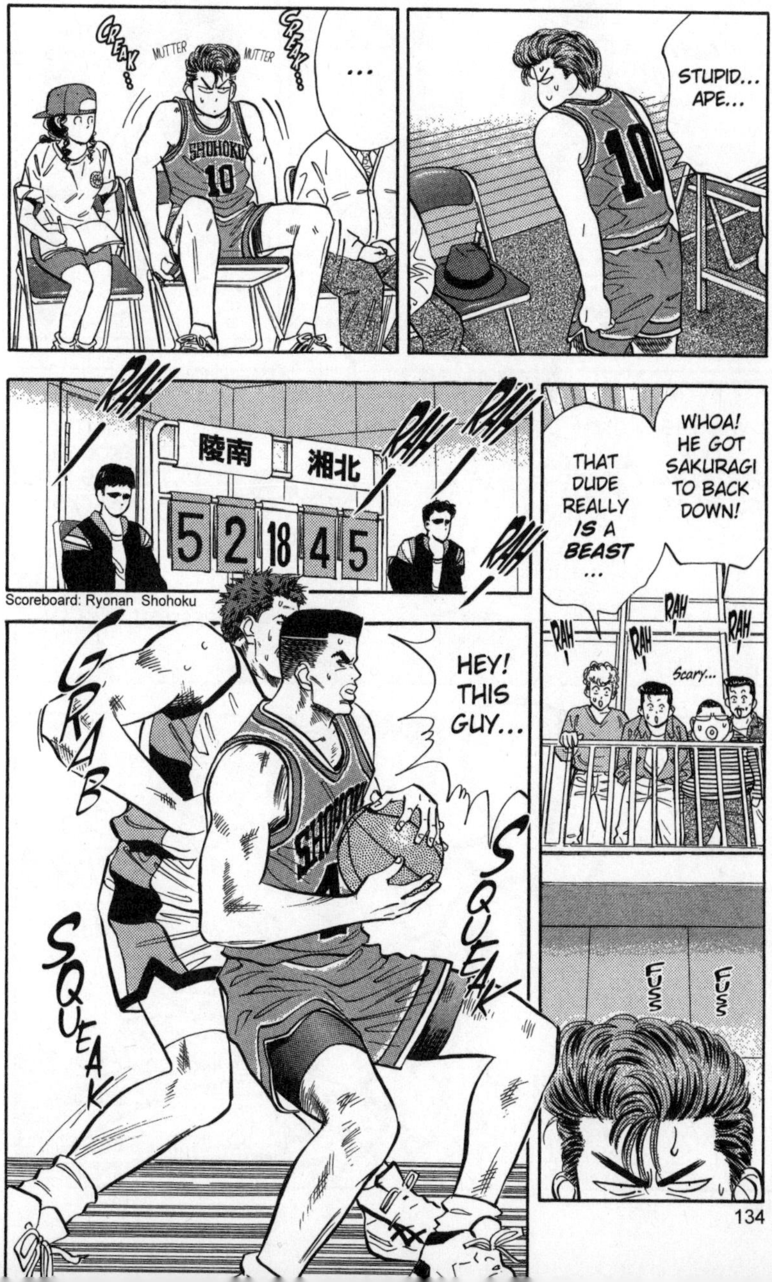
STUPID... APE...
CREAK...
MUTTER
MUTTER
CREAK...
...
WHOA! HE GOT SAKURAGI TO BACK DOWN!
THAT DUDE REALLY IS A BEAST ...
RAH
RAH
RAH
RAH
Scary...
FUSS
FUSS
RAH
RAH
RAH
RAH
陵南
湘北
5 2 18 4 5
HEY! THIS GUY...
GRAB
SQUEAK
SQUEAK
Scoreboard: Ryonan Shohoku

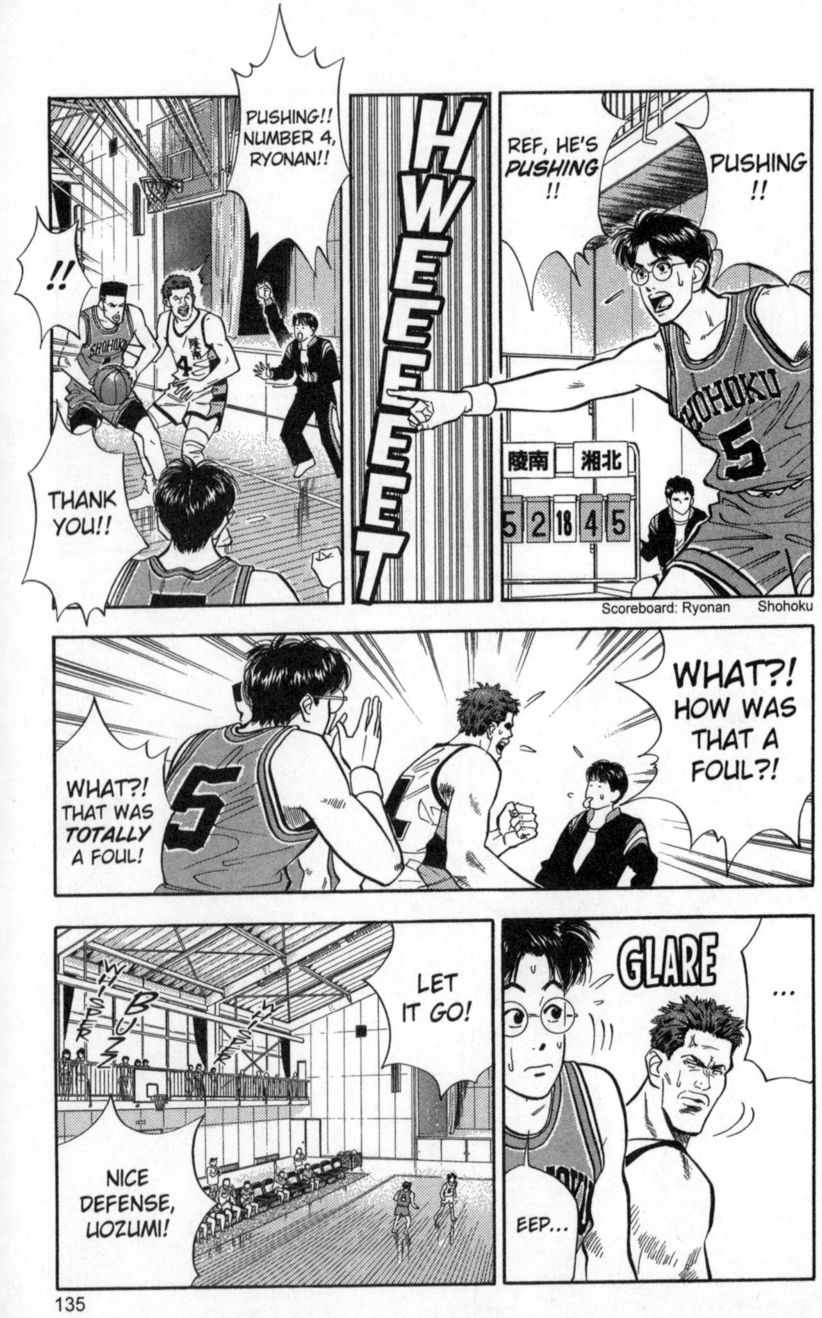
REF, HE'S PUSHING!!
PUSHING!!
陵南 湘北
5 2 18 4 5
HWEEEEEET
PUSHING!! NUMBER 4, RYONAN!!
!!
THANK YOU!!
WHAT?! HOW WAS THAT A FOUL?!
WHAT?! THAT WAS TOTALLY A FOUL!
GLARE
...
EEP...
LET IT GO!
WHISPER
BUZZ
WHISPER
NICE DEFENSE, UOZUMI!
Scoreboard: Ryonan Shohoku

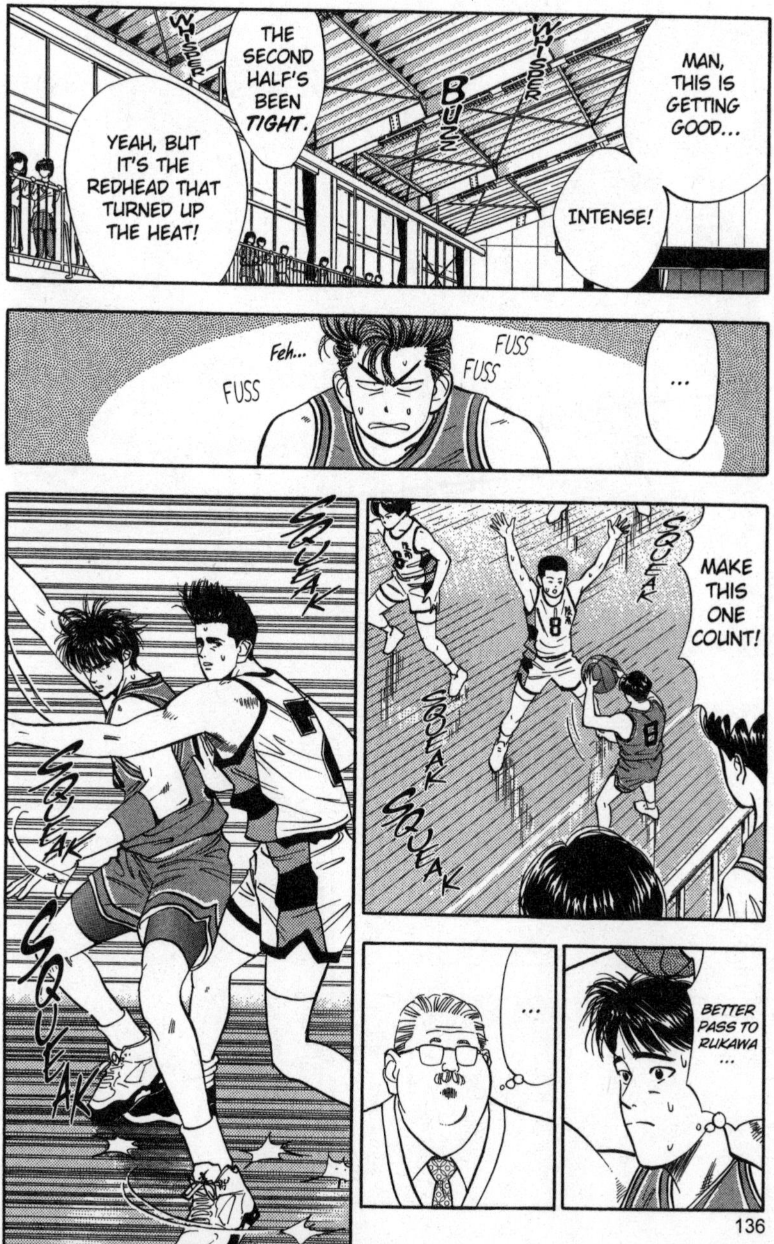
MAN, THIS IS GETTING GOOD...
INTENSE!
WHISPER
BUZZ
THE SECOND HALF'S BEEN *TIGHT*.
WHISPER
YEAH, BUT IT'S THE REDHEAD THAT TURNED UP THE HEAT!
...
FUSS
FUSS
Feh...
FUSS
MAKE THIS ONE COUNT!
SQUEAK
SQUEAK
SQUEAK
BETTER PASS TO RUKAWA ...
...
SQUEAK
SQUEAK
SQUEAK

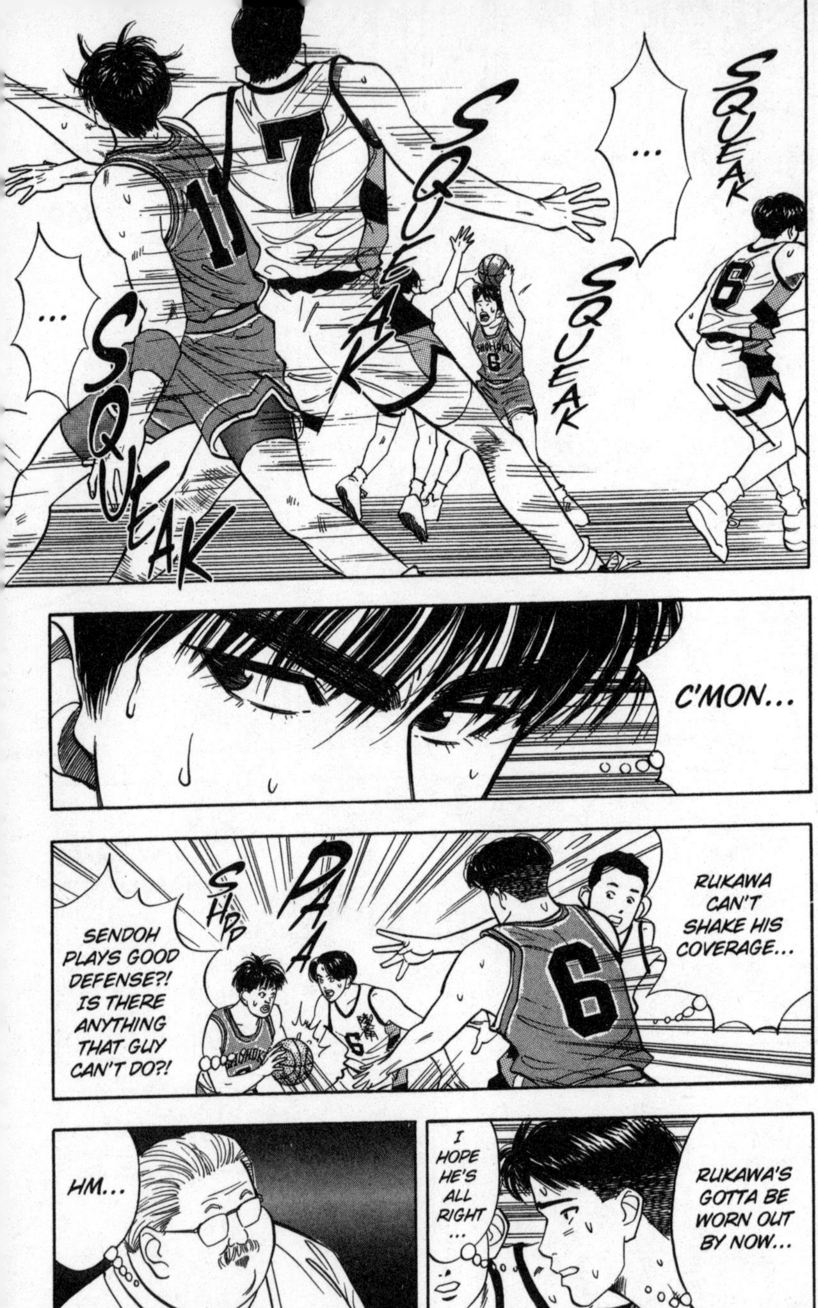
SQUEAK
...
SQUEAK
SQUEAK
...
SQUEAK
C'MON...
RUKAWA CAN'T SHAKE HIS COVERAGE...
DAA
SHPP
SENDOH PLAYS GOOD DEFENSE?! IS THERE ANYTHING THAT GUY CAN'T DO?!
RUKAWA'S GOTTA BE WORN OUT BY NOW...
I HOPE HE'S ALL RIGHT ...
HM...

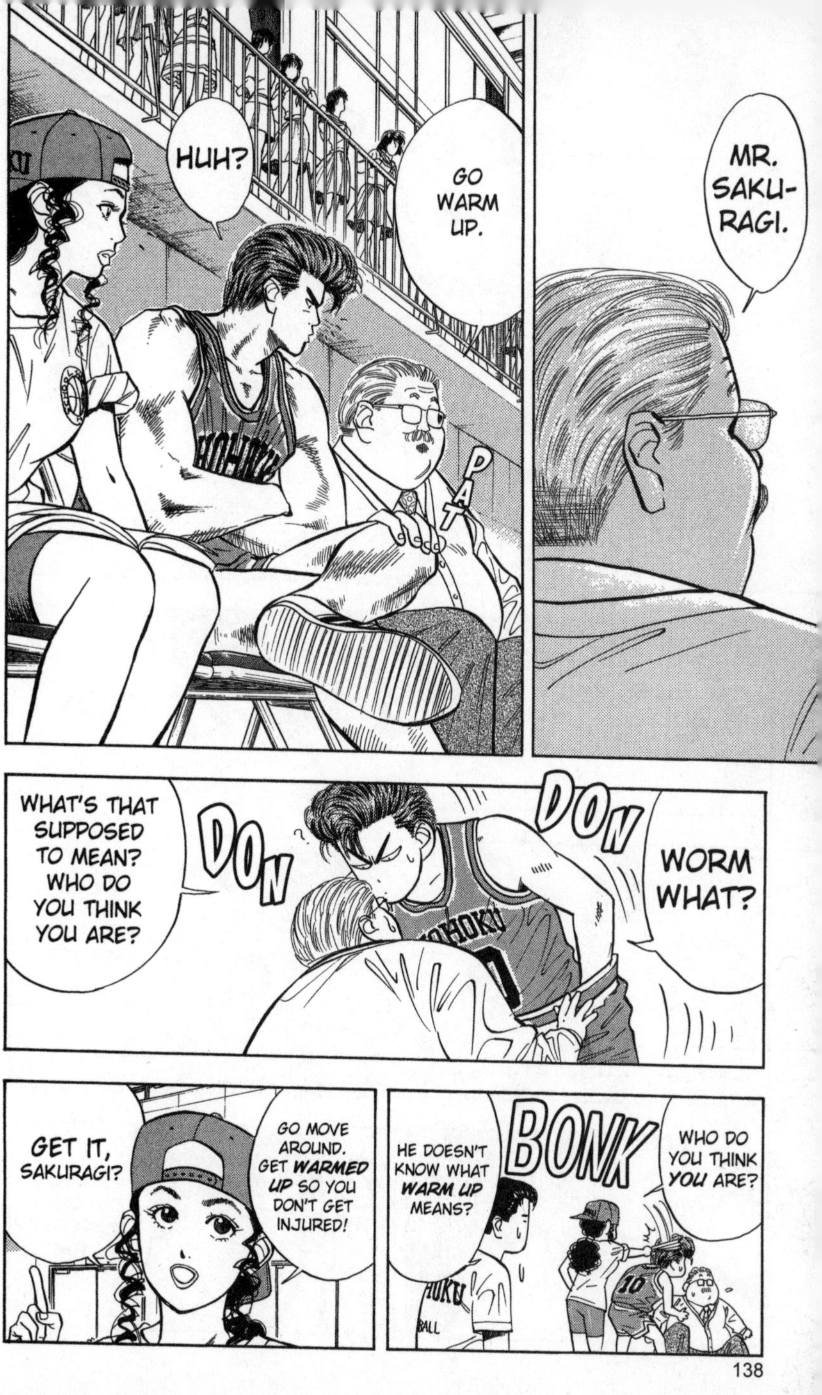
MR. SAKU-RAGI.
GO WARM UP.
HUH?
WORM WHAT?
DON
DON
WHAT'S THAT SUPPOSED TO MEAN? WHO DO YOU THINK YOU ARE?
WHO DO YOU THINK ***YOU*** ARE?
BONK
HE DOESN'T KNOW WHAT ***WARM UP*** MEANS?
GO MOVE AROUND. GET ***WARMED UP*** SO YOU DON'T GET INJURED!
GET IT, SAKURAGI?

READ THIS WAY

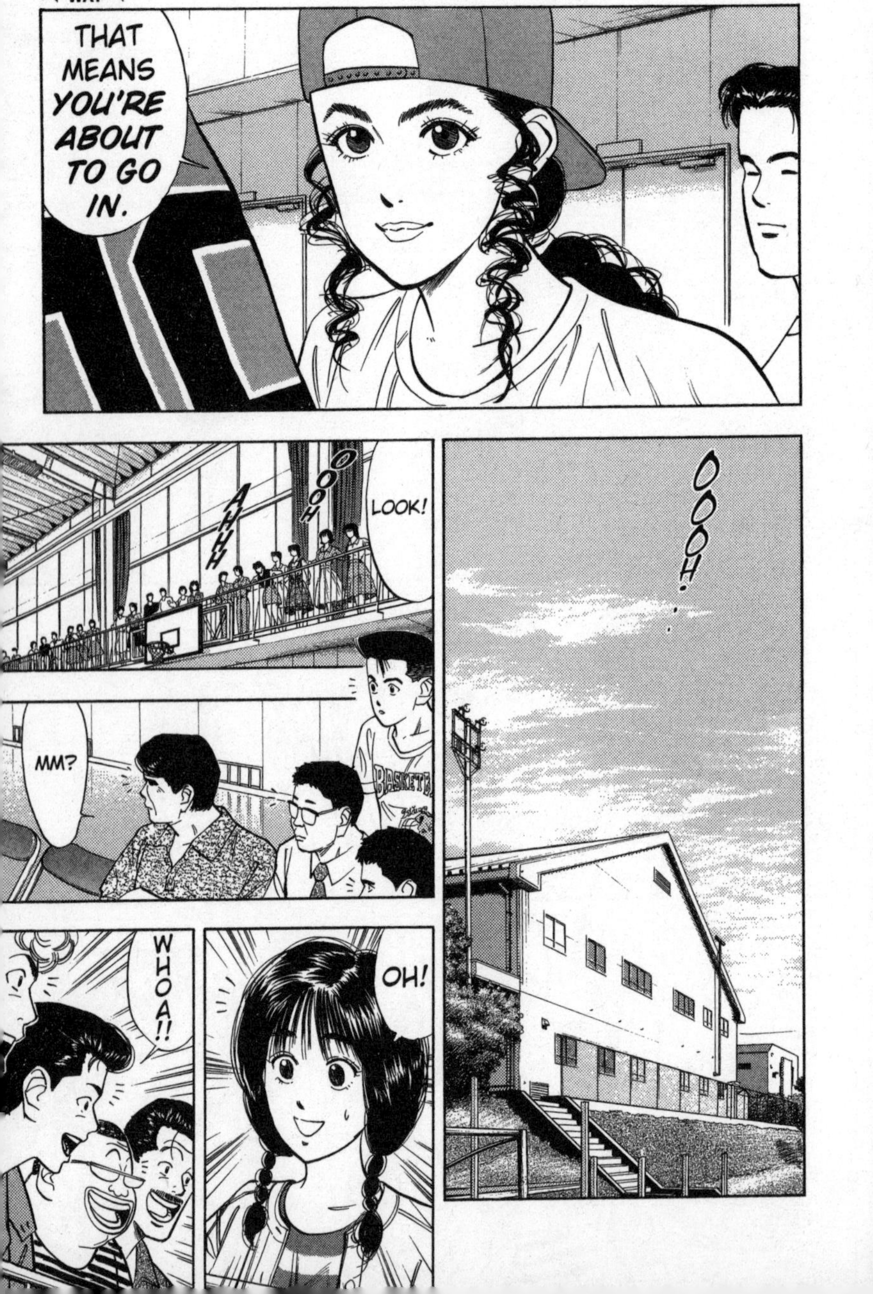
THAT MEANS YOU'RE ABOUT TO GO IN.
OOOOH...!
LOOK!
OOOOH
AHHHH
MM?
OH!
WHOA!!

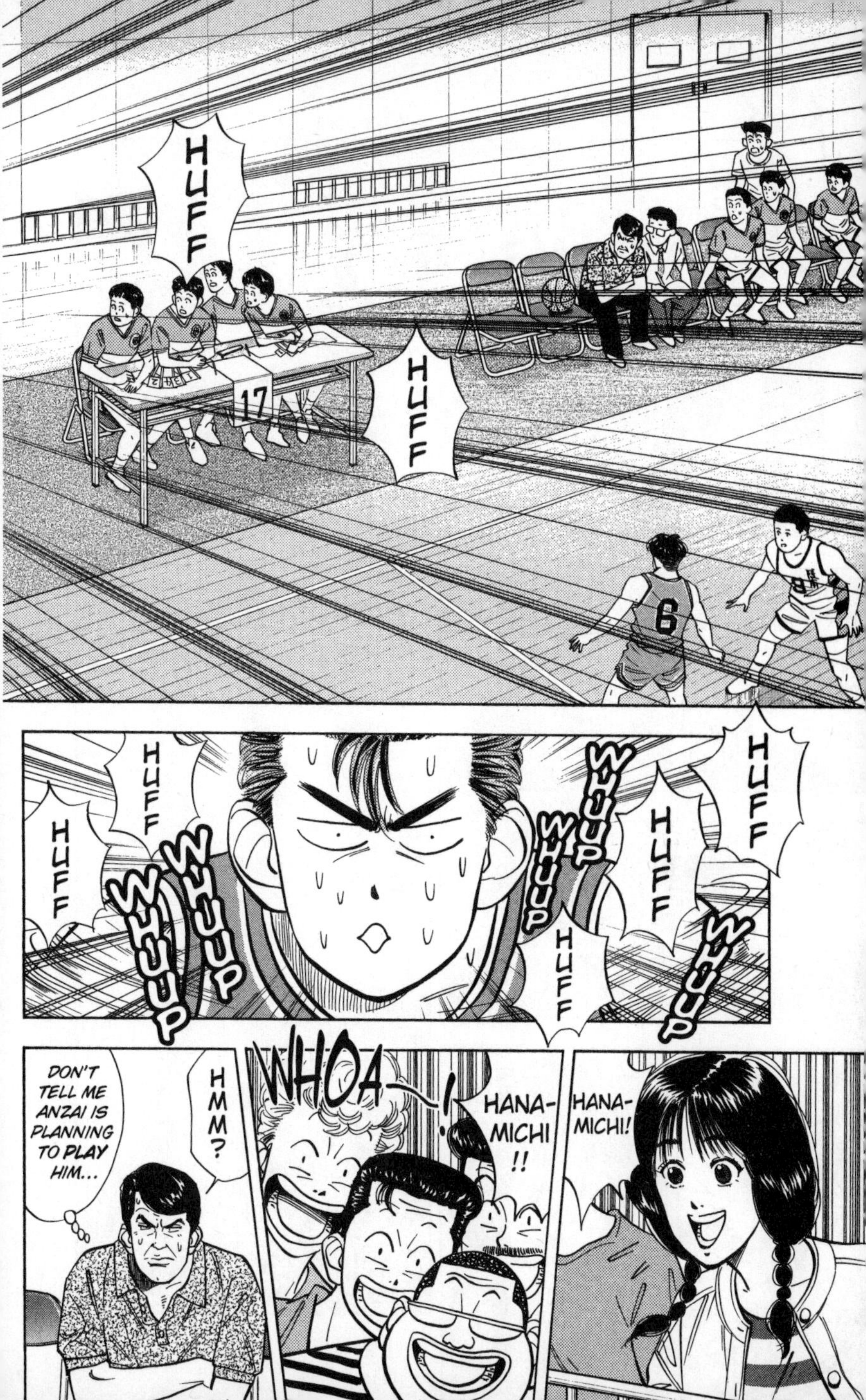
HUFF
HUFF
HUFF
WHUUP
WHUUP
HUFF
HUFF
WHUUP
HUFF
WHUUP
WHUUP
HUFF
HANA-MICHI!
WHOA—!
HANA-MICHI!!
HMM?
DON'T TELL ME ANZAI IS PLANNING TO PLAY HIM...

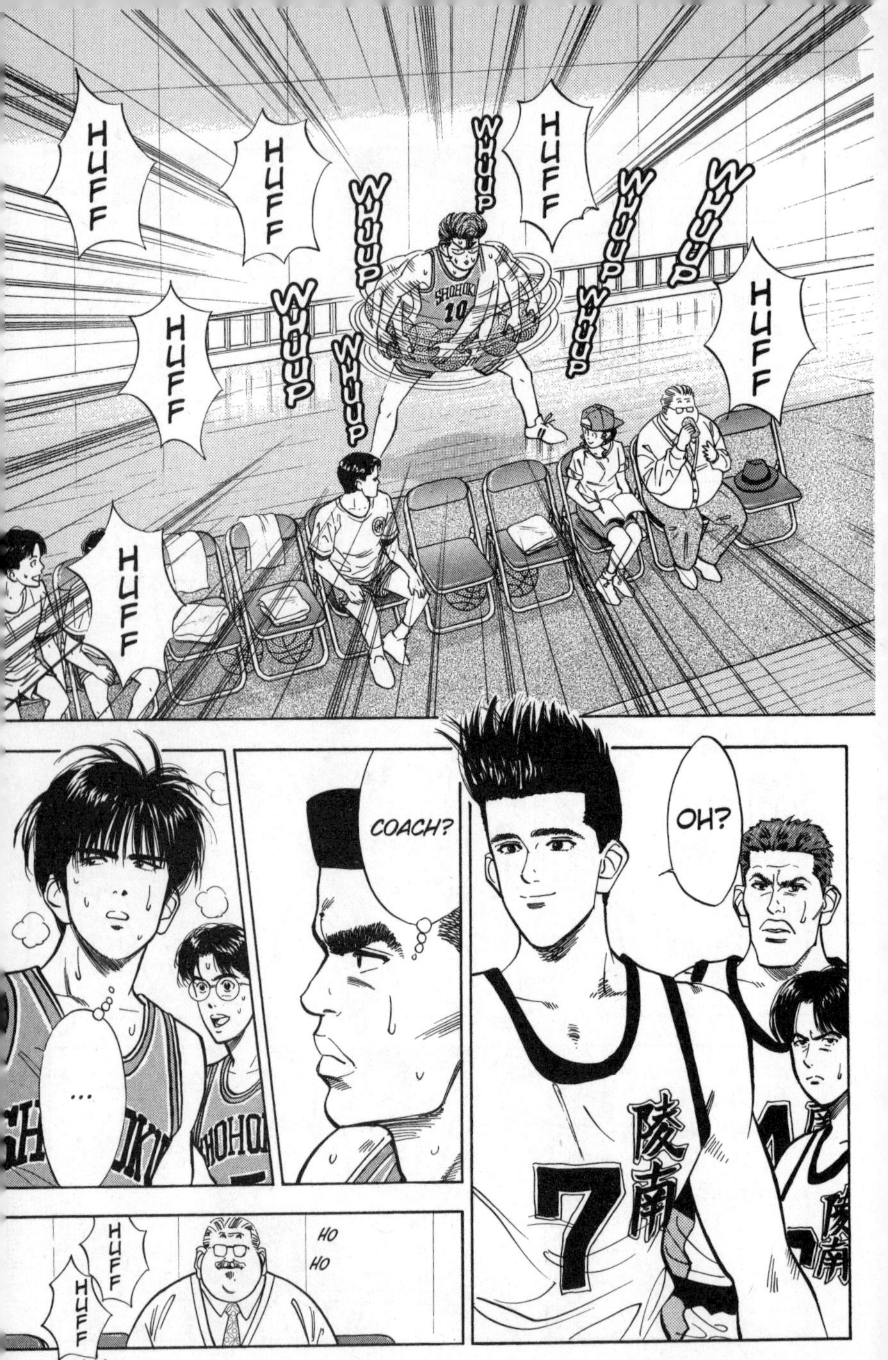

WHUUP
HUFF
WHUUP
WHUUP
HUFF
WHUUP
WHUUP
WHUUP
WHUUP
HUFF
HUFF
HUFF
HUFF
OH?
COACH?
...
HO
HO
HUFF
HUFF

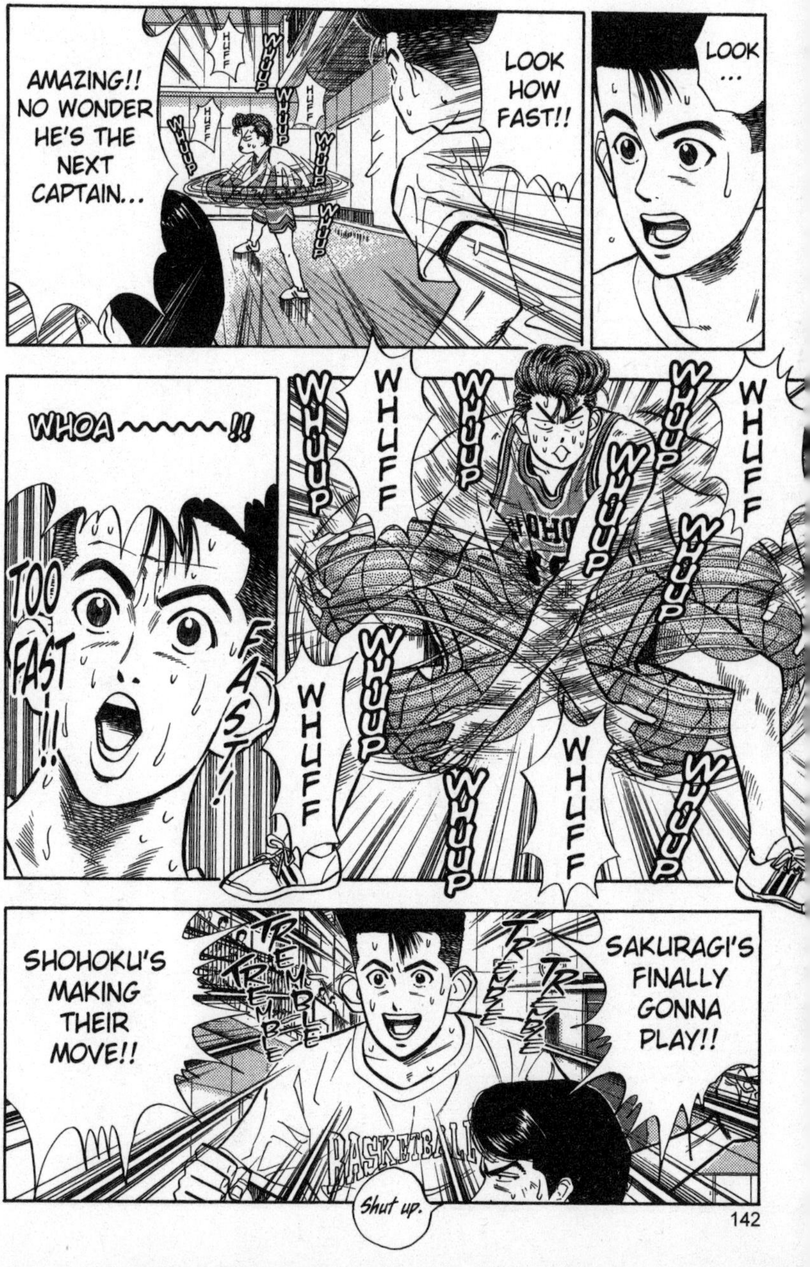
LOOK ...
LOOK HOW FAST!!
AMAZING!! NO WONDER HE'S THE NEXT CAPTAIN...
HUFF
WHUUP
HUFF
WHUUP
HUFF
WHUUP
WHUUP
WHUFF
WHUUP
WHUUP
WHUFF
WHUUP
WHUUP
WHUUP
WHUFF
WHUUP
WHUFF
WHUUP
WHOA~~~~~!!
TOO FAST!!
FAST!
SAKURAGI'S FINALLY GONNA PLAY!!
TREMBLE
TREMBLE
TREMBLE
TREMBLE
SHOHOKU'S MAKING THEIR MOVE!!
BASKETBALL
Shut up.

READ THIS WAY

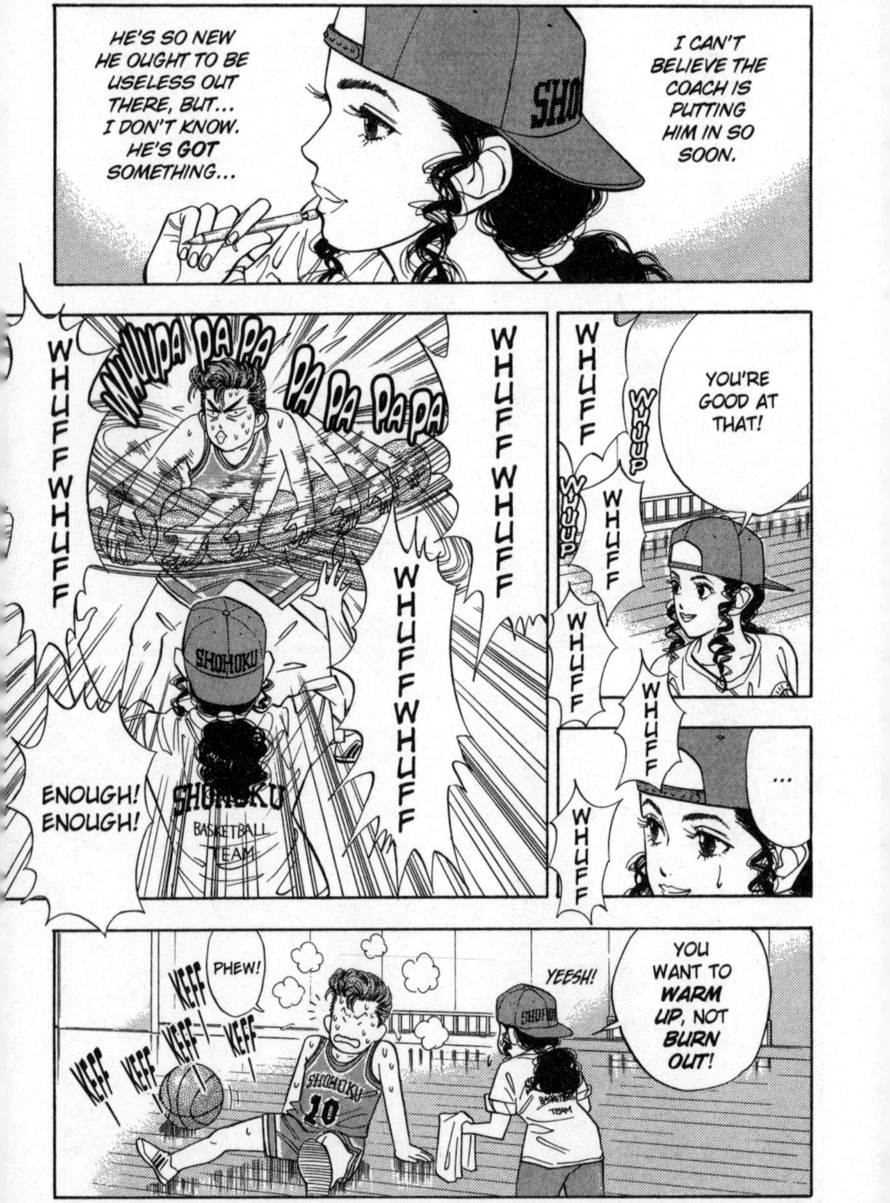

I CAN'T BELIEVE THE COACH IS PUTTING HIM IN SO SOON.
HE'S SO NEW HE OUGHT TO BE USELESS OUT THERE, BUT... I DON'T KNOW. HE'S GOT SOMETHING...
WHUFF
YOU'RE GOOD AT THAT!
WHUUP
WHUUP
WHUFF
WHUFF
WHUFF
...
WHUFF
WHUFFWHUFF
WHUUPA PA PA
PA PA PA PA
WHUFFWHUFF
WHUFFWHUFF
ENOUGH! ENOUGH!
YOU WANT TO WARM UP, NOT BURN OUT!
YEESH!
PHEW!
KEFF
KEFF
KEFF
KEFF
KEFF

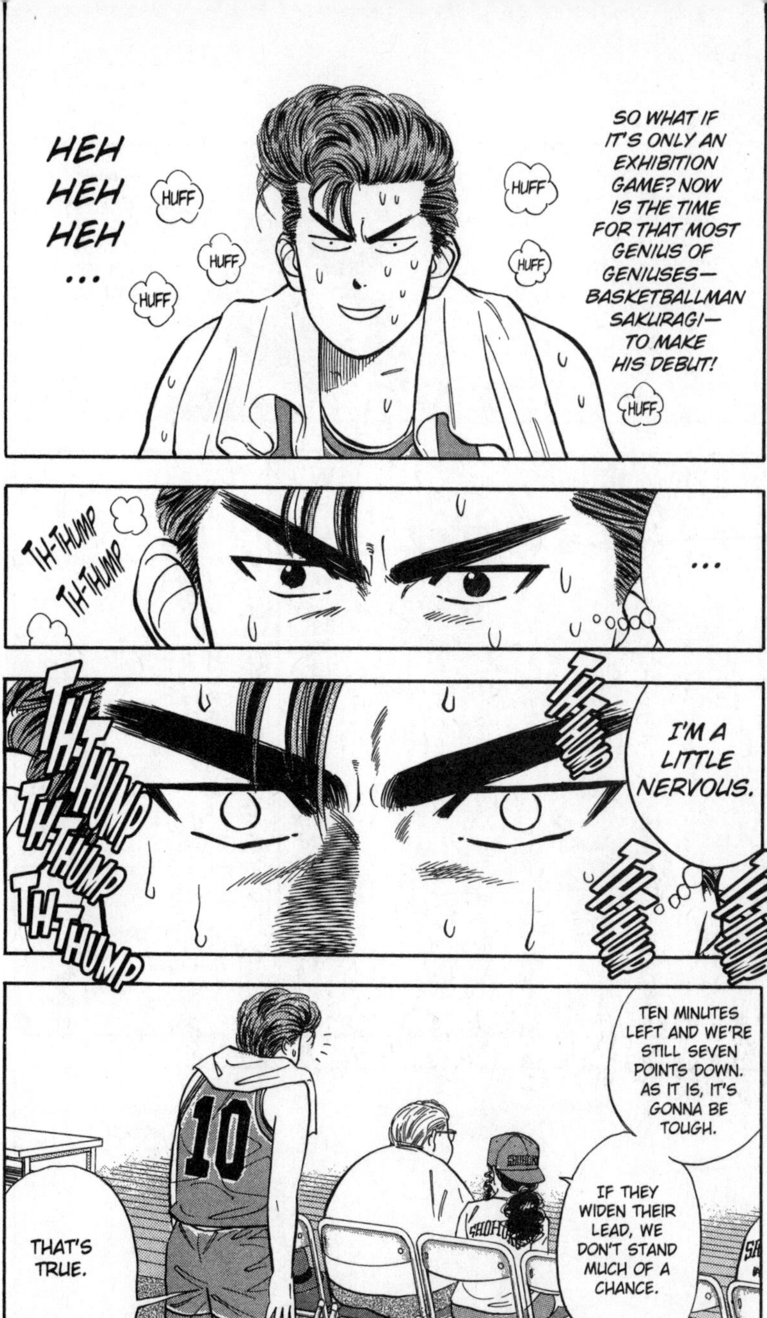
SO WHAT IF IT'S ONLY AN EXHIBITION GAME? NOW IS THE TIME FOR THAT MOST GENIUS OF GENIUSES— BASKETBALLMAN SAKURAGI— TO MAKE HIS DEBUT!
HUFF
HUFF
HUFF
HUFF
HUFF
HUFF
HEH HEH HEH ...
...
TH-THUMP
TH-THUMP
I'M A LITTLE NERVOUS.
TH-THUMP
TH-THUMP
TH-THUMP
TH-THUMP
TH-THUMP
TH-THUMP
TEN MINUTES LEFT AND WE'RE STILL SEVEN POINTS DOWN. AS IT IS, IT'S GONNA BE TOUGH.
IF THEY WIDEN THEIR LEAD, WE DON'T STAND MUCH OF A CHANCE.
THAT'S TRUE.

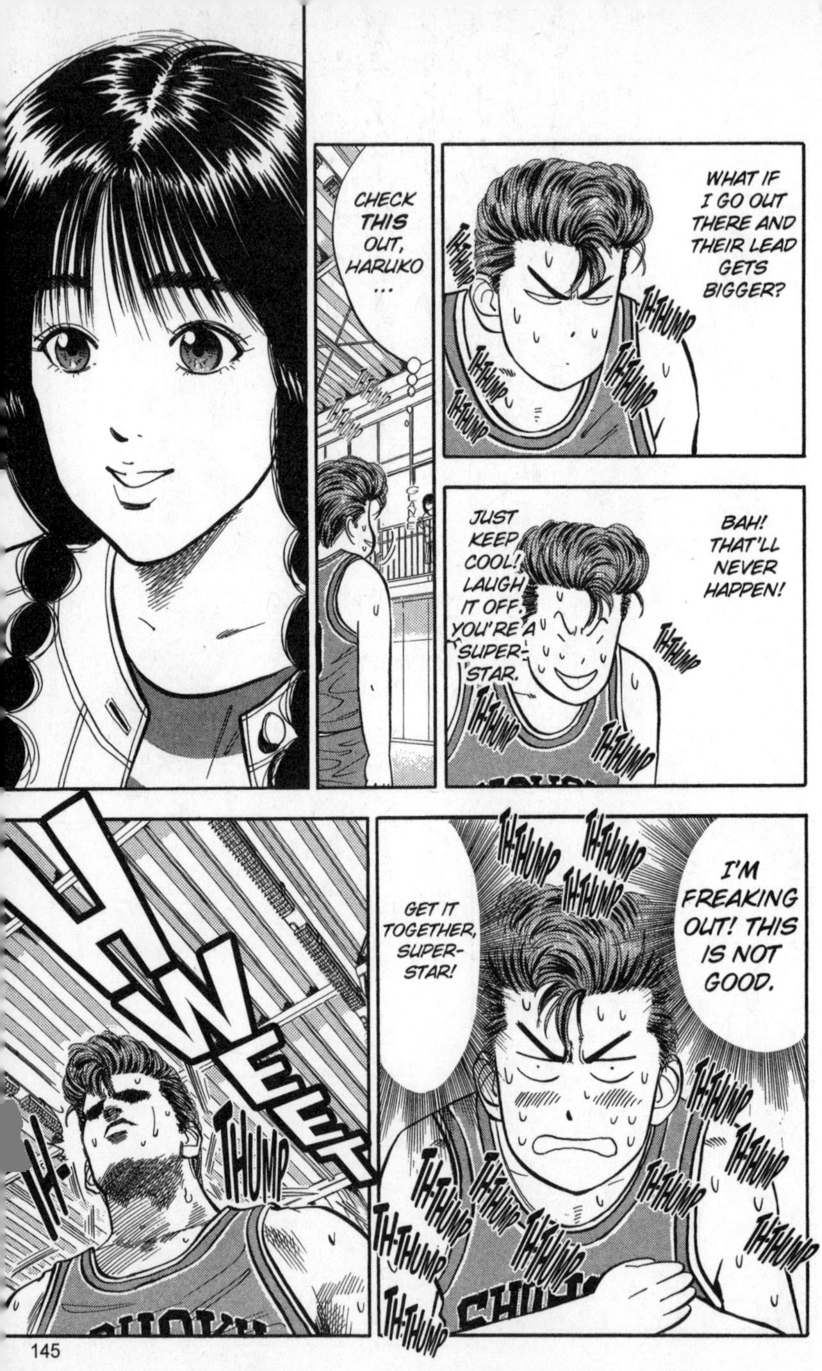
WHAT IF I GO OUT THERE AND THEIR LEAD GETS BIGGER?
TH-THUMP
TH-THUMP
TH-THUMP
TH-THUMP
TH-THUMP
BAH! THAT'LL NEVER HAPPEN!
JUST KEEP COOL! LAUGH IT OFF. YOU'RE A SUPER-STAR.
TH-THUMP
TH-THUMP
TH-THUMP
CHECK THIS OUT, HARUKO ...
TH-THUMP
TH-THUMP
GLANCE
I'M FREAKING OUT! THIS IS NOT GOOD.
GET IT TOGETHER, SUPER-STAR!
TH-THUMP
TH-THUMP
TH-THUMP
TH-THUMP
TH-THUMP
TH-THUMP
TH-THUMP
TH-THUMP
TH-THUMP
TH-THUMP
TH-THUMP

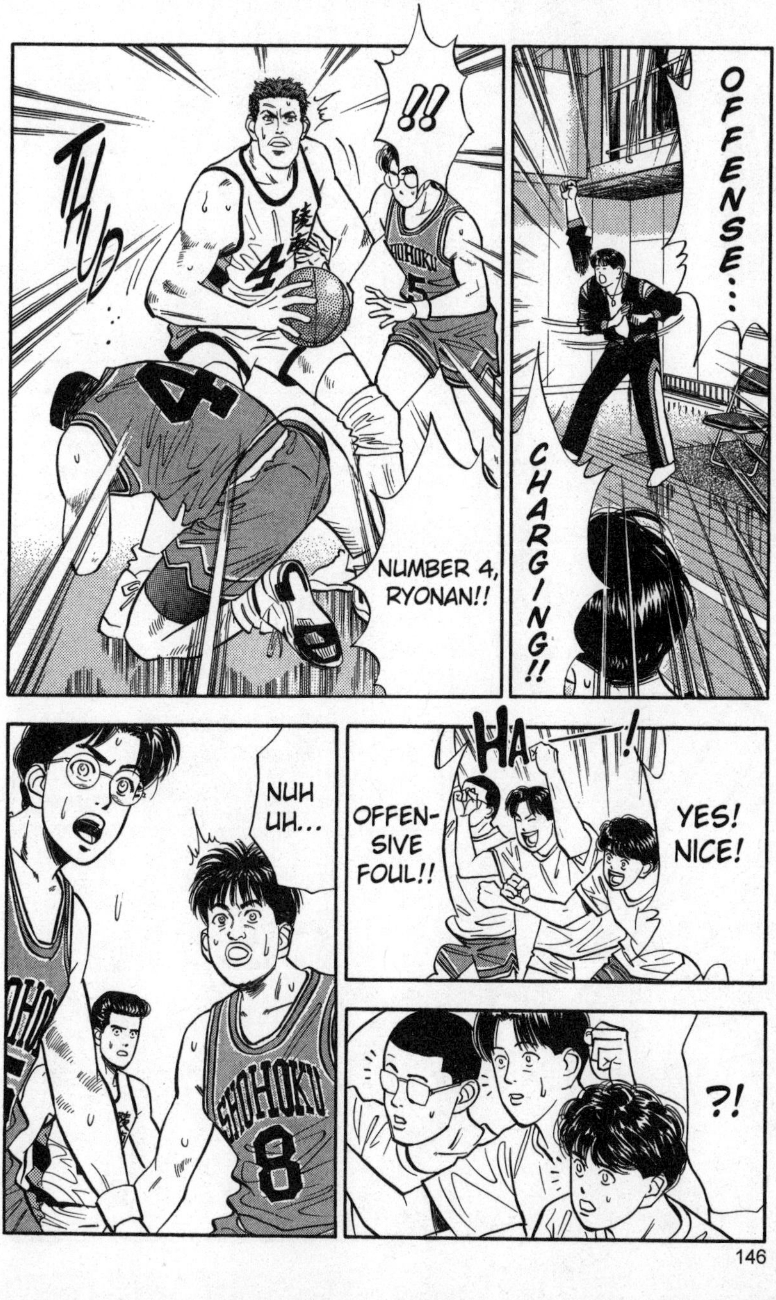

OFFENSE...
CHARGING!!
!!
THUD
NUMBER 4, RYONAN!!
HA—!
YES! NICE!
OFFEN-SIVE FOUL!!
?!
NUH UH...

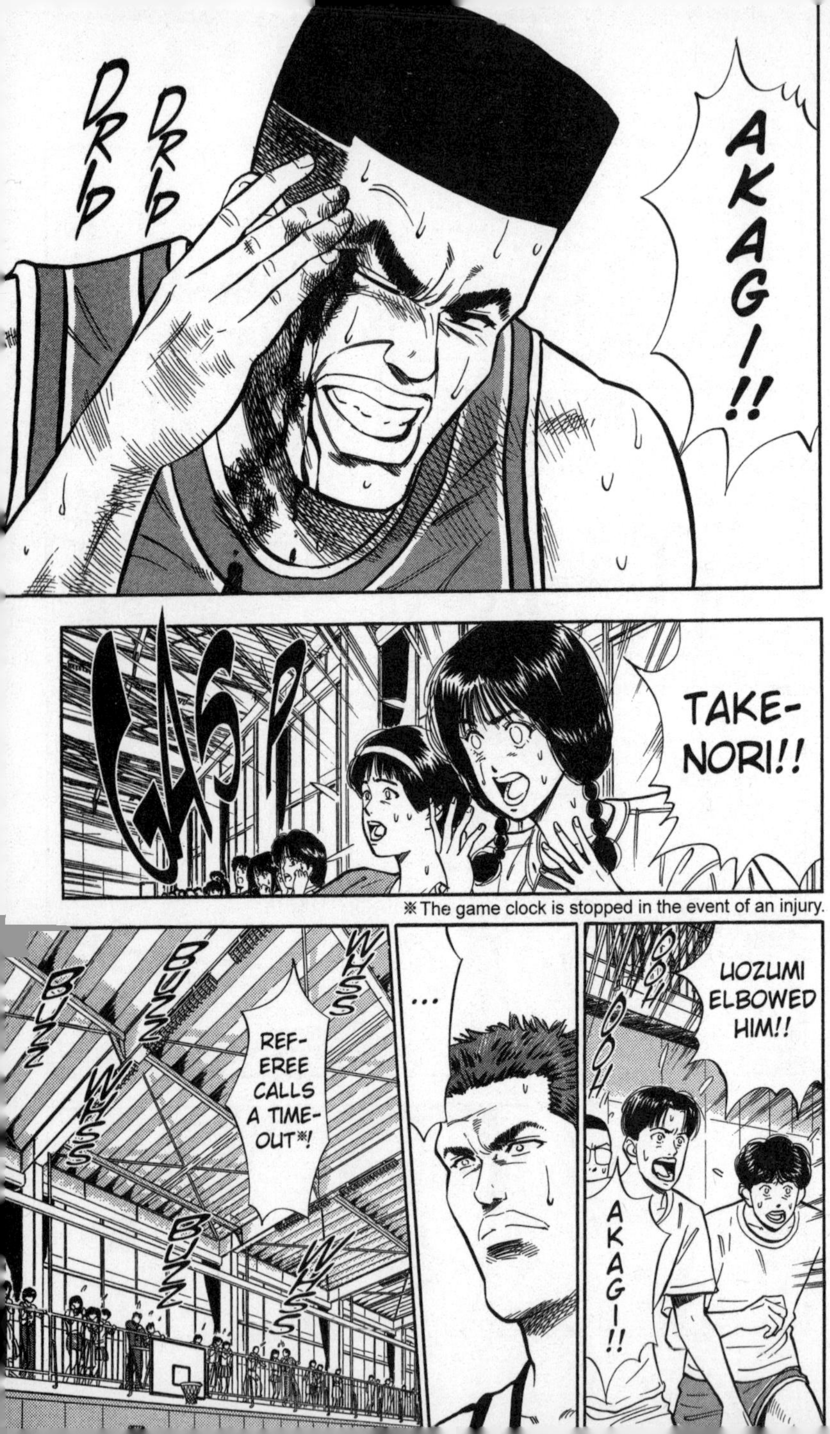
AKAGI!!
DRIP DRIP
TAKE-NORI!!
GASP
UOZUMI ELBOWED HIM!!
AKAGI!!
...
WHSS
REF-EREE CALLS A TIME-OUT※!
BUZZ BUZZ
WHSS
BUZZ
WHSS
※The game clock is stopped in the event of an injury.

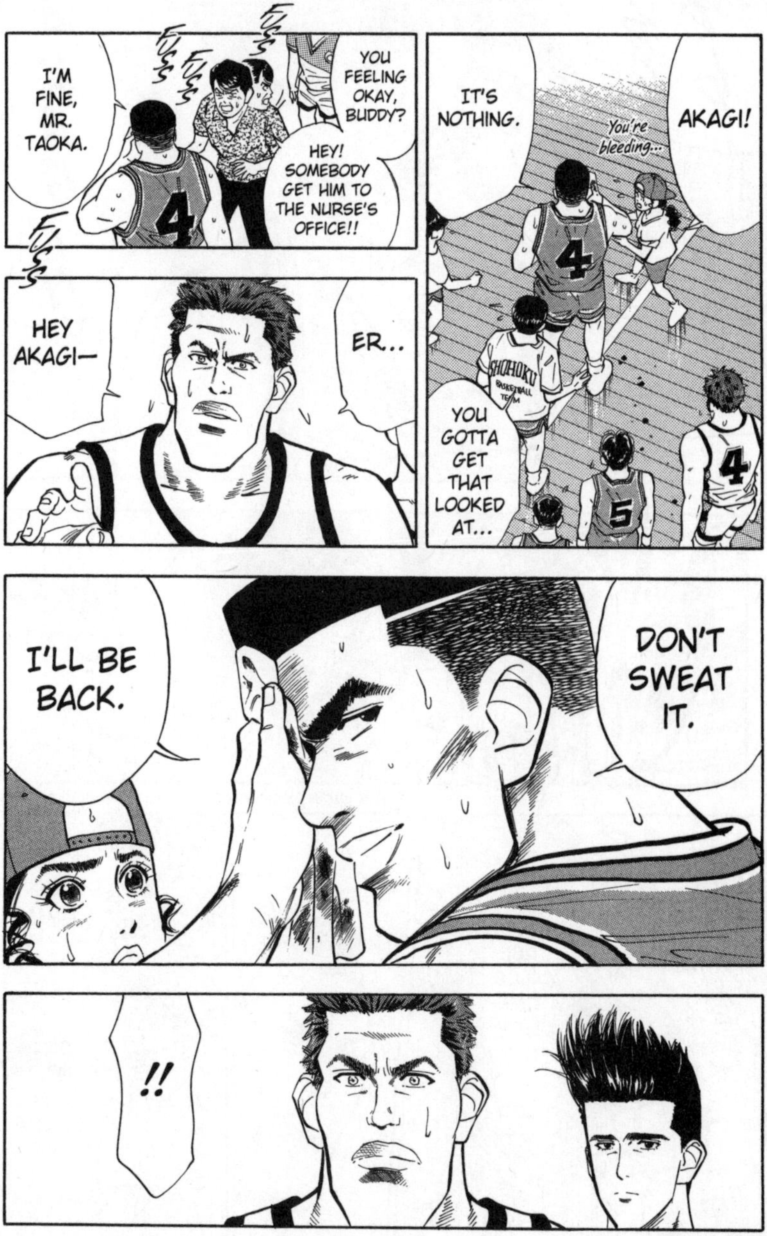
AKAGI!
You're bleeding...
IT'S NOTHING.
YOU GOTTA GET THAT LOOKED AT...
YOU FEELING OKAY, BUDDY?
FUSS FUSS FUSS
HEY! SOMEBODY GET HIM TO THE NURSE'S OFFICE!!
I'M FINE, MR. TAOKA.
FUSS
ER...
HEY AKAGI—
DON'T SWEAT IT.
I'LL BE BACK.
!!

READ THIS WAY

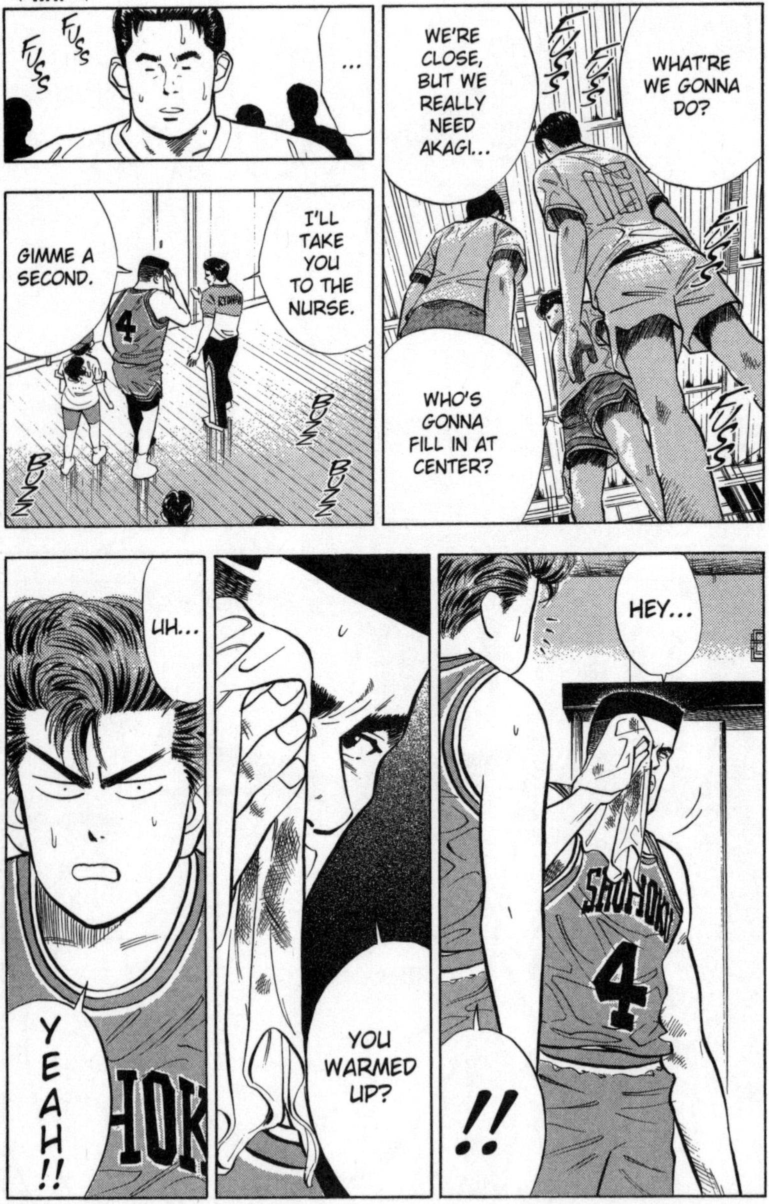

WHAT'RE WE GONNA DO?
FUSS FUSS
WE'RE CLOSE, BUT WE REALLY NEED AKAGI...
FUSS
WHO'S GONNA FILL IN AT CENTER?
FUSS
FUSS FUSS
...
I'LL TAKE YOU TO THE NURSE.
GIMME A SECOND.
BUZZ
BUZZ
BUZZ
HEY...
!!
YOU WARMED UP?
UH...
YEAH!!

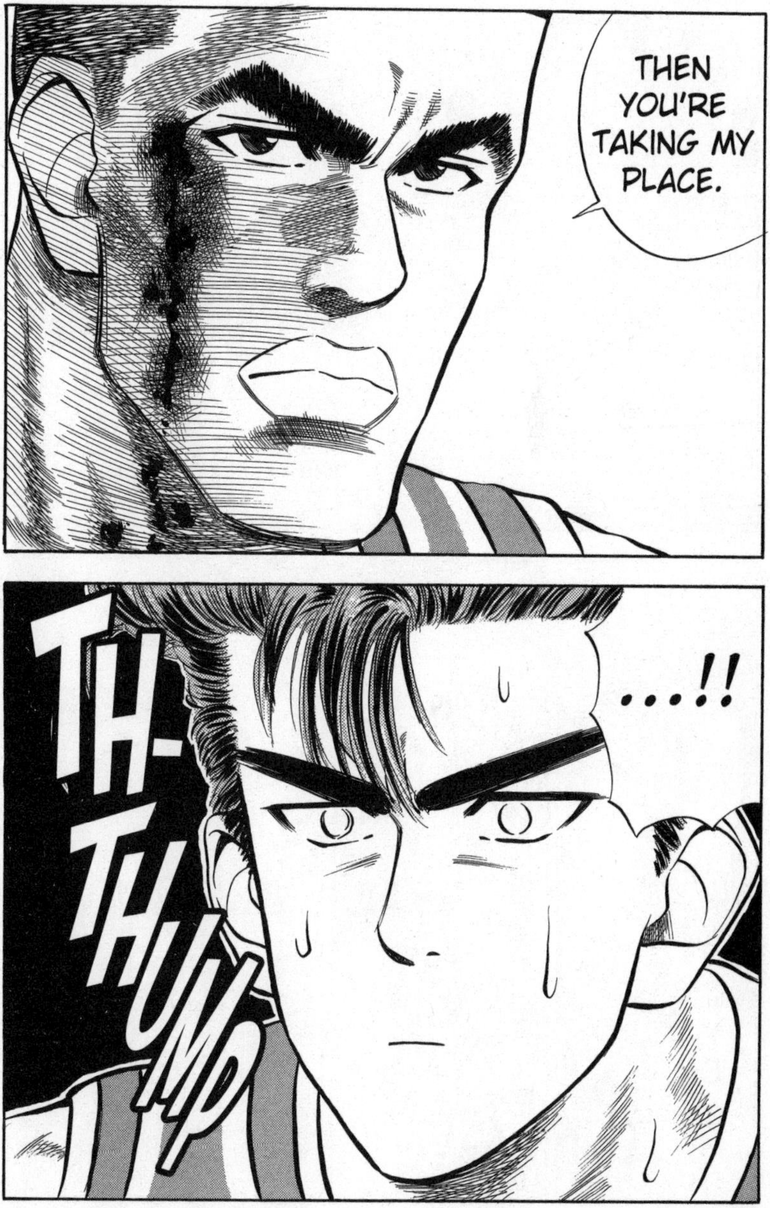
THEN YOU'RE TAKING MY PLACE.
...!!
TH-THUMP

READ THIS WAY

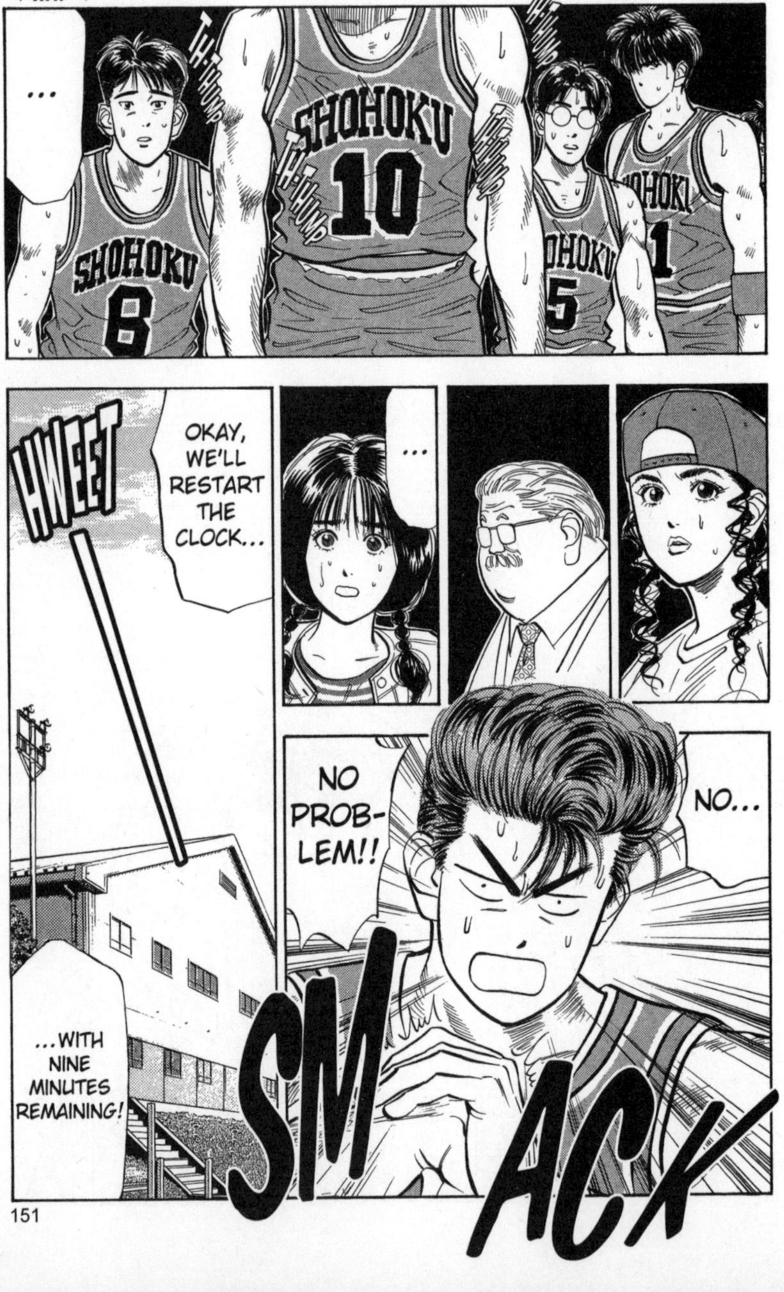

TH-THUMP
TH-THUMP
TH-THUMP
TH-THUMP
...
...
NO...
NO PROBLEM!!
SMACK
HWEET
OKAY, WE'LL RESTART THE CLOCK...
...WITH NINE MINUTES REMAINING!

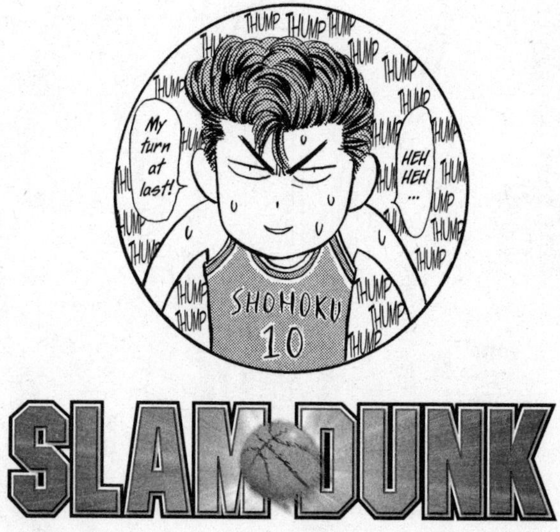
THUMP THUMP THUMP
HEH HEH ...
My turn at last!
SHOHOKU
10

SLAM DUNK

#34 ENTER THE HERO!!

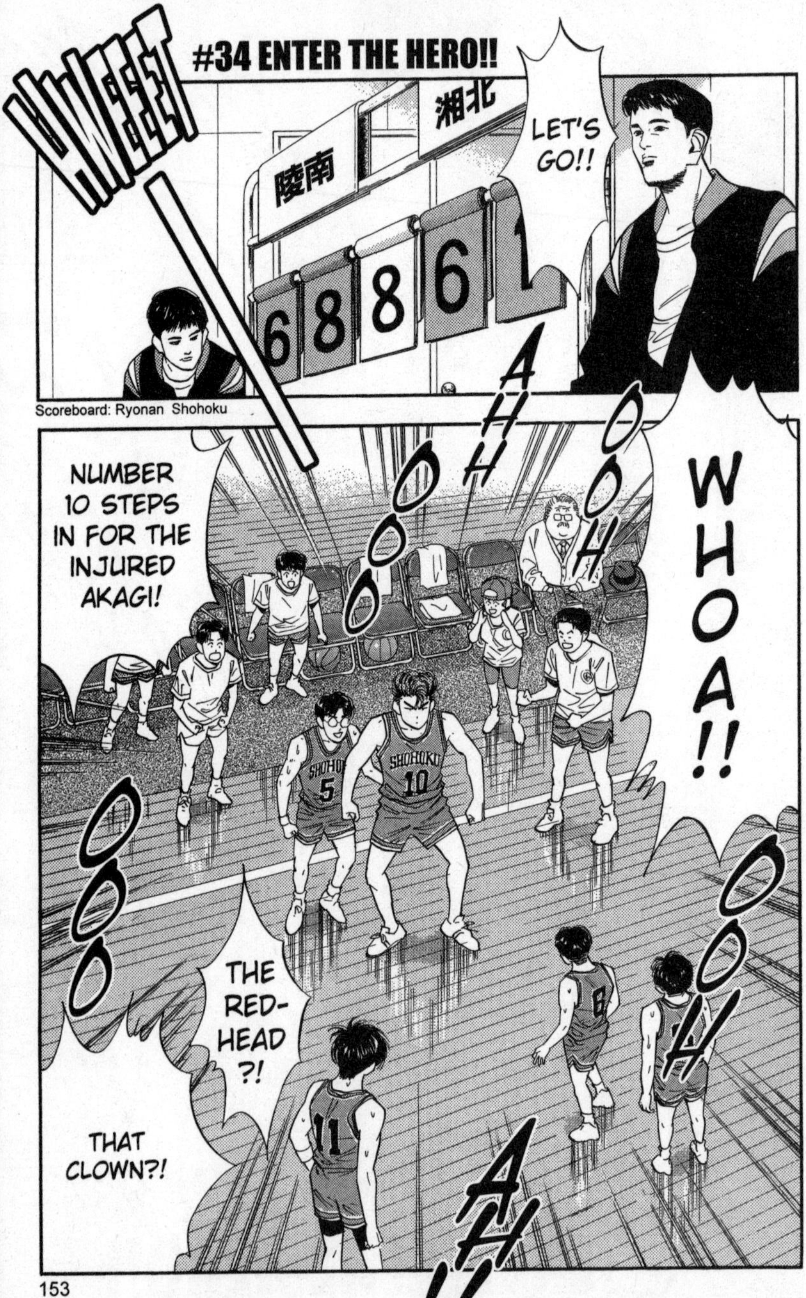
SWEEEET
LET'S GO!!
湘北
陵南
WHOA!!
OOOOH
AHH
OOOOO
NUMBER 10 STEPS IN FOR THE INJURED AKAGI!
OOOOO
THE RED-HEAD?!
OOOH
AHH
THAT CLOWN?!

Scoreboard: Ryonan Shohoku

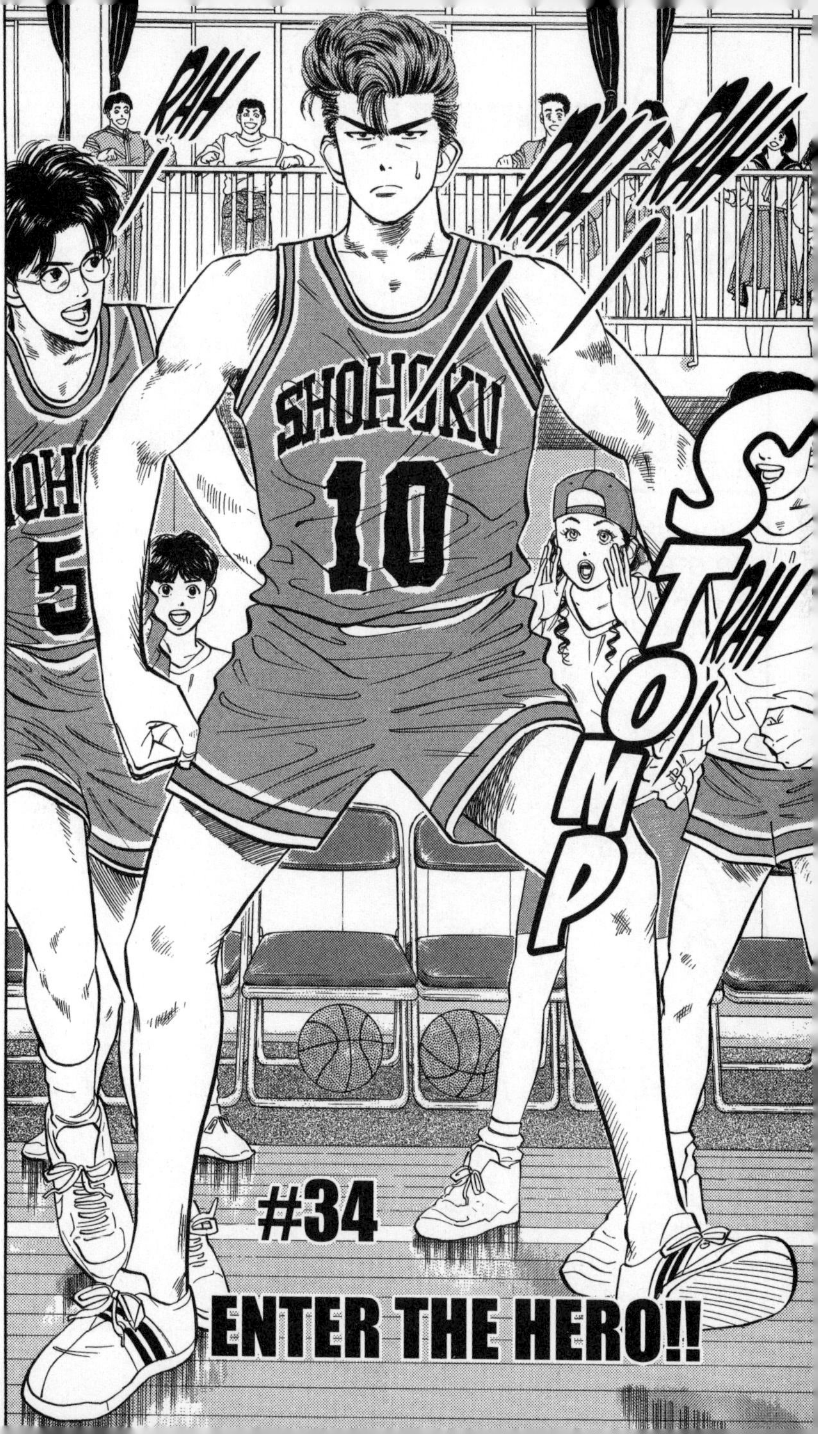
RAH! RAH!
RAH!
STOMP
RAH!

#34 ENTER THE HERO!!

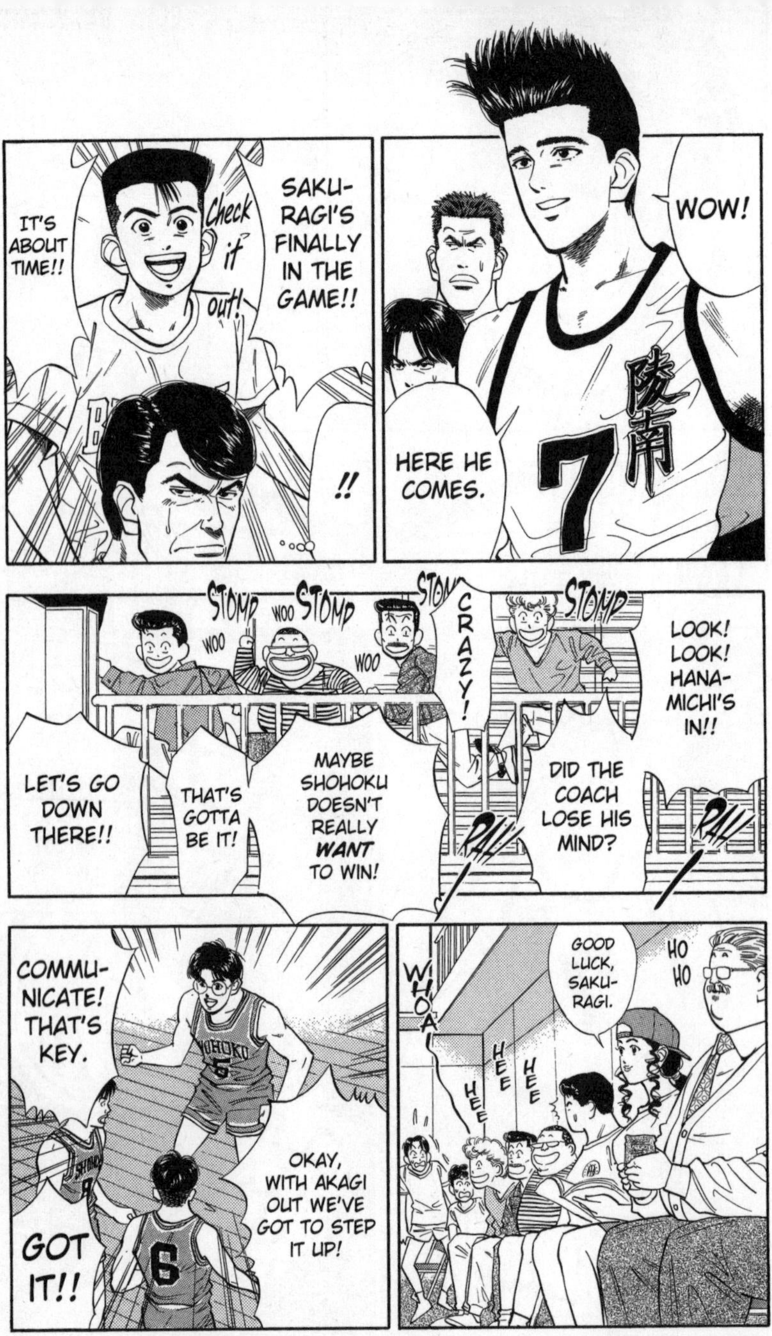
WOW!
HERE HE COMES.
SAKU-RAGI'S FINALLY IN THE GAME!!
Check it out!
IT'S ABOUT TIME!!
!!
LOOK! LOOK! HANA-MICHI'S IN!!
STOMP
CRAZY!
DID THE COACH LOSE HIS MIND?
RAL
STOMP
WOO
MAYBE SHOHOKU DOESN'T REALLY *WANT* TO WIN!
WOO STOMP
WOO
STOMP
THAT'S GOTTA BE IT!
LET'S GO DOWN THERE!!
HO HO
GOOD LUCK, SAKU-RAGI.
WHOA!
HEE HEE
HEE HEE
COMMUNICATE! THAT'S KEY.
OKAY, WITH AKAGI OUT WE'VE GOT TO STEP IT UP!
GOT IT!!

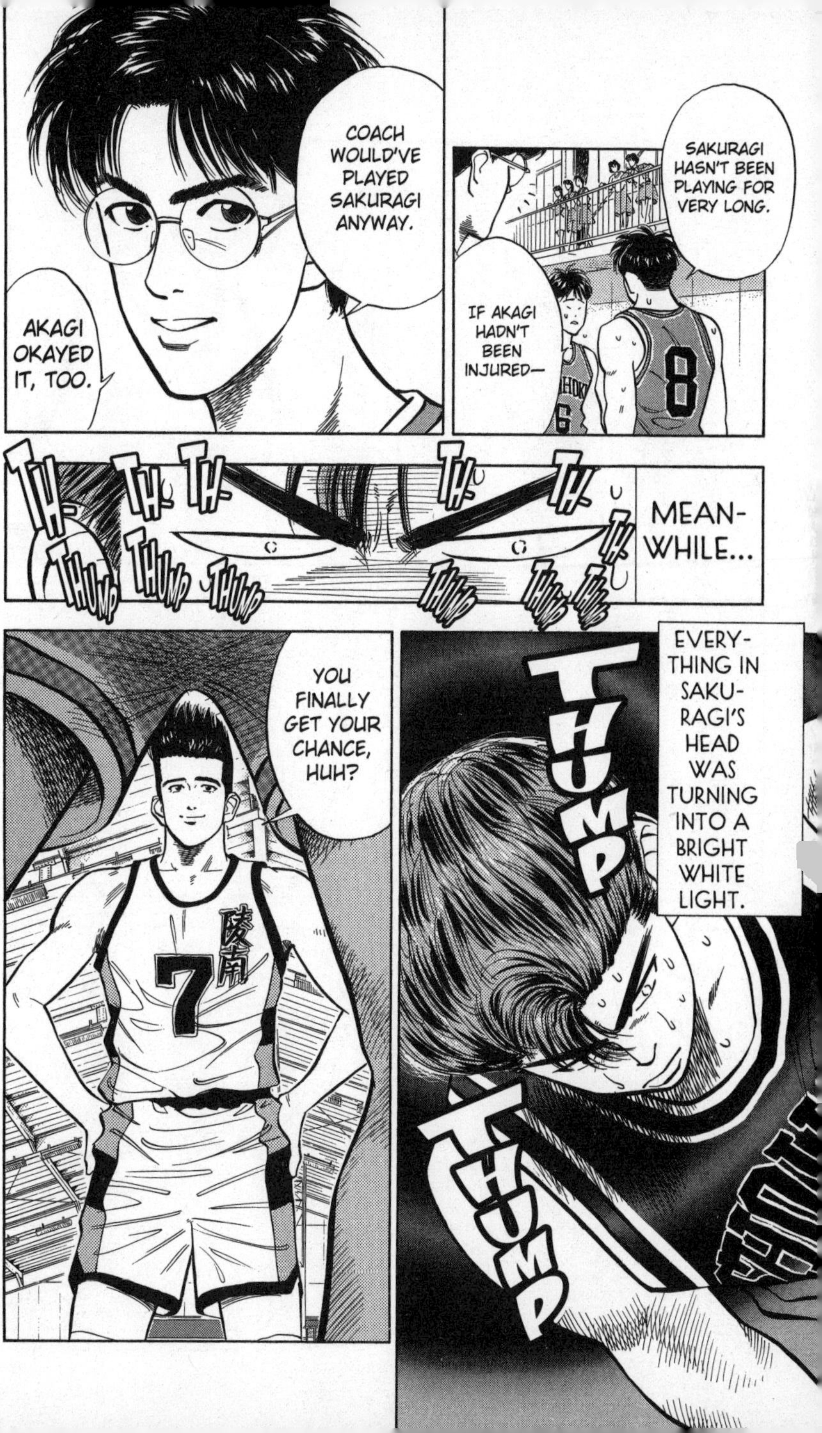
SAKURAGI HASN'T BEEN PLAYING FOR VERY LONG.
IF AKAGI HADN'T BEEN INJURED—
COACH WOULD'VE PLAYED SAKURAGI ANYWAY.
AKAGI OKAYED IT, TOO.
MEAN-WHILE...
TH- THUMP
TH- THUMP
TH- THUMP
TH- THUMP
TH- THUMP
EVERY-THING IN SAKU-RAGI'S HEAD WAS TURNING INTO A BRIGHT WHITE LIGHT.
THUMP
THUMP
YOU FINALLY GET YOUR CHANCE, HUH?

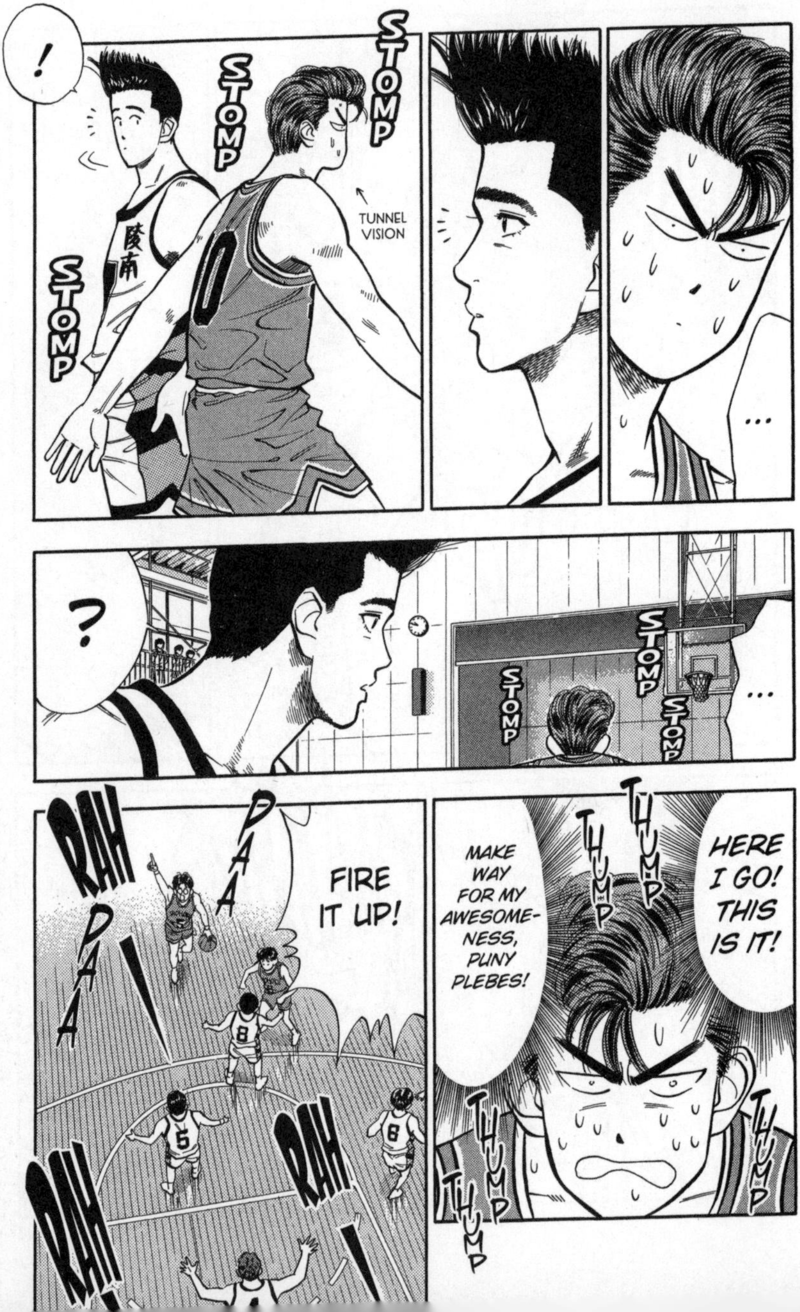
...
STOMP
STOMP
!
TUNNEL VISION
STOMP
...
STOMP
STOMP
STOMP
?
HERE I GO! THIS IS IT!
THUMP
THUMP
MAKE WAY FOR MY AWESOME-NESS, PUNY PLEBES!
THUMP
THUMP
THUMP
FIRE IT UP!
DAA
DAA
RAH
RAH
RAH

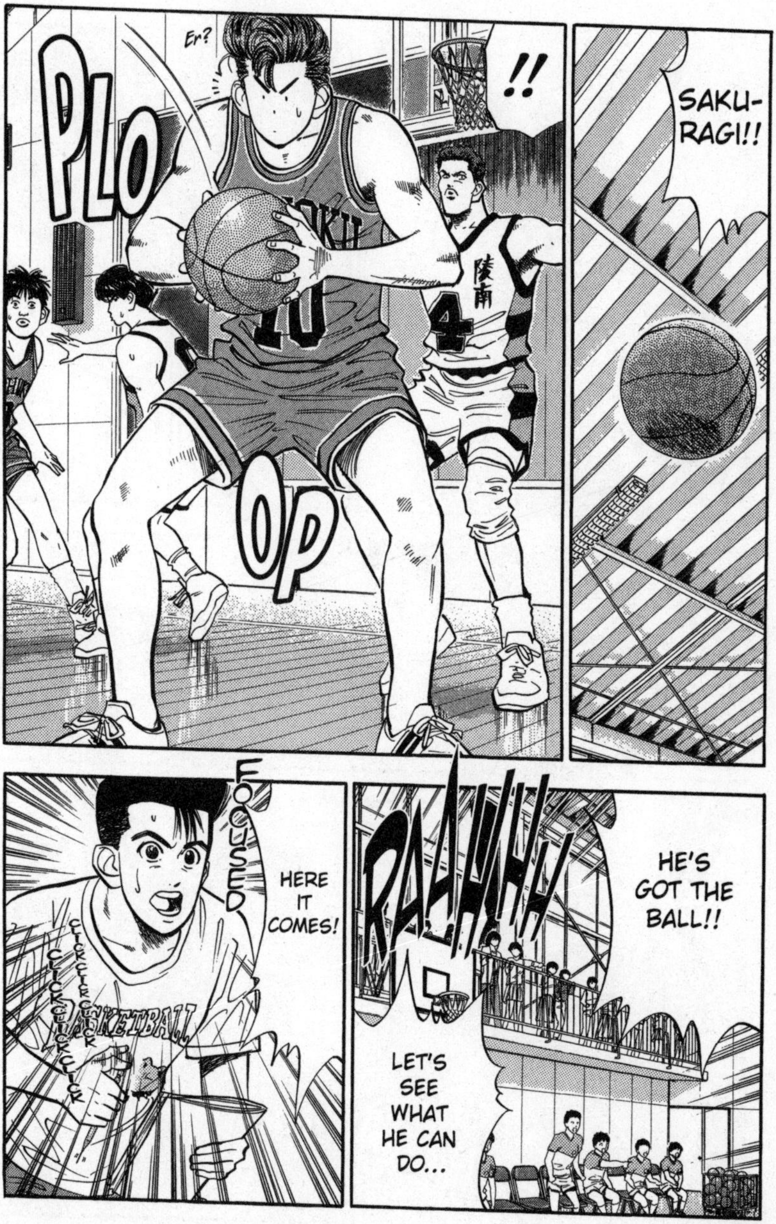
SAKU-RAGI!!
Er?
PLOP
!!
RAAHHH
HE'S GOT THE BALL!!
LET'S SEE WHAT HE CAN DO...
FOCUSED
HERE IT COMES!
CLICK CLICK CLICK
CLICK CLICK CLICK

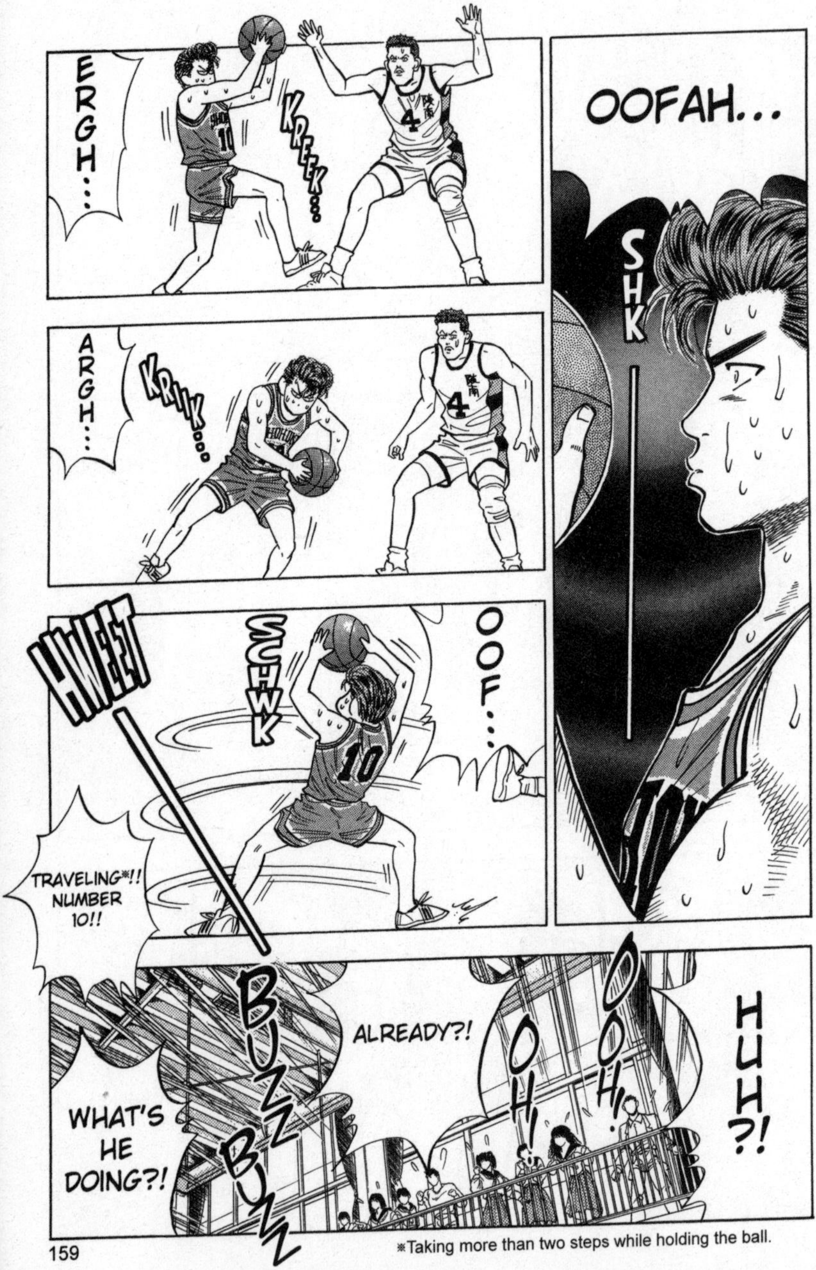
OOFAH...
SHK
KREEK...
ERGH...
KRIIK...
ARGH...
OOF...
SCHWK
HWEET
TRAVELING※!! NUMBER 10!!
HUH?!
OOOH!
OH!
ALREADY?!
BUZZ BUZZ
WHAT'S HE DOING?!

※Taking more than two steps while holding the ball.

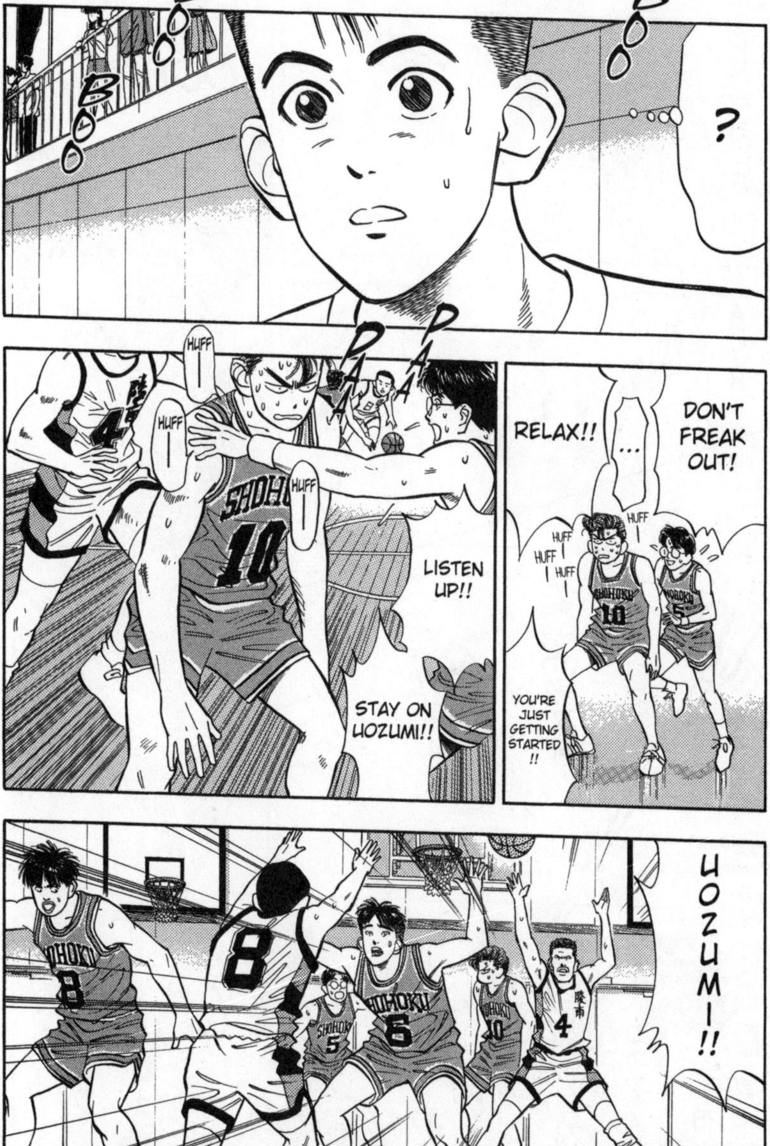
BOOO
...?
BOOO
BOOO
DON'T FREAK OUT!
...
RELAX!!
HUFF
HUFF
HUFF
HUFF
YOU'RE JUST GETTING STARTED!!
PAA
PAA
HUFF
HUFF
HUFF
LISTEN UP!!
STAY ON UOZUMI!!
UOZUMI!!

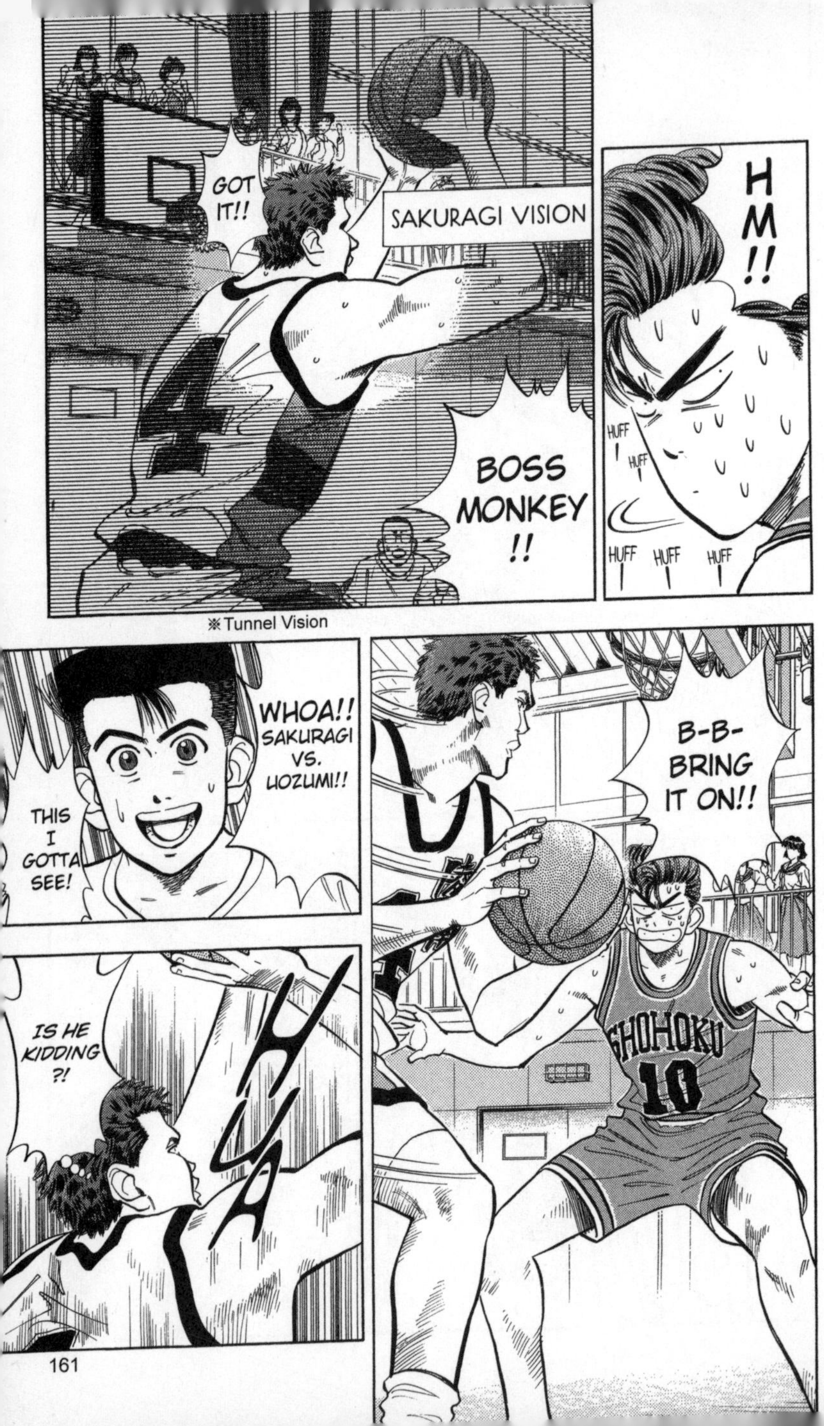
HM!!
HUFF HUFF
HUFF HUFF HUFF
SAKURAGI VISION
GOT IT!!
BOSS MONKEY!!
B-B-BRING IT ON!!
WHOA!! SAKURAGI VS. UOZUMI!!
THIS I GOTTA SEE!
HWA
IS HE KIDDING?!

※Tunnel Vision

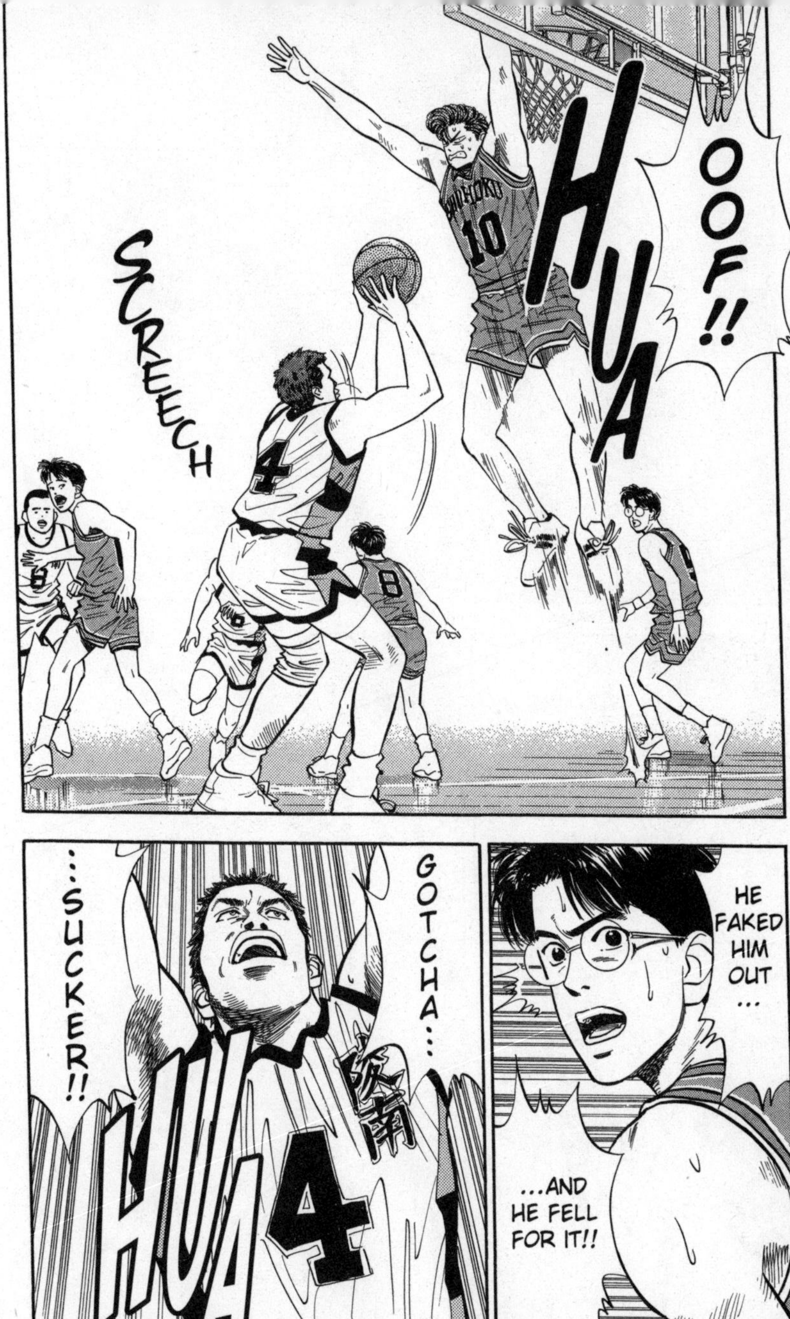
OOF!!
HUA
SCREECH
HE FAKED HIM OUT ...
...AND HE FELL FOR IT!!
GOTCHA...
...SUCKER!!
HUA

READ THIS WAY

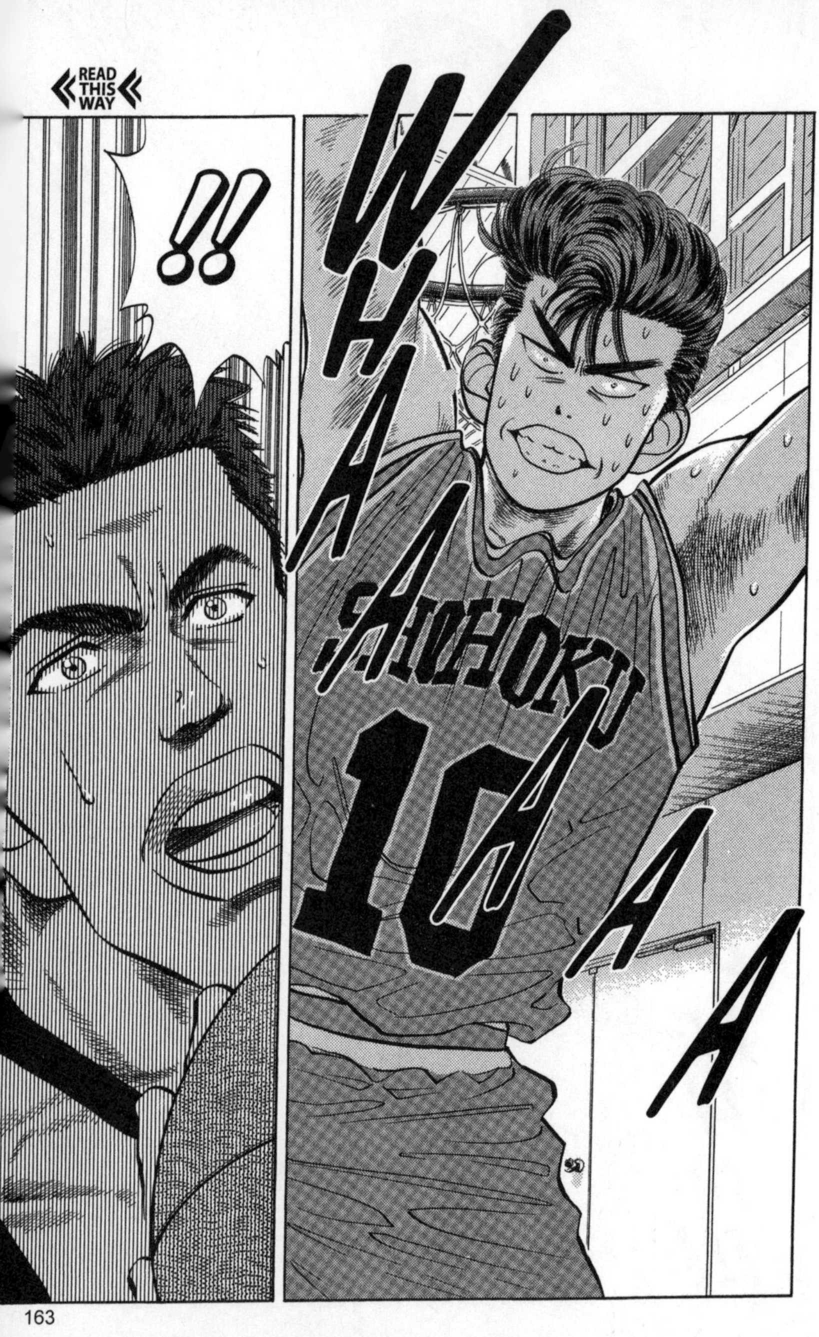
WHAAAAA
!!

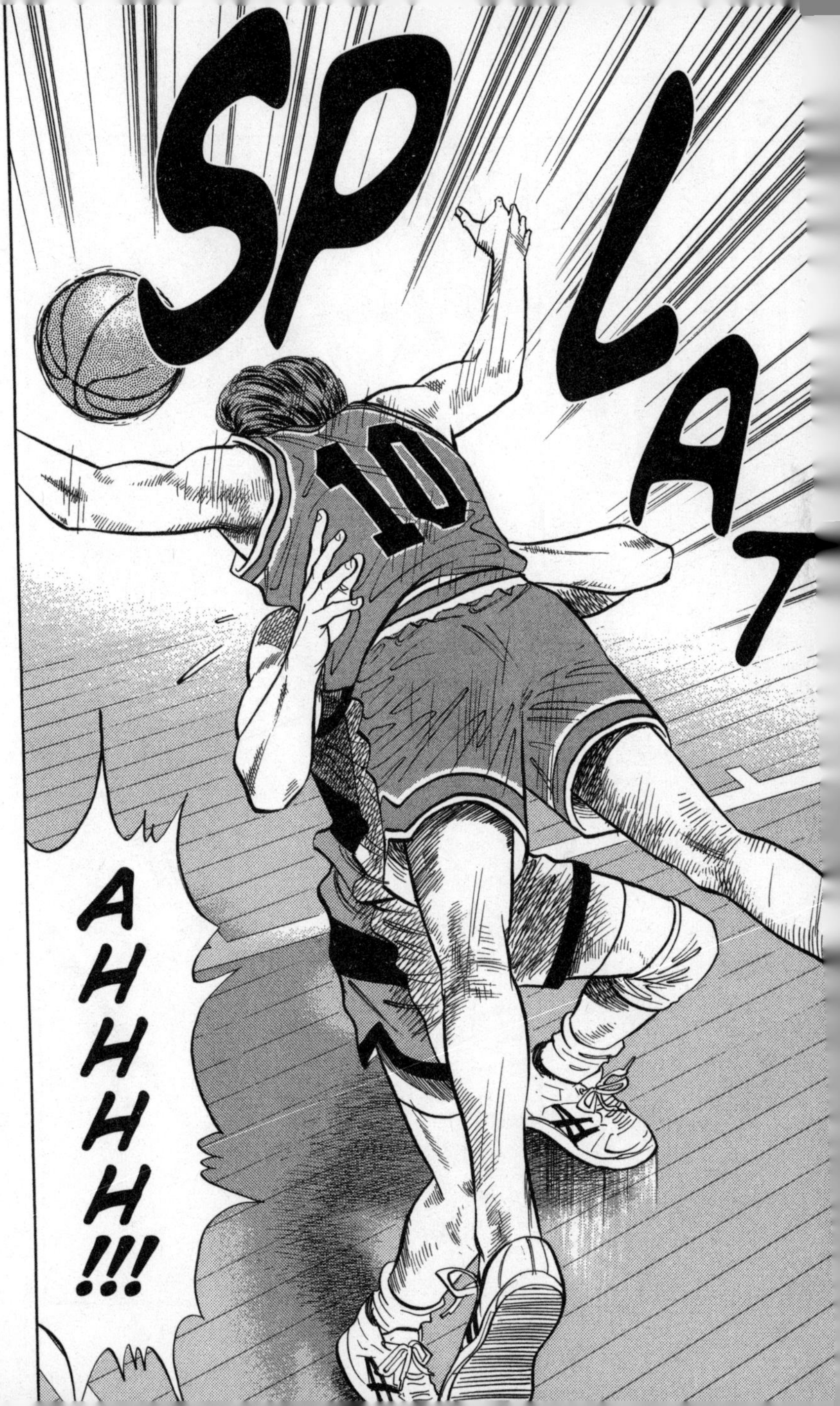
SPLAT
AHHHHH!!!

READ THIS WAY

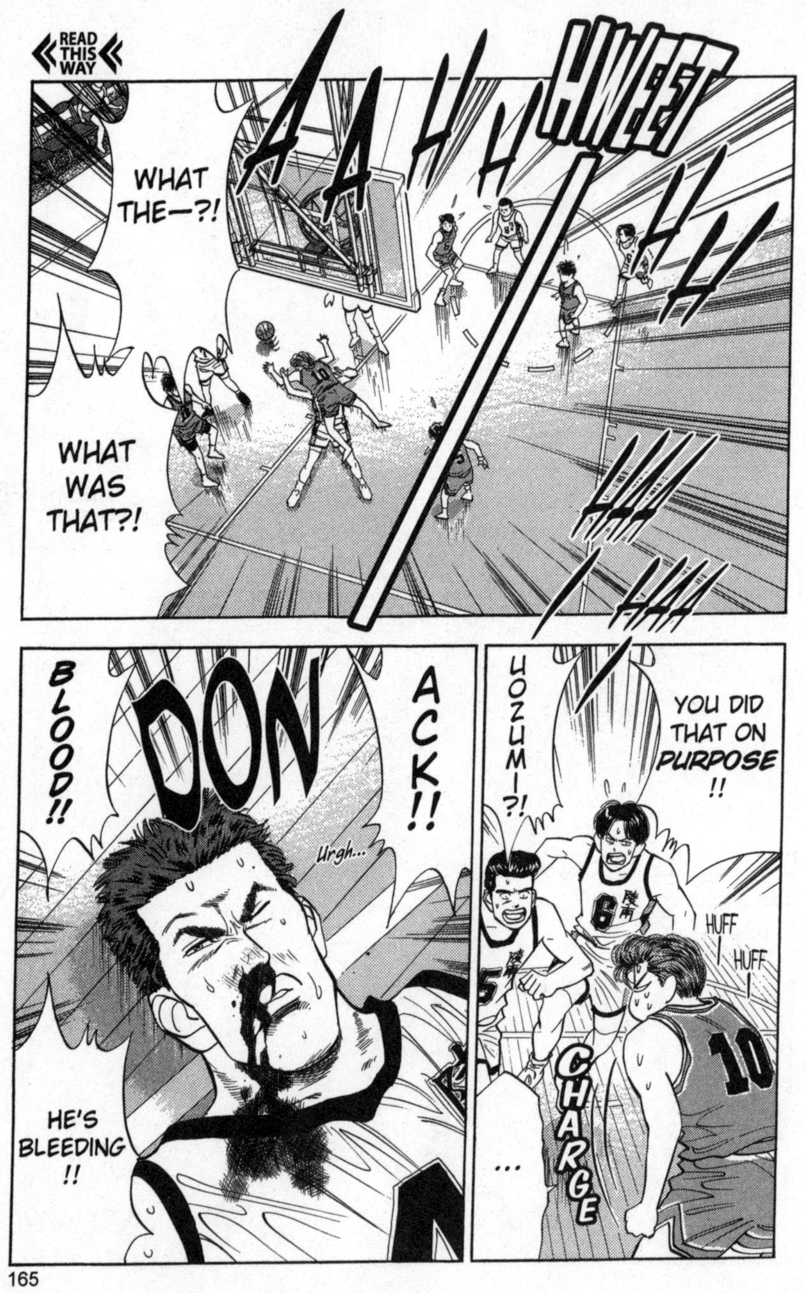

CHWEET
AAHHHHH
HAAA HAA
WHAT THE—?!
WHAT WAS THAT?!
HOZUMI?!
YOU DID THAT ON PURPOSE!!
HUFF HUFF
CHARGE
...
ACK!!
DON
BLOOD!!
Urgh...
HE'S BLEEDING!!

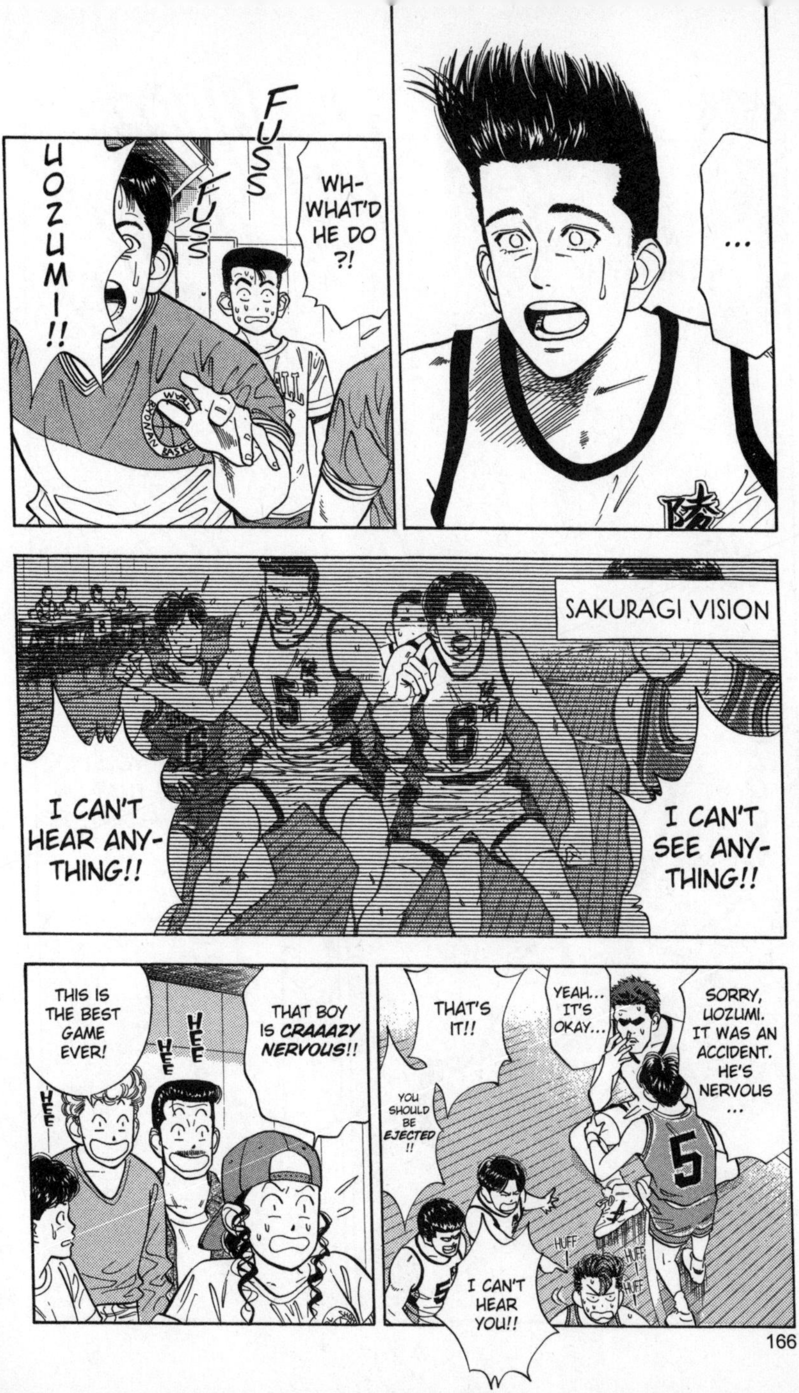
...
UOZUMI!!
FUSS
FUSS
WH-WHAT'D HE DO?!
SAKURAGI VISION
I CAN'T SEE ANYTHING!!
I CAN'T HEAR ANYTHING!!
SORRY, UOZUMI. IT WAS AN ACCIDENT. HE'S NERVOUS...
YEAH... IT'S OKAY...
THAT'S IT!!
YOU SHOULD BE EJECTED!!
HUFF!
HUFF!
HUFF!
I CAN'T HEAR YOU!!
THAT BOY IS CRAAAZY NERVOUS!!
HEE
HEE
HEE
THIS IS THE BEST GAME EVER!

READ THIS WAY

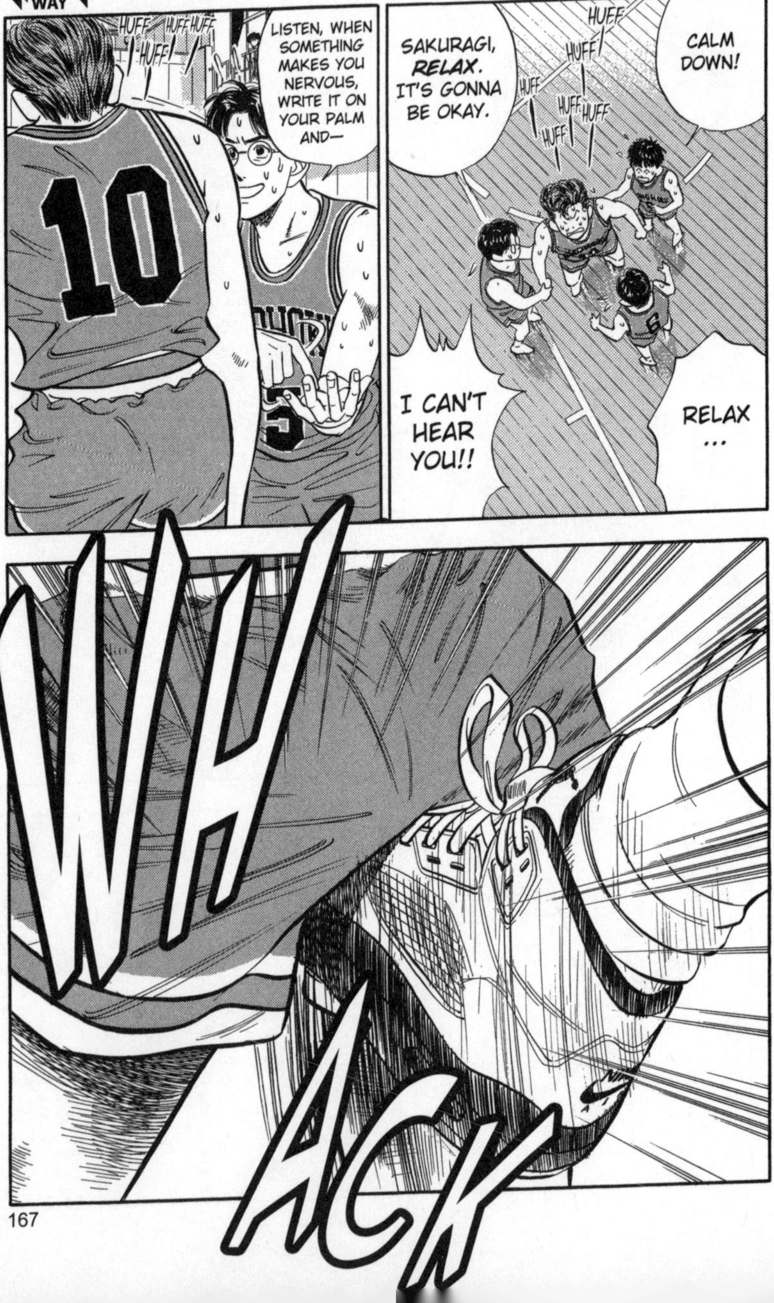

CALM DOWN!
HUFF HUFF HUFF HUFF HUFF HUFF
SAKURAGI, **RELAX**. IT'S GONNA BE OKAY.
RELAX...
I CAN'T HEAR YOU!!
HUFF HUFF HUFF HUFF
LISTEN, WHEN SOMETHING MAKES YOU NERVOUS, WRITE IT ON YOUR PALM AND—
WHACK

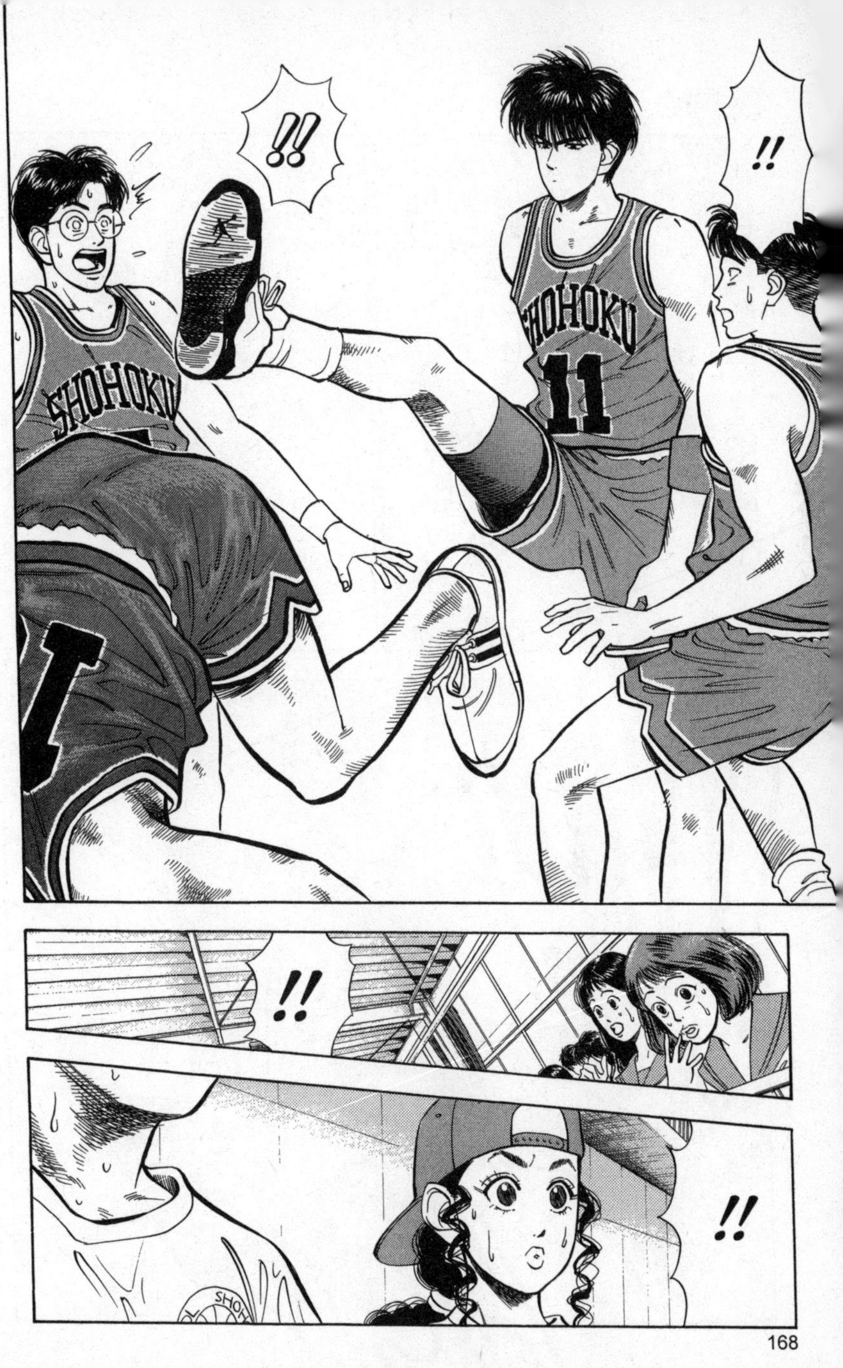
!!
SHOHOKU
11
!!
SHOHOKU
!!
!!

READ THIS WAY

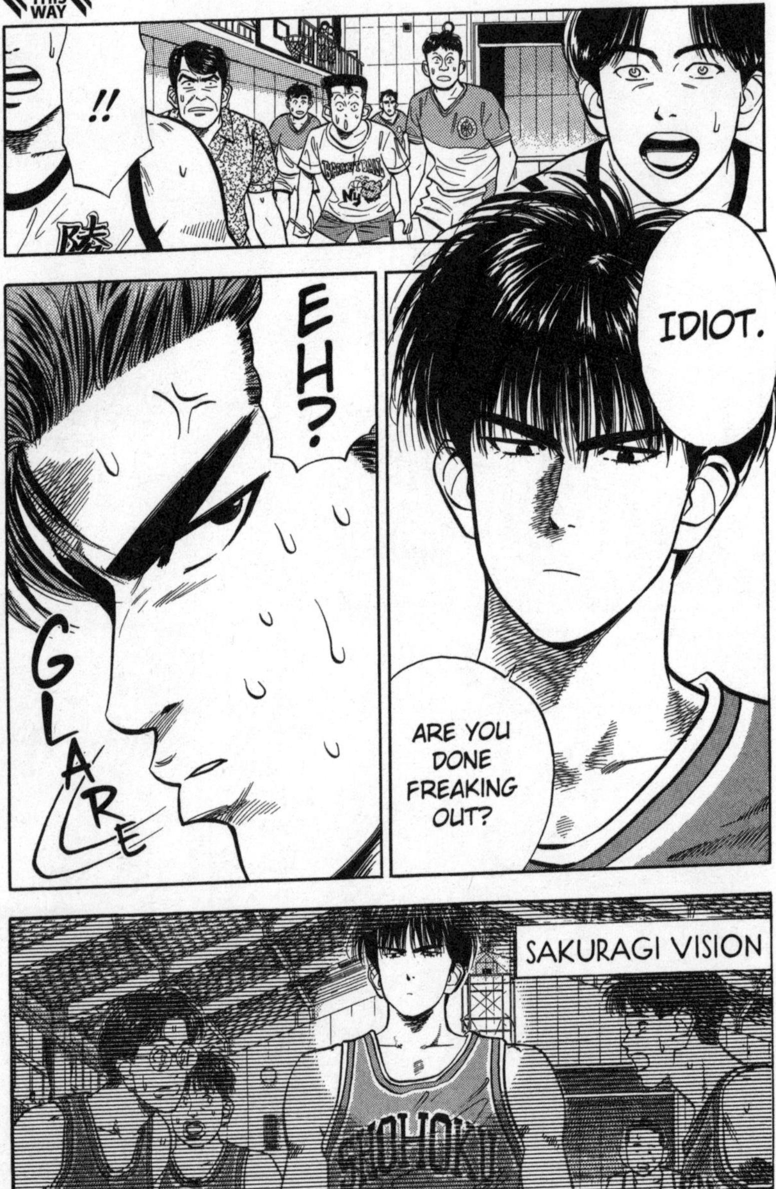
!!
IDIOT.
ARE YOU DONE FREAKING OUT?
EH?
GLARE
SAKURAGI VISION
SHOHOKU

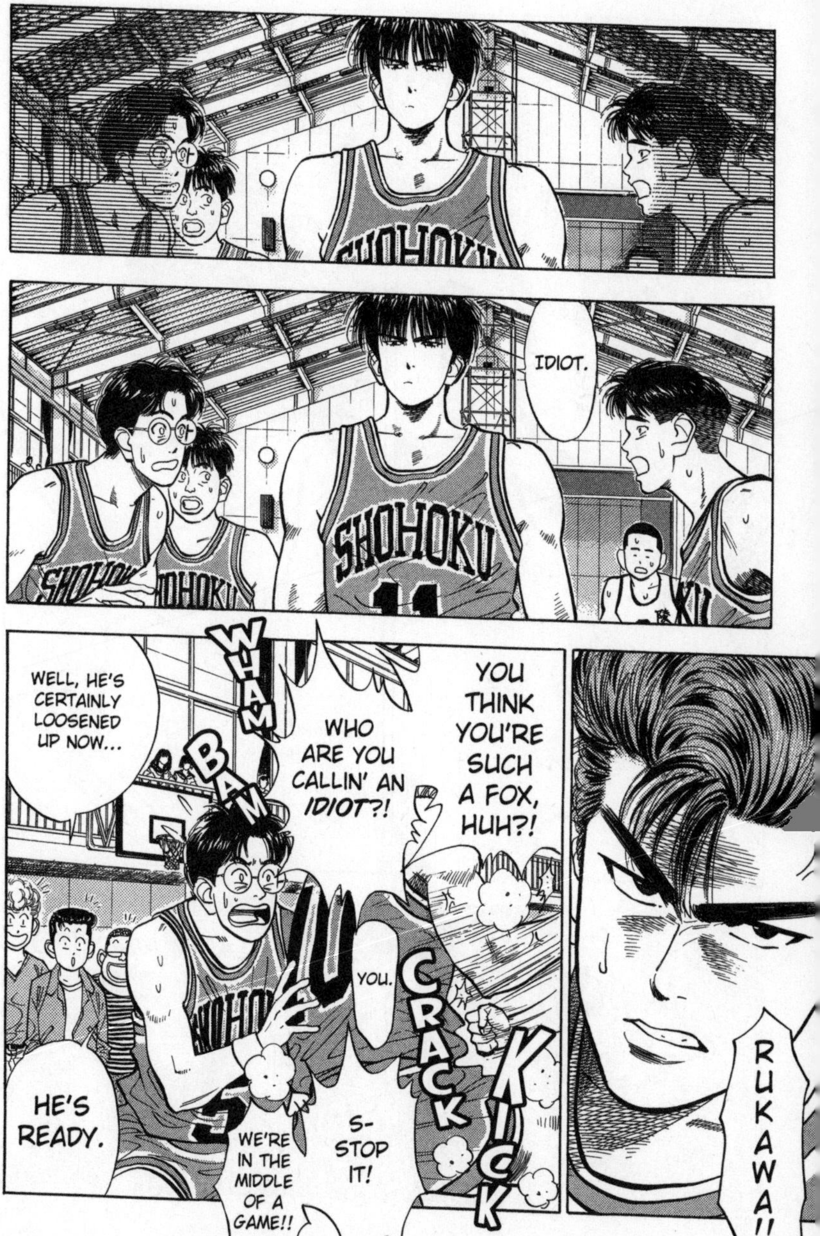
IDIOT.
RUKAWA!!
YOU THINK YOU'RE SUCH A FOX, HUH?!
WHO ARE YOU CALLIN' AN *IDIOT*?!
WHAM
BAM
WELL, HE'S CERTAINLY LOOSENED UP NOW...
YOU.
CRACK
KICK
S-STOP IT!
WE'RE IN THE MIDDLE OF A GAME!!
HE'S READY.

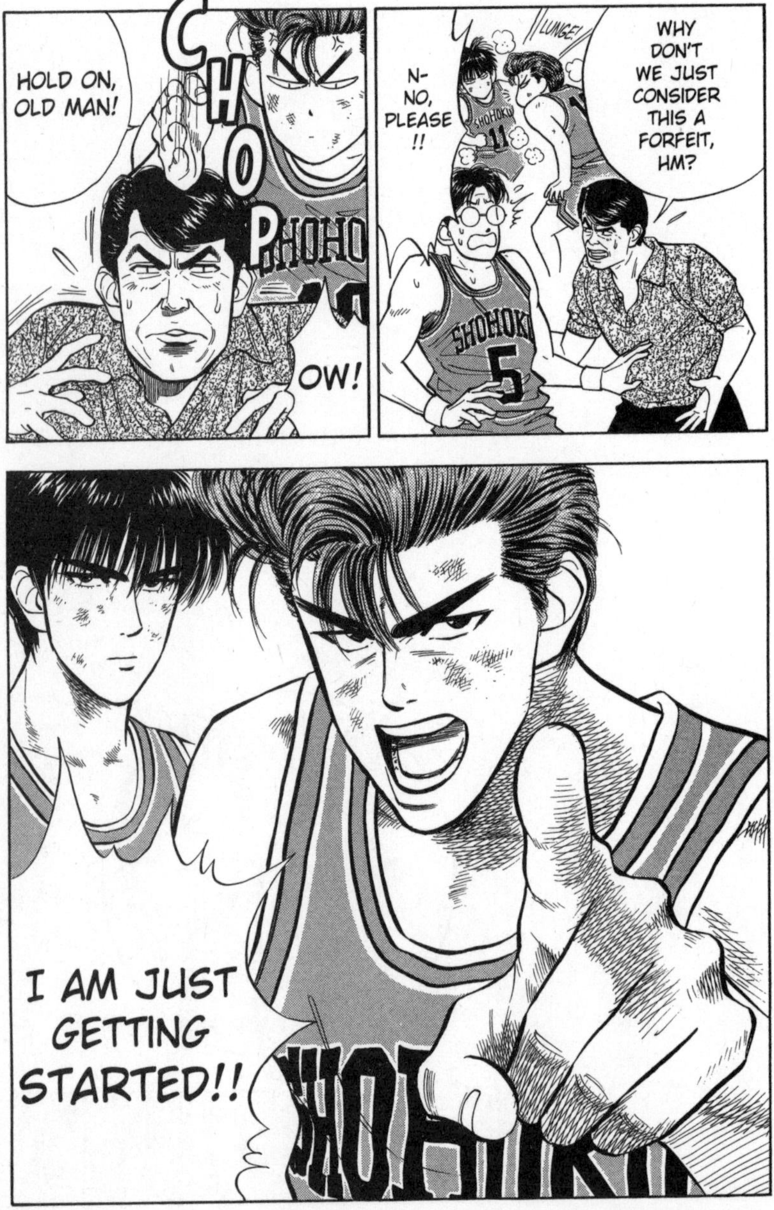
LUNGE!
WHY DON'T WE JUST CONSIDER THIS A FORFEIT, HM?
N-NO, PLEASE!!
CHOP
HOLD ON, OLD MAN!
OW!
I AM JUST GETTING STARTED!!

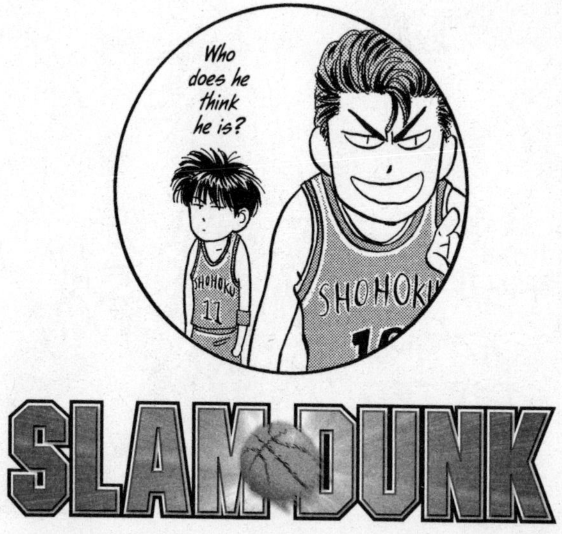
Who does he think he is?
SHOHOKU
11
SHOHOKU

SLAM DUNK

#35 WHO IS THIS GUY?

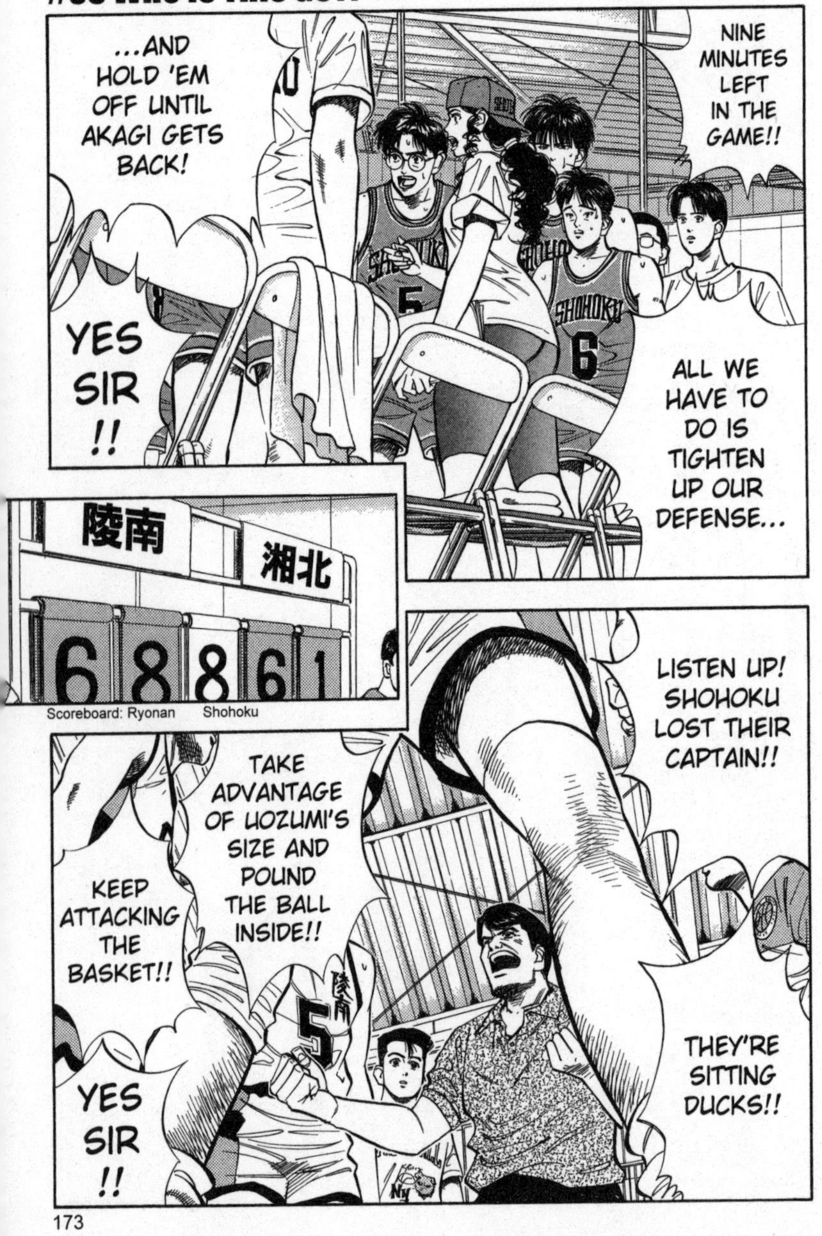
NINE MINUTES LEFT IN THE GAME!!
ALL WE HAVE TO DO IS TIGHTEN UP OUR DEFENSE...
...AND HOLD 'EM OFF UNTIL AKAGI GETS BACK!
YES SIR!!
陵南
湘北
6 8 8 6 1
Scoreboard: Ryonan Shohoku
LISTEN UP! SHOHOKU LOST THEIR CAPTAIN!!
THEY'RE SITTING DUCKS!!
TAKE ADVANTAGE OF UOZUMI'S SIZE AND POUND THE BALL INSIDE!!
KEEP ATTACKING THE BASKET!!
YES SIR!!

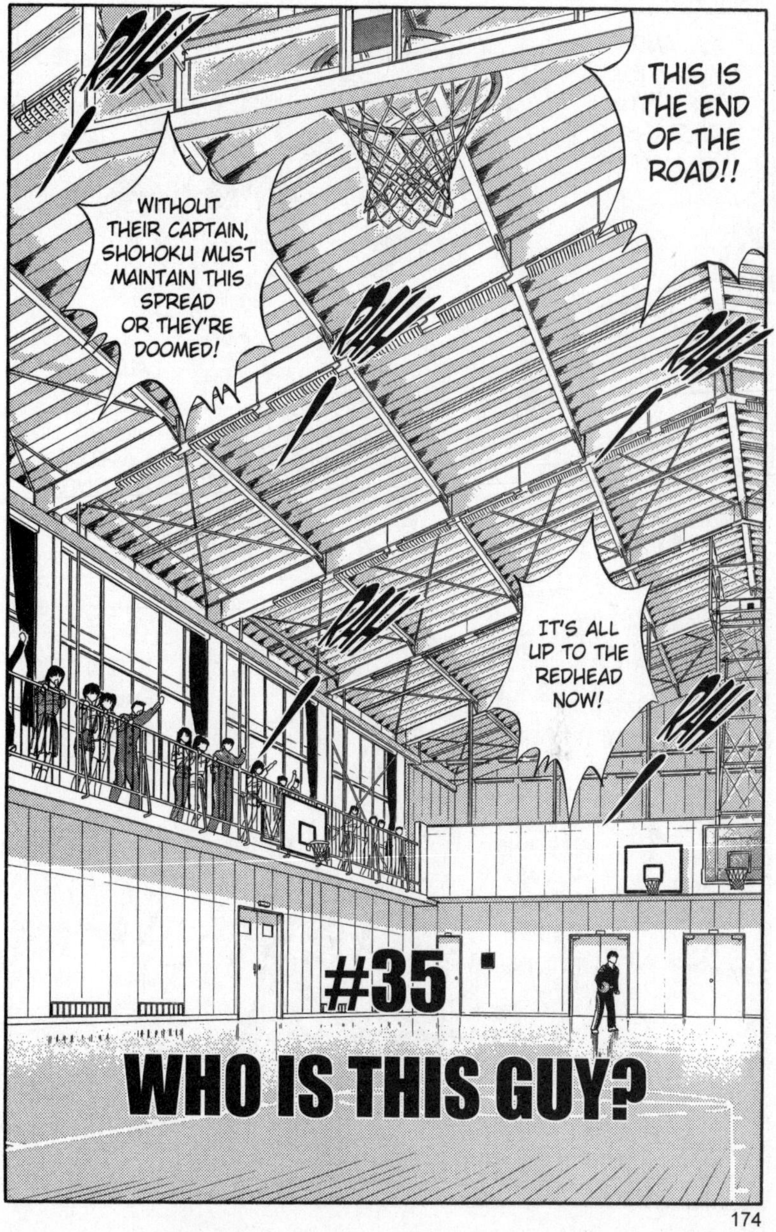
THIS IS THE END OF THE ROAD!!
RAH
RAH
WITHOUT THEIR CAPTAIN, SHOHOKU MUST MAINTAIN THIS SPREAD OR THEY'RE DOOMED!
RAH
IT'S ALL UP TO THE REDHEAD NOW!
RAH
RAH

#35 WHO IS THIS GUY?

READ THIS WAY

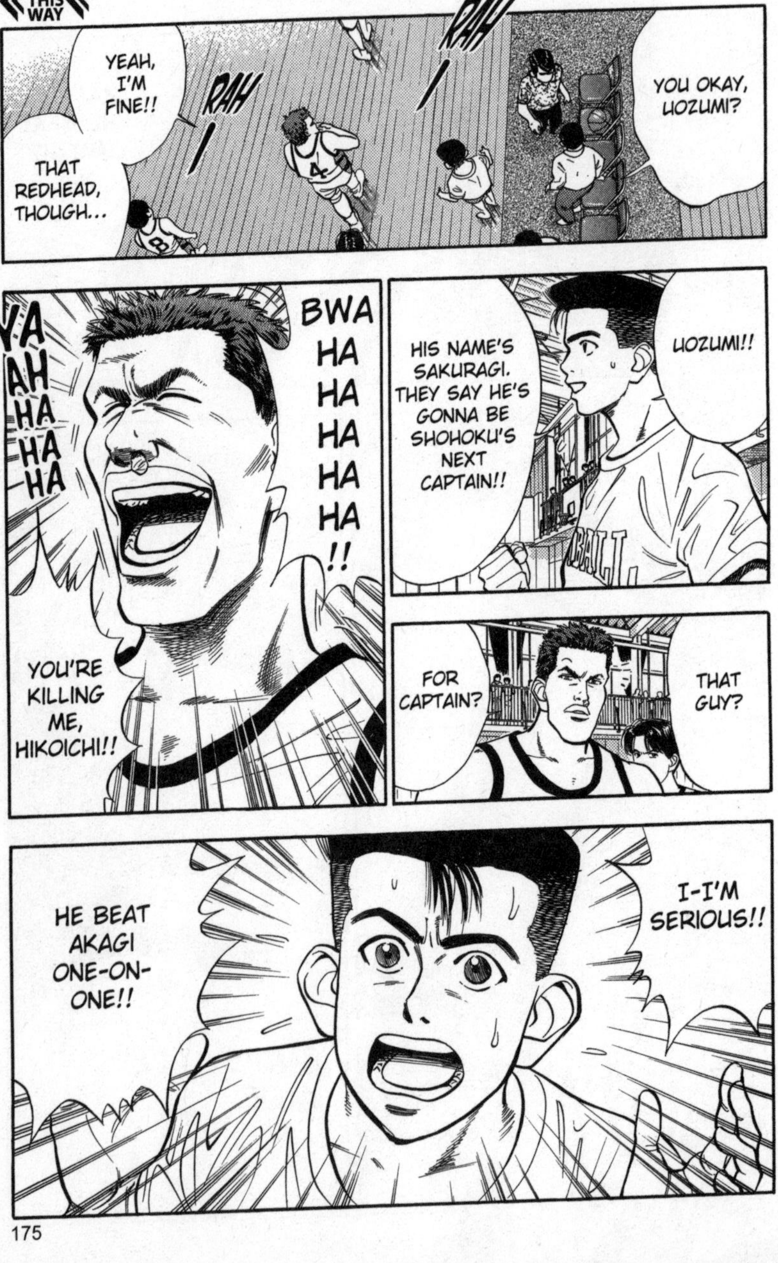

YOU OKAY, UOZUMI?
RAH—
RAH—
YEAH, I'M FINE!!
THAT REDHEAD, THOUGH...
UOZUMI!!
HIS NAME'S SAKURAGI. THEY SAY HE'S GONNA BE SHOHOKU'S NEXT CAPTAIN!!
THAT GUY?
FOR CAPTAIN?
BWA HA HA HA HA HA!!
YA AH HA HA HA HA
YOU'RE KILLING ME, HIKOICHI!!
I-I'M SERIOUS!!
HE BEAT AKAGI ONE-ON-ONE!!

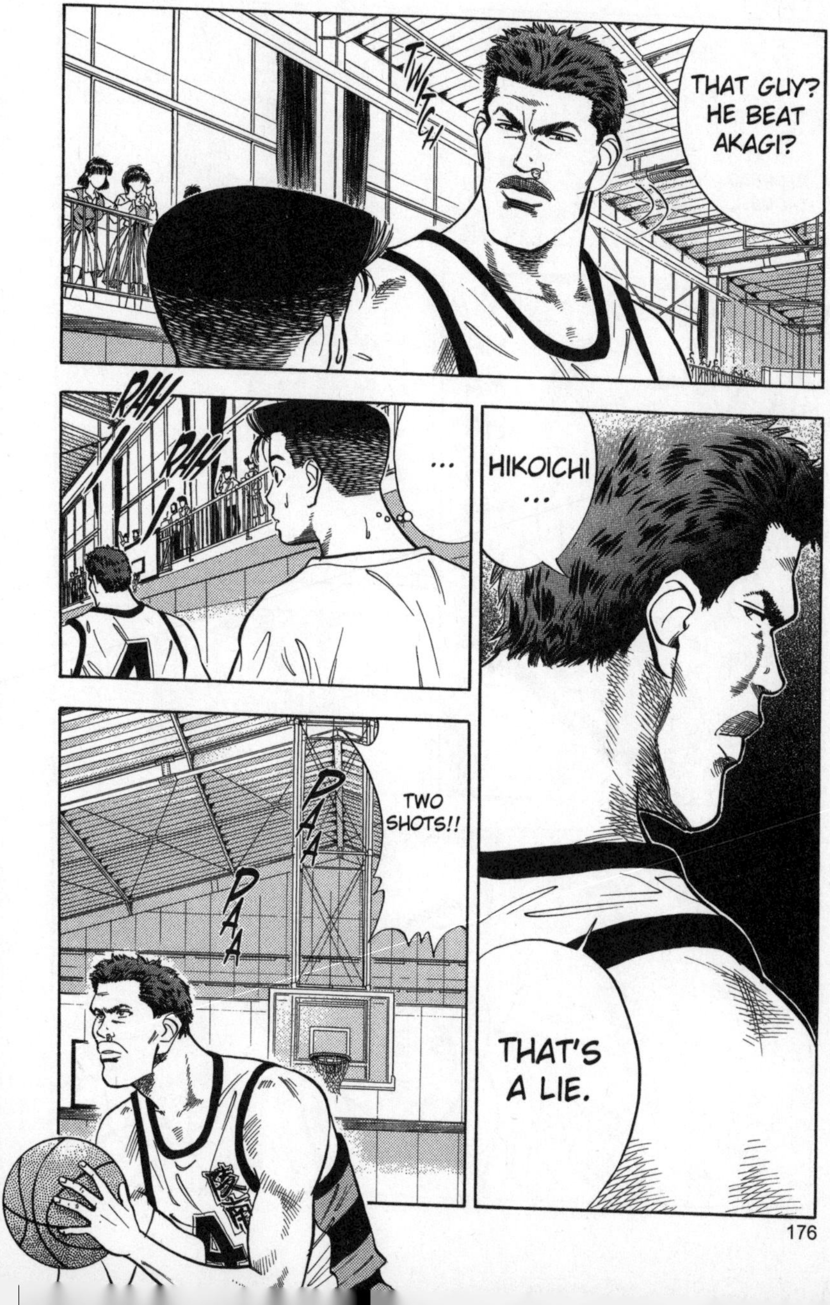
TWITCH
THAT GUY? HE BEAT AKAGI?
HIKOICHI ...
THAT'S A LIE.
...
RAH RAH
TWO SHOTS!!
PAA PAA

READ THIS WAY

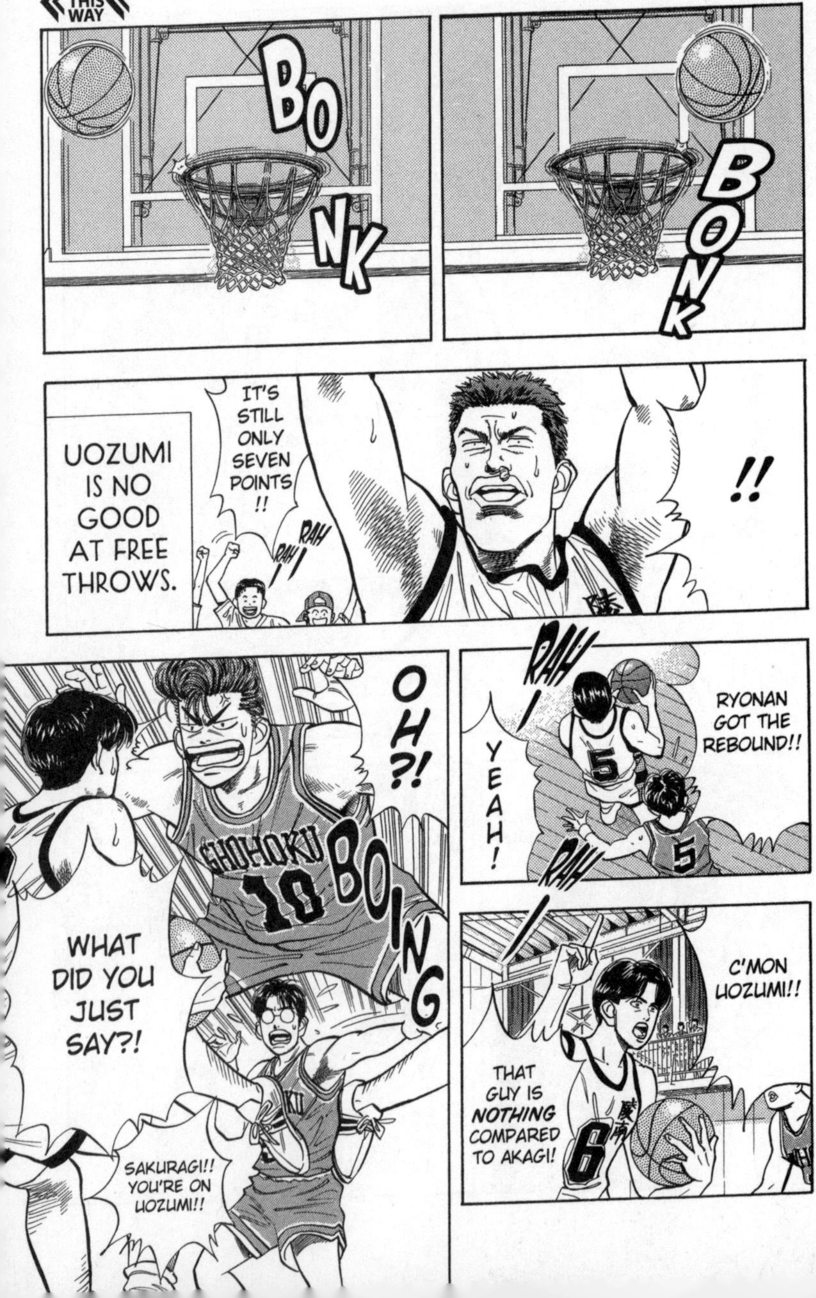
BONK
BONK
!!
IT'S STILL ONLY SEVEN POINTS!!
RAH RAH!
UOZUMI IS NO GOOD AT FREE THROWS.
RAH!
RYONAN GOT THE REBOUND!!
YEAH!
RAH!
C'MON UOZUMI!!
THAT GUY IS ***NOTHING*** COMPARED TO AKAGI!
OH?!
BOING
WHAT DID YOU JUST SAY?!
SAKURAGI!! YOU'RE ON UOZUMI!!

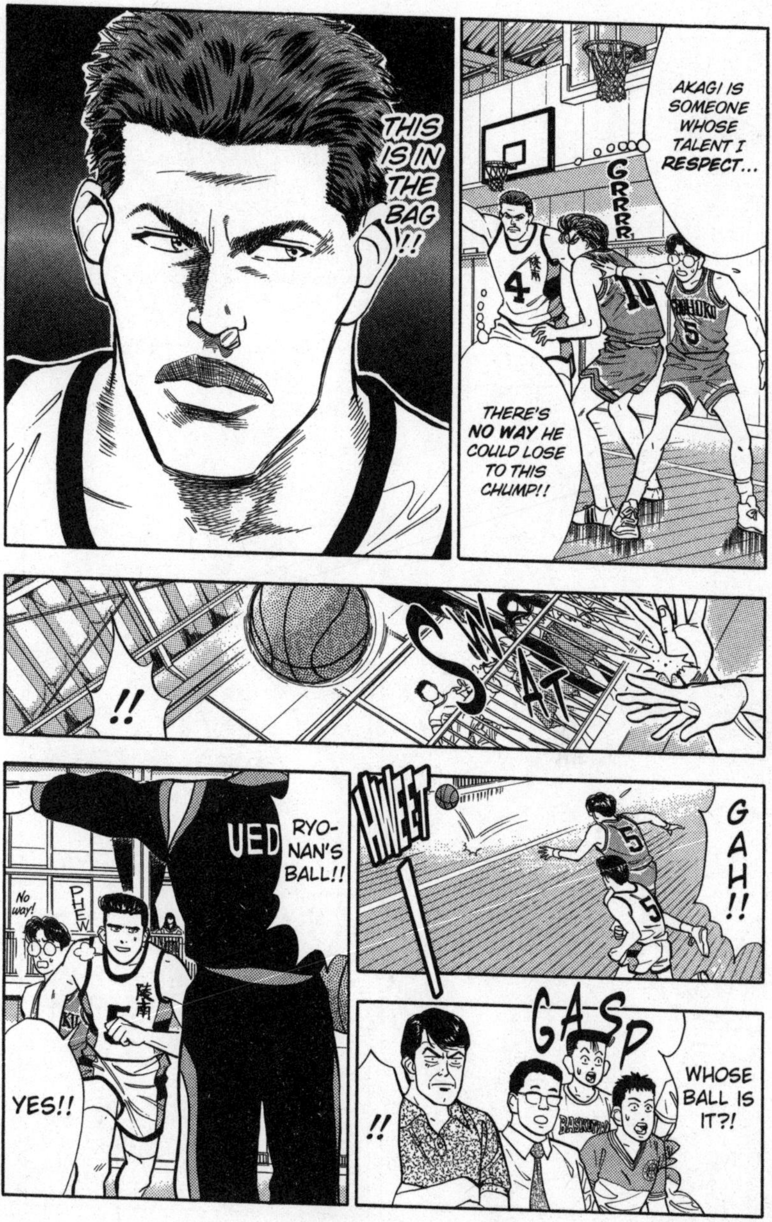

AKAGI IS SOMEONE WHOSE TALENT I RESPECT...
GRRRR
THERE'S NO WAY HE COULD LOSE TO THIS CHUMP!!
THIS IS IN THE BAG!!
SWAT
!!
HWEET
GAH!!
GASP
WHOSE BALL IS IT?!
!!
RYO-NAN'S BALL!!
UED
PHEW
No way!
YES!!

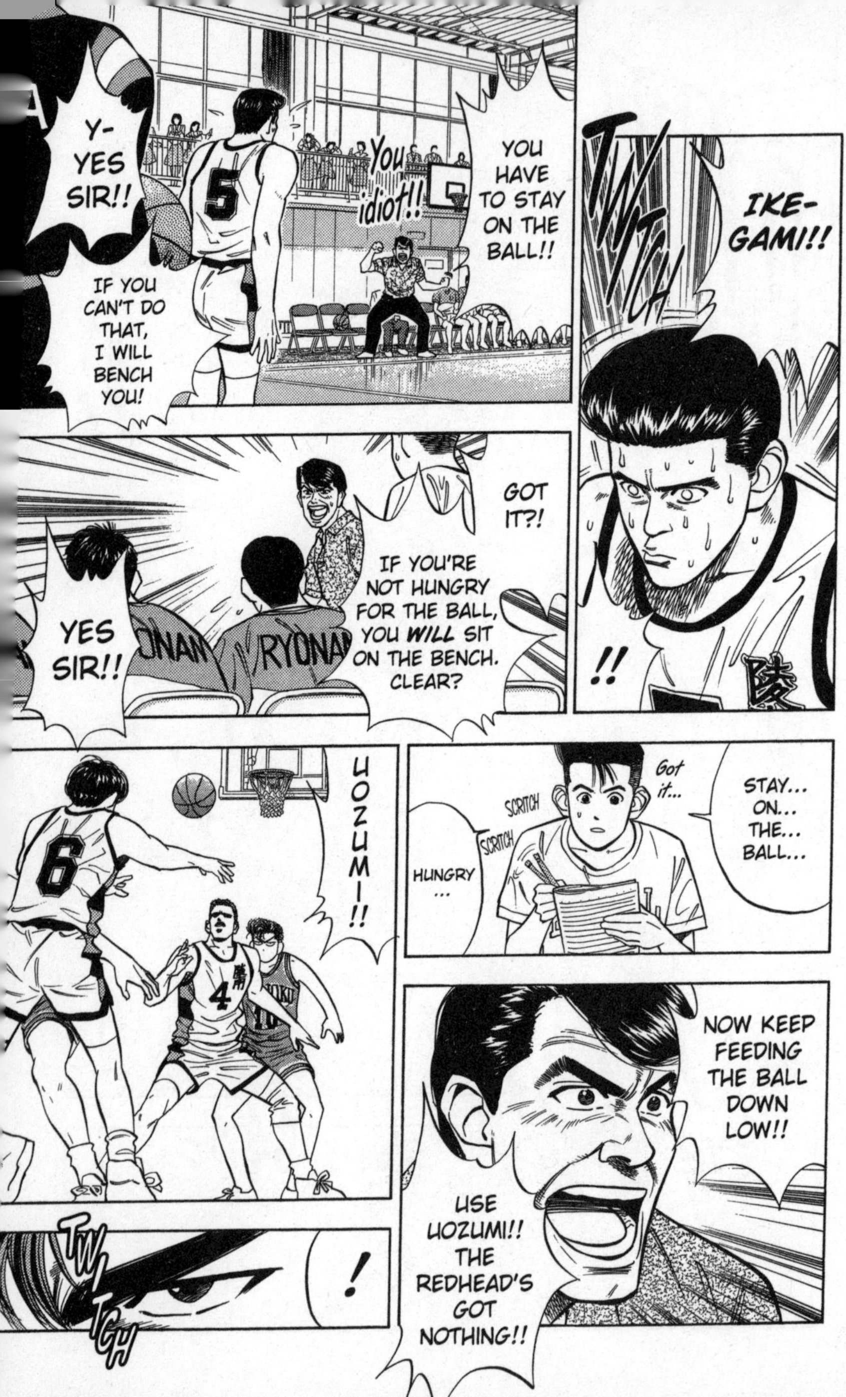
TWITCH
IKE-GAMI!!
!!
You idiot!!
YOU HAVE TO STAY ON THE BALL!!
Y-YES SIR!!
IF YOU CAN'T DO THAT, I WILL BENCH YOU!
GOT IT?!
IF YOU'RE NOT HUNGRY FOR THE BALL, YOU *WILL* SIT ON THE BENCH. CLEAR?
RYONAN
RYONAN
YES SIR!!
STAY... ON... THE... BALL...
Got it...
SCRITCH
SCRITCH
HUNGRY ...
UOZUMI!!
NOW KEEP FEEDING THE BALL DOWN LOW!!
USE UOZUMI!! THE REDHEAD'S GOT NOTHING!!
!
TWITCH

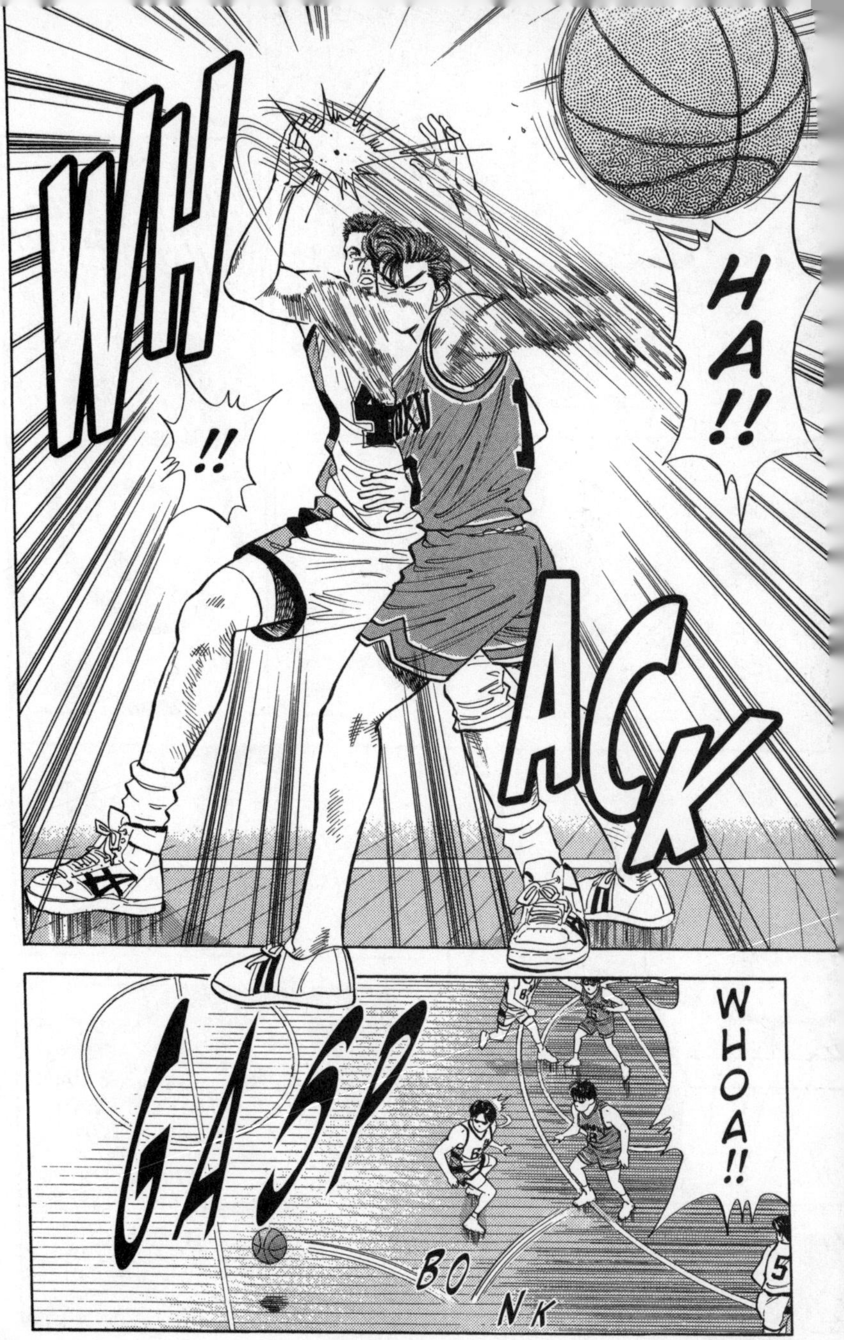
HA!!
WH
!!
ACK
WHOA!!
GASP
BO
NK

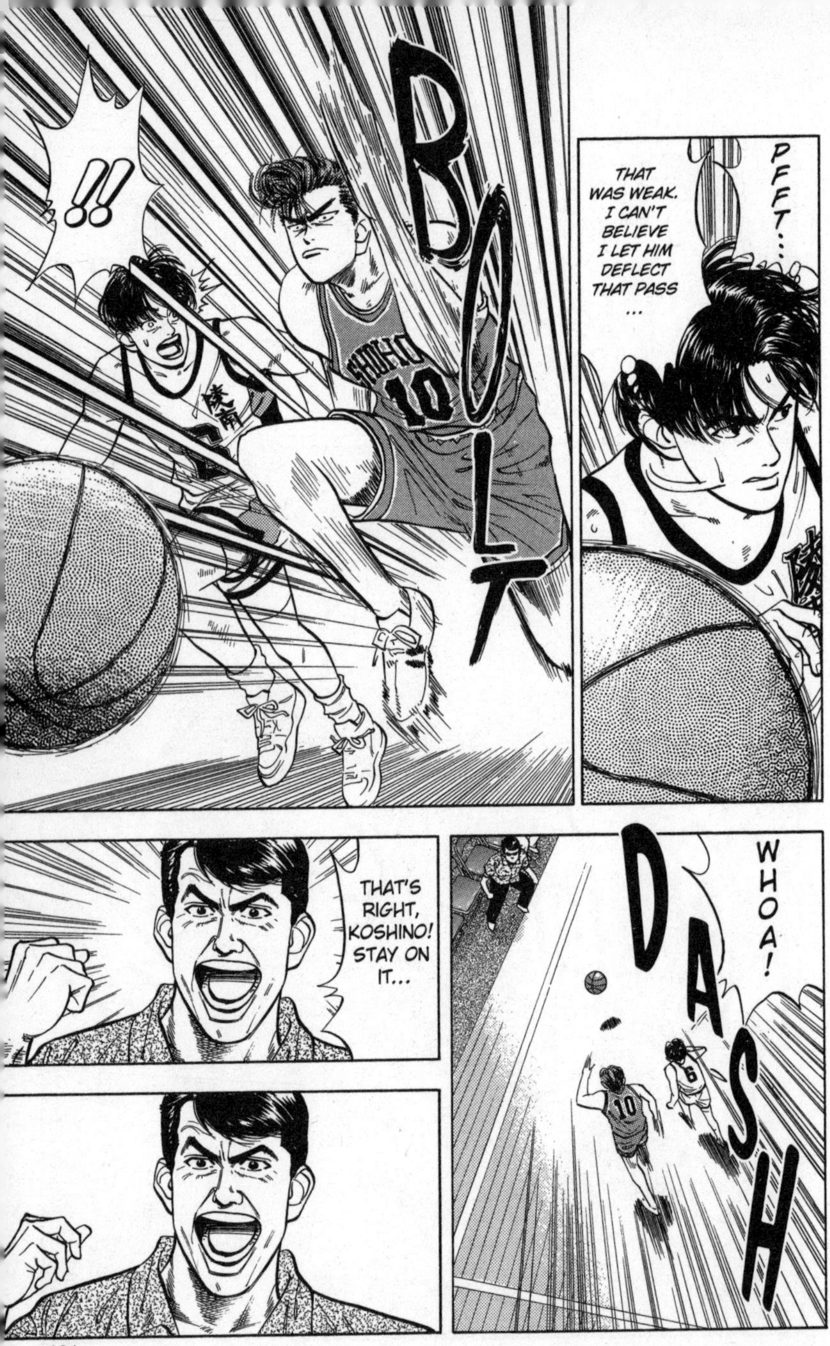
PFFT...
THAT WAS WEAK. I CAN'T BELIEVE I LET HIM DEFLECT THAT PASS ...
BOLT
!!
WHOA!
DASH
THAT'S RIGHT, KOSHINO! STAY ON IT...

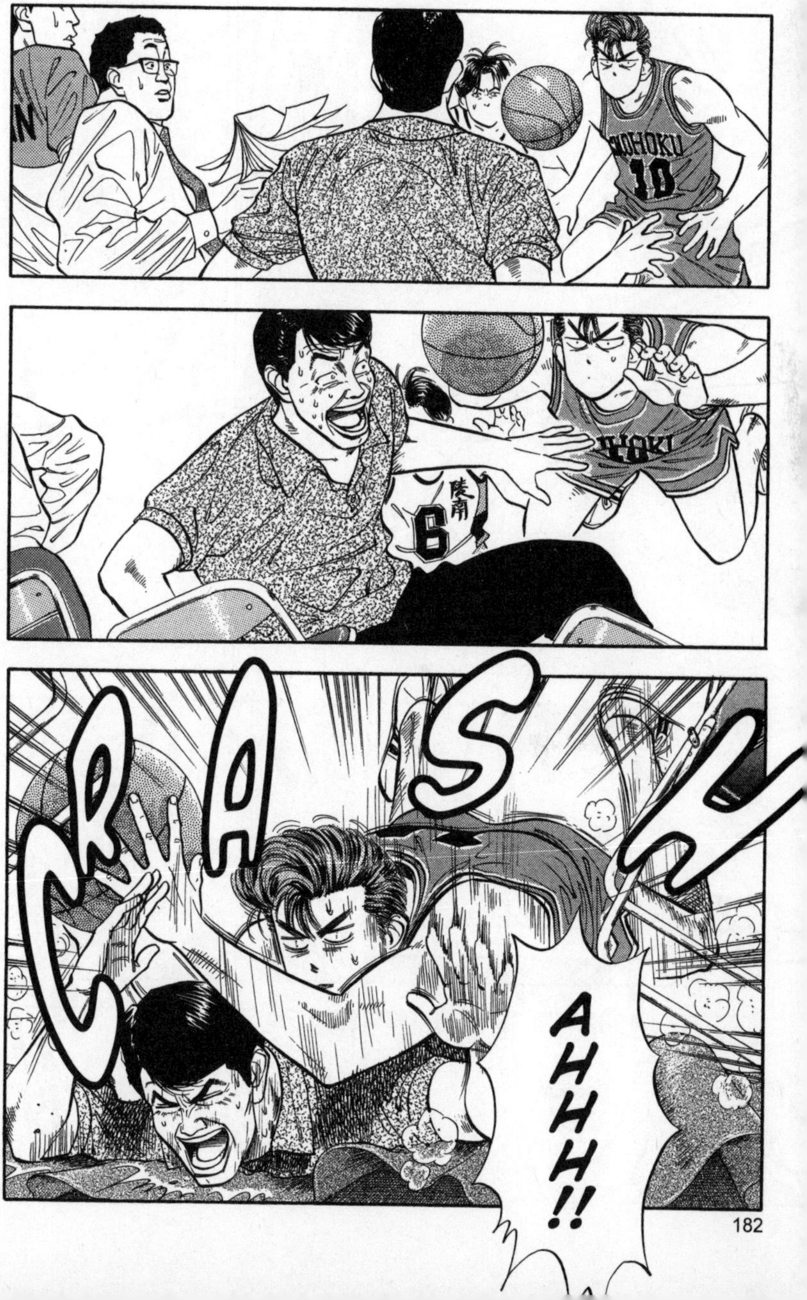
CRASH
AHHHH!!

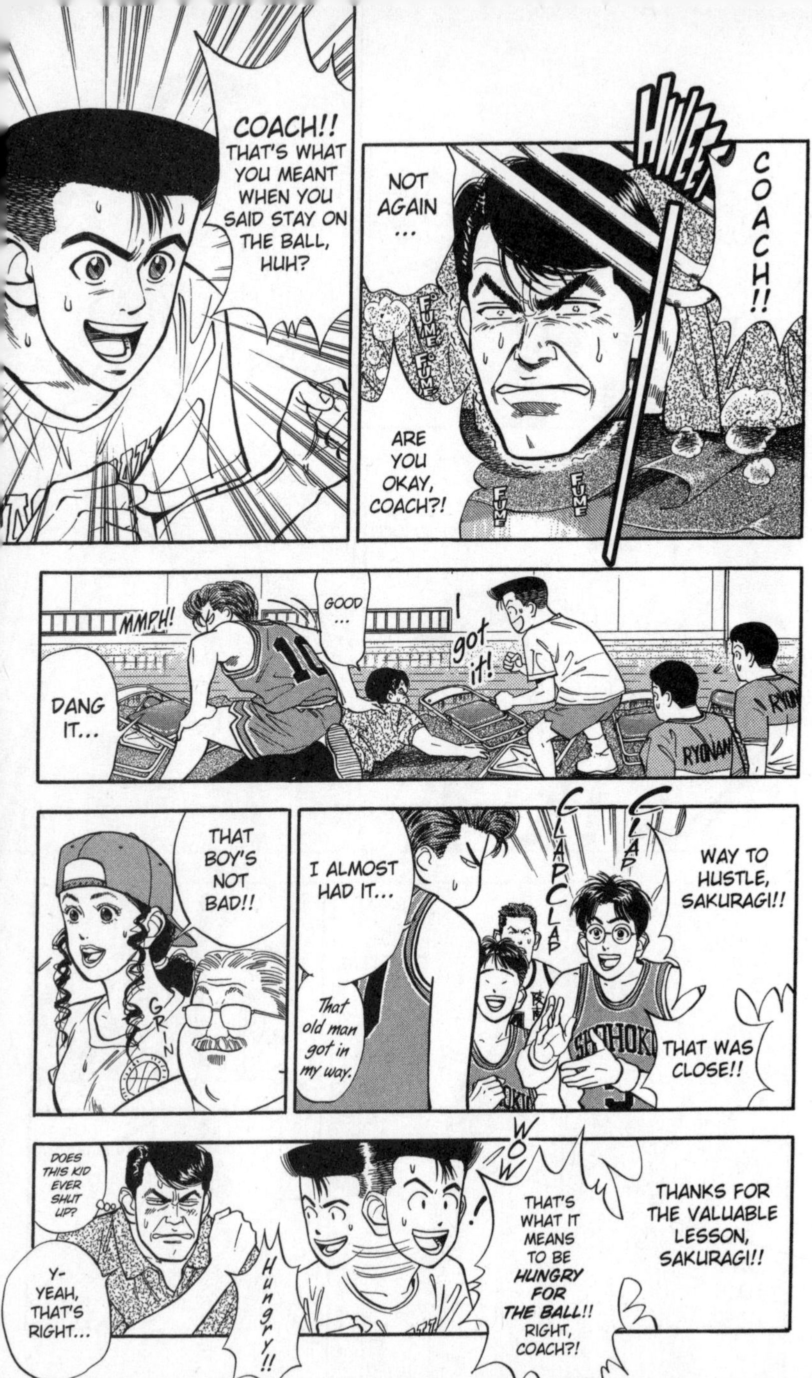
HWEE
COACH!!
NOT AGAIN ...
FUME FUME
ARE YOU OKAY, COACH?!
FUME FUME
COACH!! THAT'S WHAT YOU MEANT WHEN YOU SAID STAY ON THE BALL, HUH?
I got it!
GOOD ...
MMPH!
DANG IT...
CLAP CLAP
WAY TO HUSTLE, SAKURAGI!!
I ALMOST HAD IT...
THAT WAS CLOSE!!
That old man got in my way.
THAT BOY'S NOT BAD!!
GRIN
THANKS FOR THE VALUABLE LESSON, SAKURAGI!!
WOW
THAT'S WHAT IT MEANS TO BE HUNGRY FOR THE BALL!! RIGHT, COACH?!
!
Hungry!!
DOES THIS KID EVER SHUT UP?
Y-YEAH, THAT'S RIGHT...

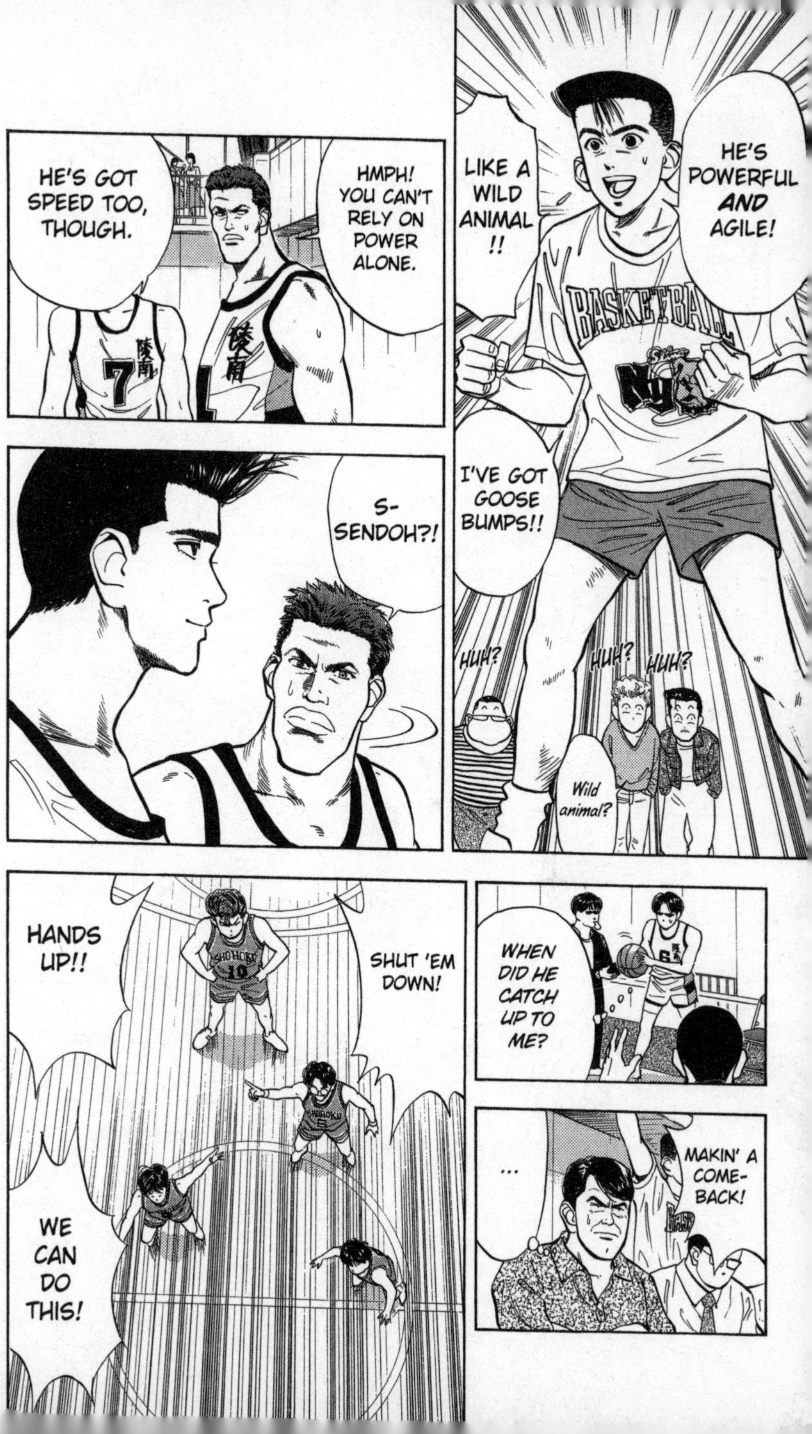
HE'S POWERFUL AND AGILE!
LIKE A WILD ANIMAL!!
I'VE GOT GOOSE BUMPS!!
HUH?
HUH?
HUH?
Wild animal?
HMPH! YOU CAN'T RELY ON POWER ALONE.
HE'S GOT SPEED TOO, THOUGH.
S- SENDOH?!
WHEN DID HE CATCH UP TO ME?
MAKIN' A COME-BACK!
...
SHUT 'EM DOWN!
HANDS UP!!
WE CAN DO THIS!

READ THIS WAY

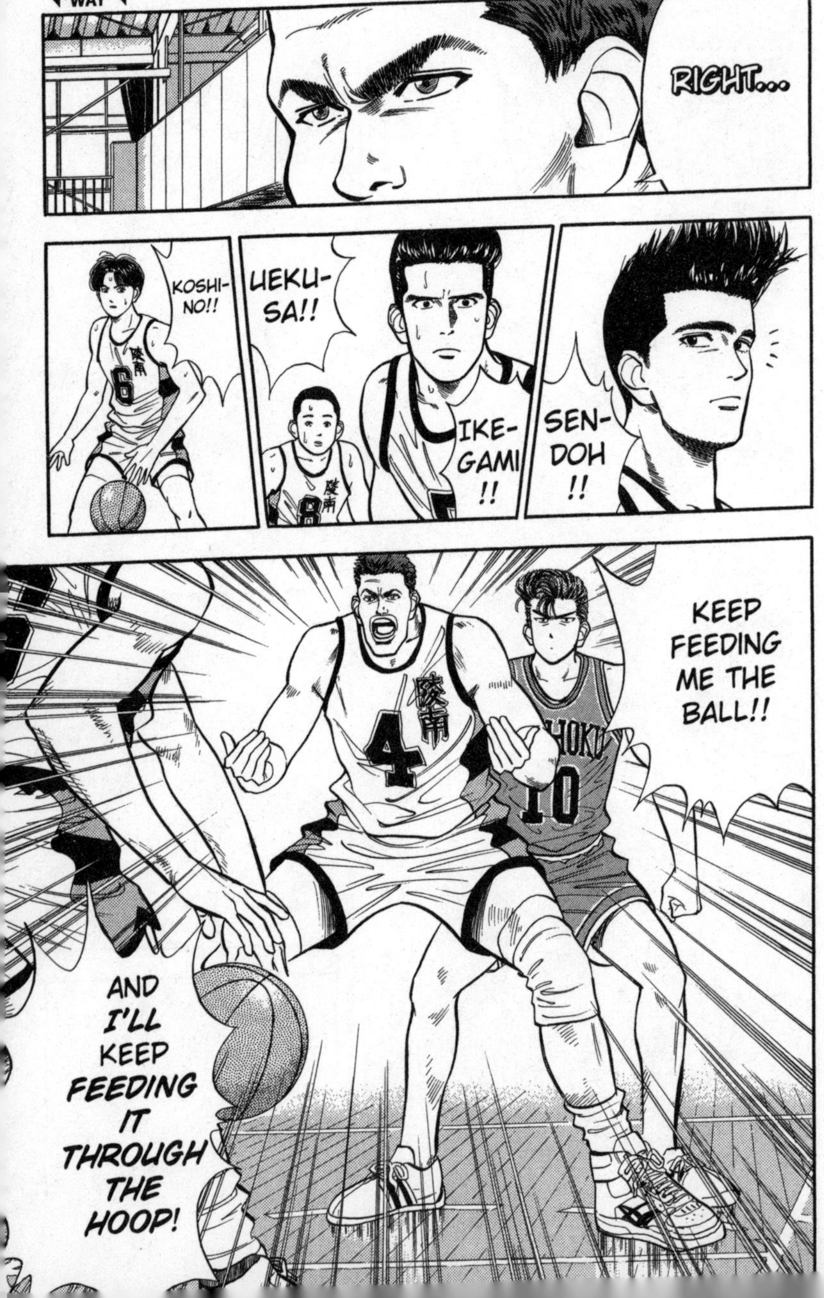
RIGHT...
SEN-DOH!!
IKE-GAMI!!
UEKU-SA!!
KOSHI-NO!!
KEEP FEEDING ME THE BALL!!
AND I'LL KEEP FEEDING IT THROUGH THE HOOP!

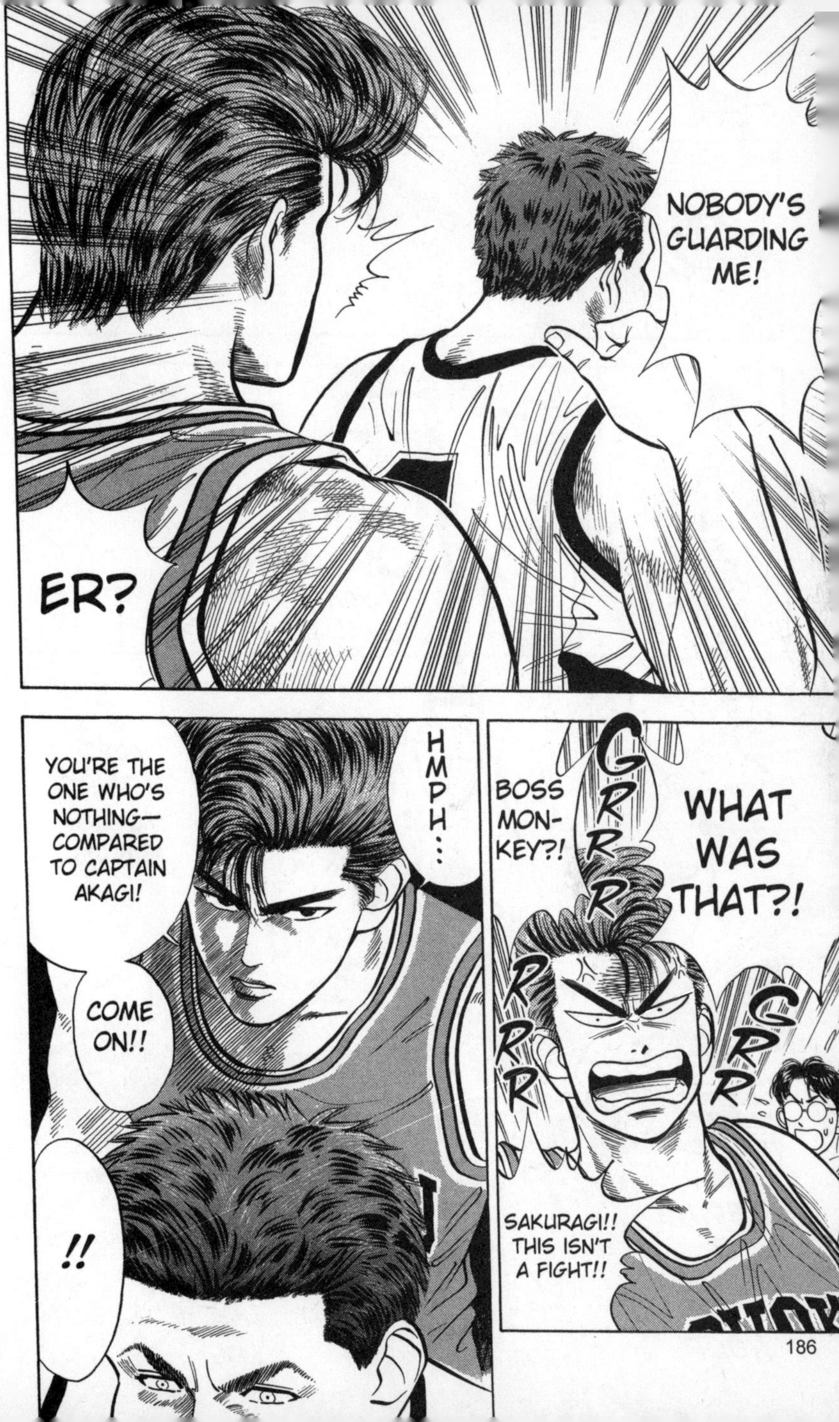

NOBODY'S GUARDING ME!
ER?
WHAT WAS THAT?!
BOSS MONKEY?!
GRRRR
RRRR
GRRR
SAKURAGI!! THIS ISN'T A FIGHT!!
HMPH...
YOU'RE THE ONE WHO'S NOTHING—COMPARED TO CAPTAIN AKAGI!
COME ON!!
!!

READ THIS WAY

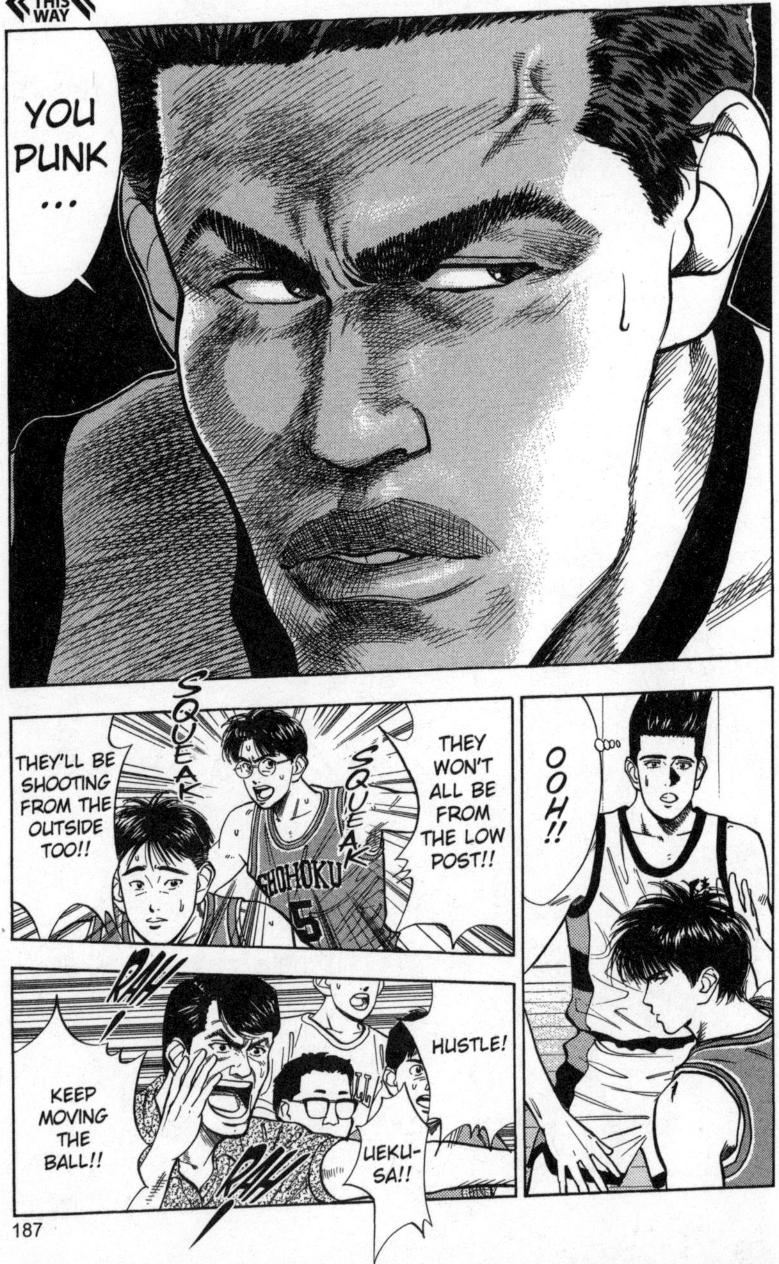
YOU PUNK...
OOH!!
SQUEAK
SQUEAK
THEY WON'T ALL BE FROM THE LOW POST!!
THEY'LL BE SHOOTING FROM THE OUTSIDE TOO!!
SHOHOKU
HUSTLE!
RAH!
KEEP MOVING THE BALL!!
UEKU-SA!!
RAH

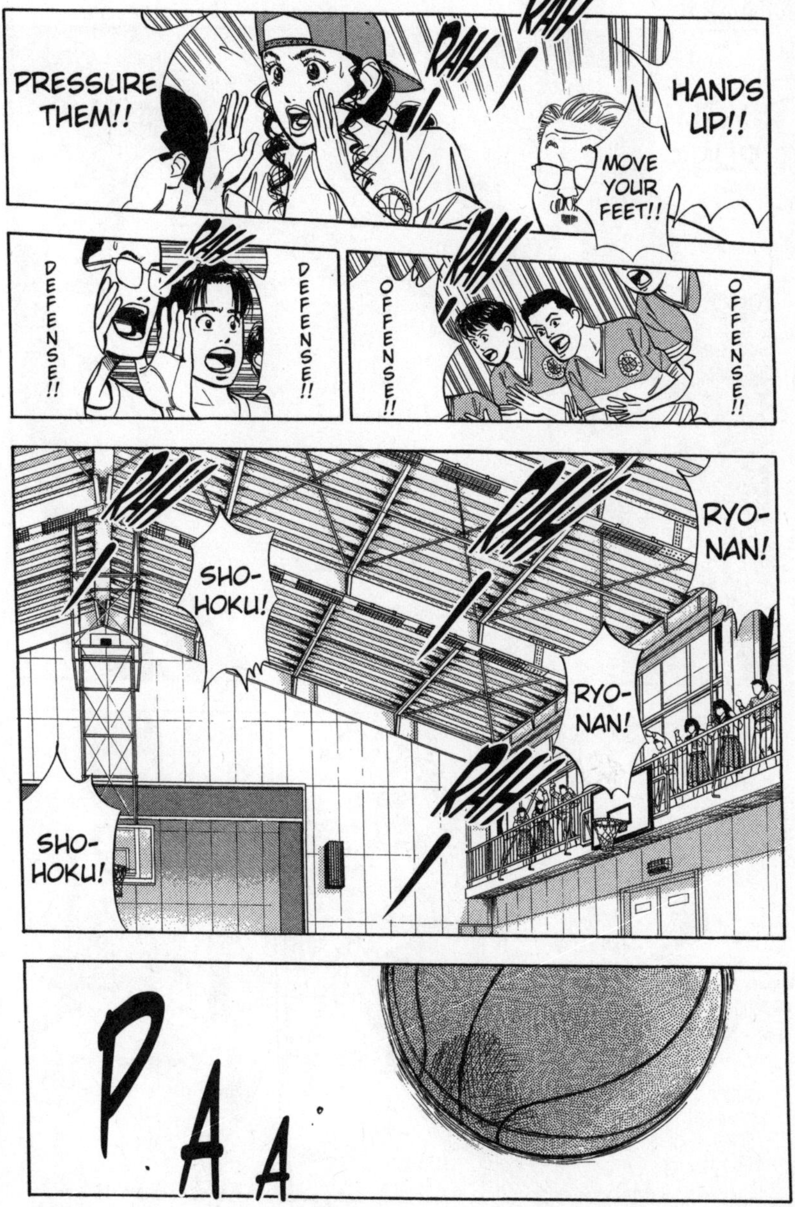
RAH RAH!
HANDS UP!!
MOVE YOUR FEET!!
PRESSURE THEM!!
RAH!
OFFENSE!!
OFFENSE!!
DEFENSE!!
RAH!
DEFENSE!!
RYO-NAN!
RAH!
RYO-NAN!
RAH!
SHO-HOKU!
RAH!
SHO-HOKU!
PAAA

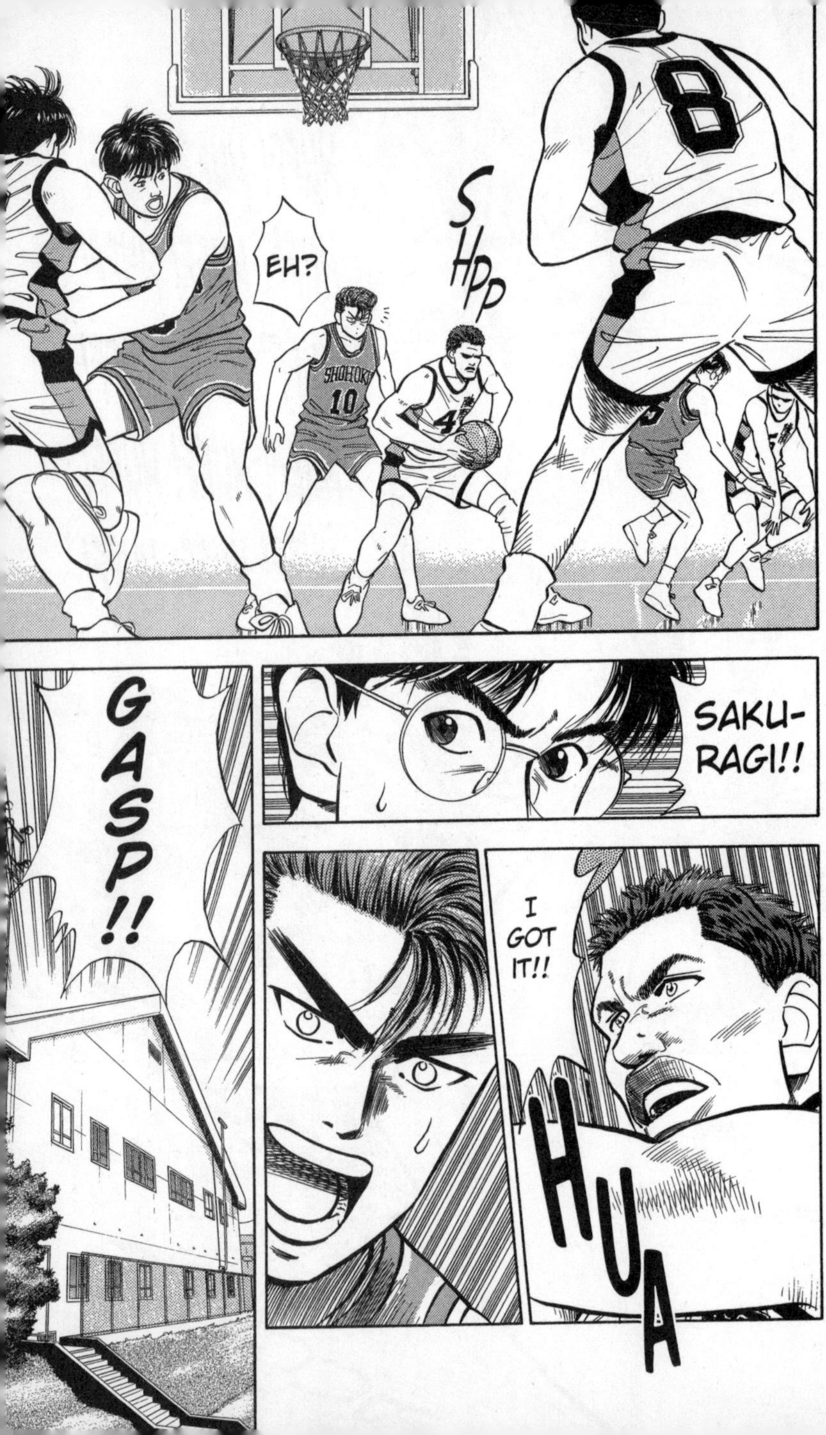
SHPP
EH?
SAKU-RAGI!!
I GOT IT!!
HUA
GASP!!

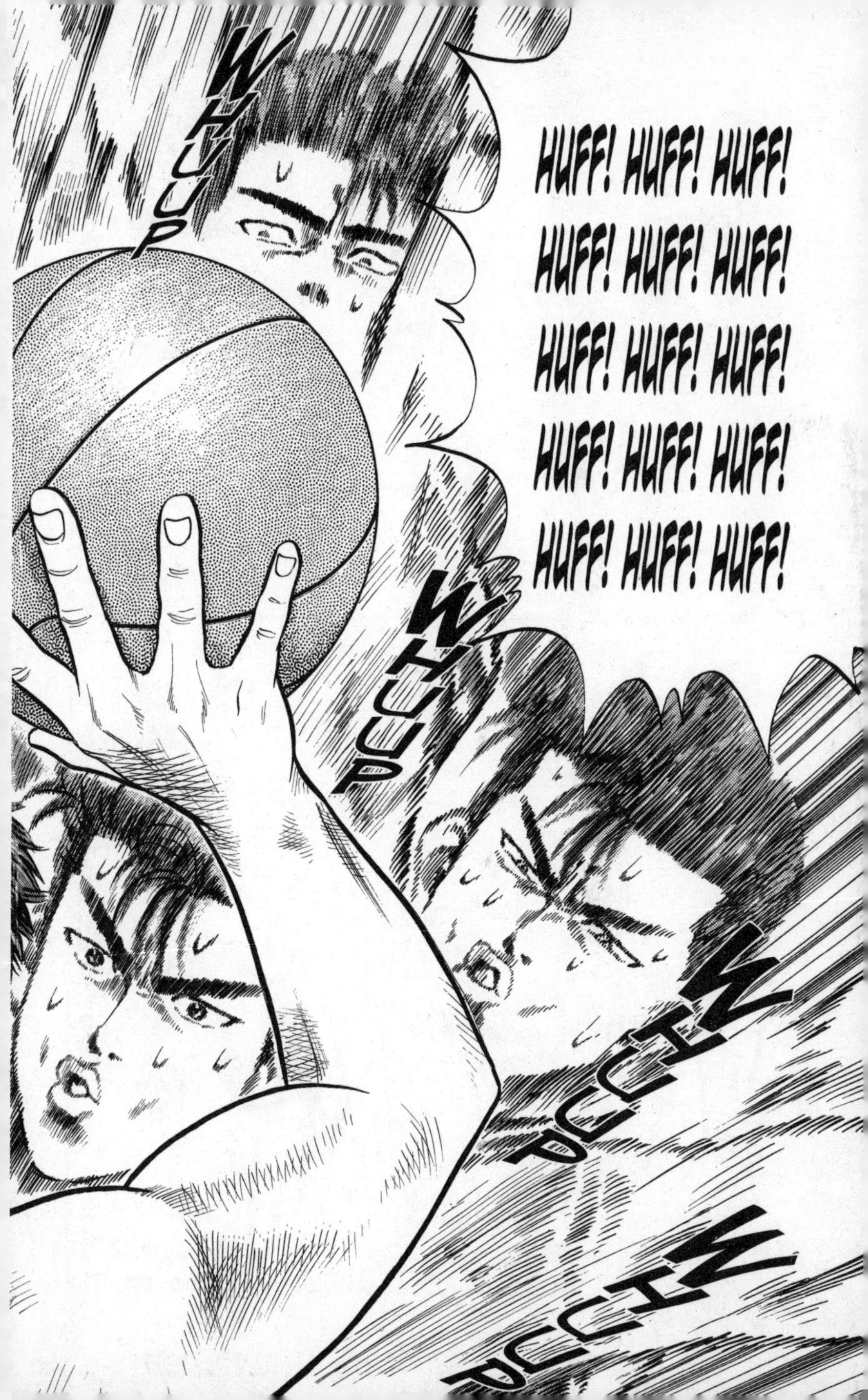

HUFF! HUFF! HUFF!
HUFF! HUFF! HUFF!
HUFF! HUFF! HUFF!
HUFF! HUFF! HUFF!
HUFF! HUFF! HUFF!
WHUUP
WHUUP
WHUUP
WHUUP

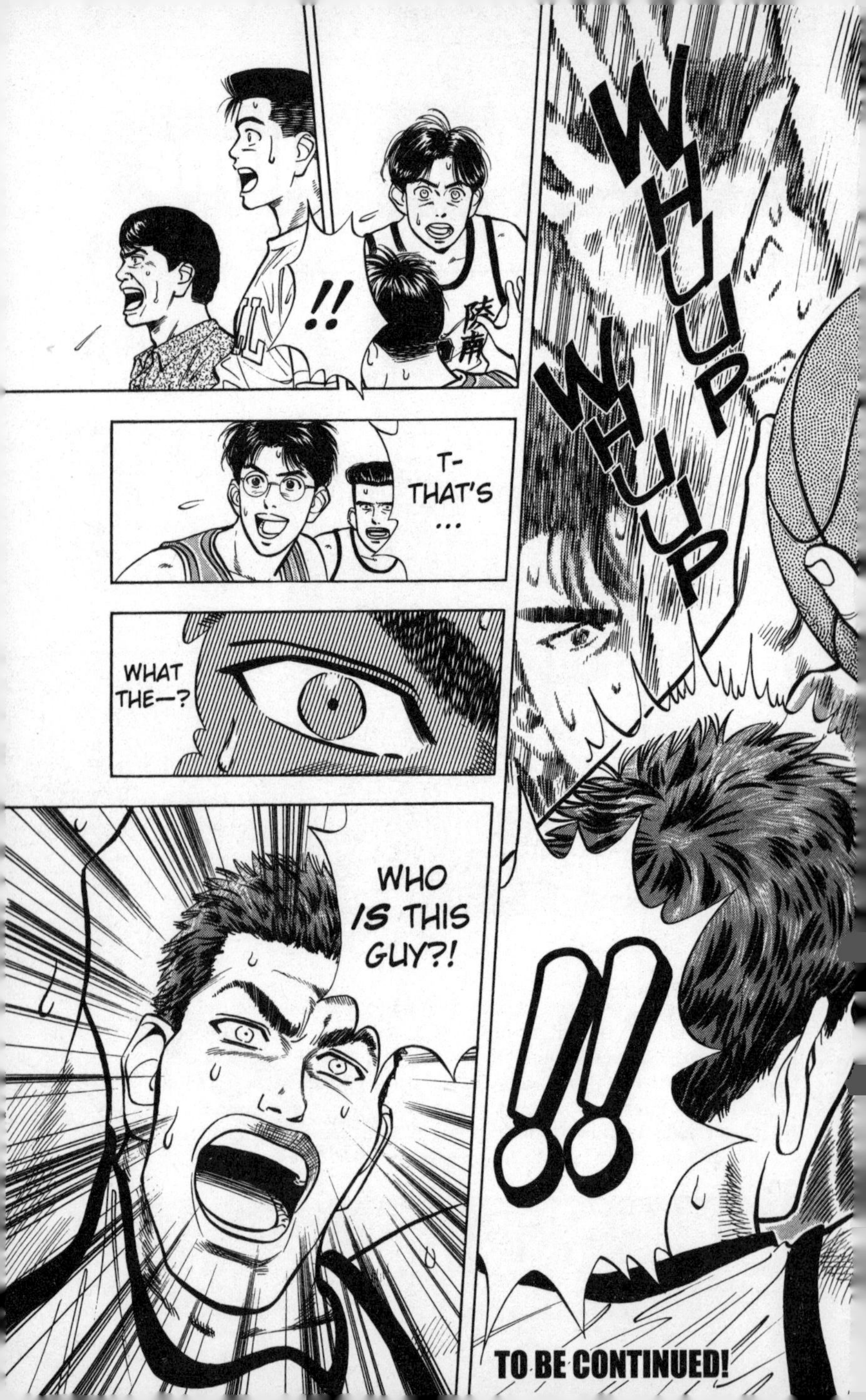
WHUUP
WHUUP
!!
!!
T-THAT'S...
WHAT THE—?
WHO *IS* THIS GUY?!

TO BE CONTINUED!

Coming Ne

SHOHOKU
11
SHOHOKU

Shohoku's practice game against rival school Ryonan is really starting to heat up, and now that Hanamichi is on the court, just about anything seems possible. Hoping to dominate the rim with his impressive rebounding skills, Hanamichi might be on the brink of leading Shohoku towards a major upset victory, but Ryonan's ace player Sendoh refuses to back down. Will the duo of Hanamichi and Rukawa be able to keep Sendoh's game in check?

ON SALE NOW